Domestic Judicial Treatment of European Court of Human Rights Case Law

The European Court of Human Rights (ECtHR) suffers from a burgeoning caseload and challenges to its authority. This two-pronged crisis undermines the ECtHR's legitimacy and consequently the functioning of the whole European human rights regime. Domestic courts can serve as welcome allies of the Strasbourg Court. They have a potential to diffuse European Convention of Human Rights norms domestically, and therefore prevent and filter many potential human rights violations. Yet we know very little about how domestic courts actually treat the Strasbourg Court's rulings. This book brings unique empirical findings on how often, how, and with what consequences domestic judges work with the ECtHR's case law. It moves beyond the narrow concept of compliance and develops a new three-level methodology for analyzing the role played by domestic courts in the implementation of ECtHR case law. Moreover, using the example of Czechia, it shifts the attention from Western countries to a more volatile Central and Eastern European region, which has recently witnessed democratic backsliding and a backlash against international checks on human rights and the rule-of-law standards. Looking at a wider social and legal context, this book identifies factors helping transitional countries to adapt to regional human rights regimes.

The work will be an essential resource for students, academics, and policy-makers working in the areas of constitutional law, politics, and human rights law. Its global appeal is enhanced by the methodological framework which is applicable in other international systems.

David Kosař is the Head of the Judicial Studies Institute, Masaryk University Faculty of Law, Czechia.

Jan Petrov is a senior researcher at the Judicial Studies Institute, Masaryk University Faculty of Law, Czechia.

Katarína Šipulová is a senior researcher at the Judicial Studies Institute, Masaryk University Faculty of Law, Czechia.

Hubert Smekal is an assistant professor at the Faculty of Social Studies and Senior Researcher at the Judicial Studies Institute, Masaryk University Faculty of Law, Czechia.

Ladislav Vyhnánek is an assistant professor at Masaryk University Faculty of Law, Czechia.

Jozef Janovský holds master's degrees in Applied Statistics (the University of Oxford), and political science (Masaryk University). He works in various quantitative roles in both the public and private sectors.

Routledge Research in Human Rights Law

Human Rights, Digital Society and the Law
A Research Companion
Edited by Mart Susi

Criminal Theory and International Human Rights Law
Steven Malby

Women's Health and the Limits of Law
Domestic and International Perspectives
Edited by Irehobhude O. Iyioha

Women and International Human Rights Law
Universal Periodic Review in Practice
Gayatri H Patel

International Law and Violence Against Women
Europe and the Istanbul Convention
Edited by Johanna Niemi, Lourdes Peroni, and Vladislava Stoyanova

The Human Rights Council
The Impact of the Universal Periodic Review in Africa
Damian Etone

Domestic Judicial Treatment of European Court of Human Rights Case Law
Beyond Compliance
David Kosař, Jan Petrov, Katarína Šipulová, Hubert Smekal, Ladislav Vyhnánek, and Jozef Janovský

For more information about this series, please visit:
www.routledge.com/Routledge-Research-in-Human-Rights-Law/book-series/HUMRIGHTSLAW

First published 2020 by Routledge

2 Park Square, Milton Park, Abingdon, Oxon OX14 4RN
605 Third Avenue, New York, NY 10017

Routledge is an imprint of the Taylor & Francis Group, an informa business

First issued in paperback 2021

Publisher's Note

The publisher has gone to great lengths to ensure the quality of this reprint but points out that some imperfections in the original copies may be apparent.

British Library Cataloguing-in-Publication Data
A catalogue record for this book is available from the British Library

Library of Congress Cataloging-in-Publication Data
A catalog record has been requested for this book

ISBN: 978-0-367-36116-7 (hbk)
ISBN: 978-1-03-217320-7 (pbk)
DOI: 10.4324/9780429343933

Typeset in Galliard
by Swales & Willis, Exeter, Devon, UK

The research leading to this book has received funding from the Czech Science Foundation under Grant Agreement No. 16-09415S, Panel P408 ("Beyond Compliance – Domestic Implementation of International Human Rights Case Law").

Contents

Illustrations

Figures

Tables

Preface

This book marks the ending of a three-year project which started out as a seemingly easy puzzle. We asked what is hidden in domestic courts' decision-making practice and to what extent the lengthy discussion over interpretation of various European Court of Human Rights (ECtHR) rulings matches domestic judges' views of the issue. Very soon, we realized that the question hides many twists and nuances and calls for a systematic analysis of national case law. We discovered that the underlying issue, how domestic courts use Strasbourg case law, has occupied the minds of scholars both in Europe and worldwide for a while.

We also soon found out that we needed an insider's knowledge of the functioning of each apex court we wanted to cover as well as in-depth specialists in quantitative methods for the automated coding in the macro level of our inquiry. Such knowledge is impossible to accumulate in one or two people. That is why we decided to write a monograph with six co-authors, which is still rare in the field of law. In our endeavor, we divided our tasks as follows (in alphabetical order):

Jozef Janovský – Chapter 4 (together with Katarína Šipulová and Hubert Smekal).

David Kosař – Chapters 1, 2, and 9 (together with Jan Petrov).

Jan Petrov – Chapter 6, and Chapters 1, 2, and 9 with David Kosař.

Hubert Smekal – Chapters 3 and 8, and Chapter 4 with Katarína Šipulová and Jozef Janovský.

Katarína Šipulová – Introduction and Chapter 5, and Chapter 4 with Jozef Janovský and Hubert Smekal.

Ladislav Vyhnánek – Chapter 7.

Nevertheless, although each substantive chapter has a different author (or authors), the chapters individually and collectively pursue the book's central argument. They are intended to stand together, not like the chapters of an edited collection united by a set of related themes, but like the chapters of a single-authored monograph. For this reason, while each chapter listed above specifies an author, the book as a whole is jointly authored.

Acknowledgements

The research leading to this book benefited greatly from external feedback and presentations of our endeavor at various venues. First of all, conferences at the European Consortium for Political Research and the Association of Human Rights Institutes, and various workshops and research stays at fellow research centers at iCourts in Denmark and PluriCourts in Norway provided us with great methodological advice and tools. Parts of the book and various methodological issues were presented at several workshops and conferences. Particularly useful for bringing this inquiry to its current state of completion have been events held in (listed alphabetically) Brno (especially a workshop co-organized with Alice Donald and Anne-Katrin Speck at the MUNI Law Faculty), Copenhagen (Marlene Wind, Mikael Rask Madsen), Oslo (Andreas Føllesdal and Geir Ulfstein), and Prague (CEELI Institute). We also learned a lot from the participants of our "Beyond Compliance" conference, which included, among others, Jiří Malenovský, the judge at the Court of Justice of the European Union, and both Czech and Slovak Government Agents for the European Court of Human Rights, Vít A. Schorm and Marica Pirošíková.

Chapter 1 and Chapter 2 elaborate on an article previously published as David Kosař and Jan Petrov, 2017, "The Architecture of the Strasbourg System of Human Rights: The Crucial Role of the Domestic Level and the Constitutional Courts in Particular", *Heidelberg Journal of International Law* 77: 585–621. Chapter 4 draws on a shorter methodology article published as Katarína Šipulová, Hubert Smekal, and Jozef Janovský, 2018, "Searching for a reference: Using automated text analysis to study judicial compliance", *Masaryk University Journal of Law and Technology* 12 (2): 131–60. The review process in both above-mentioned journals and the critical evaluations we received helped us clarify our arguments and methods and motivated us to continue developing our research.

We are also extremely grateful to the highest Czech judicial institutions (the Constitutional Court, the Supreme Court, and the Supreme Administrative Court) and their staffs. Four of the authors (have) closely cooperated with these courts in past, which enabled us to study from inside the practical application of ECtHR case law in their everyday activities. Particular acknowledgements are due to (listed alphabetically) Martina Baráková, Jan Drábek, Martina Grochová,

Radim Jílek, Alžbeta Králová, Lukáš Lehotský, Alžbeta Nemeškalová Rosinová, and Tereza Papoušková for their invaluable help in coding the collected case law.

Lukáš Hamřík made a tremendous effort in editing the book and Marni Kristin was incredibly cooperative when proofreading our texts under severe time constraints.

Finally, we would like to express our gratitude to the Czech Science Foundation, whose research grant "Beyond Compliance – Domestic Implementation of International Human Rights Case Law" made publication of this book possible.

About the authors

Jozef Janovský holds an MSc in Applied Statistics from the University of Oxford, and a master's in political science from Masaryk University. In 2011, he was awarded the Dirk Berg-Schlosser Award by the European Consortium for Political Research. He has participated in various quantitative social-scientific research projects in international law, political science, and psychology. Since 2013, he has worked in various quantitative roles in both the public and private sectors.

David Kosař is the Head of the Judicial Studies Institute at Masaryk University Faculty of Law. He was awarded a European Research Council Starting Grant to investigate "The rise of judicial self-government and repercussions for separation of powers" (2016–21). He studied law in Brno (Masaryk University, MA in law), the Central European University (LLM), and the New York University School of Law (JSD). He previously worked as a law clerk to the Vice-President of the Czech Supreme Administrative Court of the Czech Republic and to the Justice of the Czech Constitutional Court of the Czech Republic. His areas of research include various aspects of constitutional law and politics, international public law, judicial studies, transitional justice, human rights law, and constitutional theory. He is the author of *Perils of Judicial Self-Government in Transitional Societies* (2016), which won the Canada Prize from the International Academy of Comparative Law, and was an editor of the special issue on "Judicial Self-Governance in Europe" (*German Law Journal* 19 (7): 1567–2188). His recent publications have appeared in *American Journal of International Law*, *European Journal of International Law*, *Heidelberg Journal of International Law*, *International Journal of Constitutional Law*, *European Constitutional Law Review*, *Hague Journal of the Rule of Law*, *German Law Journal*, and *Utrecht Law Review*.

Jan Petrov is a senior researcher at the Judicial Studies Institute, Masaryk University. He studied law, political science, and international relations at Masaryk University. In 2018, he earned an LLM degree in International Legal Studies from New York University School of Law, where he studied as a Hauser Global Scholar. In 2019, he earned a PhD in Constitutional Law at Masaryk University. Besides his studies, he worked as a law clerk at the Czech Supreme

Administrative Court. His research interests include constitutional and international courts. More specifically, Jan has been researching on topics such as judicialization of politics, domestic judicial application of international human rights law, effectiveness of the ECtHR, and questions of populism and separation of powers. His publications have appeared in *European Journal of International Law*, *European Constitutional Law Review*, *Heidelberg Journal of International Law*, and *East European Politics and Societies.*

Katarína Šipulová earned her PhD at the Faculty of Social Studies, Department of European Studies, Masaryk University, Brno, and an MSt degree in Socio-Legal Research at the University of Oxford. Her main area of interest is transitional justice and democratization of the Central and Eastern European countries. She worked as the Head of the International Department of the Czech Supreme Court. As of now, she is a senior researcher at the Judicial Studies Institute at Masaryk University, and external consultant at the Supreme Court. She has been an active member of several research projects dealing with human rights as well as international law and its impact on domestic jurisprudence (e.g. international human rights treaties in national legal systems, implementation of ECtHR case law against Czechia). She was co-leader of a project on the application of European Union law by the Czech civil courts conducted by the Supreme Court between 2011 and 2018. Her work has appeared in *Hague Journal of the Rule of Law*, *German Law Journal*, *Netherlands Quarterly of Human Rights*, *International Community Law Review*, and *World Political Science Review.*

Hubert Smekal holds a PhD in European Studies from Masaryk University, Brno, where he currently works as an assistant professor and a senior researcher at the Judicial Studies Institute. He spent a year (2010–11) as a Fulbright–Masaryk Scholar at the Center for the Study of Law and Society, University of California, Berkeley. He co-founded the Czech Centre for Human Rights and Democratization and serves as a member of the Human Rights Council of the Czech Government. His academic interests take in the issues of human rights, the political role of the Court of Justice of the European Union and ECtHR, and judicialization of (international) politics. He has published articles in *European Constitutional Law Review*, *Netherlands Quarterly of Human Rights*, the *Journal of Mixed Methods Research*, and *German Law Journal.* He has authored two books on human rights, co-edited five volumes, and published a number of book chapters and articles in peer-reviewed journals. He has been a member of three research projects funded by Czech Grant Agency and currently also participates at a H2020 research project funded by the European Union.

Ladislav Vyhnánek is an assistant professor at Masaryk University Faculty of Law. He was awarded a prestigious grant from the Czech Grant Agency to investigate how extra-legal factors influence the Czech Constitutional Court's decision-making (2017–19). He studied law in Brno (Masaryk University, MA in law and PhD in constitutional law) and the New York University School of

Law (LLM, Fulbright Scholar). He has worked as a law clerk to the Justice of the Czech Constitutional Court. His areas of research include various aspects of constitutional law and theory, judicial studies, and human rights law. He (co) authored several books and numerous academic articles in the fields of (comparative) constitutional law, human rights law, and judicial studies. Recent publications have appeared in *European Constitutional Law Review*, *Vienna Journal on International Constitutional Law*, and *Heidelberg Journal of International Law*.

Abbreviations

ECHR/(European) Convention	European Convention on Human Rights
ECtHR/Strasbourg Court	European Court of Human Rights
CC	Constitutional Court of the Czech Republic
CEE	Central and Eastern Europe
CEI	Czech Environmental Inspectorate
CJEU	Court of Justice of the European Union
CoE	Council of Europe
EU	European Union
ICCPR	International Covenant on Civil and Political Rights
SAC	Supreme Administrative Court of the Czech Republic
SC	Supreme Court of the Czech Republic
UN	United Nations

Judicial cases

Constitutional Court of the Czech Republic

no. I. ÚS 526/98, judgment of 18 February 1999
no. Pl. ÚS 16/99, judgment of 27 June 2001
no. Pl. ÚS 36/01 *Euro-Amendment*, judgment of 25 June 2002
no. I. ÚS 367/03 *Rejžek v. Vondráčková*, judgment of 15 March 2005
no. Pl. ÚS 45/04, judgment of 22 March 2005
no. IV. ÚS 146/04 *Šlouf*, judgment of 4 April 2005
no. IV. ÚS 162/04, decision of 25 May 2005
no. I. ÚS 589/05, judgment of 2 November 2006
no. IV. ÚS 23/05 *Píchová*, judgment of 17 July 2007
no. II.ÚS 2733/08, decision of 11 June 2009
no. IV. ÚS 1921/09, decision of 17 September 2009
no. I. ÚS 1941/09, decision of 21 January 2010
no. Pl. ÚS 13/10, decision of 27 May 2010
no. I. ÚS 3438/11, judgment of 23 May 2012
no. III. ÚS 2837/12, decision of 20 February 2014
no. III. ÚS 306/14, decision of 15 May 2014
no. IV. ÚS 1511/13 *Čouka*, judgment of 20 May 2014
no. III. ÚS 1305/14, decision of 16 October 2014
no. Pl. ÚS-st 39/14, judgment [Plenary] of 25 November 2014
no. II. ÚS 2051/14 *Řápková v Hůle*, judgment of 3 February 2015
no. I. ÚS 1565/14, judgment of 2 March 2015
no. Pl. ÚS 12/14, judgment of 16 June 2015
no. III. ÚS 3913/14, decision of 1 July 2015
no. III. ÚS 1136/13 *J. S.*, judgment of 12 August 2015
no. III. ÚS 541/15, decision of 3 September 2015
no. I. ÚS 2617/15 *Kydalka*, judgment of 5 September 2015
no. III. ÚS 693/15, decision of 17 September 2015
no. III. ÚS 1033/15, decision of 8 October 2015
no. I. ÚS 860/15, judgment of 27 October 2015
no. II. ÚS 3626/13, judgment of 6 December 2015
no. I. ÚS 750/15 *Šimůnek*, judgment of 19 January 2016

no. II. ÚS 3436/14, judgment of 19 January 2016
no. I. ÚS 1042/15, judgment of 24 May 2016
no. III. ÚS 3522/15, decision of 21 July 2016
no. IV. ÚS 434/16, decision of 9 November 2016
no. IV. ÚS 2308/16, decision of 14 December 2016
no. IV. ÚS 2320/16, decision of 21 January 2017
no. Pl. ÚS 32/16, judgment of 8 August 2017

Constitutional Court of the Russian Federation

no. 21–П/2015, decision of 14 July 2015
no. 12-П/2016, decision of 19 April 2016
no. 1-П/2017, judgment of 19 January 2017

Constitutional Court of the Slovak Republic

no. PL. ÚS 21/2014, judgment of 30 January 2019

Court of Justice of the European Union

Åkerberg Fransson [GC], no. C-617/10, judgment of 26 February 2013

District Court Ostrava (Czech Republic)

no. 26 C 42/2016-124 *Z. Ž. and J. V. v. Základní škola Ostrava Muglinov*, judgment of 1 March 2017

European Court of Human Rights

Case "relating to certain aspects of the laws on the use of languages in education in Belgium" [Plenary], nos. 1474/62; 1677/62; 1691/62; 1769/63; 1994/63 and 2126/64, judgment of 9 February 1967
Engel and Others v. the Netherlands [Plenary], nos. 5100/71; 5101/71; 5102/71; 5354/72 and 5370/72, judgment of 8 June 1976
Handyside v. the United Kingdom, no. 5493/72, judgment of 7 December 1976
The Sunday Times v. United Kingdom, no. 6538/74, judgment of 26 April 1979
Marckx v. Belgium [Plenary], no. 6833/74, judgment of 13 June 1979
Le Compte, Van Leuven and De Meyre v. Belgium, nos. 6878/75 and 7238/75, judgment of 23 June 1981
Eckle v. Germany, no. 8130/78, judgment of 15 July 1982
Özturk v. Germany, no. 8544/79, judgment of 21 February 1984
Benthem v. Netherlands [Plenary], no. 8848/80, judgment of 23 October 1985
Lingens v. Austria, no. 9815/82, judgment of 8 July 1986
Lutz v. Germany, no. 9912/82, judgment of 25 August 1987
F. v. Switzerland [Plenary], no. 11329/85, judgment of 18 December 1987
Belilos v. Switzerland [Plenary], no. 10328/83, judgment of 29 April 1988

Huvig v. France, no. 11105/04, judgment of 24 April 1990
Kruslin v. France, no. 11801/85, judgment of 24 April 1990
Wassink v. Netherlands, no. 12535/86, judgment of 27 September 1990
Cruz Varas and Others v. Sweden, no. 15576/89, judgment of 20 March 1991
Vilvarajah and Others v. the United Kingdom, nos. 13163/87; 13164/87; 13165/87; 13447/87 and 13448/87, judgment of 30 October 1991
Windisch v. Austria, no. 12489/86, judgment of 28 June 1993
A. v. France, no. 14838/89, judgment of 23 November 1993
Bendenoun v. France, no. 12547/86, judgment of 24 February 1994
Van de Hurk v. the Netherlands, no. 16034/90, judgment of 19 April 1994
López Ostra v. Spain, no. 16798/90, judgment of 9 December 1994
Ruiz Torija v. Spain, no. 18390/91, judgment of 9 December 1994
Gradinger v. Austria, no. 15963/90, judgment of 23 October 1995
Schmautzer v. Austria, no. 15523/89, judgment of 23 October 1995
De Haes a Gijsels v. Belgium, no. 19983/92, judgment of 24 February 1997
Halford v. the United Kingdom, no. 20605/92, judgment of 25 June 1997
Oberschlick v. Austria (no. 2), no. 20834/92, judgment of 1 July 1997
Garyfallou AEBE v. Greece, no. 18996/91, judgment of 24 September 1997
Bowman v. the United Kingdom [GC], no. 24839/94, judgment of 19 February 1998
Kopp v. Switzerland, no. 23224/94, judgment of 25 March 1998
Güleç v. *Turkey*, no. 21593/93, judgment of 27 July 1998
Oliveria v. Switzerland, no. 25711/94, judgment of 30 July 1998
Lauko v. Slovakia, no. 26138/95, judgment of 2 September 1998
Kadubec v. Slovakia, no. 27061/95, judgment of 2 September 1998
Malige v. France, no. 27812/95, judgment of 23 September 1998
Castillo Algar v. Spain, no. 28194/95, judgment of 28 October 1998
García Ruiz v. Spain, no. 30544/96, judgment of 21 January 1999
Larkos v. Cyprus, no. 29515/95, judgment of 18 February 1999
Oğur v. Turkey, no. 21594/93, judgment of 20 May 1999
Pellegrin v. France, no. 28541/95, judgment of 8 December 1999
Scozzari and Giunta v. Italy [Plenary], nos. 39221/98 and 41963/98, judgment of 13 July 2000
Hugh Jordan v. the United Kingdom, no. 24746/94, judgment of 4 May 2001
Franz Fischer v. Austria, no. 27569/02, judgment of 29 May 2001
Feldek v. Slovakia, no. 29032/95, judgment of 12 July 2001
Hirst v. the United Kingdom, no. 40787/98, judgment of 24 July 2001
Pincová and Pinc v. the Czech Republic, no. 36548/97, judgment of 5 November 2002
Běleš v. the Czech Republic, no. 47273/99, judgment of 12 November 2002
Zvolský and Zvolská v. the Czech Republic, no. 46129/99, 12 November 2002
Bucheň v. the Czech Republic, no. 36541/97, judgment of 26 November 2002
Bořánková v. the Czech Republic, no. 41486/98, judgment of 7 January 2003
Maestri v. Italy [GC], no. 39748/98, judgment of 17 February 2004
Görgülü v. Germany, no. 74969/01, judgment of 26 February 2004

Assanidze v. Georgia [GC], no. 71503/01, judgment of 8 April 2004
Broniowski v. Poland [GC], no. 31443/96, judgment of 22 June 2004
Von Hannover v. Germany, no. 59320/00, judgment of 24 June 2004
Kopecký v. Slovakia, no. 44912/98, judgment of 28 September 2004
O.B. Heller, a. s. v. the Czech Republic, nos. 55631/00 and 55728/00, judgment of 9 November 2004
Makaratzis v. Greece, no. 50385/99, judgment of 20 December 2004
E v. the Czech Republic, no. 49962/92, judgment of 5 July 2005
Hirst (no. 2) v. the United Kingdom [GC], no. 74025/01, judgment of 6 October 2005
D.H. and Others v. the Czech Republic, no. 57325/00, 7 February 2006
Blečić v. Croatia, no. 59532/00, judgment of 8 March 2006
Apicella v. Italy [GC], no. 64890/01, judgment of 29 March 2006
Hutten-Czapska v. Poland [GC], no. 35014/97, judgment of 19 June 2006
Öllinger v. Austria, no. 76900/01, judgment of 29 June 2006
Üner v. the Netherlands, no. 46410/99, judgment of 18 October 2006
Walla and Wallová v. the Czech Republic, no. 23848/04, judgment of 26 October 2006
Vilho Eskelinen and Others v. Finland [GC], no. 63235/00, judgment of 19 April 2007
Havelka and Others v. the Czech Republic, no. 23499/06, judgment of 21 June 2007
Smatana v. the Czech Republic, no. 18642/04, judgment of 27 September 2007
D.H. and Others v. the Czech Republic [GC], no. 57325/00, judgment of 13 November 2007
Saadi v. UK [GC], no. 13229/03, judgment of 29 January 2008
Salduz v. Turkey [GC], no. 36391/02, judgment of 27 November 2008
Zolotukhin v. Russia [GC], no. 14939/03, judgment of 10 February 2009
A. and Others v. the United Kingdom [GC], no. 3455/05, judgment of 19 February 2009
Šilih v. Slovenia, no. 71463/01, judgment of 9 April 2009
Opuz v. Turkey, no. 33401/02, judgment of 9 June 2009
Herri Batasuna and Batasuna v. Spain, nos. 25803/04 and 25817/04, judgment of 30 June 2009
Verein gegen Tierfabriken Schweiz (VgT) v. Switzerland (no. 2) [GC], no. 32772/02, judgment of 30 June 2009
Varnava and Others v. Turkey, nos. 16064/90; 16065/90; 16066/90; 16068/90; 16069/90; 16070/90; 16071/90; 16072/90 and 16073/90, judgment of 18 September 2009
Rantsev v. Cyprus, no. 25965/04, judgment of 7 January 2010
Crabtree v. the Czech Republic, no. 41116/04, judgment of 25 February 2010
Oršuš and Others v. Croatia, no. 15766/03, judgment of 16 March 2010
Handölsdalen Sami Village and Others v. Sweden, no. 39013/04, judgment of 30 March 2010
Skoullos family v. Turkey, no. 55819/00, judgment of 1 June 2010
Žirovnický v. the Czech Republic, no. 23661/03, judgment of 30 September 2010

Paksas v. Latvia [GC], no. 34932/04, judgment of 6 January 2011
Golha v. the Czech Republic, no. 7051/06, judgment of 26 May 2011
Finogenov and Others v. Russia, nos. 18299/03 and 27311/03, judgment of 20 December 2011
Eremiášová and Pechová v. the Czech Republic, no. 23944/04, judgment of 16 February 2012
Yordanova v. Bulgaria, no. 25446/06, judgment of 24 April 2012
Volkov v. Ukraine, no. 21722/11, judgment of 9 January 2013
Anchugov and Gladkov v. Russia, nos. 11157/04 and 15162/05, judgment of 4 July 2013
Orion-Břeclav, s.r.o. v. the Czech Republic, no. 43783/98, judgment of 13 January 2014
Lucky Dev v. Sweden, no. 7356/10, judgment of 27 November 2014
Horncastle and Others v. the United Kingdom, no. 4184/10, judgment of 16 December 2014
Hutchinson v. the United Kingdom, no. 57592/08, judgment of 3 February 2015
Bochan v. Ukraine [GC], no. 22251/08, judgment 5 February 2015
Karácsony and Others v. Hungary [GC], nos. 42461/13 and 44357/13, judgment of 17 May 2016
Baka v. Hungary [GC], no. 20261/12, judgment of 23 June 2016
A and B v. Norway [GC], nos. 24130/11 and 29758/11, judgment of 15 November 2016
Erményi v. Hungary, no. 22254/14, judgment of 22 November 2016
A.P., Garçon a Nicot v. France, nos. 79885/12; 52471/13 and 52596/13, judgment of 6 April 2017
Moreira Ferreira v. Portugal (no. 2), no. 19867/12, judgment of 11 July 2017
Regner v. the Czech Republic [GC], no. 35289/11, judgment of 19 September 2017

French Court of Cassation

no. P16-2018-001, judgment of 10 April 2019

Italian Constitutional Court

no. 49/2015, judgment of 26 March 2015

Supreme Administrative Court of the Czech Republic

no. 5 A 145/2001-58, judgment of 4 March 2004
no. 2 As 3/2004-70, judgment of 22 April 2004
no. 6 A 126/2002-27, judgment of 27 October 2004
no. 5 Afs 185/2004-85, judgment of 23 September 2005
no. 1 Afs 86/2004-54, judgment of 26 October 2005
no. 3 As 57/2004-39, judgment of 15 December 2005
no. 4 As 2/2005-62, judgment of 20 January 2006

no. 7 Afs 29/2006-68, judgment of 13 April 2006
no. 1 As 42/2005-62, judgment of 21 June 2006
no. 5 Afs 178/2006-81, judgment of 23 February 2007
no. 1 As 32/2006-99, judgment of 28 March 2007
no. 8 As 29/2007-121, judgment of 31 May 2007
no. 6 As 55/2006-96, judgment of 11 July 2007
no. 1 Azs 36/2006-71, judgment of 25 July 2007
no. 8 As 51/2007-67, judgment of 5 November 2007
no. 8 Afs 133/2006-106, judgment of 6 November 2007
no. Pst 1/2008-66, judgment of 4 March 2009
no. 7 As 29/2008-104, judgment of 8 August 2009
no. 8 As 7/2008-116, judgment of 31 August 2009
no. 6 Ads 41/2008-67, judgment of 7 October 2009
no. Pst 1/2009-348, judgment of 17 February 2010
no. 5 As 25/2009-83, judgment of 25 February 2010
no. 2 Azs 7/2010-100, judgment of 19 March 2010
no. 6 Ads 155/2009-42, judgment of 16 June 2010
no. 5 Afs 33/2010-55, judgment of 15 July 2010
no. 9 Afs 5/2010-81, judgment of 15 July 2010
no. 1 As 53/2011-109, judgment of 27 July 2011
no. 6 Ads 1/2011-433, judgment of 31 August 2011
no. 7 As 79/2010-150, decision of 23 November 2011
no. 1 As 125/2011-163, judgment of 11 January 2012
no. 1 Ao 7/2011-526, judgment of 21 June 2012
no. 7 As 97/2012-26, judgment of 4 September 2012
no. 2 As 104/2012-35, judgment of 30 October 2012
no. 9 As 111/2012-34, judgment of 1 November 2012
no. 8 As 118/2012-45, judgment of 5 March 2013
no. 7 Azs 6/2013-105, judgment of 11 July 2013
no. 6 As 48/2013-33, judgment of 26 July 2013
no. 5 Azs 13/2013-30, judgment of 17 September 2013
no. 2 As 60/2013-26, judgment of 29 November 2013
no. 5 Afs 50/2012-39, judgment of 13 December 2013
no. 9 Azs 49/2014-27, judgment of 26 March 2014
no. 4 As 120/2014-21, judgment of 24 July 2014
no. 1 As 78/2014-41, judgment of 13 August 2014
no. 5 As 112/2014-33, judgment of 7 November 2014
no. 1 As 202/2014-28, judgment of 4 December 2014
no. 4 Afs 216/2014-32, judgment of 28 January 2015
no. 7 Azs 11/2015-32, judgment of 19 February 2015
no. 1 As 113/2012-133, judgment of 25 February 2015
no. 8 As 67/2014-69, judgment of 3 March 2015
no. 1 Azs 160/2014-37, judgment of 4 March 2015
no. 5 Azs 6/2015-31, judgment of 16 April 2015
no. 6 As 255/2014-42, judgment of 25 May 2015

no. 2 Azs 52/2015-52, decision of 27 May 2015
no. 10 Azs 53/2015-28, judgment of 28 May 2015
no. 6 As 106/2014-25, judgment of 3 June 2015
no. 6 As 114/2014-55, decision [GC] of 30 September 2015
no. 4 Afs 210/2014-57, decision [GC] of 24 November 2015
no. 6 As 167/2015-37, judgment of 2 December 2015
no. 6 As 163/2016-39,judgment of 13 December 2016
no. 6 As 256/2016-79, judgment of 1 March 2017
no. 8 As 124/2017-51, judgment of 21 March 2018
no. 2 As 199/2018-37, judgment of 30 May 2019

Supreme Court of the Czech Republic

no. Skno 1/94, decision of 31 August 1994
no. 21 Cdo 1009/98, judgment of 21 October 1998
no. 2 Cdon 804/96, decision of 24 June 1999
no. 25 Cdo 38/2000, decision of 8 February 2001
no. 11 Tdo 738/2003, judgment of 22 July 2004
no. 3 Tdo 260/2007, decision of 21 March 2007
no. 5 Tdo 1399/2007, decision of 12 December 2007
no. 6 Tdo 1478/2009, decision of 27 May 2010
no. 30 Cdo 1614/2009, judgment of 8 September 2010
no. 30 Cdo 1337/2010, judgment of 20 October 2010
no. Cpjn 202/2010, opinion of 8 December 2010
no. 31 Cdo 3916/2008, judgment [GC] of 11 May 2011
no. 30 Cdo 3964/2010, judgment of 31 August 2011
no. 30 Cdo 2357/2010, judgment of 11 January 2012
no. 29 Cdo 2012/2010, judgment of 31 May 2012
no. 30 Cdo 4277/2010 *J. S.*, judgment of 13 December 2012
no. 30 Cdo 4277/2010, judgment of 13 December 2012
no. 28 Cdo 2789/2012, judgment of 9 January 2013
no. 30 Cdo 1770/2012, judgment of 24 April 2013
no. 30 Cdo 2916/2012, judgment of 29 May 2013
no. 30 Cdo 1663/2012, judgment of 12 June 2013
no. 5 Tdo 326/2014, decision of 24 September 2014
no. 30 Cdo 1982/2012, judgment of 24 September 2014
no. 30 Cdo 3534/2014, judgment of 26 November 2014
no. 30 Cdo 1987/2014, decision of 17 December 2014
no. 30 Cdo 1290/2014, judgment of 16 September 2015
no. 30 Cdo 5172/2015, decision of 18 May 2016
no. Tpjn 300/2016, opinion of 26 October 2016
no. 30 Cdo 24/2016, judgment of 20 December 2016
no. 15 Tdo 832/2016, decision [GC] of 4 January 2017

Supreme Court of Czechoslovakia

no. R I 488/25, judgment of 16 July 1925

Introduction

1. The problem: Why is it important to understand how domestic courts treat the Strasbourg case law?

The European Court of Human Rights (ECtHR or Strasbourg Court) is generally accepted as the most successful human rights court (Anagnostou 2013) and a poster child for other regional human rights regimes. It operates under the auspices of the Council of Europe (CoE), which consists of 47 member states that are all parties to the European Convention on Human Rights (ECHR or Convention). The Committee of Ministers supervises the national implementation of adverse ECtHR judgments.[1] As the democratic character of the political regime presents one of the core conditions of membership in the CoE,[2] the states within the regime are expected to already have fairly good domestic human rights standards. Grave violations of core human rights covered by the Convention are therefore expected to appear only very rarely.

Yet compliance with and execution of ECtHR judgments is not as clear cut as it might seem.[3] On the contrary, populist attacks have swept through both Western and Eastern European countries, challenging the core principles of the Convention as well as the authority of the Strasbourg Court, and resisting both its existence and the direction of its case law (Andenæs and Bjørge 2012; Grozev 2013; Seibert-Fohr and Villiger 2015). Late reforms of the ECtHR in the 2010s, the Brighton Declaration of 2012 and resulting Protocols Nos. 15 and 16, led the CoE, for the first time in its history, to introduce a systemic rebalancing of powers between the ECtHR and the domestic courts (Madsen, Cebulak, and Wiebusch 2018).

Three major factors have challenged the effectiveness and the authority of the ECtHR recently. First, although a democratic political regime is a condition for entry into the CoE,[4] not all CoE member states necessarily remain liberal democracies. Political regimes are dynamic, and democracy is not necessarily a one-way path. Some European countries face challenges that sometimes lead to as grave and disturbing changes as we might currently witness in Central and Eastern Europe (CEE) due to the democratic backsliding instigated by populist leaders (von Bogdandy and Sonnenveg 2015; Sedelmeier 2017; Scheppele and

Pech 2018; Zoll and Wortham 2019). The group of 47 CoE member states therefore includes established democracies, (post-)transitional democracies, reversing democracies, and states where the fundamental norms of democracy and the rule of law have been failing (Harmsen 2013). Such a composition implies challenges to the ECHR system, ranging from a lack of domestic human rights awareness to serious human rights violations.

Second, implementation of some ECtHR rulings posits a challenge for all states, irrespective of the character of their political regime. Human rights as a concept is continuously evolving. The ECtHR gradually fills in the holes and adds new dimensions to original Convention provisions, which leads to criticisms of the overarching interference of the ECtHR into domestic policies, especially when ECtHR judgments significantly intrude into domestic separation of powers (Kosař and Lixinski 2015). The costs of compliance with such interferences vary. Some ECtHR rulings involve only financial compensation while others require complex legislative changes. In the past decade, several topics touched upon by the ECtHR have proved to be very salient, provoking negative reactions by several CoE member states, irrespective of their domestic human rights regime or the "old v. new" Convention party cleavage.[5] This in turn has led to increasing demands to strengthen the principle of subsidiarity within the ECtHR system.[6]

Third, although the Committee of Ministers closely monitors compliance in individual cases, the ECtHR still heavily relies on domestic actors.[7] Domestic courts, with their ability to translate the ECtHR rulings into day-to-day policies, have been singled out by scholars as one of the most important factors in the compliance equation.[8] Broad access to domestic courts, their independence, the established mechanism of decision enforcement (Roberts 2011), and common legal language shared with international courts (Benvenisti 1993) make national courts particularly important actors for the effective functioning of the ECHR system (Stone Sweet 2012; Gerards 2014). Domestic courts may also help lessen the "double-faced" caseload and legitimacy crisis faced by the ECtHR.

They diffuse the standards developed in the Strasbourg case law domestically. They can introduce and enforce ECtHR rulings and principles, and hence prevent a significant number of ECHR violations. Moreover, the engagement of domestic courts with the ECHR standards can be seen as an additional input for the ECtHR's legitimacy, as the domestic judiciaries can significantly contribute to the domestic internalization of the ECHR and the Strasbourg Court's case law (Kosař and Petrov 2017).

Given these three challenges, understanding the relationship between the ECtHR and the domestic courts, as well as the impact of domestic courts on judicial compliance and its conditions, is crucial. Their mutual relationship gains even more importance in the face of the rising backlash against the ECtHR by politicians and the mass media (Barnard 2018), as well as the current political developments in some of the CEE CoE countries (Gibler and Randazzo 2011; Sedelmeier 2014; Mechkova, Lührmann, and Lindberg 2017). While various attempts to cease the power of and exercise influence over domestic courts have been part of domestic political games for centuries, the esprit with which modern autocracies target courts and attack their legitimacy and functionality is unprecedented (Pech and Scheppele 2017; Kosař and Šipulová 2018). Never before was the research on courts more important. The wave of democratic backsliding in CEE (von Bogdandy and Sonnevend 2015; Sadurski 2018) strengthens the need for an effective external control of human rights and the rule-of-law standards. As a result, the ECtHR needs, more than ever, domestic courts as allies to foster its credibility and social legitimacy, and to diffuse its findings.

Nevertheless, domestic courts, although formally bound to implement international human rights commitments, are first and foremost autonomous actors. It therefore cannot be taken for granted that they will always give priority to the Convention or always concur with the Strasbourg Court. With a rising trend of "judicial disobedience" towards the Strasbourg Court (Krisch 2008; Foster 2009; Bates 2014; Martinico 2016; Padskocimaite 2017; Petrov 2018), it is clear that domestic courts may not only contribute to convergence with the ECtHR case law, but also resist it (Jackson 2010). The prisoners' voting rights in the *Hirst*[9] saga or *Anchugov and Gladkov v. Russia*[10] and the resulting negative reactions of UK and Russian courts are only the tip of the iceberg, which, however, clearly demonstrates that the resistance movement runs across both consolidated democratic and undemocratic countries with different levels of judicial independence.

2. The approach: How to study judicial treatment of Strasbourg case law

Reflecting the indispensable role of domestic judiciaries and its challenges, we posit a core research question: *How do domestic courts use the ECtHR's case law?* In order to answer this puzzle, we introduce a novel concept of "judicial treatment" and argue that the importance of the domestic courts' role surpasses the traditional understanding of compliance and judicial implementation of adverse rulings by respective targeted countries. More specifically, while the narrow understanding of compliance reflects merely the implementation of adverse rulings against a particular country by its domestic court, judicial treatment more generally demonstrates how domestic courts add to judicial compliance in a broader sense. It allows us to capture and understand both the positive and negative part played by domestic courts.

In the last decade, several authors reported the positive influence of independent domestic courts on human rights treaty compliance (Cross 1999; Apodaca 2002; Camp Keith 2002; Powell and Staton 2009; Conrad and Ritter 2013; Lupu 2013; Conrad 2014). However, only a very recent enrichment of legal science with social sciences methods has allowed for the emergence of new studies employing quantitative content and automated text analyses. The results, so far, seem to support the statement by showing that domestic courts increasingly use international human rights law references (Wind 2016). Nevertheless, there is much left to do. Our book shows that domestic courts refer to the ECtHR's case law quite frequently, but we argue that the mere count of references does not automatically convey a positive or significant message for the ECtHR's system. The position and significance of the ECtHR-related references in the domestic rulings need to be analyzed in a greater detail, since the manifold ways in which domestic courts actually treat the Strasbourg case law have crucial repercussions for the functioning of the subsidiarity principle and the idea of domestic embeddedness.

While we make use of new methodological development and build on pioneering studies researching the frequencies of domestic courts referencing to the ECtHR and other international courts (De Witte et al. 2016), our book also goes much deeper and looks at the *quality and impact of references* on domestic case law. By doing so it offers the very first comprehensive empirical analysis of the use of Strasbourg case law and its effect on the reasoning of domestic courts. Our concept of judicial treatment reflects the more dynamic role of the ECtHR in the Strasbourg system of human rights protection and asks how much inspiration domestic courts take from the adverse judgments against other countries, whether they wait for the cases coming from their own jurisdiction or act pre-emptively, and whether they assign the same weight and power to the ECtHR's rulings as they do to rules explicitly stemming from the Convention.

Such a broader understanding of judicial treatment allows us to pose a core research question, *How do domestic courts use the ECtHR's case law*, unpacked in the following subquestions, around which we further organize the empirical part of this book:

1. How did the patterns of how domestic apex courts treat ECtHR case law evolve in time?
2. In what instances do domestic apex courts refer to ECtHR case law?
3. Which factors influence treatment of ECtHR case law by domestic apex courts?
4. Are domestic apex courts functioning as faithful allies for the ECtHR?

In order to untangle puzzles aligned in research questions, we propose a new methodology for researching judicial treatment. While using the benefits of pioneer quantitative studies, we also argue that automated methods and simple counts of references paint only a very incomplete picture. The questions on the role of domestic courts in diffusing the ECtHR's rulings and potentially adding to its legitimacy require much deeper digging. First, automated analysis needs very careful validation, as too many negatives may occur. Second, even with careful validation, the mere count of references fails to capture the impact of the reference on the domestic courts' reasoning.

We set out a three-level research model analyzing the use of Strasbourg case law on the macro, meso, and micro level, which uses a blend of quantitative and qualitative methods (frequencies, crosstabs, content analysis), as well as more traditional legal analysis.

At the macro level, we utilize automated methods of data collection and coding, identifying the population of all domestic apex courts' rulings referring to the ECtHR. We show how frequency of judicial treatment should be measured beyond the mere count of references, taking into the consideration position of the reference within the body of the judgment, in order to eliminate the random noise, i.e. references outside of domestic courts' own reasoning. The macro level uncovers general patterns in ECtHR case law references, and their development over time, and identifies the most frequently cited rulings and the position of domestic judgments with rich ECtHR references within the rest of the case law. It searches for correlations between changes in citation patterns and internal constitutional, institutional, and personnel development within the judiciary.

At the meso level, we complement the automated analysis with sophisticated hand-coding of the role the ECtHR references play in the text of domestic rulings. We propose a typology of different levels of engagement with Strasbourg rulings, asking whether the references directly influence the reasoning of the domestic courts or whether they serve as a mere ornament to arguments based on domestic law. If the reference has substantive importance to a ruling, we further check whether the domestic court follows the ECtHR's precedent, distinguishes the case at hand from the ECtHR's precedent, or refuses to follow the ECtHR's precedent.

Lastly, the micro level relies on traditional legal analysis and discusses the most salient cases and factors involved in the differing approach of domestic apex courts towards ECtHR case law. It looks at the most important areas of law where domestic courts either used ECtHR case law to push forward desired changes, or, on the contrary, refused to follow the Strasbourg Court, giving preference to their own interpretation of the Convention's effects.

This three-level research design allows us both to observe the façade of the "dome of judicial treatment" (macro level), enter its interior (meso level), and understand the atmosphere and motives (micro level) present inside the dome and inherently needed for its successful construction. We believe that the motives of actors and the atmosphere within all three levels of the dome are necessary to understand the judicial treatment and conditions leading to judicial implementation of ECtHR or any other international human rights body case law.

3. Why Czechia? Case study on a country that mixes transitioning and non-transitioning domestic courts

The second part of our book applies the concept of judicial treatment to the case study of Czechia and its three apex courts. We opt only for apex courts as they are the actors typically identified as the most prominent intermediaries between international human rights courts and domestic judiciaries (see Chapter 4 for more details).

Czechia entered the CoE only in 1993, and since then, apart from a couple of controversial rulings such as *D.H.*, it has remained primarily off the radar of academic research. Yet there are several reasons why the analysis of Czechia and its performance works well as a pilot study.

First, Czechia is an example of a "good complier". Very few cases brought before the ECtHR end with a ruling on a violation. Out of 12,588 rulings against Czechia, the ECtHR issued a judgment finding a violation of the Convention only 186 times. In 2018, the ECtHR dealt with 347 applications concerning Czech Republic, of which 333 were declared inadmissible or struck out. Out of admissible cases, 14 were decided by judgment, with at least one violation found (ECtHR 2019a). Overall, over 62 percent of the findings of a violation concerned Article 6 (right to a fair trial), which broke down into fairness of process (28.94 percent) and length of proceedings (33.62 percent) violations. The second most commonly violated article has been Article 5 (right to liberty and security). Mirroring these judgments, the Committee of Ministers reported positive reforms and improvements relating to deprivation of liberty, quality of access to justice, appeals procedures, and remedies for compensation for excessively lengthy proceedings. Similarly, the ECtHR's rulings and the Committee of Ministers' recommendations on the protection of private and family life (custody of children, speed of proceedings on child abduction, and covert surveillance) were implemented and showed positive progress (ECtHR 2019b). This all makes Czechia an outlier in the post-communist region. Yet, Czechia has also had a few politically salient cases which spurred public debate and required systemic changes and adjustment in its domestic legal and political system, be they transitional justice issues (immaterial damage for past regime violations of human rights and controlled rents), or discrimination against Roma children in education. All these issues called for a dramatic legislative change, provoking adverse public reactions. However, the Committee of Ministers currently registers only one not-fully-implemented adverse judgment. We argue that researching domestic courts' treatment of the ECtHR's case law in a country that has overall good scores with the ECtHR adds to the hypothesis of domestic courts as allies. If the domestic courts do not comply with ECtHR case law in a broad sense, then the hypothesis cannot stand, and, obviously, other factors are in play.

Second, the very few empirical studies of the ECtHR's case law that exist have so far concentrated on Western European states, that is on countries which entered the CoE with different aims and different initial standards of human rights protection than the post-communist region. Creating a model for analysis based on the old CoE members might therefore miss certain specifics present in transitional and newly emerging democratic regimes, which are more volatile and which entered the CoE with the aim to lock in new, desired, and often unstable pro-human rights policies. Moreover, these existing studies usually examine only few important rulings, not the life of the Convention in a domestic system as such. Czechia represents a cluster of those CoE countries that entered the CoE and the Convention in the middle of their transition to democracy, and had to learn, internalize, and develop their human rights culture with the help of the ECtHR.

Third, the uniqueness of Czechia dwells in the composition and history of its apex courts. While the Czech Constitutional Court and the Czech Supreme Administrative Court emerged only after the Velvet Revolution and the fall of communism as completely new institutions, the Supreme Court was inherited from the communist era and remained untouched by any substantive personnel change. The lack of transition at the Supreme Court dwelled in the need to use the existing judiciary to handle a new bundle of laws and legal acts enacted in the transition. Yet it also meant that the Supreme Court entered the democratic regime with judges who had served under the communist regime and who were strongly influenced by a culture of socialist formalism and had enjoyed their position as the final authoritative interpreter of law (Kühn 2011). On the other hand, both the Constitutional Court (established in 1993) and the Supreme Administrative Court (established in 2003) were brand new institutions that followed a different pattern. The Constitutional Court consisted of former political dissidents and emigrants who easily embraced the concept of human rights. The Supreme Administrative Court incorporated lateral hiring (in contrast to the Supreme Court, which recruited their future colleagues exclusively from career judges) and attracted younger judges and scholars (in contrast to older judges of the Supreme Court), who had often studied abroad and were well versed in international and European Union law. Hence, the comparison of these three courts offers us a unique view on how both the new courts and the old unreformed courts use the ECtHR case law. The study therefore serves as a good model for various types of transitions.

Fourth, the research on the implementation practice in Czechia also fits well within the current explosive discourse on backsliding democracies and is particularly important in the CEE setting. The backsliding of several countries in the CEE region demonstrates the volatile character of the political system and the fragile standards of the rule of law and human rights guarantees. Therefore, it is all the more important to guarantee the effectiveness and legitimacy of the ECtHR regime and secure both the effective enforcement and implementation of its judgments domestically. The book, in this respect, represents a first step towards understanding how CEE domestic courts work with the ECtHR's case law and how heavily they rely on the Strasbourg Court in their reasoning. This, in turn, shows more genuinely how the international human rights case law in general becomes internalized domestically.

In sum, the Czech case study is instrumental to understand the role and position of domestic courts in ECHR regime, since Czech courts faced the challenge of attuning themselves to working with the ECtHR's case law after the transition from a non-democratic regime. Czechia not only illustrates the trends of the subsidiarity principle and the domestic embeddedness of the ECHR, it also provides for interesting insights as regards overcoming transitional hardships of domestic judicial treatment of international human rights law. Comparison between the three Czech apex courts, informed by their unique institutional and personal histories, sheds light on the role of access to ECHR expertise and human rights socialization.

4. The main argument

Our analysis of judicial treatment of the ECtHR's case law by Czech apex courts showed that the Strasbourg Court is a natural ally for newly created (especially constitutional) courts in the transitioning democracies. It has the potential to help the reforming transitional societies to lock in desired policies and human rights principles (Moravcsik 2000). It also offers an additional layer of legitimacy for the newly established courts. Moreover, the ECtHR serves as a great source of new human rights legal language and inspiration for how to interpret and solve certain principles and problems. Nevertheless, the actual use of the Strasbourg case law by new courts depends on the knowledge, understanding, and penetration of the Convention into domestic law sources and legal circles.

The ECtHR is also an important factor in the "human rights transformation" of old judges who remained on the bench after transition. More specifically, it pushes and binds old non-reformed courts to a higher human rights standard. However, the penetration of ECtHR case law to case law of older courts takes time and requires further external pushes (typically coming from constitutional courts, new judges, and the involvement of other actors, such as media and civil society, who exercise pressure on the old courts).

On the other hand, the ECtHR remains uncontested only up to a certain point. We argue that a period of learning naturally transgresses into a period of liberation, with domestic courts leading more pro-active dialogue and at times contesting the ECtHR. Yet we echo Madsen, Cebulak, and Wiebusch's (2018) call on the need to distinguish various forms of courts' resistance against the ECtHR, as not all negative reflections of domestic courts erode the ECtHR's legitimacy.

More specifically, our study of judicial treatment of the ECtHR's case law uncovered five findings important for the understanding of the role of domestic courts in the Strasbourg system which are applicable beyond the Czech case study. First, the three-level approach presented in the theoretical part of the book helped us isolate instances where domestic courts actively engage with the ECtHR case law and follow its reasoning. We show that the majority of references to the ECtHR are simply ornamental. Yet we argue that even these ornamental references play an important role in embedding the ECtHR's case law, as they document to what extent domestic courts internalize it in their day-to-day decision-making practice. The isolated results of the macro-level analysis, when compared to qualitative coding on the meso level, also demonstrate that a simple count of references cannot fully reflect these nuances.

Second, the use of the ECtHR case law nevertheless clearly surpasses the role that domestic courts play in the standard understanding of compliance. The data supports our claim that domestic courts act as norm diffusers, often pushing for the direct implementation of principles delivered in judgments issued against other CoE member countries. With this pre-emptive activity, domestic apex courts can actually filter a significant number of violations that otherwise might have potentially ended up before the Strasbourg Court. In other words, domestic courts act as important filters and capture situations where potential discrepancies might occur. Nevertheless, they are still embedded in the domestic arena and often combine ECHR and domestic legal argumentation, plus pragmatic and idealistic reasons for engagement with the Strasbourg case law, and use it for both changing and advocating the status quo of the domestic human rights protection. In sum, the domestic judicial treatment of the Strasbourg case law is an open-ended enterprise depending on many factors.

Third, how domestic courts approached Strasbourg case law has changed over time. Shortly after the entry of Czechia into the CoE, domestic courts referred to the ECtHR only in instances where they needed to challenge significant gaps or human rights discrepancies in national legal orders. Nowadays, apex courts use ECtHR references much more often, seemingly almost redundantly. The majority of them tend to merely support the arguments and principles that already exist in national law. However, this is not to say that such ornamental references are not important for the study of judicial implementation. On the contrary, the immediacy with which domestic judges reach into the ECtHR's jurisprudence when searching for arguments and sources of inspiration demonstrates the level of internalization of international human rights law in domestic settings. An even stronger argument arises from the frequent use of the confirmation ("blessing") technique, with domestic apex courts justifying the limits and delineation of human rights protection with the use of ECtHR references. This significantly changes the perception of the Strasbourg Court being a human rights missionary pushing the domestic courts to a very activist approach towards human rights. With rising frequency, domestic courts refer to the ECtHR when showing the limits of human rights protection and international commitments, justifying the domestic legal provisions and practice. In a sense, the apex courts perceive the ECtHR as an important authority to consult when interpreting the borders of human rights protection. Overall, the widespread use of supporting ornamental references and "blessing" references suggests that the ECHR and Strasbourg case law permeates the daily decision-making practice of domestic apex courts. This further confirms our argument that apex courts act as allies and norm diffusers at the national level, and filter potential ECHR violations. Moreover, the frequent engagement with the Strasbourg case law also adds to the ECtHR's output legitimacy.

Fourth, and most importantly, surprisingly, we did not uncover a huge cleavage between the behavior of the Constitutional Court and the general judiciary. We expected that constitutional courts should act as champions in the use of the ECtHR's case law and be far more active than apex general courts. However, the situation on the ground is more complex. While the Czech Constitutional Court, whose agenda focuses on human rights protection almost exclusively, is slightly more active in referring to Strasbourg rulings, the discrepancy between the courts is not very significant. On the other hand, we found an important cleavage between the position of the Supreme Court, representing the old, almost unreformed, post-communist court, and the two new apex judicial bodies established only after the democratic revolution (Supreme Administrative Court and Constitutional Court). While both younger courts adapted to the ECtHR regime quite quickly and adopted a pro-active stance, the Supreme Court travelled a rocky road, only gradually learning to work with the Strasbourg case law and accepting its supremacy.

The change in the position of the Supreme Court was influenced by mostly external impulses, be it case law of other courts, or new appointed judges coming from the Constitutional Court or with experience from abroad. First, the binding jurisprudence of the Constitutional Court forced the Supreme Court to adopt and accept the binding effect of the Strasbourg rulings implemented in the Constitutional Court's decisions and judgments. Second, even more importantly, the personal composition of the Supreme Court has eventually changed, with new younger judges, especially those coming from outside the general judiciary or with foreign education experience, being much more open and willing to implement the ECtHR case law. Third, the Supreme Court's general stance towards international law and European Union law was another important factor. In accepting the principles of the direct effect and supremacy of European Union law, the Supreme Court judges eventually also changed their position regarding the Strasbourg Court. Other important external factors that pushed the Supreme Court to change its position included intensive contact between Supreme Court judges and the Czech representatives of international courts, as well as the direct engagement of the Government Agent representing Czechia before the ECtHR. The Government Agent actively participated in debates with judges, especially regarding the implementation of adverse cases against Czechia, but also prompted the Supreme Court judges to work in various informal working groups distributing information on the ECtHR's newest case law in the Czech language.

Nowadays, approximately 25 years after entering the Strasbourg regime, the Supreme Court uses the ECtHR case law almost as frequently as the other two younger apex courts, although its approach is still less active and more self-restrained in terms of both frequency and impact of ECtHR references. This, however, suggests that judiciaries of countries entering international human rights regimes need additional external pushes to internalize the case law, apart from the existence and authority of the Strasbourg Court on its own.

Lastly, an in-depth analysis of domestic courts' work with the Strasbourg rulings brings very important findings that add to the most recent debates and suggestions on the rising judicial resistance and push-back against international courts. Similarly to Madsen, Cebulak, and Wiebusch (2018), we found that domestic courts in fact rarely directly challenge the legitimacy of the ECtHR. Instead they accept the existing rules of the game and act more as ECtHR partners. This applies also to the post-communist Supreme Court, whose judges initially opposed on principle the existence of another binding judicial body. It was predominantly external inputs (new incoming judges, training, internships with international organizations, etc.) that eventually helped to change the Supreme Court's stance. Generally, Czech apex courts do not challenge the legitimacy and authority of the Strasbourg Court as such, but instead, in the few cases of the most controversial and sensitive issues (questions of transitional justice, for example), they push against the direction of ECtHR case law, challenging the applicability of the reasoning and the ECtHR's findings on social, political, and legal particularities. This finding highlights the need to distinguish between various forms of challenges faced by international courts, as the disputes on the direction of the case law are a natural component of the legal discourse and do not really diminish the authority of the institutions as such.

5. Roadmap

The book consists of three parts and is structured so that the general framework can be applied to other case studies in the future. The first part lays out a general systematic framework explaining the importance of the problem and answering why and how to study domestic judicial treatment of the ECtHR's rulings. It analyzes the architecture of the Strasbourg system of human rights, identifies the role of domestic courts in this system, engages with the current compliance theories, and proposes a new three-level approach to studying judicial treatment of the Strasbourg case law. This part aims to create a roadmap on how to study compliance and implementation of the ECtHR's case law in individual member countries. The second part of the book, Chapters 4–8, is the empirical part on the treatment of Strasbourg rulings by the Czech apex courts, assessing how often and in what way the domestic courts engage with the ECtHR's case law. The third part concludes with a discussion of broader repercussions of our concept of judicial treatment in transitional democracies.

Chapter 1 first briefly sketches the basic features of the domestic effects of the Strasbourg judgments, namely the *inter partes* effect and the so-called *res interpretata* effect. It also presents the typical roles domestic authorities play in the processes of the ECtHR's case law implementation, and shows their "diffusing" and "filtering" functions vis-à-vis the Strasbourg Court. Subsequently, it problematizes the model of diffusers and filters, and provides a more nuanced account of the domestic actors' significance in the Convention system.

Chapter 2 focuses more closely on the role of courts and judges in the implementation of Strasbourg case law. First, it identifies the various actors within the domestic judiciaries who influence the implementation processes. Subsequently, it zeroes in on the role of constitutional courts and ordinary courts in implementing Strasbourg case law. It identifies different motivations of domestic judges for engaging with the Strasbourg case law, shows different strategies domestic courts use towards the ECtHR, and discusses the factors that affect the relationship between domestic courts and the ECtHR.

Chapter 3 reviews theories of compliance and synthesizes findings of empirical research on compliance. It shows why it is fruitful to look *beyond* compliance and focus on *judicial treatment* more generally. The chapter prepares the conceptual background for understanding the practice of the treatment of ECtHR case law by a domestic judiciary.

Chapter 4 proposes a novel methodology on the study of judicial treatment on the macro, meso, and micro levels. It describes qualitative and quantitative methods used in the research, with particular attention placed on the benefits and risks of automated text analysis and manual coding. The chapter also serves as a prequel to the second part of the book, briefly describing the data collection, methodology, and sources of potential inaccuracies that must be taken into account when interpreting the results of the case study on Czechia.

Chapters 5–7 are each devoted to one of the apex courts. Chapter 5 provides an analysis of the Supreme Court, the old post-communist court largely untouched by the transition. Chapter 6 examines the Supreme Administrative Court, a new apex court established only in 2003. Finally, Chapter 7 introduces the Constitutional Court, also a new court, established in 1993, endowed with, among other things, the competence of constitutional review of legislation and individual constitutional complaints.

For each court, the chapters first engage with the macro level and uncover general patterns in references to the ECtHR case law and their development over time. They indicate the most frequently cited ECtHR rulings. Subsequently, the chapters seek to explain changes in citation patterns by looking at constitutional, institutional, and personnel development in the judiciary. Second, all chapters proceed with a meso-level analysis of the treatment of Strasbourg rulings by the Czech apex courts. Building on the results of the quantitative analysis, they offer a mix of quantitative and qualitative analyses of the top courts' case law and ask *how*, *when*, and *why* the top courts refer to the ECtHR's rulings. They explore the formal qualities of references, the significance of ECtHR case law references for the domestic court's reasoning, and the legal techniques employed for dealing with the Strasbourg case law. The chapters also examine whether domestic judges follow, distinguish from, or reject Strasbourg rulings and observe trends over time, trying to find reasons for any significant changes in existing patterns. Finally, the micro levels in each chapter examine the most problematic and the most influential cases of implementation of the ECtHR's jurisprudence in domestic apex courts' case law. They point out legal areas where domestic courts have internalized and applied, or, on the contrary, have refused to apply, the Strasbourg rulings.

Chapter 8 summarizes the empirical findings. It examines commonalities and differences in the treatment of the Strasbourg case law by the three Czech apex courts: the Constitutional Court, the Supreme Court, and the Supreme Administrative Court. It elaborates on the reasons for these commonalities and differences.

Chapter 9 identifies the strategies domestic judges use when they engage with the Strasbourg case law, and analyzes when they use each strategy and with what aim, and how this shapes their relationship to the ECtHR. It discusses whether the Strasbourg Court actually makes a difference on the ground. Finally, it argues that the effectiveness of the Strasbourg system of human rights protection lies deeper than in mere compliance rates.

Notes

1 Although the Committee of Ministers lacks "hard" execution powers, it can refer to the ECtHR a question of whether a party has failed to fulfil its obligation to abide by the final judgment of the Court ECtHR (see Article 46 ECHR).

2 Article 3 of the Statute of the CoE actually does not mention democracy, but acceptance of "the principles of the rule of law and of the enjoyment by all persons within its jurisdiction of human rights and fundamental freedoms". The preamble of the Statute, however, mentions that common heritage of CoE member states, that member states are "[r]eaffirming their devotion to the spiritual and moral values which are the common heritage of their peoples and the true source of individual freedom, political liberty and the rule of law, principles which form the basis of all genuine democracy".

3 Most recently see, for example, Avbelj (2018).

4 See Articles 3 and 4 of Statute of the CoE, which require the candidates for the CoE membership to accept principles of the rule of law, and of indiscriminate enjoyment of human rights and fundamental freedoms, and to collaborate in the realization of the CoE aim.

5 Most notably *Hirst v. the United Kingdom* (no. 40787/98, judgment of 24 July 2001), *D.H. v. the Czech Republic* ([GC], no. 57325/00, judgment of 13 November 2007), *Hutchinson v. the United Kingdom* (no. 57592/08, judgment of 3 February 2015), *Anchugov and Gladkov v. Russia* (nos. 11157/04 and 15162/05, judgment of 4 July 2013), *Zolotukhin v. Russia* ([GC], no. 14939/03, judgment of 10 February 2009), and following case law *A and B v. Norway* (nos. 24130/11 and 29758/11, judgment of 15 November 2016), etc.

6 On subsidiarity in international human rights law, see Carozza (2003) and Neuman (2013). On subsidiarity in international law more generally, see Føllesdal (2013) and Jachtenfuchs and Krisch (2016). For the foundations and scope of the subsidiarity principle, see Chaplin (1997) and Føllesdal (1998).

7 See also the role of the ECtHR in the infringement procedure, Article 46 ECHR.

8 See the Interlaken, Izmir, Brighton, and Brussels declarations and Protocol No. 15 to the ECHR, which emphasizes the principle of subsidiarity. In the existing scholarship see Lauterpacht (1929), Scelle (1933), Helfer (2008), Hillebrecht (2012), Gerards and Fleuren (2014), and Kosař and Petrov (2017).

9 ECtHR, *Hirst v. the United Kingdom,* no. 40787/98, judgment of 24 July 2001; and *Hirst v. the United Kingdom (no. 2)* [GC], no. 74025/01, judgment of 6 October 2005.

10 ECtHR, *Anchugov and Gladkov v. Russia,* nos. 11157/04 and 15162/05, judgment of 4 July 2013.

References

Anagnostou, Dia, ed. 2013. *The European Court of Human Rights: Implementing Strasbourg Judgments on Domestic Policy.* Edinburgh: Edinburgh University Press.

Andenæs, Mads Tønnesson, and Eirik Bjørge. 2012. "Human Rights and Acts by Troops Abroad: Rights and Jurisdictional Restrictions". *European Public Law* 18: 473–92.

Apodaca, Clair. 2002. "The Globalization of Capital in East and Southeast Asia: Measuring the Impact on Human Rights Standards". *Asian Survey* 42 (6): 883–905.

Avbelj, Matej. 2018. "Slovenia's Supreme Court Rejects the European Court of Human Rights". *Verfassungsblog*, 26 October 2018. Accessed 20 May 2019. https://verfassungsblog.de/slovenias-supreme-court-rejects-the-european-court-of-human-rights/.

Barnard, Catherine. 2018. "The Court of Justice and National Courts: A Transparent Dialogue – Reaction". In *Binding Effect of Judicial Decisions: National and International Perspectives*, edited by Pavel Šámal, Guido Raimondi, and Koen Lenaerts, 214–18. Prague: Wolters Kluwer.

Bates, Ed. 2014. "Analysing the Prisoner Voting Saga and the British Challenge to Strasbourg". *Human Rights Law Review* 14 (3): 503–40.

Benvenisti, Eval. 1993. "Judicial Misgivings Regarding the Application of International Law: An Analysis of Attitudes of National Courts". *European Journal of International Law* 4: 159–83.

Camp Keith, Linda. 2002. "Constitutional Provisions for Individual Human Rights (1977–1996): Are They More than Mere 'Window Dressing'?" *Political Research Quarterly* 55 (1): 111–43.

Carozza, Paolo. 2003. "Subsidiarity as a Structural Principle of International Human Rights Law". *American Journal of International Law* 97: 38–79.

Chaplin, Jonathan. 1997. "Subsidiarity: The Concept and the Connections". *Ethical Perspectives* 4 (2): 117–30.

Conrad, Courtenay R. 2014. "Divergent Incentives for Dictators: Domestic Institutions and (International Promises Not To) Torture". *Journal of Conflict Resolution* 58 (1): 34–67.

Conrad, Courtenay R., and Emily Hencken Ritter. 2013. "Treaties, Tenure, and Torture: The Conflicting Domestic Effects of International Law". *Journal of Politics* 75 (2): 397–409.

Cross, Frank B. 1999. "The Relevance of Law in Human Rights Protection". *International Review of Law and Economics* 19 (1): 87–98.

De Witte, Bruno, Juan Mayoral, Urszula Jaremba, Marlene Wind, and Karolina Podstawa, eds. 2016. *National Courts and EU Law: New issues, Theories and Methods*. Cheltenham: Edward Elgar.

European Court of Human Rights. 2019a. "Press Country Profile. Czech Republic". Accessed 14 August 2019. www.echr.coe.int/Documents/CP_Czech_Republic_ENG.pdf.

European Court of Human Rights. 2019b. "The ECHR and the Czech Republic: Facts & Figures". Accessed 14 August 2019. www.echr.coe.int/Documents/Facts_Figures_Czech_ENG.pdf.

Føllesdal, Andreas. 1998. "Subsidiarity". *Journal of Political Philosophy* 6 (2): 190–218.

Føllesdal, Andreas. 2013. "Principle of Subsidiarity as a Constitutional Principle in International Law". *Global Constitutionalism* 2 (1): 37–62.

Foster, Steve. 2009. "Reluctantly Restoring Rights: Responding to the Prisoner's Right to Vote". *Human Rights Law Review* 9 (3): 489–507.

Gerards, Janneke. 2014. "The European Court of Human Rights and the National Courts: Giving Shape to the Notion of 'Shared Responsibility'". In *Implementation of the European Convention on Human Rights and of the Judgments of the ECtHR in National Case Law*, edited by Janneke Gerards and Jospeh Fleuren, 13–94. Cambridge: Intersentia.

Gerards, Janneke, and Joseph Fleuren. 2014. *Implementation of the European Convention on Human Rights and of the Judgments of the ECtHR in National Case-law*. Cambridge: Intersentia.

Gibler, Douglas M., and Kirk A. Randazzo. 2011. "Testing the Effects of Independent Judiciaries on the Likelihood of Democratic Backsliding". *American Journal of Political Science* 55 (3): 696–709.

Grozev, Yonko. 2013. "Political Opposition and Judicial Resistance to Strasbourg Case Law Regarding Minorities in Bulgaria". In *The European Court of Human Rights: Implementing Strasbourg's Judgments on Domestic Policy*, edited by Dia Anagnostou, 122–42. Edinburgh: Edinburgh University Press.

Harmsen, Robert. 2013. "The Reform of the Convention System: Institutional Restructuring and the (Geo-)politics of Human Rights". In *The European Court of Human Rights between Law and Politics*, edited by Jonas Christoffersen and Mikael Rask Madsen, 119–43. New York, NY: Oxford University Press.

Helfer, Laurence R. 2008. "Redesigning the European Court of Human Rights: Embeddedness as a Deep Structural Principle of the European Human Rights Regime". *European Journal of International Law* 19 (1): 125–59.

Hillebrecht, Courtney. 2012. "Implementing International Human Rights Law at Home: Domestic Politics and the European Court of Human Rights". *Human Rights Review* 13 (3): 279–301.

Jachtenfuchs, Marcus, and Nico Krisch. 2016. "Subsidiarity in Global Governance". *Law and Contemporary Problems* 79: 1–26.

Jackson, Vicky. 2010. *Constitutional Engagement in a Transnational Era*. New York, NY: Oxford University Press.

Kosař, David, and Katarína Šipulová. 2018. "The Strasbourg Court Meets Abusive Constitutionalism: Baka V. Hungary and the Rule of Law". *Hague Journal on the Rule of Law* 10 (1): 83–110.

Kosař, David, and Lucas Lixinski. 2015. "Domestic Judicial Design by International Human Rights Courts". *American Journal of International Law* 109 (4): 713–60.

Kosař, David, and Jan Petrov. 2017. "The Architecture of the Strasbourg System of Human Rights: The Crucial Role of the Domestic Level and the Constitutional Courts in Particular". *Heidelberg Journal of International Law* 77: 585–621.

Krisch, Nico. 2008. "The Open Architecture of European Human Rights Law". *Modern Law Review* 71 (2): 183–216.

Kühn, Zdeněk. 2011. *The Judiciary in Central and Eastern Europe: Mechanical Jurisprudence in Transformation?* Leiden: Martinus Nijhoff.

Lauterpacht, Hersch. 1929. "Decisions of Municipal Courts as a Source of International Law". *British Yearbook of International Law* 10: 65–95.

Lupu, Yonatan. 2013. "Best Evidence: The Role of Information in Domestic Judicial Enforcement of International Human Rights Agreements". *International Organization* 67 (3): 469–503.

Madsen, Mikael Rask, Pola Cebulak, and Micha Wiebusch. 2018. "Resistance to International Courts". *International Journal of Law in Context* 14 (Special Issue2): 193–6.

Martinico, Giuseppe. 2016. "National Courts and Judicial Disobedience to the ECHR: A Comparative Overview". In *Shifting Centres of Gravity in Human Rights Protection*, edited by Oddný Mjöll Arnardóttir and Antoine Buyse, 59–78. Abingdon: Routledge.

Mechkova, Valeriya, Anna Lührmann, and Staffan I. Lindberg. 2017. "How Much Democratic Backsliding?" *Journal of Democracy* 28 (4): 162–9.

Moravcsik, Andrew. 2000. "The Origins of Human Rights Regimes: Democratic Delegation in Postwar Europe". *International Organization* 54 (2): 217–52.

Neuman, Gerard. 2013. "Subsidiarity". In *The Oxford Handbook of International Human Rights Law*, edited by Dinah Shelton, 360–78. Oxford: Oxford University Press.

Padskocimaite, Ausra. 2017. "Constitutional Courts and (Non)execution of Judgments of the European Court of Human Rights: A Comparison of Cases from Russia and Lithuania". *Heidelberg Journal of International Law* 77: 651–84.

Pech, Laurent, and Kim Lane Scheppele. 2017. "Illiberalism Within: Rule of Law Backsliding in the EU". *Cambridge Yearbook of European Legal Studies* 19: 3–47.

Petrov, Jan. 2018. "Unpacking the Partnership: Typology of Constitutional Courts' Roles in Implementation of the European Court of Human Rights' Case Law". *European Constitutional Law Review* 14 (3): 499–531.

Powell, Emilia J., and Jeffrey K. Staton. 2009. "Domestic Judicial Institutions and Human Rights Treaty Violation". *International Studies Quarterly* 53 (1): 149–74.

Roberts, Anthea. 2011. "Comparative International Law? The Role of National Court in Creating and Enforcing International Law". *International and Comparative Law Quarterly* 60: 57–96.

Sadurski, Wojciech. 2018. "How Democracy Dies (In Poland): A Case Study of Anti-Constitutional Populist Backsliding". *Sydney Law School Research Paper No 18/01.* https://papers.ssrn.com/sol3/papers.cfm?abstract_id=3103491.

Scelle, Georges. 1933. "Règles Générales Du Droit De La Paix". *Recueil Des Cours De l'Académie de La Haye* 46: 334–6.

Scheppele, Kim Lane, and Laurent Pech. 2018. "What Is Rule of Law Backsliding?" *Verfassungsblog*, 2 March 2018. Accessed 4 May 2019. https://verfassungsblog.de/what-is-rule-of-law-backsliding/.

Sedelmeier, Ulrich. 2014. "Anchoring Democracy from Above? The European Union and Democratic Backsliding in Hungary and Romania after Accession". *Journal of Common Market Studies* 52 (1): 105–21.

Sedelmeier, Ulrich. 2017. "Political Safeguards against Democratic Backsliding in the EU: The Limits of Material Sanctions and the Scope of Social Pressure". *Journal of European Public Policy* 24 (3): 337–51.

Seibert-Fohr, Anja, and Mark E. Villiger. 2015. *Judgments of the European Court of Human Rights - Effects and Implementation.* New York, NY: Routledge.

Stone Sweet, Alec. 2012. "A Cosmopolitan Legal Order: Constitutional Pluralism and Rights Adjudication in Europe". *Global Constitutionalism* 1 (1): 53–90.

Von Bogdandy, Armin, and Pál Sonnevend. 2015. *Constitutional Crisis in the European Constitutional Area: Theory, Law and Politics in Hungary and Romania.* Oxford: Hart Publishing.

Wind, Marlene. 2016. "Do Scandinavians Care about International Law? A Study of Scandinavian Judges' Citation Practice to International Law and Courts". *Nordic Journal of International Law* 85 (4): 281–302.

Zoll, Fryderyk, and Leah Wortham. 2019. "Judicial Independence and Accountability: Withstanding Political Stress in Poland". *Fordham International Law Journal* 42 (3): 875–948.

Part I

Implementation of the Strasbourg rulings

Theoretical framework

1 Architecture of the Strasbourg system of human rights

The authority of the European Court of Human Rights (ECtHR or Strasbourg Court) has changed profoundly since its establishment. At the beginning of its functioning, the Strasbourg Court faced the problem of a limited caseload and the reluctance of certain signatory parties to accept its jurisdiction. By the 1980s all signatory parties recognized the competence of the ECtHR to receive petitions from individuals, the number of applications rose exponentially, and the authority of the ECtHR increased significantly (Bates 2010; Madsen 2013, 2016). Towards the end of the millennium, the Strasbourg Court turned into a permanent international court with a caseload comprising tens of thousands of applications every year, a court representing "the most effective human rights regime in the world" (Stone Sweet and Keller 2008a, 11).

Nowadays, the ECtHR delivers rulings that deal with the crucial legal, political, and societal issues of our day and influences domestic legal orders of the Council of Europe (CoE) member states on a regular basis. In reaction to the judgments of the ECtHR, the CoE member states often amend legislation, change domestic case law, alter their public policies, and even revisit the fundamental features of their constitutional and political systems (Barkhuysen and van Emmerik 2005; Lambert-Abdelgawad 2008; Kosař 2012; Helfer and Voeten 2014; Kosař and Lixinski 2015; Kosař and Petrov 2018; Smekal and Vyhnánek 2018). This development allowed the former president of the Strasbourg Court Rolv Ryssdal to claim that the judgments of the Strasbourg Court had "not only generally but always been complied with by the Contracting States concerned" (Harris et al. 2014, 30).

However, a more detailed analysis of the situation shows that since the second half of the 1990s the overall rate of compliance with the ECtHR's judgments has decreased (von Staden 2018),[1] and the Strasbourg human rights regime has witnessed more instances of lengthy compliance processes. Some of those processes resulted in partial or minimalist compliance and sometimes even in overt non-compliance with the ECtHR's case law.[2]

This combination of floods of new cases and the growing resistance to the Strasbourg case law pushed the ECtHR between a proverbial "rock and a hard place". On the one hand, signatory parties identified failures and delays in the execution and full implementation of the ECtHR's judgments, resulting in a high number of repetitive cases and the overloading of the Strasbourg Court, as the major challenges for the practical functioning of the European Convention on Human Rights (ECHR or Convention) system.[3] This voice calls for a more proactive implementation of Strasbourg jurisprudence and more profound changes to domestic legal systems. On the other hand, the increasing impact of the Strasbourg Court on national legal systems led to the domestic criticism of the ECtHR, which is no longer limited to discontent with particular rulings only, but opens up the debates questioning the legitimacy of the Strasbourg Court as such (Flogaitis, Zwart, and Fraser 2013; Bates 2014; Gerards and Fleuren 2014, 3–6; Oomen 2016; Føllesdal 2016; Popelier, Lambrecht, and Lemmens 2016; Madsen 2019). More recently, this kind of criticism has been intensified by numerous populist leaders in Europe who portray the Strasbourg Court as a foreign elitist obstacle compromising the enforcement of authentic popular will (Petrov 2020). All these voices call for less intervention by the ECtHR into domestic law.

These two demands show that effective implementation of the ECtHR's rulings is a critical point of the ECHR system's architecture. The Strasbourg Court's ability to induce systemic change of domestic policies is crucial both for its legitimacy and the practical functioning of the entire Convention system. At the same time, however, it seems to be one of the most challenging and controversial features of the system. The current implementation crisis shows that the ECtHR, despite being labelled as the most effective international human rights court in the world (Stone Sweet and Keller 2008a, 11), is still only an international court with no influence over "either the sword or the purse" (Hamilton 2003, 464). International courts are empowered to interpret the law in their rulings, but they have no power to execute their rulings and have only a few formal instruments to force governments to comply with their rulings (Koh 1999; Hathaway and Shapiro 2011).

1.1 The domestic effects of the Strasbourg case law

The Strasbourg Court's case law has had a major influence on the domestic law of most of the CoE member states in various areas (Algan 2008; Krisch 2008; Johnson 2010; Helfer and Voeten 2014; Hillebrecht 2014a; Kosař 2018).[4] The ECtHR's judgments regularly influence not only the legal order of a respondent state, the direct addressee of the ECtHR's ruling, but also provoke reforms in states which were not party to the proceedings. This section briefly explains the legal grounding of the ECtHR's domestic impact. First, it discusses the *inter partes* binding force of the ECtHR's judgments and the recent shift from the ECtHR's classical remedial strategy to a more proactive specification of individual and general measures required from the "convicted" signatory parties. Subsequently, it deals with the doctrine of the *res interpretata* effect, which explains what normative implications the Strasbourg jurisprudence has for the states which were not party to the original dispute.

1.1.1 *Inter partes* binding force of the ECtHR's judgments

The Convention contains several provisions regulating the execution of the ECtHR's judgments. Article 41 ECHR grants the Strasbourg Court the power, if necessary, to award just satisfaction. Moreover, Article 46(1) ECHR requires the signatory parties to abide by the final judgment of the ECtHR in any case to which they are party. The effect of this provision reaches beyond the situation of a particular applicant who was successful at the Strasbourg Court. The Convention's purpose was not only to redress concrete wrongs committed by the states, but also to secure a certain minimal standard of human rights protection within the territory of the parties to the Convention (Gerards 2014, 19).

As a result, Article 46(1) ECHR urges the states to respond to the ECtHR's judgment in the case of the individual applicant, and on the general level, if necessary, in order to prevent future human rights violations of the same kind. Accordingly, the Strasbourg Court held that

> As regards the requirements of Article 46, it should first be noted that a respondent State found to have breached the Convention or its Protocols is under an obligation to abide by the Court's decisions in any case to which it is a party. In other words, a total or partial failure to execute a judgment of the Court can engage the State Party's international responsibility. The State Party in question will be under an obligation not just to pay those concerned the sums awarded by way of just satisfaction, but also to take individual and/or, if appropriate, general measures in its domestic legal order to put an end to the violation found by the Court and to redress the effects, the aim being to put the applicant, as far as possible, in the position he would have been in had the requirements of the Convention not been disregarded.[5]

This means that the responding state faces three levels of obligations resulting from the "conviction" of the state by the Strasbourg Court: (1) the duty to pay just satisfaction to the injured party, if awarded by the ECtHR (Article 41 ECHR); (2) the duty to adopt individual measures; and (3) the duty to adopt general measures to avoid repetition of the rights violation. As the duty to pay just satisfaction does not require changes in the domestic law, we leave it aside. The necessity to adopt individual measures may in some instances be important for changes in the domestic legal order as compliance with certain individual measures might require systemic changes in the domestic law.[6] However, it is the duty to adopt general measures that is essential for the purposes of this book, as it regularly implies not only amending domestic legislation, but also revisiting domestic case law and changing administrative practices. The ECtHR made clear that the member states have committed themselves to adjust their legal orders so that they comply with the Convention.[7]

The ECtHR often declares that it cannot engage in the abstract or concrete review of legislation and that it does not have the power to quash the piece of legislation in question. The Strasbourg Court therefore limits its review on the result of the law's application and on declaring whether there was a violation of the Convention or not.[8] This self-perception led to the ECtHR's restrained approach towards remedies in which the Strasbourg Court has concentrated solely on finding a violation of the Convention and left the rest to the states. Under this traditional model of remedies, the ECtHR would not specify what measures should be taken to comply with its judgment as the domestic authorities would be seen as better placed to decide on the appropriate way to prevent repetition of the human rights violation (Hawkins and Jacoby 2010, 40; Hillebrecht 2012a, 281).[9]

This practice has changed though. In recent years, the Strasbourg Court has stepped beyond its classical remedial strategy and started indicating more specific individual and also general measures (Leach 2013; Jahn 2014; Keller and Marti 2015), which can have further implications for implementation processes. On the one hand, indication of remedial measures can facilitate implementation as it assists the domestic actors in interpreting what the Strasbourg judgment requires domestically (Stiansen 2019a). On the other hand, the specific remedial measures are more intrusive and regularly increase demands on the states parties, which can lead to further challenges of the ECtHR's authority and create additional implementation difficulties. Furthermore, specification of general measures by the ECtHR and subsequent compliance with them is the essential element of the pilot judgment procedure.[10] In fact, the pilot judgment procedure aims at disposing of a large number of similar cases in order to reduce the ECtHR's backlog, which inevitably requires general measures on the state level.

However, the pilot procedure focuses only on cases emanating from the same signatory party. It is an important tool for increasing the effectiveness of the Strasbourg system, but it would hardly be sufficient to reduce the backlog of the ECtHR's cases in itself. In order to ensure the effectiveness of the Strasbourg system, the ECtHR's case law needs to be taken into account also by the signatory parties that were not a party to the case adjudicated by the ECtHR. This brings us to the doctrine of the *res interpretata* effect.

1.1.2 Res interpretata effect

The case law of the ECtHR is binding for the parties to a particular dispute. Regarding these parties, the judgment of the ECtHR gains the status of *res judicata*. The impact of the Strasbourg Court, however, is broader and reaches beyond the states which were parties to the proceedings. In fact, the ECtHR judgments often influence legal orders of the states which were not the direct addressees of the rulings, and thus de facto have an *erga omnes* effect. For instance, Ireland, Latvia, and Cyprus changed their regulation of prisoners' voting rights in response to the *Hirst (no. 2) v. the United Kingdom* judgment.[11] The Grand Chamber judgment in *Salduz v. Turkey*[12] had already led to reforms of custodial legal assistance in France, Belgium,

Ireland, Scotland, and the Netherlands (Giannoulopoulos 2016). In response the pilot judgment in *Hutten-Czapska v. Poland*,[13] the Czech Republic adopted a new Act on unilateral rent increases.[14] These are just a few examples. Other states also regularly monitor the developments in the Strasbourg case law beyond the cases against their own governments and adjust their legal orders accordingly.[15]

These examples are instances of the Strasbourg Court's general interpretative authority over the Convention (Article 32 ECHR) and its implications for the states which were not the direct addressees of a Strasbourg judgment. The case law of the ECtHR thus acquires the so-called *res interpretata* effect.[16] According to the *res interpretata* effect, via its rulings the ECtHR provides for abstract interpretation of the Convention rights, which shall be taken into account by all the signatory parties if relevant for their domestic legal orders. *Res interpretata* is not explicitly stated in the text of the Convention. It has been inferred from the very construction of the European system of human rights protection[17] and mentioned in the case law of the ECtHR[18] as well as in political declarations[19] and various CoE documents.[20]

In sum, the effects of a single judgment of the Strasbourg Court go far beyond the situation of a concrete successful applicant. The ECtHR's judgment is supposed to be projected into the national legal system of a violating state through adoption of general measures of non-repetition, eventually along the lines proposed by the Strasbourg Court, if it resorted to indicating what measures would remedy the situation. Furthermore, other signatory parties are likewise supposed to react to the ECtHR's judgment if it provides for an interpretation of the Convention related to a situation which is relevant for them. Having sketched the legal basis for the effects of the Strasbourg case law in the CoE member states, both in parties to the dispute and the third states, it is now possible to unpack a member state into multiple domestic actors and show how these actors influence the implementation process.

1.2 Domestic-level matters: "Diffusing" and "filtering" role of the domestic authorities

The previous section of this chapter showed that the impact of the Strasbourg case law on national legal systems has been grounded mainly in the obligation to execute the ECtHR's judgments under Article 46(1) ECHR and in the doctrine of *res interpretata*. However, the ECtHR is empowered only to interpret the Convention in its rulings, and on its own has little formal power to trigger domestic reform or to change domestic laws and case law in order to put national legal orders into compliance with its rulings.[21] In this regard, the ECtHR, to a large extent, has to rely on national legal and political authorities who may serve as levers of the Strasbourg Court. As Courtney Hillebrecht (2012a) put it, "domestic political institutions, particularly domestic democratic institutions, play an important role in facilitating compliance with international human rights law".[22]

This section thus aims to offer a more detailed explanation of how the domestic level matters for the implementation of the ECtHR's judgments and for the Convention system as such. Regarding the *inter partes* binding effect and the *res interpretata* effect of the Strasbourg case law, the domestic institutions fulfil two main roles in the Convention system – the role of "diffusers" of the Strasbourg case law and the role of "filters" of the Strasbourg Court.

Figure 1.1 illustrates the first phase,[23] in which the national authorities act as the "diffusers" of the ECtHR's conclusions. Within this function, the domestic authorities are expected to reflect the Strasbourg Court's rulings and adopt domestic rules – via a statutory amendment or a change of domestic practice, especially through the case law of the apex courts with (quasi-)precedential effects – which respect the conclusions of the ECtHR. These domestic rules are general and apply to all rights holders at the national level. In other words, the domestic authorities act as "diffusers" as they spread the effects of an ECtHR ruling. The domestic authorities thereby transform the ECtHR's conclusions from a case of one particular applicant to a general domestic rule applicable to all similar situations. The model case depicted in Figure 1.1 expects respondent State A to adopt general measures fully respecting the Strasbourg case law. Other states (B and C in Figure 1.1) are presupposed, first, to respect the *res interpretata* effect and, second, to comply fully with the judgments of the ECtHR.

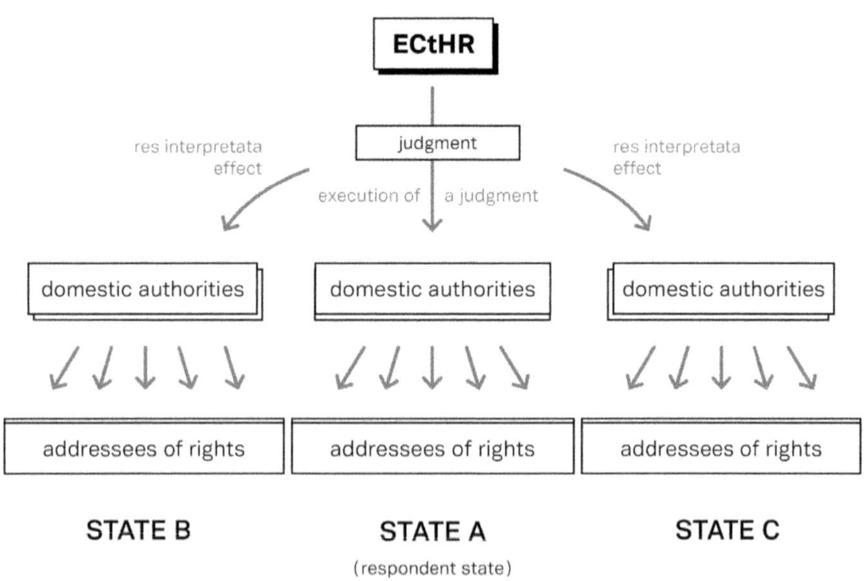

Figure 1.1 Domestic authorities as "diffusers" in the Convention system.
Source: authors.

In he second phase, the domestic authorities – especially the administrative bodies and the national courts – fulfil the role of "filters" within the processes of the application of law. They are supposed to respect the general rules adopted in the first phase in order to comply with the Strasbourg judgments (during the "diffusing" phase) and apply these general rules to concrete cases. In doing so, the national authorities should prevent violations of the Convention rights, or at least remedy them, already at the national level. As a result, the national authorities may act as "filters" vis-à-vis the Strasbourg Court and de facto become, to some extent, the ECtHR's substitutes.[24] The Convention then becomes embedded at the national level (Helfer 2008), which implies granting protection of the Convention rights – as interpreted by the ECtHR – already at the national level and preventing applications from being filed at the Strasbourg Court, or at least significantly lowering their total number. The filtering role of the national authorities is depicted in Figure 1.2.

Among other implications, the described model shows that not only the establishment of a domestic general rule complying with the EC(t)HR, but also the subsequent practice of the law-applying authorities is crucial from the point of view of the overall effectiveness of the Convention system. This brings us to the importance of various actors involved in the domestic implementation process that will be addressed in the section that follows.

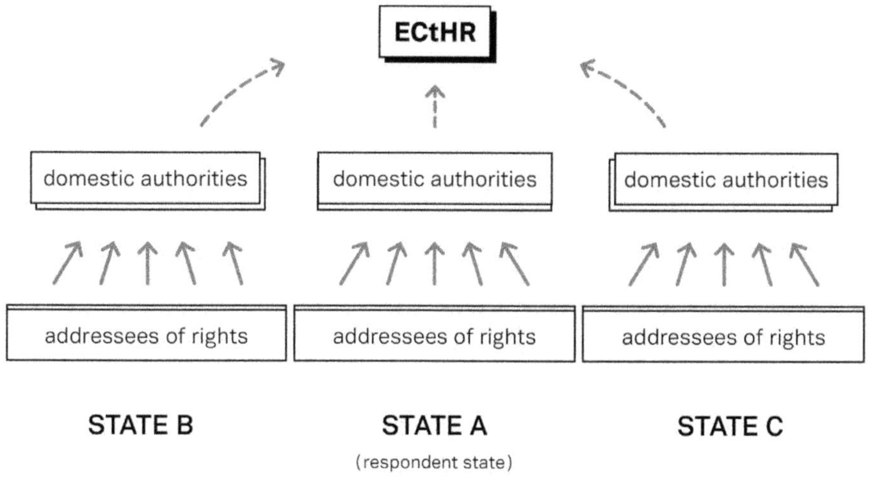

Figure 1.2 Domestic authorities as "filters" in the Convention system.
Source: authors.

1.3 Implementation processes of the Strasbourg case law: Particular actors within the domestic arena matter

The model presented in the previous section structures the basic features of the ECtHR's judgments implementation and illustrates the ties between the Strasbourg level and the domestic level of the Convention system. Yet it is notable that these links between the ECtHR and domestic layers of the Strasbourg human rights regime are, in fact, more diverse and heterogeneous. In practice, the system is not so strictly built along hierarchical lines (Krisch 2008; O'Cinneide 2010) and, especially at the domestic level, implementation is more open-ended as to the processes and their final outcomes.

As regards the processes of implementation, the domestic layer of the Convention system is far from being monolithic. On the contrary, domestic implementation processes are distinguished by (1) the plurality of actors, (2) who may have different attitudes towards the Strasbourg judgments, (3) are entangled in the web of mutual relations and interactions among each other, and (4) may have different powers and willingness to employ them. As the recent instances of backlash against the ECtHR have demonstrated, implementation of the Strasbourg case law may become a "hot" political issue. Ultimately, domestic responses depend primarily on the ability and willingness of domestic actors to push through such change. Therefore, in order to understand the implementation properly we need to open "the black box" of the domestic authorities element in the model scheme of the ECtHR's case law implementation processes.

First, regarding the plurality of actors, both national and international actors can possibly take part in the implementation processes. At the international level they include, among other actors, third states, governmental and non-governmental international organizations criticizing non-compliance by the respondent state.[25] International actors can also play the expertise-providing role. The European Commission for Democracy through Law (Venice Commission) is a particularly illustrative case. It provides states with opinions on their (draft) legislation or with reports on topical issues.[26] At the same time, some constitutional courts have even required *amicus curiae* opinions from the Venice Commission on comparative and international legal aspects of the cases they were dealing with. Such *amicus curiae* briefs regularly contain passages on the ECtHR's case law,[27] which enhances the constitutional courts' knowledge of the Strasbourg Court's jurisprudence and may contribute to its smoother implementation.

At the domestic level, especially the executive, the legislature, domestic courts, the Ombudsman, and the Government Agent before the ECtHR are engaged in ECHR rights implementation processes. Civil society actors, especially the domestic non-governmental organizations (NGOs), also importantly influence implementation processes. Even though they do not possess sufficient formal powers to change the status quo, they can mobilize around an ECtHR judgment, provide expertise, and generate pressure on the state authorities to act (Miara and Prais 2012).

Usually, at least in the high-profile cases, a plurality of actors is engaged. As Courtney Hillebrecht (2014a, 25) states, "[n]o single domestic actor, not even the strongest executive, can satisfy all of the tribunals' mandates, legally or logistically".[28] Different authors then emphasize roles of different institutions: Some rely on the power of the civil society and NGOs (Miara and Prais 2012), or pressure groups (Trachtman 2010), while others stress the power of the judiciary (Nollkaemper 2012; Gerards and Fleuren 2014), legislature (Donald and Leach 2016, 99–108; Stiansen 2019b) or the executive (Koh 1997, 2657; Huneeus 2011, 517) to push through the policy change. Therefore, the domestic implementation process is a complex endeavor that typically involves a number of actors. In fact, it is a complicated system consisting of an ever-changing set of actors whose steps might be important for the implementation of a Strasbourg Court judgment.[29]

Second, these actors who engage in the implementation processes are likely to have different interests, preferences, and attitudes towards human rights as such and towards the issue at stake in particular. Not all of these actors are necessarily in favor of the ECtHR's rulings in all of the cases. Domestic responses to the ECtHR's judgments do not take place automatically. Implementation of the ECtHR's rulings thus can be described as a political battle (Marmo 2008), or more generally as a competition between the pro-compliance forces and the compliance-opposing camp. In practice, however, the positions of particular actors will hardly be "black or white", which makes the trajectory of the implementation process even more complicated and unpredictable.

Furthermore, one must take into account the fact that the Convention system consists of 47 members and includes, according to Harmsen (2013, 141–42), three types of states (according to their human rights situation): established democracies, (post-)transition democracies, and hybrid regimes in which the basic norms of democratic governance and the rule of law have not been fully accepted. The smooth functioning of the model presented in Section 1.2 of this chapter presupposes a high level of expertise in human rights law, including knowledge of the Strasbourg case law concerning other countries so that the *res interpretata* effect is effectively guaranteed, and the respective language skills[30] of domestic officials. These assumptions still cannot be taken for granted, at least not in all of the 47 signatory parties to the Convention. As a result, especially in (post-)transition democracies and hybrid regimes, the obstacles of effective implementation may result not only from the (in)action of anti-compliance forces, but also from ignorance of the ECtHR's rulings, insufficient engagement with the issues addressed by the Strasbourg Court, or from a lack of enforcement capacity or will in the "filtering" phase.

Third, there are mutual relations and interactions between domestic actors. The proverbial "implementation ball" may move from one domestic institution to another as a result of their actions. For instance, if the constitutional court strikes down a statute for violating the Convention, the ball moves to the parliament, which can no longer be inactive as it must fill the gap in the law. This may nudge or force the parliament to leave the compliance-opposing camp and implement the relevant Strasbourg judgment. However, the parliament may also opt for minimalist compliance with the constitutional court's judgment and the ball then moves to the courts again. Due to the divergent preferences and priorities of domestic institutions regarding human rights, the ECtHR's judgments may also "ignite domestic battles over human rights, state sovereignty and the role of international law in domestic politics" (Hillebrecht 2012a, 293). Such Strasbourg judgments may sometimes even result in reshuffling the power of domestic actors, for instance by introducing judicial review in a certain area,[31] by reducing the autonomy of one branch of government,[32] by changing the composition of a constitutional organ,[33] or by introducing a new independent body to review police misconduct.[34] Such transfers of power require lengthy discussion, careful deliberation, and sometimes even quid pro quo solutions among the domestic actors involved.

Finally, the capacities and powers of the actors involved matter. As Sonia Cardenas (2007, 13) put it, the domestic battle over compliance may be affected more by the distribution of institutional power than by the greatest commitment to international human rights law. In the same vein, Courtney Hillebrecht (2014a, 25) concurs and argues that "[i]nternational law, and particularly the tribunals' rulings, can provide an impetus for action for individual actors or coalitions of actors, but their ability to act on that impetus will be limited – or enhanced – by their domestic political power". For instance, when domestic constraints on the executive (such as independent judiciaries, political competition, free media, and civil society) are weak, as they are in Russia, then a single actor – the executive – can dominate the implementation process (Hillebrecht 2012a, 288–9). In contrast, when several strong institutions take part in the implementation process, as in the United Kingdom, the eventual result of this process very much depends on the ability to reach consensus (Hillebrecht 2012a, 293–7). Similarly, implementation of the *D.H. and Others v. the Czech Republic* judgment concerning the segregation of Roma children in primary education shows how much the relative power of each domestic actor involved matters. For several years the implementation process reached an impasse as equally powerful pro- and anti-compliance coalitions, both ready to act, blocked any significant action (Smekal and Šipulová 2014). It was only when the new Minister of Education went over to the pro-compliance camp that the balance tilted towards the pro-compliance position and implementation moved forward (Kosař and Petrov 2018, 414).

In sum, it is possible to conclude that the implementation process and its outcome depend on (1) the number of (domestic) actors taking part in the implementation process, (2) their stances towards the ECtHR's judgment to be implemented, (3) mutual relations and interactions among these actors, and (4) their respective power within the system and their ability and readiness to act.

Therefore, the actors involved may play different roles in the implementation processes. We acknowledge that every actor possesses a certain spectrum of de facto possible options regarding how to react to the Strasbourg judgment

(Stone Sweet and Keller 2008b, 22). According to its preferences, powers, and possible interactions with other actors a particular actor may essentially influence the dynamics of the implementation process and, therefore, affect its outcome – the level of compliance with the ECtHR's ruling.

However, all those actors operate within a broader ecosystem – the state – that is shaped by macro-level factors. Fundamental state-level features of the polity and their implications for the implementation of international commitments have been widely studied.[35] Socio-political macro-level factors such as regime type (Slaughter 1995), length of democracy,[36] legal infrastructure and domestic institutional capacity (Anagnostou and Mungiu-Pippidi 2014; Hillebrecht 2014b, 1117), states' reputational concerns (Guzman 2002), or generally spread human rights expertise and awareness (Hillebrecht 2012a; Anagnostou and Mungiu-Pippidi 2014, 221) have been reported to influence compliance with international human rights law. At the same time, legal macro-level factors like the status of international law in domestic law, and particularly the de facto domestic status of the ECHR and the ECtHR's case law (Keller and Stone Sweet 2008, 683),[37] separation of powers doctrine, and configuration of constitutional review (Gerards and Fleuren 2014, 363), or prevailing perceptions of legal and political culture and the concept of democracy among judges in a given country[38] should be taken into account. That is to say that the macro-level factors can contribute to explanations of variations in the implementation of international human rights law over time and across countries (Hillebrecht 2012b, 963), and that they also shape the starting position of particular actors in the individual implementation processes at the meso level (domestic politics).

Having provided this general framework, Chapter 2 turns to analyzing the role of an allegedly natural ally of the ECtHR – the domestic judiciary – in implementing the Strasbourg case law.

Notes

1 For the discussion of decreasing rates of compliance with the ECtHR's judgment see also Shany (2012, 262–5).
2 Various reasons that may explain this resistance have been put forward: See, for example, Hillebrecht (2012a) and Anagnostou and Mungiu-Pippidi (2014).
3 See the respective declarations adopted at the High Level Conferences on the Future of the European Court of Human Rights in Interlaken (2010), Izmir (2011), Brighton (2012), Brussels (2015) and Copenhagen (2018). See also the annual reports on the supervision of the execution of the ECtHR's judgments by the Committee of Ministers, available at: www.coe.int/bg/web/execution/annual-reports.
4 See also Barkhuysen and van Emmerik (2005); Lambert-Abdelgawad (2008); Kosař (2012) and Kosař and Lixinski (2015).
5 ECtHR [GC], *Verein gegen Tierfabriken Schweiz (VgT) v. Switzerland (no. 2)*, no. 32772/02, judgment of 30 June 2009, § 85. See also e.g. *Castillo Algar v. Spain*, no. 28194/95, judgment of 28 October 1998, § 60; *Assanidze v. Georgia* [GC], no. 71503/01, judgment of 8 April 2004, § 198; and *Maestri v. Italy* [GC], no. 39748/98, judgment of 17 February 2004, § 47.
6 For further details see Jahn (2014).

7 See, for example, ECtHR [GC], *Maestri v. Italy*, no. 39748/98, judgment of 17 February 2004, § 47; *Apicella v. Italy* [GC], no. 64890/01, judgment of 29 March 2006, § 123; *Yordanova v. Bulgaria*, no. 25446/06, judgment of 24 April 2012, § 163; *Paksas v. Latvia* [GC], no. 34932/04, judgment of 6 January 2011, § 119.

8 See Article 34 ECHR; and, for example, *F. v. Switzerland* [Plenary], no. 11329/85, judgment of 18 December 1987, § 43; *Marckx v. Belgium* [Plenary], no. 6833/74, judgment of 13 June 1979, § 58.

9 In the case law of the Strasbourg Court see, for example, *Marckx v. Belgium* [Plenary], no. 6833/74, judgment of 13 June 1979, § 58; *Belilos v. Switzerland* [Plenary], no. 10328/83, judgment of 29 April 1988, § 78; *Scozzari and Giunta v. Italy* [Plenary], nos. 39221/98 and 41963/98, judgment of 13 July 2000, § 249.

10 For the description of pilot judgments procedure see, for example, Buyse (2009) and Fyrnys (2011). In short, the pilot judgments procedure is the ECtHR's judicial innovation which aims to trigger domestic legal reform in the areas afflicted by structural human rights dysfunctions.

11 *Hirst (no. 2) v. the United Kingdom* [GC], no. 74025/01, judgment of 6 October 2005.

12 *Salduz v. Turkey* [GC], no. 36391/02, judgment of 27 November 2008, Merits and Just Satisfaction.

13 *Hutten-Czapska v. Poland* [GC], no. 35014/97, judgment of 19 June 2006.

14 Act No. 107/2006 Coll. It should be added that another impulse for adopting this new statute was the case law of the Czech Constitutional Court. See Wintr (2012).

15 For other examples, see Bodnar (2014), Drzemczewski (2011) and Gerards (2014, 21–7).

16 See Bodnar (2014), Drzemczewski (2011), and Gerards (2014).

17 A *res interpretata* effect is inferred from the joint reading of Articles 1, 19, and 32 ECHR. See Drzemczewski (2011).

18 See, for example, *Opuz v. Turkey*, no. 33401/02, judgment of 9 June 2009, § 163; *Rantsev v. Cyprus*, no. 25965/04, judgment of 7 January 2010, § 197 and the case law cited therein.

19 See above.

20 For further details on *res interpretata* effect, see Drzemczewski (2011, 243–7), Bodnar (2014), and Gerards (2014, 21–7).

21 But see the new infringement procedure enshrined in Article 46(4) and (5) ECHR, which is, nevertheless, a rather extraordinary instrument.

22 See also Hillebrecht (2012b, 964–72, 984–5), regarding the Inter-American Court of Human Rights.

23 In some cases, the two phases might merge into one.

24 On the substituting role of national courts in relation to international courts, see Nollkaemper (2012).

25 See, for example, ECtHR [GC], *D.H. and Others v. the Czech Republic*, no. 57325/00, judgment of 13 November 2007; and Smekal and Šipulová (2014), who discuss the subsequent implementation process in the Czech Republic.

26 See, for example, De Visser (2015) and Volpe (2016). The Venice Commission is not the only relevant actor in this respect. See also the activities of the European Union actors, in particular the Commission and the Court of Justice who can push the states for greater compliance with ECHR principles.

27 For example, *Amicus Curiae* Brief for the Constitutional Court of Georgia on individual application by public broadcasters, adopted by the Venice Commission at its 98th Plenary Session (Venice, 21–22 March 2014), §§ 49–60; Joint *Amicus Curiae* Brief for the Constitutional Court of Moldova on the compatibility with European Standards of Law No. 192 of 12 July 2012 on the prohibition of the use of symbols of the totalitarian communist regime and of the promotion of totalitarian ideologies of the Republic of Moldova, adopted by the Venice Commission at its 94th Plenary Session (Venice, 8–9 March 2013); *Amicus Curiae*

Brief on the Compatibility with Human Rights Standards of certain articles of the Law on Primary Education of the Sarajevo Canton of the Federation of Bosnia and Herzegovina, adopted by the Venice Commission at its 91st Plenary Session (Venice, 15–16 June 2012), §§ 23–9.

28 See also Dai (2007).

29 See also Alter (2014, 19).

30 Even though the ECtHR has recently significantly improved access to its case law in more than the two original languages and has started to publish translations of its judgments into various languages on its website, HUDOC (see http://hudoc.echr.coe.int). As of 12 June 2019, the number of translated judgments varied from 17 (Latvian) to 3,317 (Turkish).

31 The ECtHR has, among other things, required the Netherlands to allow full judicial review of the Crown's administrative decisions (*Benthem v. Netherlands* [Plenary], no. 8848/80, judgment of 23 October 1985, §§ 32–44). See also van Dijk (1987).

32 For instance, the ECtHR has significantly narrowed the scope of parliamentary immunity (see *Karácsony and Others v. Hungary* [GC], nos. 42461/13 and 44357/13, judgment of 17 May 2016; and earlier case law discussed in Kosař [2012, 46–55]).

33 For instance, the ECtHR has de facto forced Ukraine to change the composition of the Ukrainian High Council of Justice (see *Volkov v. Ukraine*, no. 21722/11, judgment of 9 January 2013, § 91, §§ 109–117, 200). For further details see Kosař and Lixinski (2015, 737–8, 756).

34 See, for example, ECtHR, *Güleç v. Turkey*, no. 21593/93, judgment of 27 July 1998, §§ 76, 80; *Hugh Jordan v. the United Kingdom*, no. 24746/94, judgment of 4 May 2001, § 120; and *Eremiášová and Pechová v. the Czech Republic*, no. 23944/04, judgment of 16 February 2012, §§ 137, 151–60.

35 The following list of macro-level factors does not aspire to completeness. Rather, we mention the factors most relevant for the focus of this book.

36 See the discussion in Grewal and Voeten (2015).

37 In detail, see Paris (2017).

38 See, *mutatis mutandis*, Wind (2010) or Mayoral and Jaremba (2016, 10–11).

References

Algan, Bülent. 2008. "The Brand New Version of Article 301 of Turkish Penal Code and the Future of Freedom of Expression Cases in Turkey". *German Law Journal* 9 (12): 2237–52.

Alter, Karen J. 2014. *New Terrain of International Law*. Princeton, NJ: Princeton University Press.

Anagnostou, Dia, and Alina Mungiu-Pippidi. 2014. "Domestic Implementation of Human Rights Judgments in Europe: Legal Infrastructure and Government Effectiveness Matter". *European Journal of International Law* 25 (1): 205–27.

Barkhuysen, Tom, and Michiel L. van Emmerik. 2005. "A Comparative View on the Execution of Judgments of the European Court of Human Rights". In *European Court of Human Rights: Remedies and Execution of Judgments*, edited by Theodora Christou and Juan Pablo Raymond, 1–23. London: British Institute of Comparative and International Law.

Bates, Ed. 2010. *The Evolution of the European Convention on Human Rights: From Its Inception to the Creation of a Permanent Court of Human Rights*. Oxford: Oxford University Press.

Bates, Ed. 2014. "Analysing the Prisoner Voting Saga and the British Challenge to Strasbourg". *Human Rights Law Review* 14 (3): 503–40.

Bodnar, Adam. 2014. "Res Interpretata: Legal Effect of the European Court of Human Rights' Judgments for Other States than Those Which Were Party to the Proceedings". In *Human Rights & Civil Liberties in the 21st Century*, edited by Yves Haeck and Eva Brems, 223–62. Dordrecht: Springer.

Buyse, Antoine. 2009. "The Pilot Judgment Procedure at the European Court of Human Rights: Possibilities and Challenges". *The Greek Law Journal* 57 (8): 1890–1902.

Cardenas, Sonia. 2007. *Conflict and Compliance: State Responses to International Human Rights Pressure*. Philadelphia, PA: University of Pennsylvania Press.

Dai, Xinyuan. 2007. *International Institutions and National Policies*. New York: Cambridge University Press.

De Visser, Maartje. 2015. "A Critical Assessment of the Role of the Venice Commission in Processes of Domestic Constitutional Reform". *American Journal of Comparative Law* 63 (4): 963–1008.

Donald, Alice, and Philip Leach. 2016. *Parliaments and the European Court of Human Rights*. Oxford: Oxford University Press.

Drzemczewski, Andrew Z. 2011. "Quelques Réflexions Sur L'autorité De La Chose Interprétée Par La Cour De Strasbourg". In *La Conscience Des Droits: Mélanges En L'honneur De Jean-Paul Costa*, edited by Jean Barthélemy, et al., 243–7. Paris: Dalloz.

Flogaitis, Spyridon, Tom Zwart, and Julie Fraser, eds. 2013. *The European Court of Human Rights and Its Discontents: Turning Criticism into Strength*. Cheltenham: Edward Elgar.

Føllesdal, Andreas. 2016. "Squaring the Circle at the Battle of Brighton: Is the War between Protection of Human Rights or Respecting Sovereignty Over, or Has It Just Begun?" In *Shifting the Centres of Gravity in Human Rights Protection: Rethinking Relations between the ECHR, EU, and National Legal Orders*, edited by Oddný Mjöll Arnardóttir and Antoine Buyse, 189–204. Abingdon and New York: Routledge.

Fyrnys, Markus. 2011. "Expanding Competences by Judicial Lawmaking: The Pilot Judgment Procedure of the European Court of Human Rights". *German Law Journal* 12 (5): 1231–60.

Gerards, Janneke. 2014. "The European Court of Human Rights and the National Courts: Giving Shape to the Notion of 'Shared Responsibility'". In *Implementation of the European Convention on Human Rights and of the Judgments of the ECtHR in National Case Law*, edited by Janneke Gerards and Jospeh Fleuren, 13–94. Cambridge: Intersentia.

Gerards, Janneke, and Joseph Fleuren, eds. 2014. *Implementation of the European Convention on Human Rights and of the Judgments of the ECtHR in National Case Law*. Cambridge: Intersentia.

Giannoulopoulos, Dimitrios. 2016. "Strasbourg Jurisprudence, Law Reform and Comparative Law: A Tale of the Right to Custodial Legal Assistance in Five Countries". *Human Rights Law Review* 16 (1): 103–29.

Grewal, Sharanbir, and Erik Voeten. 2015. "Are New Democracies Better Human Rights Compliers?". *International Organization* 69 (2): 497–518.

Guzman, Andrew T. 2002. "A Compliance-Based Theory of International Law". *California Law Review* 90 (6): 1823–87.

Hamilton, Alexander. 2003. "Federalist No. 78". In *The Federalist Papers*, edited by Clinton Rossiter, 463–70. New York: Signet Classic.

Harmsen, Robert. 2013. "The Reform of the Convention System: Institutional Restructuring and the (Geo-)politics of Human Rights". In *The European Court of Human Rights between Law and Politics*, edited by Jonas Christoffersen and Mikael Rask Madsen, 119–43. New York: Oxford University Press.

Harris, David J., Michael O'Boyle, Ed Bates, and Carla Buckley, eds. 2014. *Law of the European Convention on Human Rights*. 3rd edition. Oxford: Oxford University Press.

Hathaway, Oona A., and Scott J. Shapiro. 2011. "Outcasting: Enforcement in Domestic and International Law". *Yale Law Journal* 121: 252–349.

Hawkins, Darren, and Wade Jacoby. 2010. "Partial Compliance: A Comparison of the European and Inter-American Courts of Human Rights". *Journal of International Law and International Relations* 6 (1): 35–85.

Helfer, Laurence. 2008. "Redesigning the European Court of Human Rights: Embeddedness as a Deep Structural Principle of the European Human Rights Regime". *European Journal of International Law* 19 (1): 125–59.

Helfer, Laurence, and Eric Voeten. 2014. "International Courts as Agents of Legal Change: Evidence from LGBT Rights in Europe". *International Organization* 68 (1): 77–110.

Hillebrecht, Courtney. 2012a. "Implementing International Human Rights Law at Home: Domestic Politics and the European Court of Human Rights". *Human Rights Review* 13 (3): 279–301.

Hillebrecht, Courtney. 2012b. "The Domestic Mechanisms of Compliance with International Human Rights Law: Case Studies from the Inter-American Human Rights System". *Human Rights Quarterly* 34 (4): 959–85.

Hillebrecht, Courtney. 2014a. *Domestic Politics and International Human Rights Tribunals: The Problem of Compliance*. New York: Cambridge University Press.

Hillebrecht, Courtney. 2014b. "The Power of Human Rights Tribunals: Compliance with the European Court of Human Rights and Domestic Policy Change". *European Journal of International Relations* 20 (4): 1100–23.

Huneeus, Alexandra. 2011. "Courts Resisting Courts: Lessons from the Inter-American Court's Struggle to Enforce Human Rights". *Cornell International Law Journal* 44 (3): 493–533.

Jahn, Jannika. 2014. "Ruling (In)directly through Individual Measures? Effect and Legitimacy of the ECtHR's New Remedial Power". *Heidelberg Journal of International Law* 76: 1–39.

Johnson, Paul. 2010. "'an Essentially Private Manifestation of Human Personality': Constructions of Homosexuality in the European Court of Human Rights". *Human Rights Law Review* 10 (1): 67–97.

Keller, Helen, and Cedric Marti. 2015. "Reconceptualizing Implementation: The Judicialization of the Execution of the European Court of Human Rights' Jurisprudence". *European Journal of International Law* 26 (4): 829–50.

Keller, Helen, and Alec Stone Sweet. 2008. "Assessing the Impact of the ECHR on National Legal Systems". In *A Europe of Rights: The Impact of the ECHR on National Legal Systems*, edited by Alec Stone Sweet and Helen Keller, 677–712. Oxford: Oxford University Press.

Koh, Harold H. 1997. "Why Do Nations Obey International Law?" *Yale Law Journal* 106 (8): 2599–659.

Koh, Harold H. 1999. "How Is International Human Rights Law Enforced?". *Indiana Law Journal* 74 (4): 1397–417.

Kosař, David. 2012. "Policing Separation of Powers: A New Role for the European Court of Human Rights?". *European Constitutional Law Review* 8 (1): 33–62.

Kosař, David. 2018. "The Strasbourg Court and Domestic Judicial Politics". In *International Courts and Domestic Politics*, edited by Marlene Wind, 71–92. Cambridge: Cambridge University Press.

Kosař, David, and Lucas Lixinski. 2015. "Domestic Judicial Design by International Human Rights Courts". *The American Journal of International Law* 109 (4): 713–60.

Kosař, David, and Jan Petrov. 2018. "Determinants of Compliance Difficulties among 'Good Compliers': Implementation of International Human Rights Rulings in the Czech Republic". *The European Journal of International Law* 29 (2): 397–425.

Krisch, Nico. 2008. "The Open Architecture of European Human Rights Law". *Modern Law Review* 71 (2): 183–216.

Lambert-Abdelgawad, Elizabeth. 2008. *The Execution of Judgments of the European Court of Human Rights*. Strasbourg: Council of Europe.

Leach, Philip. 2013. "No Longer Offering Fine Mantras to a Parched Child? the European Court's Developing Approach to Remedies". In *Constituting Europe: The European Court of Human Rights in a National, European and Global Context*, edited by Andreas Føllesdal, Birgit Peters, and Geir Ulfstein, 142–80. Cambridge: Cambridge University Press.

Madsen, Mikael Rask. 2013. "The Protracted Institutionalization of the Strasbourg Court: From Legal Diplomacy to Integrationist Jurisprudence". In *The European Court of Human Rights between Law and Politics*, edited by Jonas Christoffersen and Mikael Rask Madsen, 43–60. New York: Oxford University Press.

Madsen, Mikael Rask. 2016. "The Challenging Authority of the European Court of Human Rights: From Cold War Legal Diplomacy to the Brighton Declaration and Backlash". *Law & Contemporary Problems* 79: 141–78.

Madsen, Mikael Rask. 2019. "Resistance to the European Court of Human Rights: The Institutional and Sociological Consequences of Principled Resistance". In *Principled Resistance to ECtHR Judgments – A New Paradigm?* edited by Marten Breuer, 35–52. Heidelberg: Sringer.

Marmo, Marinella. 2008. "The Execution of Judgments of the European Court of Human Rights – A Political Battle". *Maastricht Journal of European and Comparative Law* 15 (2): 235–58.

Mayoral, Juan A., and Urszula Jaremba. 2016. "Perspectives on Europeanization of National Judiciaries: Old and New Questions". *iCourts Working Paper Series*, No. 59: 1–31.

Miara, Lucja, and Victoria Prais. 2012. "The Role of Civil Society in the Execution of Judgments of the European Court of Human Rights". *European Human Rights Law Review*, 2012, n. 5: 528–37.

Nollkaemper, André. 2012. "The Role of National Courts in Inducing Compliance with International and European Law – A Comparison". In *Compliance and the Enforcement of EU Law*, edited by Marise Cremona, 157–93. Oxford: Oxford University Press.

O'Cinneide, Colm. 2010. "Human Rights within Multi-Layered Systems of Constitutional Governance: Rights Cosmopolitanism and Domestic Particularism in Tension". *Irish Yearbook of International Law* 3: 19–44.

Oomen, Barbara M. 2016. "A Serious Case of Strasbourg-bashing? an Evaluation of the Debates on the Legitimacy of the European Court of Human Rights in the Netherlands". *The International Journal of Human Rights* 20 (3): 407–25.

Paris, Davide. 2017. "Allies and Counterbalances. Constitutional Courts and the European Court of Human Rights: A Comparative Perspective". *Heidelberg Journal of International Law* 77 (3): 623–49.

Petrov, Jan. 2020. The Populist Challenge to the European Court of Human Rights. *International Journal of Constitutional Law* 18 (forthcoming).

Popelier, Patricia, Sarah Lambrecht, and Koen Lemmens, eds. 2016. *Criticism of the European Court of Human Rights.* Cambridge: Intersentia.

Shany, Yuval. 2012. "Assessing the Effectiveness of International Courts: A Goal-Based Approach". *American Journal of International Law* 106 (2): 225–70.

Slaughter, Anne-Marie. 1995. "International Law in a World of Liberal States". *The European Journal of International Law* 6 (3): 503–38.

Smekal, Hubert, and Katarína Šipulová. 2014. "*DH v Czech Republic* Six Years Later: On the Power of an International Human Rights Court to Push through Systemic Change". *Netherlands Quarterly of Human Rights* 32 (3): 288–321.

Smekal, Hubert, and Ladislav Vyhnánek, eds. 2018. *Beyond Compliance – Implementace Rozhodnutí Mezinárodních Lidskoprávních Těles Na Národní Úrovni [Beyond Compliance: Domestic Judicial Implementation of the International Human Rights Case Law].* Prague: Wolters Kluwer.

Stiansen, Øyvind. 2019a. Directing Compliance? Remedial Approach and Compliance with European Court of Human Rights Judgments. *British Journal of Political Science* (forthcoming).

Stiansen, Øyvind. 2019b. "Delayed but Not Derailed: Legislative Compliance with European Court of Human Rights Judgments". *International Journal of Human Rights* 23 (8): 1221–47.

Stone Sweet, Alec, and Hellen Keller. 2008a. "The Reception of the ECHR in National Legal Orders". In *A Europe of Rights: The Impact of the ECHR on National Legal Systems,* edited by Alec Stone Sweet and Hellen Keller, 3–28. New York: Oxford University Press.

Stone Sweet, Alec, and Hellen Keller, eds. 2008b. *A Europe of Rights: The Impact of the ECHR on National Legal Systems.* New York: Oxford University Press.

Trachtman, Joel P. 2010. "International Law and Domestic Political Coalitions: The Grand Theory of Compliance with International Law". *Chicago Journal of International Law* 11 (1), Article 6: 127–58.

van Dijk, Pieter. 1987. "The Benthem Case and Its Aftermath in the Netherlands". *Netherlands International Law Review* 34 (1): 5–24.

Volpe, Valentina. 2016. "Drafting Counter-Majoritarian Democracy The Venice Commission's Constitutional Assistance". *Heidelberg Journal of International Law* 76: 811–843.

von Staden, Andreas. 2018. *Strategies of Compliance with the European Court of Human Rights.* Philadelphia, PA: University of Pennsylvania Press.

Wind, Marlene. 2010. "The Nordics, the EU and the Reluctance Towards Supranational Judicial Review". *Journal of Common Market Studies* 48 (4): 1039–63.

Wintr, Jan. 2012. ""Vliv Evropské Úmluvy Na Český Ústavní pořádek" ["impact of the European Convention on the Czech Constitutional order"]". *Jurisprudence* 21 (7–8): 7–8.

2 The role of domestic courts in the Strasbourg system

The previous chapter showed that several domestic actors are usually involved in the process of implementation of the European Court of Human Rights' (ECtHR or Strasbourg Court) case law, and that their attitudes towards the Strasbourg judgments, their mutual relationship, and their relative powers to a large extent determine the direction and speed of the implementation processes. Among those actors, domestic courts are considered the most natural allies of the Strasbourg Court who may help the ECtHR to secure compliance with its judgments and to enhance its legitimacy (Sadurski 2009; Dothan 2014, 111–12; Paris 2017; Petrov 2018). This chapter concentrates on the domestic judiciaries and examines the role of various judicial actors in detail. Subsequently, it analyzes separately the role of the apex courts in the mechanisms of implementing the ECtHR's case law.

2.1 Domestic judiciaries: The driving force of implementation?

Domestic judiciaries share the ECtHR's *legal* language and working methods. National courts, and the apex courts in particular, can help to monitor the enforcement of Strasbourg judgments in their own states and, by issuing similar rulings, even increase the support within their own states for those judgments (Dothan 2014, 111). That also explains why the ECtHR forged a compliance partnership with domestic judges[1] and empowered them vis-à-vis other branches of the government (Kosař and Lixinski 2015, 747–9).

However, the domestic judiciary is not a monolithic block. The domestic judicial landscape is much more complicated than usually assumed in the debates about the future of the European Convention on Human Rights (ECHR or Convention) system. This chapter shows the complexity of the domestic judicial level of the Strasbourg system and demonstrates that there are numerous structural and contingent factors potentially affecting the domestic judicial treatment of the ECtHR's case law. Consequently, a positive contribution of domestic (apex) courts to ECtHR case law implementation is not automatic and cannot be taken for granted. That makes the case for studying actual domestic judicial treatment of the Strasbourg case law more closely (see Part II of this book) even stronger.

There are at least five actors within the domestic judiciaries. These actors are the constitutional court (if it exists in a given country), top ordinary courts (the Supreme Court, the Supreme Administrative Court, the Council of State, and other courts of the same stature), lower courts, court presidents, and judicial associations. These actors, each in their own way, influence the implementation of the Strasbourg jurisprudence into the domestic case law. They may, like domestic actors within the other two branches of the government, have different interests, preferences, and attitudes towards the Strasbourg case law in general as well as towards particular judgments. The position of each of these actors depends, among other things, on their openness to supranational sources, values, and beliefs that may or may not place a special premium on legal certainty and the stability of the legal system; knowledge of foreign languages; promotion incentives; expectations of their key audience; and on power considerations. Moreover, the position of each actor within the judiciary may change over time.

The significance of the role of apex courts – i.e., constitutional courts and top ordinary courts – is addressed in detail below. In a nutshell, constitutional courts can reinterpret statutes through the Convention-conforming interpretation or strike down laws that fail to meet the domestic fundamental rights standards, which are often heavily influenced by Strasbourg case law. Some constitutional courts went even further. They de facto constitutionalized the Convention (see, for example, Stone Sweet and Keller 2008, 686; Martinico 2010, 12–14) and started to use it as a benchmark, separately from the domestic constitutional norms, for judging domestic laws (van de Heyning 2013; Paris 2017). Top ordinary courts are also powerful players as they may employ Convention-conforming interpretations and prioritize positions that engage more with the Strasbourg case law (Gerards and Fleuren 2014). By doing so, they also impose their Strasbourg-friendly positions on the lower courts. Hence, constitutional courts and top ordinary courts may operate as great "diffusers" and "filters" in the Convention system.[2] On the other hand, they also wield a significant "negative power" that can be unleashed. They can impose a narrow reading of the Strasbourg case law on the lower courts that may lead to minimalist compliance.[3] In some countries, they may even block the compliance processes by finding the Strasbourg position incompatible with the domestic constitution,[4] as in such scenarios other political actors will very probably not openly defy the position of their own apex court.[5]

The role of lower courts, court presidents, and judicial associations is less visible and often underestimated. Lower courts do not necessarily have to share the top courts' views of the Strasbourg Court (Mańko 2014). For instance, in Poland they seem to be more resistant to the Strasbourg influence than the Polish Constitutional Tribunal and the Supreme Court (see, for example, Koncewicz 2016a, 2016b). In the Czech Republic, one might witness an even more complex situation – the so-called "sandwich scenario": Judges appointed after the fall of communism, often fluent in English and French and more keen to implement the Strasbourg case law, sit in the lowest courts and in the

Constitutional Court (established as a part of democratic transition), whereas judges who were appointed in the communist era (or educated in the communist era and appointed in the early 1990s), not well versed in foreign languages and often skeptical of the purposive and value-oriented ECtHR reasoning, occupy the seats at appellate courts and at the Supreme Court.[6] In other words, the Strasbourg skeptics on the bench are "sandwiched" by the pro-Strasbourg judges (Kosař 2016, 107–8).

Court presidents are even less visible yet important actors. They are the key players within the Central and Eastern European judiciaries,[7] who influence judicial appointments and decide on promotion, case assignment, and other perks (Piana 2010, 43–44; Solomon 2010, 354; Müller 2012, 965; Kosař 2016, 390–8), and hence their stance towards the Strasbourg Court also matters. For instance, a court president who is skeptical about international human rights courts might prioritize the appointment of less Strasbourg-enthusiastic judges to his court or informally tone down current judges' engagement with the Strasbourg case law. Finally, judicial associations, although rarely built on the pro- and anti-Strasbourg axis, may also induce judges to exercise restraint or openness towards the ECtHR, as they influence promotion in several countries, such as France[8] and Italy (Guarnieri and Pederzoli 2002, 54; Guarnieri 2013, 348).

2.2 Apex courts and the Strasbourg Court: A far more complicated relationship than it seems

Out of the actors identified in Section 2.1, this book focuses on the role of apex courts – constitutional courts and top ordinary courts – as the existing literature treats them as the ECtHR's main allies or "faithful trustees" (Bjorge 2015) who have taken the lead in implementing the ECHR (Stone Sweet and Keller 2008, 687; Dzehtsiarou and Mavronicola 2016).

The apex courts' contribution to implementation of the ECtHR's case law is undeniable. With their competence to quash unconstitutional legislation and to reinterpret statutes, constitutional courts have imposed human rights standards on the legislatures in many areas.[9] Additionally, constitutional courts that are empowered to review individual acts (judicial and administrative decisions) in the constitutional complaint mechanism have also contributed to mainstreaming human rights in the process of law application, particularly in ordinary courts (Petrov 2019). More generally, however, supervision and unification of domestic judicial practice is the domain of top ordinary courts (supreme and supreme administrative courts). Since their rulings have significant normative force and influence on general directions of the domestic jurisprudence (MacCormick and Summers 1997), they are crucial actors in tackling human-rights-defective practices in the law application process. As a result, apex courts function both as significant diffusers of the ECtHR's jurisprudence and filters vis-à-vis the Strasbourg Court, thereby contributing to domestic embeddedness of the Convention (Helfer 2008).

However, apex courts are far from being mere marionettes (Gerards 2014) or transmission belts of the ECtHR. Especially in the past decade, they have played a more active role in shaping the ECHR rights. In fact, the developments in the ECHR system emphasizing the principle of subsidiarity[10] have strengthened this role of apex courts. Apex courts and the Strasbourg Court have a "shared responsibility" for protecting and implementing the Convention.[11] Accordingly, domestic courts' (and other bodies') engagement with and implementation of ECHR rights have been seen as "vital to the proper functioning of the Convention system".[12] The Strasbourg Court itself has developed an emerging doctrine of responsible courts, which ascribes high significance to domestic judicial decision-making. To put it briefly, the main point of the doctrine is that the width of the margin of appreciation conferred by the ECtHR to the state is co-determined by the quality and weight given to the ECHR in the preceding domestic judicial procedure. If the state proves that the domestic courts have paid sufficient attention to human rights standards, the ECtHR should be more deferential and grant a wider margin of appreciation to the state party.[13] This (semi-)procedural approach of the ECtHR strengthens the role of domestic courts in the ECHR system, the apex courts' role in particular. On the other hand, it is still a rather recent and unsettled approach that is not applied coherently yet.

Another mechanism allowing for a greater engagement of domestic apex courts with the ECtHR is the advisory opinion mechanism introduced by Protocol No. 16 to ECHR. Under this mechanism, domestic apex courts are entitled to request that the ECtHR gives advisory opinions on questions of principle relating to the interpretation or application of the Convention rights and freedoms.[14] The advisory opinion mechanism, however, is too novel to assess its impact on the ECHR system architecture.[15]

Besides the rosy picture of apex courts as allies and partners in interpreting and implementing the ECHR, there is a competing narrative. Apex courts may also perceive the ECtHR as a competitor and, therefore, prefer not to engage much with the Convention in order to guard their own playing field (Stone Sweet and Keller 2008, 28). The ECtHR might even become a subversive force that challenges the prominent position of apex courts within the domestic constitutional order, disrupts the status quo, or undermines the national sovereignty.[16] Under this narrative, apex courts embrace the Strasbourg case law only if it suits their own goals.

In fact, the number of instances of tensions between domestic apex courts and the Strasbourg Court has increased. Such tensions have been of different quality and intensity. They have ranged from disagreements over the particular legal questions, and over general delimiting of the ECtHR's case law effects in the domestic constitutional order, to contestations of the Strasbourg Court's position in the ECHR system.

These signs of resistance come from both established and new democracies. For instance, the Italian Constitutional Court held in 2015 that only the "settled case law" of the ECtHR is binding upon Italian ordinary courts.[17] The

Russian Constitutional Court went even further, and in a series of judgments from 2015 and 2016 stressed the supremacy of the Russian Constitution over the Convention and openly rejected the implementation of the ECtHR's *Anchugov and Gladkov v. Russia* judgment dealing with the voting rights of prisoners,[18] and later also the *Yukos* case that concerned high satisfaction awarded by the ECtHR to the applicants.[19] Even the German Constitutional Court, which has stopped short of open revolt so far, has shown considerable reservations about fully embracing the Strasbourg case law in the so-called preventive detention saga (see, for example, Merkel 2010, 1046–7; Andenas and Bjorge 2011; Giegerich 2014, 225; Klein 2014, 207; Paulus 2014, 274–5), the *Görgülü* case (e.g., Tomuschat 2010, 520–6; Hartwig 2011, 145–6) and the *Von Hannover* case (Hoffmann-Riem 2006, 497–9; Papier 2006, 3; Coors 2010, 533–5; Tomuschat 2010; Hartwig 2011).

In addition, this contagion seems to be spreading to top ordinary courts as well.[20] The UK Supreme Court famously persuaded the ECtHR to adjust its "sole and decisive" test in the context of hearsay evidence in the *Horncastle* saga (López Guerra 2017, 407–8). The Swiss Federal Supreme Court decided not to follow the ECtHR's case law on a few occasions and once even stated that the Strasbourg Court's ruling at stake may have been issued *ultra vires* (Altwicker 2016, 407; Ammann 2018). The Czech Supreme Administrative Court recently refused to follow the ECtHR's judgment in *A.P., Garçon and Nicot v. France* regarding the rights of transgender persons, simply due to an allegedly differing view of the majority of Czech society.[21] More generally, a recent socio-legal study on the legitimacy of the ECtHR in the eyes of domestic judges yielded similar results and confirmed the rise of opposition to the Strasbourg Court within the judiciary (Çali, Koch, and Bruch 2011, 2013; Popelier, Lambrecht, and Lemmens 2016).

A less visible shift took place in Central and Eastern Europe, whose constitutional courts were adamant supporters of the Strasbourg Court in their early years. That was understandable, as for them the ECtHR's case law was, in the absence of the developed case law based on the domestic catalogues of fundamental rights, an important inspiration,[22] or even operated as a "shield"[23] against the post-communist semi-authoritarian regimes (see, for example, Procházka 2002a, 218; Bobek and Kosař 2010). But times have changed. Some constitutional courts in the region, such as the Hungarian Constitutional Court and the Polish Constitutional Tribunal, came under pressure from the ruling parties that see the Strasbourg Court and the Council of Europe (CoE) more broadly as the supporters of their opposition (Bugarič and Ginsburg 2016; Kovács and Scheppele 2018; Sadurski 2019). Other constitutional courts have built a considerable amount of their own case law within the last 20 years and, at least in certain areas of law, no longer need to look to Strasbourg for guidance. The Czech Constitutional Court in particular has become more assertive and increasingly aware of, and willing openly to advance, the distinctive Czech constitutional identity.[24] Neither the pressure and court-packing in Hungary and Poland nor the new self-esteem in Czechia has so far materialized in an open challenge to the Strasbourg Court. However, it is significantly more likely that this may happen in the future, especially if the ECtHR increases the number of highly divisive judgments against these countries that would resonate with the ruling political forces and the public at large.[25]

In sum, domestic judicial treatment of the ECtHR's case law is manifold and ranges from complete embracement over unawareness and ignorance to occasional contestation or even overt rejection. As a result, following and giving full effect to the Strasbourg Court's rulings by the domestic apex courts in all cases cannot be taken for granted these days. Explaining the differing positions of apex courts towards the ECtHR's case law is difficult and depends on numerous factors beyond the scope of this book. For better understanding of the institutional factors, one should take into account not only the other actors interacting with apex courts (see Chapter 1), but also the inner differentiation of apex courts and the existence of different actors *within* apex courts.

Apex courts' internal structure is diverse. It is well known that many constitutional courts sit not only as a full court, but also in smaller panels.[26] The German *Bundesverfassungsgericht* is a typical example. It is de facto not one, but two courts,[27] because its 16 judges virtually never sit together to decide cases on the merits. Novel cases are decided in two separate eight-member senates, whereas repetitive and less important cases are adjudicated by three-member panels (Kommers 2012, 18–22). Czech, Romanian, Slovak, and many other constitutional courts decide cases either in plenary sessions or in smaller (usually three-member) panels (see, for example, Procházka 2002b, 33–75; Kosař 2008, 348–51; Sadurski 2014, 22). It is thus quite possible that the smaller decision-making units *within* a given constitutional court may diverge regarding their openness towards the Strasbourg case law. Top ordinary courts are usually even larger courts consisting of dozens of judges and numerous panels.

However, these tensions among the panels of the same court should not be exaggerated, and most apex courts have developed mechanisms for unifying the divergent case law anyway.[28] Therefore, it is important to look beyond the dynamics between the plenary and the panels and among the panels. Depending on legal culture, the perception of the role of a constitutional court and its justices, the maturity of constitutional adjudication and institutional design in a given country, there are at least five more players *within* the apex court whose role might be critical for the embeddedness of the Strasbourg case law: the court president, the Secretariat, a separate analytical department specializing in international and comparative law, individual justices, and law clerks.

The powers and roles of chief justices vary from one country to another.[29] In some countries chief justices decide unilaterally on case assignment,[30] have a major say in the composition of panels on multi-panel courts,[31] preside over and set the agendas of plenary and grand chamber meetings,[32] decide on the use of courts' resources (Blisa and Kosař 2018), and may even influence the selection of new apex court judges as they are often formally involved[33] or informally consulted in this process.[34] In sum, chief justices wield not only media and ambassadorial powers, but also significant jurisprudential, administrative, and financial powers as well as power over the judicial careers of other apex court judges.[35] None of this entails a direct take on the Strasbourg case law, but it is clear that chief justices are powerful figures in many countries and their view of the Strasbourg Court may heavily influence the position of individual judges towards the ECtHR.[36]

The role of the Secretariats and Registries of apex courts in implementing Strasbourg judgments is rarely studied, but it might matter too. The Registry may play the "sifting" role in processing the individual constitutional complaints[37] and provide research support for the justices regarding Strasbourg case law.[38] Some apex courts even decided to create a specialized analytical department that focuses primarily on the analysis of international law, European Union law, and foreign law. Such departments were created, for instance, in all three Czech apex courts.

For instance, the Analytical Department (*analytický odbor*) of the Czech Constitutional Court employs five analysts,[39] who are purposefully selected from different backgrounds[40] and to ensure language diversity.[41] It is formally subordinated to the General Secretary of the Czech Constitutional Court, but its role in "translating" the Strasbourg case law into the Czech constitutional context is so important that it must be treated separately from the rest of the Secretariat. More specifically, the Analytical Department alerts the justices when a new Strasbourg judgment against the Czech Republic is issued, provides the justices with monthly summaries of the new Strasbourg judgments against other countries, and, at the request of an individual justice, conducts individualized research on the Strasbourg jurisprudence tailored to a particular case.[42] At the Supreme Administrative Court, the Department of European Law providing in-house expertise in European Union, international, and comparative law – including the Strasbourg case law – was established in 2004. In 2007, it was transformed into the Analytical Department (Supreme Administrative Court of the Czech Republic 2010, 34–5). As regards the Supreme Court, a similar body, the Foreign Department of the Supreme Court (nowadays "the Department for Analytics and Comparative Law"), which fulfils the expertise-providing function with respect to European Union law and international human rights law, was created in 2007 to catch up with the other two Czech apex courts (Šipulová and Sulitka 2018, 90).

It is thus clear that a well-staffed Secretariat or a specialized analytical department can significantly improve the use of the Strasbourg case law. This is particularly true in Central and Eastern Europe, where many top jurists in their fifties and sixties, including apex court justices, do not speak foreign languages fluently (Malenovský 2011; Kosař 2015, 143–44). As a result, they become dependent on reliable "translators" of the ECtHR's case law. Such justices, not confident in their own foreign language skills, are of course more willing to consult "in-house" specialists rather than members of academia and other "outsiders".[43]

Individual justices' attitudes and expertise in and openness towards ECHR law may also affect the constitutional court's treatment of the ECtHR's case law. A judge who is knowledgeable about the ECtHR's case law and engages with it thoroughly may serve as a "hub" or an "entry point" for the Strasbourg jurisprudence. The former career of a judge is particularly important here – these "entry point" justices often come from academia and top ordinary courts, but some countries even intentionally[44] facilitated such "hubs" by appointing ex-Strasbourg judges[45] to the constitutional court.[46] From these "entry points" the Strasbourg case law travels into the subsequent judgments of the given constitutional court and radiates to the ordinary courts. Even if these Strasbourg-friendly justices are in the minority at the moment, they bring new arguments into the deliberation and, if separate opinions are allowed, may castigate the majority in their dissenting opinions. Such dissenting opinion also has an important signaling function: It signals to the party that lost before the constitutional court that it makes sense to lodge the application to the ECtHR. In addition, it sends a signal to the ECtHR itself, which will surely subject such judgment of the constitutional court to serious scrutiny. This dual signaling function constrains the majority, as most apex courts will think twice before challenging the ECtHR openly.[47]

Finally, mainly in the post-communist countries that have (re-)introduced effective judicial enforcement of human rights only in the post-1989 period and often showed lower human rights awareness, even law clerks can make the difference, especially if they are fluent in English and French (Vyhnánek 2017). As explained above, the language skills of apex court justices in many Central and Eastern European countries are insufficient for them to engage fully with the Strasbourg jurisprudence (Šipulová and Sulitka 2018). Having a law clerk who is able to do so can overcome this deficiency. Some justices go even further and intentionally hire former members of the ECtHR's Registry,[48] which gives them a clear competitive edge regarding the knowledge of the Strasbourg case law.

The significance of the inner actors and structure is common to constitutional and top ordinary courts. Still, there are important differences that may affect the role of constitutional courts on the one hand and top ordinary courts on the other hand in implementing the ECtHR's case law. First of all, several CoE member states did not create constitutional courts. For instance, the Dutch Constitution explicitly prohibits judicial review of legislation (see, for example, van der Schyff 2010; Mak 2015). The common law member states, the United Kingdom[49] and Ireland,[50] have supreme courts that can be perceived as constitutional courts in the broader sense (Häberle 2006, 67), but their role is different from the specialized Kelsenian constitutional courts on the Continent (Garlicki 2007; Comella 2009). Nordic countries do have some form of constitutional review, but despite recent developments it has been used sparingly and reluctantly (Husa 2010).[51] In the absence of the specialized constitutional court, other bodies have to play its role. In the Netherlands and common law jurisdictions, the supreme courts are most likely to fill this vacuum and act as "constitutional courts light",[52] whereas in Nordic countries it is the parliament that tends to play the key role in implementing the Strasbourg case law.

In countries with both a Kelsenian constitutional court and a supreme court (or even several supreme courts), differences in their role in implementing the Strasbourg case law may arise easily, given the variations in institutional design, personal aspects, docket, and resources. Constitutional courts are usually separate from the rest of the judiciary due to their specific position involving judicial and political elements (Shapiro and Stone Sweet 2002, 344). Accordingly, the design of constitutional courts usually sets a different mode for selection of constitutional judges, requires a different minimal age, and imposes term limits. As explained above, all these features affecting the inner structure and composition of a constitutional court can have repercussions for the treatment of the ECtHR's case law when compared to the top ordinary courts. More generally, constitutional courts' specialized nature is also important. Their exclusive focus on constitutional and human rights issues implies constitutional judges' familiarity with human rights jurisprudence. As noted above, however, such a specialization may lead both to more frequent and thorough use of the Strasbourg case law, but also to guarding domestic constitutional order from external influences (Stone Sweet and Keller 2008, 28; Komárek 2014, 532–5). Implications for a supreme court in a system where a constitutional court exists may also vary. On the one hand, reliance on the constitutional court's expertise in human rights might lead the supreme court judges to largely ignore human rights dimensions of their cases, assuming that someone else (constitutional court justices) will address these dimensions.[53] On the other hand, the supreme court can also use the ECtHR's case law as a means to strengthen its own voice in human rights issues and get around (or even revolt against) the constitutional court's opinion.

Finally, it is important to see the role of apex courts in implementing the ECtHR's case law in the broader political context. This brings us back to the complexities of the domestic implementation process that depends on the plurality of actors with different interests, various degrees of Strasbourg enthusiasm, complicated mutual relationships, and divergent powers.[54] For instance, if a Strasbourg-friendly apex court has the support of a pro-Strasbourg coalition of other domestic actors,[55] it can diffuse the Strasbourg standards smoothly. But if such a court faces an anti-Strasbourg coalition, its impact on the implementation process is diminished.[56] In the worst case scenario, the ruling anti-Strasbourg coalition may exercise pressure on the pro-Strasbourg justices or even try to paralyze the entire apex court.[57] The opposite scenario, a pro-Strasbourg coalition facing an anti-Strasbourg apex court, is unlikely, but it cannot be excluded.[58] Finally, if the apex court joins the anti-Strasbourg domestic alliance, it may effectively block the implementation process altogether without the fear of any consequences.[59]

2.3 Conclusion

This chapter unpacked the domestic judiciary and identified its varied roles in the ECtHR's case law implementation. It explained the high capacity of domestic judiciary to contribute to the effectiveness and domestic embeddedness of the Strasbourg Court's judgments. However, it also showed that the domestic judiciary has to be further differentiated. There are numerous structural, institutional, and contingent factors that may largely influence how the given court treats the Strasbourg Court's rulings. Even on the level of apex courts, there are several *internal* actors with potentially differing preferences and positions that may affect the treatment of the ECtHR's case law by apex courts.

This was not to say that every study of domestic judicial treatment of the Strasbourg jurisprudence must analyze all these actors and nuances. This would be a daunting task that could hardly be accomplished in a single book. We rather suggest that any researcher should be aware of these factors, even if she eventually focuses only on selected aspects. In fact, we should encourage more studies focusing on a particular layer as well as methodological plurality[60] to tackle the different problems on each level. Different approaches contribute, each in their own way, to the bigger picture and our understanding of the Convention system of human rights. This book looks closely at the ways and means domestic apex court judges treat the Strasbourg case law (Part II) and revisits the significance of some of the factors addressed here in Chapters 8 and 9.

Notes

1 See Helfer (2008, 158). On the importance of national courts in ensuring compliance with international human rights rulings more generally, see Nollkaemper (2012, 164–5), Koh (1999, 1413), and Hathaway (2005, 506, 520–5).
2 See Section 1.2 above.
3 For instance, see the unwillingness of the UK and Swiss courts to accept the ECtHR's rulings on the issue of confrontation (see Jackson and Summers [2013]), and the narrow reading of the ECtHR's case law on the role of advocates general by the French *Conseil d'État* (see Bell [2008]; Krisch [2008, 194–6]).
4 See Aksenova and Marchuk (2018) and the discussion on the implementation of the 2013 *Anchugov and Gladkov v. Russia* judgment below.
5 For a rare exception, see ECtHR [GC], *A. and Others v. the United Kingdom*, no. 3455/05, 19 February 2009, § 157.
6 Note that the composition of the Czech Supreme Administrative Court differs from the Czech Supreme Court, as the former was established only in 2003 and lured several young judges who studied abroad. See Chapter 6 below.
7 While court presidents in West Europe have undergone a profound transformation since World War II (see, for example, Solomon [2012, 918–21]) and exercise less influence than their counterparts in post-communist Europe, they still have their say in some established democracies (see, for example, Garapon and Epineuse [2012, 285–6] and Salomon [2012]). In detail, see Blisa and Kosař (2018).
8 In France professional organizations control the *commissions d'avancément* (promotion commissions). For further details regarding the *commissions d'avancément*, see Garapon and Epineuse (2012, 285–6).
9 For numerous examples, see Petrov (2018).

10 See Protocol No. 15 to ECHR and Føllesdal (2016).
11 Council of Europe (2018), § 9.
12 Council of Europe (2018), § 6.
13 In detail, see Çali (2016, 144). More generally, see also Spano (2018).
14 Article 1, Protocol No. 16 to ECHR. See also Dzehtsiarou and O'Meara (2014).
15 For the first case see Advisory opinion concerning the recognition in domestic law of a legal parent-child relationship between a child born through a gestational surrogacy arrangement abroad and the intended mother Requested by the French Court of Cassation (no. P16-2018-001, judgment of 10 April 2019).
16 For a similar argument in the context of European Union law, see Komárek (2014, 532–5).
17 See Italian Constitutional Court, no. 49/2015, judgment of 26 March 2015; and Pin (2015).
18 See Russian Constitutional Court, no. 12-П/2016, decision of 19 April 2016 (available also in English at www.ksrf.ru/en/Decision/Judgments/Documents/2016_April_19_12-P.pdf), in which the Russian Constitutional Court ruled that enforcement of the 2013 *Anchugov and Gladkov v. Russia* judgment is "impossible", because it is contrary to the Russian Constitution. For further implications of this judgment see Aksenova (2016), Chaeva (2016) and Nuzov (2016). See also the earlier decision of the Russian Constitutional Court of 14 July 2015 (no. 21–П/2015); Aksenova and Marchuk (2018).
19 Russian Constitutional Court, no. 1-П/2017, judgment of 19 January 2017.
20 See *Moreira Ferreira v. Portugal (no. 2)*, no. 19,867/12, judgment of 11 July 2017, in which the Portuguese Supreme Court rejected a request for revision following a judgment delivered by the ECtHR (the case is currently pending before the Grand Chamber). See also Jackson and Summers (2013) discussing the unwillingness of the UK and Swiss courts to accept the ECtHR's rulings on the issue of confrontation; and Martinico (2016) for further examples.
21 SAC, no. 2 As 199/2018-37, judgment of 30 May 2019, and Chapter 6 below.
22 See, *mutatis mutandis*, Bobek (2013, 255–69).
23 Or a proverbial "straw" the drowning constitutional courts attempted to clutch.
24 For instance, the Czech Constitutional Court has recently found the judgment of the European Court of Justice "*ultra vires*" (see Zbíral [2012]; Bobek [2014]) and openly departed from the position taken by the German *Bundesverfassungsgerichhof* on the same issue (see, for example, Komárek and the Editors [2009] and Smekal and Vyhnánek [2016]), which was unheard of just few years ago.
25 This is already happening against Hungary (see, for example, *Karácsony and Others v. Hungary* [GC], nos. 42,461/13 and 44,357/13, judgment of 17 May 2016; and *Baka v. Hungary* [GC], no. 20,261/12, judgment of 23 June 2016). In the Czech Republic, the only Strasbourg judgment that has resonated significantly within the domestic political sphere (and partly also among the people) is the Grand Chamber judgment in *D.H. v. the Czech Republic* (see Majerčík [2016, 131–52]). Regarding Poland, see Kowalik-Bańczyk (2016).
26 In fact, constitutional courts that decide cases only in plenary session (such as the Italian *Corte Constituzionale* and the French *Conseil Constitutionnel*) are becoming rare in Europe.
27 See more generally Leiss (2015).
28 This has become a necessity given the number of judgments they issue. For broader implications of this problem see, *mutatis mutandis*, Bobek (2009).
29 See Blisa and Kosař (2018). See also Piana (2010, 43–44), Solomon (2010, 354), Müller (2012, 965), Kosař (2016, 390–8).
30 This is the case, for instance, at the Italian Constitutional Court (see Barsotti et al. [2016, 47]).

31 For instance, the presidents of all three Czech apex courts studied in this book (the Czech Constitutional Court, Supreme Court, and the Supreme Administrative Court) have such power. See Blisa, Papoušková and Urbániková (2018) on the Czech Supreme Court and the Supreme Administrative Court, and Kosař and Vyhnánek (2019) on the Czech Constitutional Court.

32 Virtually every apex court president presides over a grand chamber or a plenary and is thus able to exploit his agenda-setting role. This jurisprudential power consists of, among other things, determining the rules of the debate during judicial deliberation, deciding on the voting order, and opinion assignment (see Blisa and Kosař [2018]).

33 For instance, presidents of the Czech Supreme Court and the Supreme Administrative Court must approve assignment of any judge to "their" courts (see Kosař [2016, 174–5] and Blisa, Papoušková, and Urbániková [2018, 1954]).

34 For instance, at the beginning of the Czech President Miloš Zeman's term, the president of the Czech Constitutional Court heavily influenced the composition of the so-called "third" Czech Constitutional Court (2013 to now) due to their good informal relationship. This relationship, however, deteriorated throughout the term and the influence of the Constitutional Court's president on the Constitutional Court's composition decreased accordingly. For further details, see Šimíček (2016, 230–31) and Kosař and Vyhnánek (2019).

35 For further details on this taxonomy of powers of chief justices, see Blisa and Kosař (2018).

36 See Piana (2010), Solomon (2010), Müller (2012), Kosař (2016).

37 This role of the General Registry of the *Bundesverfassungsgericht* is well known. For further details, see Kommers (2012, 18–20).

38 See the four notes that follow.

39 The Analytical Department consists of 13 employees: the head of the department, five analysts, one advisor, three librarians, two people working on the Court's Collection of Judgments and Decisions and on the national gazette, and two assistants.

40 The members of the Analytical Department include academics, former members of the ECtHR's Registry, former law clerks to justices of the Czech Constitutional Court, former law clerks at top ordinary courts, and lawyers who practised law in the Czech Republic.

41 This means that English, French, German, and Spanish must be covered all the time. However, members of the Analytical Department often speak several other languages.

42 Apart from its major analytical task, the Analytical Department also runs the library of the Czech Constitutional Court and is responsible for publishing the official Collection of Judgments and Decisions of Czech Constitutional Court.

43 But, as we mentioned above, constitutional courts in some countries have requested the Venice Commission for *amicus curiae* briefs on comparative and international human rights issues. See Chapter 1, Section 3.

44 However, it is not entirely clear whether these governments appointed the ex-Strasbourg justices primarily in order to strengthen the influence of the Strasbourg case law or rather because they thought that the ex-Strasbourg justices were the best available candidates (and the increasing awareness of the Strasbourg case law was merely a "side effect") or both.

45 This is even encouraged by the CoE organs that have argued that the fact that judges return from the ECtHR to their home state has several positive effects, since "former [Strasbourg] judges are likely to enrich the legal profession's knowledge of Strasbourg case law with their uniquely acquired European experience" (Council of Europe: Parliamentary Assembly – Committee on Legal Affairs and Human Rights 2008, § 38).

46 Note that several ECtHR judges from Central and Eastern Europe were in their 30s and early 40s when they joined the Strasbourg Court (for the explanation of this

phenomenon, see Šipulová and Sulitka [2018]). That means that once their Strasbourg term had expired, they were still in their 40s or 50s and thus looking for another job. The Baltic States in particular tend to appoint their former ECtHR judges to their constitutional courts. For instance, Danutė Jočienė became a justice of the Constitutional Court of Lithuania in 2014 and Ineta Ziemele joined the Constitutional Court of Latvia in 2015.

47 As mentioned above, this does not mean that the apex courts will necessarily decide to opt for a Strasbourg-friendly position.

48 For instance, a Justice of the Czech Constitutional Court, Kateřina Šimáčková, has had at least one law clerk who previously worked at the ECtHR's Registry in her team since her appointment in 2013.

49 The Supreme Court of the United Kingdom may not only engage in Convention-conforming interpretation, but also issue the so-called "declaration of incompatibility" (see, for example, Delaney [2014, 556–61]). This broader understanding of constitutional adjudication is also closely connected to the debates on the "new commonwealth constitutionalism" (see, for example, Gardbaum [2010]) and the "weak judicial review" (see, for example, Dixon [2012]).

50 The Irish Supreme Court can even conduct judicial review in abstract review procedure (see, for example, Howlin [2005]; Ó'Tuama [2008]; Carolan [2014]).

51 See also the special issue on Nordic constitutionalism in Nordisk Tidsskrift For Menneskerettigheter (27 [2]: 131–311), particularly Føllesdal and Wind (2009), and the Symposium on Nordic Juristocracy in *International Journal of Constitutional Law* (9 [2]: 449–547).

52 But the absence of a constitutional court seems to increase the role of national parliaments too. See the reform proposal of MP Taverne in the Netherlands (see Lambrecht [2015]) and the discussions on the repeal (and possible replacement) of the Human Rights Act in the United Kingdom (see Lambrecht [2015]; Lock and Dzehtsiarou [2015]; Masterman [2016]).

53 This was the case with some post-communist supreme courts in Central and Eastern Europe, especially in the 1990s. See, for example, Kühn (2011) and Uzelac (2010).

54 See Chapter 1, Section 3.

55 This has been a standard scenario in most established democracies in West Europe. See the chapters on Austria, Belgium, Germany, Italy, and Sweden in Popelier, Lambrecht, and Lemmens (2016).

56 This has happened, to a certain extent, for instance in Mečiar's Slovakia in the 1990s (see, for example, Procházka (2002a, 218)) and in post-Orbán Hungary (see Polgári [2016]).

57 The former was employed in Poland by the Kaczyński brothers in 2005–2007 and the latter by Jaroslav Kaczyński after his "Law and Justice" party won the elections in 2015.

58 For instance, if authoritarian leaders manage to pack the constitutional court, which will then defy the newly elected pro-Strasbourg political coalition. In any case, the ECtHR has already held that there is no prohibition on a government to challenge the decisions of its own highest courts before the ECtHR (see *A. and Others v. the United Kingdom* [GC], no. 3455/05, judgment of 19 February 2009, § 157) and thus, if the anti-Strasbourg judgment of the domestic constitutional court is challenged before the ECtHR, the Government may decide not to defend the judgment of its constitutional court and even ask the ECtHR to find a violation of the Convention.

59 See the Russian scenario described in Aksenova and Marchuk (2018.

60 We should thus go beyond the doctrinal and normative understanding of the Convention and Strasbourg case law that operates primarily on the macro level. Interactions among meso-level actors call for insights from political science, and micro-level functioning of the constitutional courts is a fertile soil for socio-legal studies – for an example of a wonderful socio-legal study of a top domestic court, see Latour (2010).

References

Aksenova, Marina. 2016. "Anchugov and Gladkov Is Not Enforceable: The Russian Constitutional Court Opines in Its First ECtHR Implementation Case". *Opinio Iuris*, 25 April 2016. Accessed 15 August 2019. http://opiniojuris.org/2016/04/25/anchugov-and-gladkov-is-not-enforceable-the-russian-constitutional-court-opines-in-its-first-ecthr-implementation-case/.

Aksenova, Marina, and Iryna Marchuk. 2018. "Reinventing or Rediscovering International Law? the Russian Constitutional Court's Uneasy Dialogue with the European Court of Human Rights". *International Journal of Constitutional Law* 16 (4): 1322–46.

Altwicker, Tilmann. 2016. "Switzerland: The Substitute Constitution in Times of Popular Dissent". In *Criticism of the European Court of Human Rights*, edited by Patricia Popelier, Sarah Lambrecht, and Koen Lemmens, 385–412. Cambridge: Intersentia.

Ammann, Odile. 2018. "International Law in Domestic Courts through an Empirical Lens: The Swiss Federal Tribunal's Practice of International Law in Figures". *Swiss Review of International and European Law* 28: 489–516.

Andenas, Mads, and Eirik Bjorge. 2011. "Preventive Detention, No. 2 BvR 2365/09". *American Journal of International Law* 105 (4): 768–74.

Barsotti, Vittoria, Paolo G. Carozza, Marta Cartabia, and Andrea Simoncini. 2016. *Italian Constitutional Justice in Global Context*. New York: Oxford University Press.

Bell, John. 2008. "'interpretative Resistance' Faced with the Case-law of the Strasbourg Court". *European Public Law* 14 (2): 137–42.

Bjorge, Eirik. 2015. *Domestic Application of the ECHR: Courts as Faithful Trustees*. Oxford: Oxford University Press.

Blisa, Adam, and David Kosař. 2018. "Court Presidents: The Missing Piece in the Puzzle of Judicial Governance". *German Law Journal* 19 (7): 2031–76.

Blisa Adam, Papoušková Tereza, and Urbániková Marína. 2018. "Judicial Self-Government in Czechia: Europe's Black Sheep?". *German Law Journal* 19 (7): 1951–76.

Bobek, Michal. 2009. "Quantity or Quality? Re-Assessing the Role of Supreme Jurisdictions in Central Europe". *American Journal of Comparative Law* 57 (1): 33–65.

Bobek, Michal. 2013. *Comparative Reasoning in European Supreme Courts*. Oxford: Oxford University Press.

Bobek, Michal. 2014. "*Landtová, Holubec*, and the Problem of an Uncooperative Court: Implications for the Preliminary Rulings Procedure". *European Constitutional Law Review* 10 (1): 54–89.

Bobek, Michal, and David Kosař. 2010. "The Application of European Union Law and the Law of the European Convention of Human Rights in the Czech Republic and Slovakia: An Overview". In *The National Judicial Treatment of the ECHR and EU Laws. A Comparative Constitutional Perspective*, edited by Giuseppe Martinico and Oreste Pollicino, 117–50. Groningen: Europa Law Publishing.

Bugarič, Bojan, and Tom Ginsburg. 2016. "The Assault on Postcommunist Courts". *Journal of Democracy* 27 (3): 69–82.

Çali, Başak. 2016. "From Flexible to Variable Standards of Judicial Review: The Responsible Courts Doctrine at the European Court of Human Rights". In *Shifting Centres of Gravity in Human Rights Protection*, edited by Oddný Mjöll Arnardóttir and Antoine Buyse, 144–60. Abingdon: Routledge.

Çali, Başak, Anne Koch, and Nicola Bruch. 2011. "The Legitimacy of the European Court of Human Rights: The View from the Ground". Accessed 15 August 2019. https://ecthrproject.files.wordpress.com/2011/04/ecthrlegitimacyreport.pdf.

Çali, Başak, Anne Koch, and Nicola Bruch. 2013. "The Social Legitimacy of Human Rights Courts: A Grounded Interpretivist Theory of the Elite Accounts of the Legitimacy of the European Court of Human Rights". *Human Rights Quarterly* 35 (3): 955–84.
Carolan, Eoin. 2014. "Evaluating the Judicial Role in Developing the Irish Constitution". In *75 Years of the Constitution of Ireland: An Irish-Italian Dialogue*, edited by Giuseppe Franco Ferrari and John O'Dowd, 63–81. Dublin: Clarus Press.
Chaeva, Natalia. 2016. "The Russian Constitutional Court and Its Actual Control over the ECtHR Judgement in Anchugov and Gladkov". *EJIL Talk!*, 26 April 2016. Accessed 15 August 2019. www.ejiltalk.org/the-russian-constitutional-court-and-its-actual-control-over-the-ecthr-judgement-in-anchugov-and-gladko/.
Comella, Victor Ferreres. 2009. *Constitutional Courts and Democratic Values: A European Perspective*. New Haven, CT: Yale University Press.
Coors, Corinna. 2010. "Headwind from Europe: The New Position of the German Courts on Personality Rights after the Judgment of the European Court of Human Rights". *German Law Journal* 11 (5): 527–37.
Council of Europe. 2018. "Copenhagen Declaration on the Reform of the European Convention on Human Rights System". Accessed 12 June 2019. https://rm.coe.int/copenhagen-declaration/16807b915c.
Council of Europe: Parliamentary Assembly – Committee on Legal Affairs and Human Rights. 2008. "Nomination of Candidates and Election of Judges in the European Court of Human Rights". 1 December 2008, Doc. 11767. Accessed 15 August 2019. http://semantic-pace.net/tools/pdf.aspx?doc=aHR0cDovL2Fzc2VtYmx5LmNvZS5pbnQvbncveG1sL1hSZWYvWDJILURXLWV4dHIuYXNwP2ZpbGVpZD0xMjIxOSZsYW5nPUVO&xsl=aHR0cDovL3NlbWFudGljcGFjZS5uZXQvWHNsdC9QZGYvWFJlZi1XRC1BVC1YTUwyUERGLnhzbA==&xsltparams=ZmlsZWlkPTEyMjE5.
Delaney, Erin F. 2014. "Judiciary Rising: Constitutional Change in the United Kingdom". *Northwestern University Law Review* 108 (2): 543–606.
Dixon, Rosalind. 2012. "Weak-Form Review & American Exceptionalism". *Oxford Journal of Legal Studies* 32 (3): 487–506.
Dothan, Shai. 2014. *Reputation and Judicial Tactics: A Theory of National and International Courts*. Cambridge: Cambridge University Press.
Dzehtsiarou, Kanstantsin, and Noreen O'Meara. 2014. "Advisory Jurisdiction and the European Court of Human Rights: A Magic Bullet for Dialogue and Docket-control?". *Legal Studies* 34 (3): 444–68.
Dzehtsiarou, Konstantsin, and Natasa Mavronicola. 2016. "Relation of Constitutional Courts/Supreme Courts to the ECtHR" In *Max Planck Encyclopedia of Comparative Constitutional Law*, edited by Rainer Grote, Frauke Lachenmann, and Rüdiger Wolfrum. Accessed 8 May 2019. http://oxcon.ouplaw.com/view/10.1093/law-mpeccol/law-mpeccol-e572?rskey=7PcDZV&result=47&prd=MPECCOL.
Føllesdal, Andreas. 2016. "Squaring the Circle at the Battle of Brighton: Is the War between Protection of Human Rights or Respecting Sovereignty Over, or Has It Just Begun?". In *Shifting the Centres of Gravity in Human Rights Protection: Rethinking Relations between the ECHR, EU, and National Legal Orders*, edited by Oddný Mjöll Arnardóttir and Antoine Buyse, 189–204. Abingdon and New York: Routledge.
Føllesdal, Andreas, and Marlene Wind. 2009. "Introduction: Nordic reluctance towardsjudicial review under siege". *Nordisk Tidsskrift For Menneskerettigheter* 27 (2): 131–41.
Garapon, Antoine, and Harold Epineuse. 2012. "Judicial Independence in France". In *Judicial Independence in Transition*, edited by Anja Seibert-Fohr, 273–305. Heidelberg: Springer.

Gardbaum, Stephen. 2010. "Reassessing the New Commonwealth Model of Constitutionalism". *International Journal of Constitutional Law* 8 (2): 1–41.

Garlicki, Lech. 2007. "Constitutional versus Supreme Courts". *International Journal of Constitutional Law* 5 (1): 44–68.

Gerards, Janneke. 2014. "The European Court of Human Rights and the National Courts: Giving Shape to the Notion of 'Shared Responsibility'". In *Implementation of the European Convention on Human Rights and of the Judgments of the ECtHR in National Case Law*, edited by Janneke Gerards and Jospeh Fleuren, 13–94. Cambridge: Intersentia.

Gerards, Janneke, and Joseph Fleuren, eds. 2014. *Implementation of the European Convention on Human Rights and of the Judgments of the ECtHR in National Case Law*. Cambridge: Intersentia.

Giegerich, Thomas. 2014. "The Struggle by the German Courts and Legislature to Transpose the Strasbourg Case Law on Preventive Detention into German Law". In *Judgments of the European Court of Human Rights – Effects and Implementation*, edited by Anja Seibert-Fohr and Mark E. Villiger, 207–36. Baden-Baden: Nomos.

Guarnieri, Carlo. 2013. "Judicial Independence in Europe: Threat or Resource for Democracy?". *Representation* 49 (3): 347–59.

Guarnieri, Carlo, and Patrizia Pederzoli. 2002. *The Power of Judges: A Comparative Study of Courts and Democracy*. Oxford: Oxford University Press.

Häberle, Peter. 2006. "Role and Impact of Constitutional Courts in a Comparative Perspective". In *The Future of the European Judicial System in a Comparative Perspective*, edited by Ingolf Pernice, Juliane Kokott, and Cheryl Saunders, 65–77. Baden-Baden: Nomos Verlag.

Hartwig, Matthias. 2011. "Much Ado about Human Rights: The Federal Constitutional Court Confronts the European Court of Human Rights". In *Comparative Law as Transnational Law*, edited by Russel A. Miller and Peer C. Zumbansen, 145–46. Oxford: Oxford University Press.

Hathaway, Oona A. 2005. "Between Power and Principle: An Integrated Theory of International Law". *The University of Chicago Law Review* 72 (2): 469–536.

Helfer, Laurence R. 2008. "Redesigning the European Court of Human Rights: Embeddedness as a Deep Structural Principle of the European Human Rights Regime". *European Journal of International Law* 19 (1): 125–59.

Hoffmann-Riem, Wolfgang. 2006. "Kontrolldichte Und Kontrollfolgen Beim Nationalen Und Europäischen Schutz Von Freiheitsrechten in Mehrpoligen Rechtsverhältnissen". *Europaische Grundrechte-Zeitschrift* 33 (17–18): 492–98.

Howlin, Niamh. 2005. "Shortcomings and Anomalies: Aspects of Article 26". *Irish Student Law Review* 13 (1): 26–48.

Husa, Jaakko. 2010. "Nordic Constitutionalism and European Human Rights – Mixing Oil and Water?". *Scandinavian Studies in Law* 55: 101–24.

Jackson, John, and Sarah Summers. 2013. "Confrontation with Strasbourg: UK and Swiss Approaches to Criminal Evidence". *Criminal Law Review* 60 (2): 115–31.

Klein, Eckart. 2014. "Germany". In *Implementation of the European Convention on Human Rights and of the Judgments of the ECtHR in National Case Law*, edited by Jenneke Gerards and Joseph Fleuren, 185–216. Cambridge: Intersentia.

Koh, Harold H. 1999. "How Is International Human Rights Law Enforced?". *Indiana Law Journal* 74 (4): 1397–417.

Komárek, Jan. 2014. "National Constitutional Courts and the European Constitutional Democracy". *International Journal of Constitutional Law* 12 (3): 525–44.

Komárek, Jan, and the Editors. 2009. "The Czech Constitutional Court's Second Decision on the Lisbon Treaty of 3 November 2009". *European Constitutional Law Review* 5 (3): 345–52.

Kommers, Donald P. 2012. *The Constitutional Jurisprudence of the Federal Republic of Germany.* 3rd edition. London and Durnham: Duke University Press.

Koncewicz, Tomasz Tadeusz. 2016a. "'emergency Constitutional Review': Thinking the Unthinkable? A Letter from America". *Verfassungsblog*, 29 March 2016. Accessed 18 August 2019. http://verfassungsblog.de/emergency-constitutional-review-thinking-the-unthinkable-a-letter-from-america/.

Koncewicz, Tomasz Tadeusz. 2016b. "*Polish Judiciary and Constitutional Fidelity: Beyond the Institutional "Great yes"?*" *Verfassungsblog*, 12 June 2016. Accessed 19 August 2019.

Kosař, David. 2008. "Conflicts between Fundamental Rights in the Jurisprudence of the Czech Constitutional Court". In *Conflicts Between Fundamental Rights*, edited by Eva Brems, 345–76. Oxford: Intersentia.

Kosař, David. 2015. "Selecting Strasbourg Judges: A Critique". In *Selecting Europe's Judges A Critical Review of the Appointment Procedures to the European Courts*, edited by Michal Bobek, 120–61. Oxford: Oxford University Press.

Kosař, David. 2016. *Perils of Judicial Self-Government in Transitional Societies.* Cambridge: Cambridge University Press.

Kosař, David, and Vyhnánek. Ladislav. 2019. The Czech Constitutional Court. In *Constitutional Courts*, edited by Armin von Bogdandy. Oxford: Oxford University Press (forthcoming).

Kosař, David, and Lucas Lixinski. 2015. "Domestic Judicial Design by International Human Rights Courts". *The American Journal of International Law* 109 (4): 713–60.

Kovács, Kriszta, and Kim Lane Scheppele. 2018. "The Fragility of an Independent Judiciary: Lessons from Hungary and Poland–And the European Union". *Communist and Post-Communist Studies* 51 (3): 189–200.

Kowalik-Bańczyk, Krystyna. 2016. "Poland: The Taming of the Shrew". In *Criticism of the European Court of Human Rights*, edited by Patricia Popelier, Sarah Lambrecht, and Koen Lemmens, 199–238. Cambridge: Intersentia.

Krisch, Nico. 2008. "The Open Architecture of European Human Rights Law". *Modern Law Review* 71 (2): 183–216.

Kühn, Zdeněk. 2011. *The Judiciary in Central and Eastern Europe: Mechanical Jurisprudence in Transformation?* Leiden: Martinus Nijhoff Publishers.

Lambrecht, Sarah. 2015. "HRA Watch: Reform, Repeal, Replace? Criticism of the European Court of Human Rights: A UK Phenomenon?" *UK Constitutional Law Association Blog*, 27 July 2015. Accessed 5 April 2019. https://ukconstitutionallaw.org/2015/07/27/hra-watch-reform-repeal-replace-sarah-lambrecht-criticism-of-the-european-court-of-human-rights-a-uk-phenomenon/.

Latour, Bruno. 2010. *The Making of Law: An Ethnography of the Conseil D'état.* Cambridge: Polity Press.

Leiss, Johann Ruben. 2015. "One Court, Two Voices". *German Law Journal* 16 (4): 901–15.

Lock, Tobias, and Kanstantsin Dzehtsiarou. 2015. "The Legal Implications of a Repeal of the Human Rights Act 1998 and Withdrawal from the European Convention on Human Rights". *Oxford Human Rights Hub Blog*, 15 May 2015. Accessed 14 May 2019. http://ohrh.law.ox.ac.uk/the-legal-implications-of-a-repeal-of-the-human-rights-act-1998-and-withdrawal-from-the-european-convention-on-human-rights/.

López Guerra, Luis. 2017. "Dialogues between the Strasbourg Court and National Courts". In *Judicial Dialogue and Human Rights*, edited by Amrei Müller, 401–09. Cambridge: Cambridge University Press.

Majerčík, Lubomír. 2016. "Czech Republic: Strasbourg Court Undisputed". In *Criticism of the European Court of Human Rights*, edited by Patricia Popelier, Sarah Lambrecht, and Koen Lemmens, 131–52. Cambridge: Intersentia.

Mak, Elaine. 2015. "Constitutional Review and Democracy in the Netherlands: Balancing Legislative and Judicial Powers in an Internationalised Legal Order". In *Constitutional Review and Democracy*, edited by Miodrag Jovanovic, 185–205. Hague: Eleven International Publishing.

Malenovský, Jiří. 2011. "L'indépendance Des Juges Internationaux". In *Recueil Des Cours De l'Académie De Droit International De La Haye*, Vol. 349. Leiden: Martinus Nijhoff.

Mańko, Rafał. 2014. "'War of Courts' as a Clash of Legal Cultures: Rethinking the Conflict between the Polish Constitutional Tribunal and the Supreme Court over 'Interpretive Judgments'". In *Law, Politics, and the Constitution: New Perspectives from Legal and Political Theory*, edited by Antonia Geisler, Michael Hein, and Siri Hummel, 79–94. Vienna: Peter Lang.

Martinico, Giuseppe. 2010. "National Judges and Supranational Laws: Goals and Structure of the Research". In *The National Judicial Treatment of the ECHR and EU Laws. A Comparative Constitutional Perspective*, edited by Giuseppe Martinico and Oreste Pollicino, 117–50. Groningen: Europa Law Publishing.

Martinico, Giuseppe. 2016. "National Courts and Judicial Disobedience to the ECHR: A Comparative Overview". In *Shifting Centres of Gravity in Human Rights Protection*, edited by Oddný Mjöll Arnardóttir and Antoine Buyse, 59–78. Abingdon: Routledge.

Masterman, Roger. 2016. "The United Kingdom: From Strasbourg Surrogacy Towards a British Bill of Rights". In *Criticism of the European Court of Human Rights*, edited by Patricia Popelier, Sarah Lambrecht, and Koen Lemmens, 449–79. Cambridge: Intersentia.

Merkel, Grischa. 2010. "Incompatible Contrasts? Preventive Detention in Germany and the European Convention on Human Rights". *German Law Journal* 11 (9): 1046–66.

Müller, Lydia F. 2012. "Judicial Administration in Transitional Eastern Countries". In *Judicial Independence in Transition*, edited by Anja Seibert-Fohr, 937–69. Heidelberg: Springer.

Neil, MacCormick D., and Robert S. Summers, eds. 1997. *Interpreting Precedents.* Aldershot: Ashgate.

Nollkaemper, André. 2012. "The Role of National Courts in Inducing Compliance with International and European Law – A Comparison". In *Compliance and the Enforcement of EU Law*, edited by Marise Cremona, 157–93. Oxford: Oxford University Press.

Nuzov, Ilya. 2016. "Russia's Constitutional Court Declares Judgment of the European Court "Impossible" to Enforce". *International Journal of Constitutional Law Blog*, 13 May 2016. Accessed 14 May 2019. www.iconnectblog.com/2016/05/russias-constitutional-court-declares-judgment-of-the-european-court-impossible-to-enforce/.

Ó'Tuama, Seamus. 2008. "Judicial Review under the Irish Constitution: More American than Commonwealth". *Electronic Journal of Comparative Law* 12 (2): 1–22.

Papier, Hans-Jürgen. 2006. "Umsetzung Und Wirkung Der Entscheidungen Des Europäischen Gerichtshofes Für Menschenrechte Aus Der Perspektive Der Nationalen Deutschen Gerichte". *Europaische Grundrechte-Zeitschrift* 33 (1–4): 1–3.

Paris, Davide. 2017. "Allies and Counterbalances. Constitutional Courts and the European Court of Human Rights: A Comparative Perspective". *Heidelberg Journal of International Law* 77: 623–49.

Paulus, Andreas L. 2014. "From Implementation to Translation: Applying the ECtHR Judgments in the Domestic Legal Orders". In *Judgments of the European Court of Human Rights – Effects and Implementation*, edited by Anja Seibert-Fohr and Mark E. Villiger, 267–84. Baden-Baden: Nomos.

Petrov, Jan. 2018. "Unpacking the Partnership: Typology of Constitutional Courts' Roles in Implementation of the European Court of Human Rights' Case Law". *European Constitutional Law Review* 14 (3): 499–531.

Petrov, Jan. 2019. "Role of Constitutional Courts in the Mechanisms of Implementation of the ECtHR Case Law". Ph.D. Thesis, Brno: Masaryk University.

Piana, Daniela. 2010. *Judicial Accountabilities in New Europe: From Rule of Law to Quality of Justice*. Farnham: Ashgate.

Pin, Andrea. 2015. "A Jurisprudence to Handle with Care: The European Court of Human Rights' Unsettled Case Law, Its Authority, and Its Future, according to the Italian Constitutional Court". *International Journal of Constitutional Law Blog* No. 49/2015, 30 April 2015. Accessed 11 July 2019. www.iconnectblog.com/2015/04/mini-symposium-on-cc-judgment-49-2015/.

Polgári, Eszter. 2016. "Hungary: 'Gains and Losses'. Changing the Relationship with the European Court of Human Rights". In *Criticism of the European Court of Human Rights*, edited by Patricia Popelier, Sarah Lambrecht, and Koen Lemmens, 295–326. Cambridge: Intersentia.

Popelier, Patricia, Sarah Lambrecht, and Koen Lemmens, eds. 2016. *Criticism of the European Court of Human Rights*. Cambridge: Intersentia.

Procházka, Radoslav. 2002a. ""Európsky Dohovor O Ľudských Právach V Slovenskom Ústavnom poriadku" ["The ECHR in the Slovak Constitutional order"]". *Časopis Pro Právní Vědu a Praxi* 10 (3): 215–19.

Procházka, Radoslav. 2002b. *Mission Accomplished: On Founding Constitutional Adjudication in Central Europe*. Budapest: Central European University Press.

Sadurski, Wojciech. 2009. "Partnering with Strasbourg: Constitutionalization of the European Court of Human Rights, the Accession of Central and East European States to the Council of Europe, and the Idea of Pilot Judgments". *Human Rights Law Review* 9 (4): 450–83.

Sadurski, Wojciech. 2014. *Rights before Courts: A Study of Constitutional Courts in Postcommunist States of Central and Eastern Europe*. 2nd edition. Heidelberg: Springer.

Sadurski, Wojciech. 2019. *Poland's Constitutional Breakdown*. Oxford: Oxford University Press.

Shapiro, Martin M., and Alec Stone Sweet. 2002. *On Law, Politics and Judicialization*. New York: Oxford University Press.

Šimíček, Vojtěch. 2016. ""Výběr Kandidátů Na Soudce Ústavního Soudu a Jejich Schvalování senátem" ["selection of the Constitutional Court's Justices and Their Appointment by the senate"]". In *Dvacet Let Senátu Parlamentu České Republiky V Souvislostech [20 Years of the Senate of the Parliament of the Czech Republic]*, edited by Jan Kysela, 225–40. Prague: Leges.

Šipulová, Katarína, and Dušan Sulitka. 2018. ""ESLP A České Nejvyšší Soudy: Koncert Bez dirigenta?" ["ECtHR and the Czech Apex Courts: A Concert without the conductor?"]". In *Beyond Compliance: Implementace Rozhodnutí Mezinárodních Lidskoprávních Těles Na Národní Úrovni [Beyond Compliance: Domestic Judicial Implementation of the International Human Rights Case Law]*, edited by Hubert Smekal and Ladislav Vyhnánek, 81–100. Prague: Wolters Kluwer.

Smekal, Hubert, and Vyhnánek Ladislav. 2016. “Equal Voting Power under Scrutiny: Czech Constitutional Court on the 5% Threshold in the 2014 European Parliament Elections”. *European Constitutional Law Review* 12 (1): 148–63.

Solomon, Peter H. 2010. “Authoritarian Legality and Informal Practices: Judges, Lawyers and the State in Russia and China”. *Communist and Post-Communist Studies* 43 (4): 351–62.

Solomon, Peter H. 2012. “The Accountability of Judges in Post Communist States: From Bureaucratic to Professional Accountability”. In *Judicial Independence in Transition*, edited by Anja Seibert-Fohr, 909–35. Heidelberg: Springer.

Spano, Robert. 2018. “The Future of the European Court of Human Rights – Subsidiarity, Process-Based Review and the Rule of Law”. *Human Rights Law Review* 18 (3): 473–94.

Stone Sweet, Alec, and Hellen Keller, eds. 2008. *A Europe of Rights: The Impact of the ECHR on National Legal Systems.* New York: Oxford University Press.

Supreme Administrative Court of the Czech Republic. 2010. *Report of Activities from 2003–2009.* Brno: The Supreme Administrative Court.

Tomuschat, Christian. 2010. “Effects of the Judgments of the European Court of Human Rights According the German Constitutional Court”. *German Law Journal* 11 (5): 513–26.

Uzelac, Alan. 2010. “Survival of the Third Legal Tradition?”. *Supreme Court Law Review* 49 (2): 377–96.

van de Heyning, Catherine. 2013. “Constitutional Courts as Guardians of Fundamental Rights: The Constitutionalization of the Convention through Domestic Constitutional Adjudication”. In *The Role of Constitutional Courts in Multilevel Governance*, edited by Patricia Popelier, Armen Mazmanyan, and Werner Vandenbruwaene, 21–48. Cambridge: Intersentia.

van der Schyff, Gerhard. 2010. “Constitutional Review by the Judiciary in the Netherlands: A Bridge Too Far?” 2010 *German Law Journal* 11 (2): 275–90.

Vyhnánek, Ladislav. 2017. “A Holistic View of the Czech Constitutional Court Approach to the ECtHR’s Case Law”. *Heidelberg Journal of International Law* 77 (3): 715–44.

Zbíral, Robert. 2012. “A Legal Revolution or Negligible Episode? Court of Justice Decision Proclaimed Ultra Vires (Czech Constitutional Court, Judgment of 31 January 2012, Pl. ÚS 5/12)”. *Common Market Law Review* 49 (4): 1475–91.

3 Navigating the field of judicial compliance, effectiveness, implementation, and judicial treatment of international law

Domestic courts have become indispensable allies for international courts. As a former judge of the European Court of Human Rights (ECtHR or Strasbourg Court), Lech Garlicki (2008, 521), puts it: "The Strasbourg Court cannot function without a constant dialogue with and the support of the domestic courts". The increasingly pronounced role of domestic courts in relation to international courts coincides with the heightened scholarly interest in interactions between the two levels of the judiciary. The research field, immersed in debates over compliance, effectiveness, and implementation, has become increasingly complicated, partially due to conceptual overlaps and differing understandings of individual concepts. This chapter briefly summarizes the scholarship on interactions between international law and national practice and then explains why our three-level approach to judicial treatment goes beyond the existing state of the art.

Our research on judicial treatment contributes to the understanding of the influence of ECtHR case law on national practice. The European Convention on Human Rights (ECHR or Convention) and its interpretation by the ECtHR significantly affected the case law of domestic courts, national legislation, the concept of separation of powers, and political systems as such (Keller and Stone Sweet 2008; Kosař and Lixinski 2015; Motoc and Ziemele 2016). Our project goes beyond the traditional assessment of compliance in individual cases. Instead, it seeks to more systematically evaluate both direct and indirect influences which follow from long-term trends and are hard to detect from closely studying only a few cases. In order to depict the complexity of the influence of ECtHR case law on domestic apex courts, we propose a three-level inquiry into the judicial treatment of the international case law. The three-level approach enables a macro-analysis of the frequency of the use of ECtHR case law and its development over time as well as a closer meso-analysis of how the apex courts use ECtHR case law. Finally, the micro-analysis deals with particular cases selected because they are able to provide us with more insight into the impact of ECtHR case law.

This chapter thus prepares a theoretical background for understanding the broader influence of ECtHR case law on judicial domestic practice. First, it provides an overview of mainstream approaches which work especially with the concept of compliance. Then, it discusses the specifics of judicial interactions. Finally, a closer explanation of what we mean by the *beyond compliance* perspective ensues in which we introduce the concept of judicial treatment. We elaborate on distinctions among concepts of judicial compliance, effectiveness, implementation, and treatment. We describe our innovative three-level approach in more detail and show how it advances the existing research toolkit. We highlight the applicability of our approach both outside the field of international case law and outside the European context.

3.1 Mapping interactions between international law and domestic practice

In the post-World War II era, the international arena became a system with densely formalized interactions (Goldstein 2001). States concluded hundreds of thousands of international treaties (Alter and Raustiala 2018), and some portion of those treaties created supervisory bodies overseeing compliance with treaty norms (Terris, Romano, and Swigart 2007; Alter 2014; Romano, Alter, and Shany 2014b). International courts receive growing numbers of petitions and increasingly hear disputes involving contentious issues (Dunoff and Pollack 2018, 47–8). International law rapidly developed despite a lack of a strong central authority with undisputed powers of enforcement (Waltz 2001, 159; Alter 2014, 3). This defining feature of the international arena has not prevented states from investing in the creation of international courts, which are based on international treaties and have functions and working methods similar to national courts.[1] Their strong court-like appearance at the same time creates issues because effective courts induce changes in member states' practices which in turn provoke criticism concerning interference in state sovereignty (Spano 2015; Madsen, Cebulak, and Wiebusch 2018). Such criticism is especially pronounced in the case of international courts dealing with sensitive issues (e.g., human rights) and with disputes between states and individuals (Sandholtz, Bei, and Caldwell 2018). Recently, the backlash against international judgments and courts has been voiced not only by governments but also by judicial peers sitting at national courts (Tomuschat 2010; Mälksoo 2016). In the case of the ECtHR, the criticism even left the usual political and legal arena and spread to the mass media (Popelier, Lambrecht, and Lemmens 2016). Dissatisfaction with expanding powers of international judiciary swells also outside Europe (Alter, Gathii, and Helfer 2016; Daly and Wiebusch 2018; Soley and Steininger 2018).

All these developments, which have placed the international judiciary into the political and media spotlight, add to the timeliness of this book. In a time of critical exposure, international courts need allies who can increase their legitimacy. Hence, cooperative domestic courts may come in very handy. Unfortunately, not much is systematically known about the treatment of international case law by national courts,[2] and we aspire to close this gap.

3.1.1 Concept of compliance and its alternatives

Political and legal scholars approach interactions between international law and domestic political and legal systems differently. Legal scholarship focuses on to what extent, how, and based on what international legal standards are domestically observed. Louis Henkin (1979, 47) famously stated that "it is probably the case that almost all nations observe almost all principles of international law and almost all of their obligations almost all of the time". Social science scholars accept this statement, but pose a different question: Is compliance with a norm caused by the ratification of an international treaty?[3] Or would a state behave the same, even in the absence of an international treaty? Rather, social science scholarship zeroes in on the effects that international law produces.

Political and legal scholars share their preoccupation with the concept of compliance when studying interactions between international law and domestic reality. *Compliance* usually means a state of conformity of practice with legal norms.[4] However, such a definition has not received universal acceptance. For example, Courtney Hillebrecht (2017, 53–54) calls compliance a nebulous concept and points to the stream of scholarship which adopts a richer understanding of compliance as a process. In addition to the perception of compliance as a state of conformity or as a process, the third approach to compliance includes causal considerations.[5]

The causal focus of the third approach to compliance comes close to the research on effectiveness, which deals with the effects of legal norms.[6] Concepts of compliance and effectiveness often coincide, but we can also imagine cases when compliance, understood as a state of conformity between norms and practice, scores high, but effectiveness is low, and vice versa. Take, for instance, an exemplary liberal democracy that complies with an international human rights norm but had complied with the norm a long time before the treaty was ratified. The ratification, therefore, did not cause compliance. On the other hand, imagine a country that ratified an international treaty and consequently significantly changed its behavior towards an international-law-conforming way which, however, fell short of full compliance. The effects of the ratification were significant, yet did not amount to compliance.

Some authors try to reconcile the two camps by pointing out that law and compliance are conceptually linked. Legal rules set the standard, presume compliance, and explicitly aim to produce it (Raustiala and Slaughter 2002, 538). It follows that compliance is something to be achieved. The legal scholarship helps particularly in the interpretation of norms and assessment of facts, and hence in determining *what* the norm expects and *if* the observed behavior conforms to the norm (i.e., if an actor complies). Social science research seeks to explain *why* compliance happens, typically by establishing which factors contribute to compliance, and how.

In addition to concepts of compliance and effectiveness, the literature dealing with the relationship between international legal norms and national practice works with a concept of implementation. It relates both to the concept of compliance and effectiveness but captures a different aspect of the issue. *Implementation* means the process of putting international commitments into practice, usually via legislation, creation of institutions, and enforcement of rules (Raustiala and Slaughter 2002).

Compliance stands as the most used concept out of the triad introduced above and as one of the decisive factors in the evaluation of the performance of international courts (Squatrito et al. 2018).[7] However, as such, it also invites scholarly skepticism. Critiques point not only to difficulties with measuring compliance (Kingsbury 1997; Hillebrecht 2009; Kapiszewski and Taylor 2013; Squatrito 2018), but question even the concept of compliance as such. Strongly influenced by constructivist writings, authors dislike treating norms as variables because it obscures the continuous creation of norms and identities in the process of intersubjective communication (Kingsbury 1997). Empirical research on compliance acts as if a stable and agreed-upon meaning of a rule exists and usually ignores the centrality of interpretation to the generation of legal meaning (Howse and Teitel 2010). Lisa Martin (2013) titled her chapter outright "Against Compliance", calling it a poor substitute for understanding the effectiveness of international law. According to her, compliance is a legal concept and as such it is ill suited for the social-scientific pursuit of identifying causal effects.

3.1.2 Findings of compliance research

Despite their strengthening and autonomization, on their own, international court's have no formal power to enforce their rulings themselves and may employ only a few instruments to force governments to comply with their rulings (Hathaway and Shapiro 2011). International courts, therefore, need the cooperation of the national institutions, which have retained the instruments of coercion and enforcement (Heyns and Viljoen 2002, 6; Slaughter and Burke-White 2006, 343; Hillebrecht 2012). Even the ECtHR – i.e., "the world's most successful system of international law for the protection of human rights" (Janis, Kay, and Bradley 2008, 3; similarly Moravcsik 2000, 243) – relies on domestic actors. They "hold the key to the Court's ability to affect human rights on the domestic level" (Hillebrecht 2014b, 1108).

Individual studies emphasize different domestic actors as crucial for pushing through policy change and safeguarding compliance. Some rely on the power of the civil society and non-governmental organizations (NGOs) (Simmons 2009; Cichowski 2013), or pressure groups (Trachtman 2010), while others stress the power of the judiciary (Roberts 2011; Nollkaemper 2012; Gerards and Fleuren 2014), legislature (Donald and Leach 2016, 99–108; Krommendijk 2018), or the executive (Huneeus 2011, 517; Hillebrecht 2012). However, actors do not operate in isolation (Carrubba and Gabel 2017, 59) and the cooperation of a strong pro-compliance coalition is needed for a successful response to an international court's ruling (Hillebrecht 2014a, 25; Kosař and Petrov 2017).

In addition to the activities of various actors, it is also important to consider a wider legal context, especially the type of legal tradition and legal culture in a given country (Delcourt 2013). Lawyers further emphasize a general approach towards international law (monist or dualist) and whether international law is self-executing (Tzanakopoulos and Tams 2013, 534–6).[8] Surprisingly, in the case of the ECHR, empirical findings seem not to confirm the importance of its legal status in the domestic legal system, which is not consequential for the applicability of the ECHR or of ECtHR case law (Anagnostou 2014, 212).

The international and national levels continuously interact; on the one hand, the ECtHR relies on domestic actors, but on the other hand, its rulings influence the functioning and the balance of national branches of power (Kosař and Lixinski 2015). ECtHR case law is seemingly capable of contributing to a transformative change, even in sensitive issues such as LGBT rights, although it takes some time and spill-over to third states (i.e., those who were not parties to the initial dispute before the ECtHR) has its limits (Helfer and Voeten 2014). In Central and Eastern Europe, Strasbourg Court rulings have arguably even assisted in the process of cultural change after the 1989 revolutions when domestic courts learned through the ECtHR's rulings about the "Western" norms of liberal democracy, rule of law, and the human rights perspective (Ziemele 2016).

To sum up, international courts interpret international law and decide whether states' behavior conforms to the law or not. Thereby, international rulings provide incentives for domestic policy changes and, considering the rule-of-law principles, make the potential non-compliance costlier. Still, the actual decision whether to comply and how rests on all relevant domestic political actors and on the dynamics of their mutual capacities, priorities, positions, and relations (Cardenas 2007, 13). The scholarship increasingly recognizes the importance of domestic courts for compliance (Simmons 2009). Moreover, the international dynamic and increased normative pressure can provide important input to the domestic configuration and contribute to changes over time (Lupu 2013). Processes of social learning and international socialization contribute to changes in perceptions; therefore, results of a cost-and-benefit calculation of non-compliance decisions can shift over time (von Stein 2013).

3.2 Judicialization and specifics of judicial interactions[9]

Our project focuses on the use of international case law by domestic courts, which count among the most important partners of international courts (Andenas and Bjorge 2013, 259).[10] We use the adjective "judicial" (treatment, compliance, etc.) to denote that courts act in relation to the phenomenon at hand. Judicial interactions have some specifics when compared to other interactions between the domestic and international level. Judges worldwide use similar tools and logic to resolve cases; therefore, the solution or inspiration on how to solve a similar problem can travel from one jurisdiction to another. Such "travelling" is even more probable when courts are part of one international regime and interpret the same international norms, especially when there is one court specialized in the interpretation of such norms (the ECtHR in our case). Transnational interactions among judges increase when they socialize on the international level using a common (legal) language and sharing some liberal notions and institutional/professional identity (Slaughter 2003). An emerging global network of judges as a distinct community contributes also to growing familiarity with international norms.

In addition to the rising international interconnectedness of courts, another well-documented process has developed in recent decades: The courts as institutions have strengthened, both domestically and internationally (Hirschl 2007; Alter 2014). The process of judicialization includes not only the transfer of decision-making from other branches of power to the courts but also the spread of judicial decision-making methods outside the judicial province (Vallinder 1995, 13).

In particular, international courts have undergone a significant transformation during the past decades. With regard to their proliferation and strengthening (Romano, Alter, and Shany 2014a), some even talk about a paradigm change (Alter 2014, 3). International courts nowadays have a higher degree of independence from the states' control, wider access, compulsory jurisdiction, and further domestic embeddedness (Keohane, Moravcsik, and Slaughter 2000; Romano 2006).[11] Besides the traditional role of dispute settlement, they have also acquired the functions of enforcement, administrative review, and constitutional review (Alter 2008a). Hence, recent international courts with strong authority resemble trustees rather than mere agents of the states (Alter 2008b; Stone Sweet and Brunell 2013).

Despite the rise in power of the judiciary, the other branches still retain important instruments for disciplining the judiciary – from the influence over the composition of the judiciary, through its financing, to the implementation and enforcement of rulings (Staton and Moore 2011). The judiciary, therefore, builds the base of its power on the possession of legal expertise.[12] Judges need the support of the public, which helps in preventing hostile interventions by the legislative or executive branch (Vanberg 2010). Judges wield a reputation as independent umpires in legal disputes and learned interpreters of law as the dominant regulatory tool in modern states (Garoupa and Ginsburg 2017, 14–49). As a part of their exclusive expertise, they use references to previous case law so that new rulings are substantiated by citations of precedent.[13]

Our project zooms in on the top of the domestic court system. Disputes before apex courts serve as an indication of particular problems in society because litigants have to exhaustingly go through the judicial hierarchy to its top (Shapiro 1986, 49–51). Unlike hierarchically lower courts, the apex courts regularly deal with important cases, often loaded with sensitive human rights rhetoric, and they usually have means such as law clerks or analytical units which help them with processing international case law. Exhaustingly rich literature exists on determinants of judicial decision-making, which can be synthesized thus: "[J]udges' decisions are a function of what they prefer to do, tempered by what they think they ought to do, but constrained by what they perceive is feasible to do" (Gibson 1983, 9). This statement also applies very well to the situation of a judge pondering if she should use international case law. We now elaborate on this specific question.

Recently, domestic courts have considerably changed their approach towards international law (Oppong and Barreto 2017, 286). In most systems, the legislature or the executive is in charge of implementing international legal obligations (Council of Europe: European Commission for Democracy through Law 2014). Traditionally, national courts strategically avoided international law in their judgments (Dothan 2018, 234) or they deferred to the government (Schreuer 1975, 154; Benvenisti 2008, 241). Courts usually chose a narrow interpretation of constitutional provisions which imported international law into national law, the government-friendly interpretation of international law, or "avoidance doctrines" which shielded governments against judicial review under international law (Benvenisti 1993, 160–61). Judges opted for deference to governments probably from a concern that they would hurt national interests in international politics by binding the executive to rules which do not constrain foreign actors (Benvenisti 1993, 173). However, the judicial deference to other branches of power can no longer be taken for granted. National courts assist in enforcement, interpretation, and gradually also in the development of international law (Tzanakopoulos 2011). Increasingly, judges regard the application of international law as part of their constitutional role as guardians of the rule of law (Shany 2009, 6–15).

The rise of the international judiciary with its gradually more frequent and threatening interferences with national sovereignty also brought about more space for conflicts with domestic judges. National judiciaries are far from being a monolith sharing the same views (Kosař and Petrov 2017), and a truly unified global community of cooperating courts remains a myth rather than a reality. National judges do not always follow their international counterparts. Domestic courts increasingly signal limits to their openness towards international case law and start to act as "gatekeepers" (Kunz 2019, 3). Courts lose authority when they are regularly disobeyed; therefore, they presumably make decisions with an eye on future compliance. International courts can take the hint that using a less interventionist approach would be conducive to compliance.

Development of international case law brings new possibilities for domestic courts because it enables them to pragmatically pick a norm which they apply to resolve a dispute. Application of international case law presupposes that a judge knows international case law (Schreuer 1974, 692–94), or at least searches if it exists when deciding on cases. Both acquiring knowledge and searching for the international case law requires a lot of time and effort, therefore judges might carefully consider such an investment. If an international ruling exists and the judge knows it, and if at the same time it contradicts national legislation or practice, then the judge faces a potentially unpleasant dilemma: either give preference to an international ruling and side-line domestic norms, or abide by domestic law and turn a blind eye to an international ruling.[14]

One of two basic logics of human action guides judges when making a reference: They cite international case law either because they think it is appropriate or because they believe it will bring about desired consequences. What makes a reference attractive for a domestic judge? National judges have their own agendas that they want to push forward, and ECtHR case law might be instrumental in satisfying those agendas. Arguably, no actor in a liberal democracy wishes to be perceived as a human rights violator. This makes the court's reference to ECtHR case law, solidifying the argument that the state practice violated human rights norms, particularly powerful. Citing an ECtHR ruling thus increases the persuasive potential of a domestic ruling.

Bahdi (2002, 557–8) lists five reasons why judges invoke international law: (1) concern for the rule of law; (2) desire to promote universal values; (3) reliance on international law to help uncover values inherent within the domestic regime; (4) willingness to invoke the logic of judges in other jurisdictions; and (5) concern to avoid negative assessments from the international community. The problem is that this captures only a small part of all references to international law, because it examines the reasons offered by national judges to explain their references to international law. However, the clear majority of rulings do not include such justifications and the references appear there in a much more cursory way. How then to explain the motivations behind such references? Here, research on social learning (Checkel 2001) informs our endeavor – it has become a standard behavior that judges refer to ECtHR case law. Arguably, referring to international case law is evaluated positively – it can improve the persuasiveness of domestic rulings and moreover it signals the international horizons of a judge. As increasing numbers of judges invoke international law and the judicial community becomes more opened towards such practice, the other judges then simply mimic such behavior and join the stream. Nevertheless, the details of referring practice will differ wildly, with judges sincerely interested in ECtHR case law engaging with it more deeply, while judges who have not internalized a welcoming approach towards ECtHR case law will stick to a minimalist form of referencing, based merely on copying-and-pasting references to suitable rulings, without any deeper elaboration and without giving Strasbourg case law a more significant role.

The domestic judge-rapporteur drafting the ruling addresses four audiences at the same time. First, a judge can use references to persuade other members of the panel to decide the case according to her preferences.[15] Second, references may add persuasiveness to apex courts' reasoning by showing that the current practice of other branches of government violates international human rights case law. This decreases the probability of domestic legislative or executive override because the other branches negotiated and ratified membership in the international regime.[16] When embedded in rulings of domestic courts, international case law can subsequently trigger domestic legislative or executive response in order to comply with the position of both international and domestic judges.

Third, once domestic apex courts accept international case law, then both the opinions and even the ways to achieve those opinions (e.g., a proportionality test) (Andenas and Bjorge 2013, 260) spread to lower levels of judicial hierarchy. The judge-rapporteur can thus have other domestic courts in sight when including a reference to international case law.

Finally, the circle closes and the judge-rapporteur sends signals via citations of ECtHR case law to the ECtHR itself, which should be more easily persuaded about the compliance of the domestic ruling with ECtHR case law.

In the long run, a trigger coming from ECtHR case law, embraced by national apex courts and then diffused to lower levels of the judicial hierarchy, and subsequently accepted by the executive and legislative, can bring about a social change.[17] In such a case, the use of references empowers both levels of the judicial community – domestic courts can push through their preferences via citations of ECtHR case law, and in return, the ECtHR's authority increases when its case law contributes to a change in national practices.[18]

Use of international case law by apex courts creates pressure on other actors to become familiar with it because otherwise their practices can be contested before the courts. Moreover, increased referencing to international rulings as an important form of legal justification might also be relevant for actors outside judicial and political audiences, such as NGOs, advocates, media, and even members of the wider public who may find ECtHR case law useful for substantiating their claims. Once ECtHR case law penetrates broader legal discourse, the pressure on courts to cope with it increases.

Nevertheless, given the sheer volume of ECtHR case law and lack of education in international law, especially in the older generation of judges who sit at apex courts in new Council of Europe (CoE) member states, the familiarity with ECtHR case law is not to be taken for granted. This is particularly relevant for Central and Eastern Europe due to language barriers (Kosař and Petrov 2018). It is thus crucial to find the connecting link between apex judges and ECtHR case law. There are several ways these connections can be made – either a judge,[19] when deciding domestic cases, routinely searches if ECtHR case law exists, or she can be informed by the court's research units or directly by litigants. However, to recall the discussion above, knowledge of international case law does not automatically translate to its use. Even a judge knowledgeable about international law can be an ardent opponent of its domestic use. Therefore, the use of international law generally presupposes a knowledgeable judge who is willing to cite it.

We have summed up the main streams of research on the relationship between domestic practice and international law and discussed the growing role of courts and the specifics of judicial interactions. The scholarship revolves particularly around the concept of compliance, with less common elaborations on concepts of effectiveness and implementation. None of these main concepts perfectly fits our questions of interest (see the Introduction), although they quite frequently show overlaps. The following section explains advantages of our concept of judicial treatment and how it relates to the concepts of compliance, effectiveness, and implementation.

3.3 Going beyond compliance: A three-level approach to judicial treatment

Scholarship dealing with domestic factors of compliance in unison stresses the importance of an independent judiciary, but the question of how often and especially how international case law is used by national courts has not been systematically examined to date. Similarly, many works document important domestic consequences of the ECHR and Strasbourg case law,[20] yet none of them have done so systematically. We know quite a lot about spectacular cases of big successes or failures, but much less about how often national judges make use of ECtHR case law and how they use it in their daily practice. We seek to uncover deeper impacts of ECtHR case law on the practice of domestic courts, which go beyond assessing judicial compliance with few well-known individual rulings against the home country.

Our approach is in line with the conceptualization of the international court's authority in fact developed by Alter, Helfer, and Madsen (2016). They distinguish between narrow authority, which presupposes compliance in specific dispute; the intermediate authority under which compliance partners consider prospective litigations and, for example, change laws in order to prevent disputes; and extensive authority when whole legal fields accept the authority of international law. We found inspiration also in distinguishing between case-specific and *erga omnes* effectiveness and in the concept of embeddedness effectiveness (Helfer 2014), which captures the extent to which international courts anchor their rulings in domestic legal orders. This prevents a case from making it to the international stage because it is solved at home. We share with Alter et al. and Helfer the ambition to examine broader trends, but differ in our clear focus on domestic courts.

In the coming sections, we introduce our approach to judicial treatment. We discuss the shortcomings of mainstream concepts of judicial compliance, effectiveness, and implementation when elaborated separately. Then, we examine differences between judicial treatment and other concepts. Finally, we describe the potential of our new approach to judicial treatment beyond the frontiers of Europe and international human rights case law.

3.3.1 Judicial treatment of ECtHR case law

Our approach to the judicial treatment of ECtHR case law has a high potential to enrich the existing analysis of compliance, effectiveness, and implementation. It brings detailed information on how domestic courts work with Strasbourg case law, particularly how often they use it, how important a role ECtHR case law plays in the reasoning of domestic courts, how often domestic courts follow Strasbourg case law, and what its broader repercussions are for domestic judicial practice. The book thus presents the first systematic analysis of the judicial treatment of ECtHR case law.

This subsection introduces our three-level approach to studying the treatment of the Strasbourg case law by domestic apex courts. We claim that the three-level approach adequately depicts both how extensively and intensively domestic apex courts work with ECtHR case law because it captures, (1) on the whole population of domestic apex court rulings, how often and in what parts of rulings domestic apex courts refer to the international case law; (2) on the representative sample of domestic rulings, how important the use of the international case law is on the result of the domestic case, and what the function of the reference to international case law is; and (3) how use of international case law influences domestic practice in selected fields of law over time.

We believe that this quantitative-qualitative mix of legal and social sciences methods can bring a better understanding of the treatment of ECtHR case law than existing approaches. To begin with, knowledge of the law and its principles is necessary to determine what should be observed. A systematic quantitative perspective on the whole population of references to ECtHR case law helps to paint the big picture. At the meso level, a representative sample is construed based on fine distinguishing of legal techniques,[21] while still preserving its systemic features. Micro-level analyses then utilize legal expertise to closely study selected issues and compensate for trends not visible in the quantitative analysis of references.[22]

The macro-level analysis generally measures the level of penetration of ECtHR case law in domestic judicial practice. It examines development in the number of references over time, which provides us with crude information about whether domestic judges use ECtHR rulings routinely or only accidentally. The whole mass of references does not have an equal value; some play a more important role than others. It is therefore risky to treat all references equally. The position in which a reference appears in a ruling plays a role – if in the reasoning of the court, or only in the narrative part, which summarizes the previous procedure and arguments of parties to the dispute. A dominant occurrence of references only in the narrative part would hint towards a lower authority of the ECtHR among domestic courts when compared to a dominant occurrence of references in the reasoning. It makes a difference if the parties raise arguments based on Strasbourg case law that are then not then explicitly dealt with by domestic judges, or if domestic judges explain why they have not applied ECtHR case law pointed to by the parties.

Finally, the macro-level analysis helps to uncover if domestic courts perceive the authority of the ECtHR broadly and recognize its whole case law regardless of the defendant state, or if they refer only to the ECtHR rulings against their home states.

It is widely accepted that in the post-communist CoE member states that joined the ECHR regime in the 1990s, the references to ECtHR case law have been rare in the first two decades since then (Emmert 2012). This holds true also for higher courts in the hierarchy, which were generally reluctant to refer to ECtHR case law. This might have been due to the fact that older judges, who usually occupy positions at higher courts, have not received systematic training on international human rights law, and also due to the lack of translations of the case law (Emmert 2012, 600). Moreover, many judges remained in their positions even after the fall of authoritarian regimes (Černič 2018, 132). We expect the number of references to change when these elements change. Moreover, it takes some time to accumulate ECtHR rulings against the home state, whose knowledge then spreads among the domestic legal community. Only after becoming familiar with the ECHR regime does the awareness of the general ECtHR case law increase. Thus, we expect a gradual shift from references against the home state to cases against the third countries.

The meso-level analysis builds on legal expertise and moves us from how much Strasbourg case law is used to how it is used and what impact it has on the outcome of the domestic case. Our unique dataset provides us with indications on the authority of the ECtHR and how it develops over time as the country becomes more and more embedded in the ECHR regime. We are interested in whether ECtHR case law serves as an important normative source. Again, we reiterate that references are not equal; they differ particularly in their importance for deciding the dispute. We distinguish between substantive references which make ECtHR case law the decisive source substantively influencing the result of the domestic dispute and supporting references that were added to domestic rulings only to support findings based primarily on domestic law (such as: "By the way, the Strasbourg Court says the same"). We do not dismiss the relevance of supporting references, because they show that domestic courts consider it appropriate to cite Strasbourg case law even when it is not necessary for deciding the dispute. However, references with substantive influence are important, because they are the ones that often change how a domestic dispute is decided.

A closer examination of references reveals whether domestic courts follow ECtHR case law or if they oppose it. One other situation, which we call "distinguishing", warrants closer attention. When domestic judges take care to explain why they cannot use ECtHR case law, it suggests high authority of Strasbourg Court rulings. Apparently, in such cases, judges perceive that they should explain why they do not apply an ECtHR ruling – i.e., they act as though the application of an ECtHR ruling was a default option.

We can partially build on previous observations that found that courts in new CoE member states have extremely rarely engaged in an open discussion of ECtHR case law (Emmert 2012, 601). Again, this may change with increasing familiarity with international law and with younger judges at apex courts. If so, ECtHR case law will arguably be more thoroughly discussed in courts' argumentation.

Lastly, we can exploit the unique structure of the Czech judiciary, which has three apex courts, each of them having different tasks and historical legacies. Observing variations among them helps to understand how the specific setting of a given court influences its judicial treatment of ECtHR case law. Similarly to Roberts, we challenge the frequent presumption that domestic courts function as impartial enforcers of international law. But we do not go as far she does in stating that domestic courts seek to create and shape international norms (Roberts 2011, 60). Our careful multi-method research shows that treatment of international law and motivations of courts to use it varies greatly, not only among judges and courts, but also over time. While in some, rather seldom, cases domestic courts might have such high ambitions as Roberts posits, in a great majority of less spectacular cases domestic courts will use international law only as a supportive argument. Moreover, the judges at domestic apex courts, especially at constitutional courts, are by no means a uniform sort of lawyer. They differ in terms of their specialization, previous occupation, age, gender, education, etc. All these characteristics may influence the exposure of a judge to ECtHR case law and her stance towards it. Younger judges with an interest in human rights who were often educated abroad will probably feel more comfortable in encounters with Strasbourg case law. As a result, they will likely use it more often in a more elaborate way than a judge who worked in pre-1989 Czechoslovakia and was socialized into a formalist system (Kühn 2011) emphasizing national legal sovereignty.

Finally, the micro-level analysis makes use of legal doctrinal analysis and focuses on only a few noteworthy domestic legal fields. It compensates for the strictly reference-based nature of research in the macro- and meso-level. The micro-level can capture whatever development has not been spotted by the quantitative macro- and meso-level analyses. Therefore, it requires close knowledge of the jurisdiction under review. The micro-level analysis examines instances in which domestic courts used ECtHR case law differently than is their typical mode of use identified by the meso-level. It focuses on fields where ECtHR case law had a transformative influence on domestic jurisprudence or, on the contrary, fields where domestic courts had difficulties in accommodating ideas from Strasbourg Court rulings. Such analysis helps in uncovering factors playing important parts in such non-standard scenarios. The micro-level research informs us about situations in which domestic judges change their usual positions and either revolt against an ECtHR ruling, or instead embrace ECtHR case law (if they were previously suspicious towards the Strasbourg Court).

3.3.2 Judicial treatment, compliance, effectiveness, and implementation

Our research on judicial treatment is predominantly based on the use of references. It fares well when courts cite ECtHR case law, but experiences some issues when judges do not refer to Strasbourg case law. In order to offset for this drawback, we include the micro-level analysis, which builds on detailed knowledge of Czech judicial practice. Thus, we can assess situations in which judges have not referred to ECtHR case law, although they could have.

Figure 3.1 serves as a starting point for distinguishing judicial treatment from concepts of judicial compliance, effectiveness, and implementation. As noted, judicial treatment works mainly with references, while judicial compliance does not necessarily need them. To achieve a state of judicial compliance, it suffices to deliver rulings in conformity with ECtHR case law, regardless of explicit

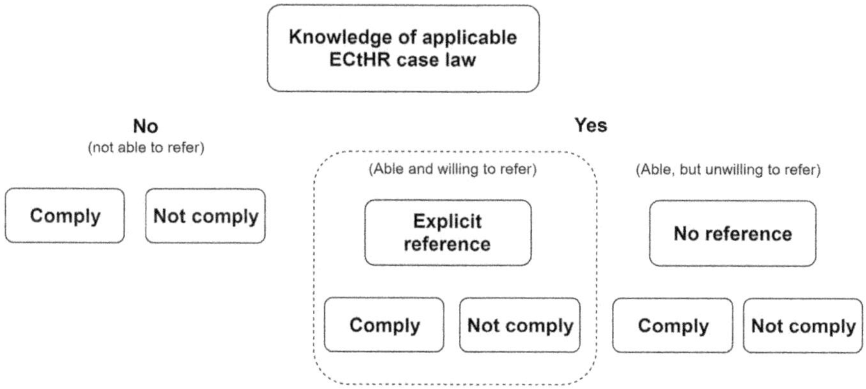

Figure 3.1 Judicial compliance, effectiveness, implementation, and treatment.
Source: authors.

citations, or even without knowing it. On the contrary, in the case of judicial treatment, domestic judges must be able and willing to use ECtHR case law. When a domestic judge is able to use Strasbourg Court rulings (i.e., she knows about them), she might be willing to cite them, when she finds doing so appropriate or consequential. Our more sophisticated concept of judicial treatment allows us also to distinguish among different uses of references.[23]

The concept of judicial effectiveness zooms in on the substantive impact of ECtHR case law, typically when a domestic court substantially uses a Strasbourg Court ruling in order to change domestic practice. In such cases, ECtHR case law produces effects. We can say that ECtHR case law produces effects only if the domestic court has knowledge about it; if a court complied without awareness of the applicable Strasbourg Court rulings, then they have not caused the domestic change. One can imagine that an ECtHR ruling can induce a domestic court to deliver a judgment that changes domestic practice without explicitly referring to the Strasbourg Court ruling, but such cases are close to impossible to explore on a systematic basis. A researcher would probably have to do interviews with judges and try to find out why they decided the way they did or to compare passages from ECtHR and domestic rulings and ascertain that domestic courts copied from ECtHR case law without a proper acknowledgement.

As opposed to judicial effectiveness, judicial treatment is interested not only in the employment of Strasbourg Court rulings that had substantial impact on the result of the case at hand, but equally on instances in which an ECtHR ruling was only of a supporting significance and when domestic courts explained why they would not use ECtHR case law. Despite having no immediate effect, such treatment of ECtHR case law shows that domestic judges take it seriously and recognize its authority and legitimacy as an important source of norms.

Finally, judicial implementation typically involves cases when domestic judges put adverse ECtHR rulings against their home state into national practice. Similarly to effectiveness, judicial implementation does not necessarily require explicit citations of ECtHR case law, but the absence of references makes any research very difficult. The pure form of judicial implementation also focuses on instances when ECtHR case law had substantive influence. When the ECtHR ruling has only a supporting influence, then the main work is done by the executive or legislative, and judicial implementation only follows what has already been done by other branches.

The strength of our concept of judicial treatment stands out especially in cases when the ECtHR did not find any violation against Czechia and despite this Czech courts subsequently refer to this ECtHR ruling. For other concepts, such an ECtHR ruling does not stand as relevant – Czechia complied before and keeps on complying after, there is no implementation needed, and no causal effect of the ECtHR ruling on domestic judicial practice is identifiable. Nevertheless, from the judicial treatment perspective, such a practice is important because courts use references to ECtHR rulings to justify their practice to various actors in the domestic legal arena, particularly to litigants. Domestic courts thereby strengthen the persuasiveness of their rulings and at the same time increase the authority of the ECtHR, whose outputs penetrate national practice more and more. The maximum boost to the ECtHR authority comes in situations when neither national nor international law gives a clear answer and a domestic court adopts an "ECtHR mindset" and ponders how the Strasbourg Court would decide the dispute. Such an approach makes sense, because the dispute can end up before the ECtHR eventually and courts generally do not like their rulings being overturned.

In sum, the strong points of the concept of judicial treatment as compared to other concepts are as follows. The research on the influence of international law on domestic practice usually revolves around the concept of compliance, whose dominant version analyzes to what extent domestic rulings conform to international case law, and eventually why they do not (see, for example, Smekal and Šipulová 2014). Typically, domestic judicial practice is assessed on a small sample of international judgments against the given state. Such an approach provides us with valuable information on the conformity of domestic case law with ECtHR judgments, but we do not learn much about the depth and breadth of penetration of ECtHR rulings into domestic courts' practice. This shortcoming also applies to concepts of effectiveness and implementation.

Moreover, when focusing on compliance, we do not know what the influence of Strasbourg case law was on domestic courts when deciding the dispute – they might have decided the case in accordance with an ECtHR ruling, but from reasons completely unrelated to the ECtHR ruling. Our judicial treatment approach captures whether an ECtHR ruling played a substantive role for a finding of a domestic court, much as the concept of effectiveness does.

To be sure, judicial treatment can be indicative of the level of compliance. Frequent references to Strasbourg Court rulings signal domestic judicial compliance. Nevertheless, the frequency of references does not serve as a perfect indicator of compliance[24] because domestic courts can refer to Strasbourg Court rulings without actually complying with them. Conversely, domestic courts can comply with ECtHR case law without referring to it. Unfortunately, such cases cannot be dealt with systematically in the research based on references, but we offset for this shortcoming at least partially. Based on our detailed knowledge of the domestic legal system and familiarity with sensitive issues where compliance with Strasbourg case law remains problematic, the micro-level analysis also examines situations of missing referencing and spectacular compliance, or non-compliance.

Finally, judicial treatment pays not only attention to the findings of domestic courts, but the micro-level analysis also examines the diffusion of interpretative techniques and concepts that domestic courts adopted from ECtHR practice. In contrast, compliance research might not notice the tectonic change in domestic jurisprudence (i.e., the introduction of the ECtHR-style proportionality test) due to its narrow focus on substantive conformity between ECtHR and domestic rulings.

3.3.3 Promises of judicial treatment

After years of scholarly doubts about the contribution of international human rights treaties to the quality of human rights protection (Hathaway 2001; Hafner-Burton and Tsutsui 2005), new research brings some reasons for optimism (Fariss 2014, 2018, 2019). Domestic courts are one of the main drivers of change in putting treaty provisions into practice (Simmons 2009). Apex courts, standing on the top of national judicial hierarchy, play a crucial role in this endeavor. For a better understanding of how international human rights norms penetrate domestic practice, a study of the use of ECtHR case law in domestic apex courts' rulings proves very valuable. This is even more true in the case of countries after transitioning to democracy, where participation in a strong international human rights regime is supposed to lock in the newly established liberal features (Moravcsik 2000).

Our three-level approach to judicial treatment allows us to observe trends in the extent of the use of ECtHR case law; that is, the purpose, manner, and form of its use, as well as its effects in selected fields of law. Moreover, thanks to the detailed knowledge of the domestic compliance system, it is possible to evaluate the effects of developments in judicial treatment of ECtHR case law on the wider political and legal system, especially by documenting its institutional and procedural innovations.

The concept of judicial treatment is of interest to scholars studying interactions of international law and domestic practice. Our three-level approach goes beyond research on compliance, effectiveness, and implementation of international law. On the conceptual level, it operates simultaneously with other key concepts. It can prove especially helpful when researchers of compliance, effectiveness, and implementation recognize that they do not completely capture the phenomenon of influence of international law on domestic practice and they can enrich their analysis by including considerations of judicial treatment. The focus on "beyond compliance" should shed light on how domestic apex courts learn to use international case law and what the consequences of these processes are.

The good news is that the three-level approach stands as universally applicable. We invite the use of our framework for other ECHR countries, which could subsequently enable a grand comparative synthesis. One can easily imagine its application also in the African or Inter-American human rights regime. However, the approach is transferrable to any analysis of the influence of whatever element (e.g., Court of Justice of the European Union case law, international treaties on environmental protection) in any jurisdiction.

Notes

1 Von Bogdandy and Venzke (2013) claim that the functions of international courts go beyond traditional dispute settlement and include the stabilization of normative expectations, law-making, and the control and legitimation of authority exercised by others. See also, for example, Caron (2006).
2 This comment was made in relation to the Court of Justice of the European Union (Bobek 2015, 200–201), but it applies also to the ECtHR.
3 This does not stipulate that all the social science literature discusses causal relations, but rather that empirical social science strives for discovering a causal relationship, either focusing on the causal effect (King, Keohane, and Verba 1995) or on the causal mechanism (Brady and Collier 2010).
4 For an overview of meanings of compliance, see Kingsbury (1997).
5 Yuval Shany defines *compliance* as "a causal relationship between the contents of judicial decisions and state practice, leading to a convergence of the two" (Shany 2012, 261).
6 See definitions of an international tribunal's effectiveness as its ability "to enhance compliance with the associated substantive obligation" (Guzman 2008, 188) or "to compel compliance with its judgments by convincing domestic government institutions, directly and through pressure from private litigants, to use their power on its behalf" (Helfer and Slaughter 1997, 290). For examples of different approaches, see Huneeus (2014).
7 Courts themselves have increasingly paid attention to how their rulings are followed and even indicate measures required to comply with a ruling (Keller and Marti 2015).
8 For example, the ECHR with national legal systems: (1) coexists – i.e., is not applicable; (2) cooperates – i.e., the ECHR and its interpretation by the ECtHR provide complementary standards to the national; and (3) integrates – i.e., the ECHR is incorporated so that it effectively forms the bill of rights directly applied by courts (Djeffal 2016, 178).
9 The section makes use of Kosař and Petrov (2018).
10 See Chapter 2 of this book.
11 International human rights courts, especially the ECtHR, are closer to the transnational type than to the traditional interstate type (Keohane, Moravcsik, and Slaughter 2000, 469).
12 Compare the conception of legal field – Bourdieu (1986).
13 Case studies hint that courts in the process of emancipation from other branches of power rely more on sources from inside the expert legal community than on those outside the judicial realm (Dothan 2016).
14 Here, ignorance is bliss – those judges who do not know international case law do not face such a dilemma.

15 We leave the issue of individual motivations for using the reference open. The judge may consider the practice of using ECtHR case law appropriate or approach it strategically, either for pushing forward its position in given case or, for example, for personally motivated reasons such as self-presentation to the legal and political community as an expert in ECtHR case law.
16 Critics point out that the ECtHR, through its "living instrument" doctrine, read into the ECHR more than the states previously subscribed to (Sumption 2019).
17 But for a sceptical look at courts as drivers of social changes, see Rosenberg (2008).
18 See Chapter 2 ("filters" and "diffusers").
19 Meaning whole teams of individual judges, including their clerks.
20 The most comprehensive is arguably in Keller and Stone Sweet (2008).
21 Our detailed codebook makes the research replicable in other settings.
22 See details on the methodology in Chapter 4.
23 For more on different questions asked on the three levels of analysis, see the Introduction and Chapter 4.
24 Similarly, references can be considered only a very crude indicator of the ECtHR's legitimacy (see such use in Wind 2016).

References

Alter, Karen J. 2008a. "Delegating to International Courts: Self-Binding Vs. Other-Binding Delegation". *Law and Contemporary Problems* 71 (1): 37–76.

Alter, Karen J. 2008b. "Agents or Trustees? International Courts in Their Political Context". *European Journal of International Relations* 14 (1): 33–63.

Alter, Karen J. 2014. *The New Terrain of International Law: Courts, Politics, Rights.* Princeton, NJ: Princeton University Press.

Alter, Karen J., James T. Gathii, and Laurence R. Helfer. 2016. "Backlash against International Courts in west, East and Southern Africa: Causes and Consequences". *European Journal of International Law* 27 (2): 293–328.

Alter, Karen J., Lauence R. Helfer, and Mikael Rask Madsen. 2016. "How Context Shapes the Authority of International Courts the Variable Authority of International Courts". *Law and Contemporary Problems* 79: 1–36.

Alter, Karen J., and Kal Raustiala. 2018. "The Rise of International Regime Complexity". *Annual Review of Law and Social Science* 14 (1): 329–49.

Anagnostou, Dia. 2014. "Politics, Courts and Society in the National Implementation and Practice of the European Court of Human Rights Case Law". In *European Court of Human Rights: Implementing Strasbourg's Judgments on Domestic Policy*, edited by Dia Anagnostou, 211–31. Edinburgh: Edinburgh University Press.

Andenas, Mads, and Eirik Bjorge. 2013. "National Implementation of ECHR Rights". In *Constituting Europe: The European Court of Human Rights in a National, European, and Global Context*, edited by Andreas Føllesdal, Birgit Peters and Geir Ulfstein, 181–262. New York: Cambridge University Press.

Bahdi, Reem. 2002. "Globalization of Judgment: Transjudicialism and the Five Faces of International Law in Domestic Courts". *George Washington International Law Review* 34 (3): 555–604.

Benvenisti, Eyal. 1993. "Judicial Misgivings Regarding the Application of International Law: An Analysis of Attitudes of National Courts". *European Journal of International Law* 4: 159–83.

Benvenisti, Eyal. 2008. "Reclaiming Democracy: The Strategic Uses of Foreign and International Law by National Courts". *The American Journal of International Law* 102 (2): 241–74.

Bobek, Michal. 2015. "Of Feasibility and Silent Elephants: The Legitimacy of the Court of Justice through the Eyes of National Courts" In *Judging Europe's Judges. The Legitimacy of the Case Law of the European Court of Justice*, edited by Maurice Adams, Henri de Waele, Johan Meeusen and Gert Straetmans, 197–234. Oxford: Hart.

Bourdieu, Pierre. 1986. "The Force of Law: Toward a Sociology of the Juridical Field". *The Hastings Law Journal* 38: 805–63.

Brady, Henry E., and David Collier, eds. 2010. *Rethinking Social Inquiry: Diverse Tools, Shared Standards.* 2nd edition. Lanham, MD: Rowman & Littlefield Publishers.

Cardenas, Sonia. 2007. *Conflict and Compliance: State Responses to International Human Rights Pressure.* Philadelphia, PA: University of Pennsylvania Press.

Caron, David D. 2006. "Towards a Political Theory of International Courts and Tribunals". *Berkeley Journal of International Law* 24: 401–22.

Carrubba, Clifford J., and Matthew Gabel. 2017. "International Courts: A Theoretical Assessment". *Annual Review of Political Science* 20 (1): 55–73.

Černič, Jernej Letnar. 2018. "Impact of the European Court of Human Rights on the Rule of Law in Central and Eastern Europe". *Hague Journal on the Rule of Law* 10 (1): 111–37.

Checkel, Jeffrey T. 2001. "Why Comply? Social Learning and European Identity Change". *International Organization* 55 (3): 553–88.

Cichowski, Rachel A. 2013. "Civil Society and the European Court of Human Rights". In *The European Court of Human Rights between Law and Politics*, edited by Jonas Christoffersen and Mikael Rask Madsen, 77–97. Oxford: Oxford University Press.

Council of Europe: European Commission for Democracy through Law (Venice Commission). 2014. "Report on the Implementation of International Human Rights Treaties in Domestic Law and the Role of Courts". 8 December 2014, Study 690/2012. Accessed 21 December 2018. www.venice.coe.int/webforms/documents/default.aspx?pdffile=CDL-AD(2014)036-e.

Daly, Tom Gerald, and Micha Wiebusch. 2018. "The African Court on Human and Peoples' Rights: Mapping Resistance against a Young Court". *International Journal of Law in Context* 14 (02): 294–313.

Delcourt, Barbara. 2013. "Compliance, Theory Of". In *Max Planck Encyclopedia of Public International Law.* Accessed 1 September 2019. http://opil.ouplaw.com/view/10.1093/law:epil/9780199231690/law-9780199231690-e1043.

Djeffal, Christian. 2016. "Dynamic and Evolutive Interpretation of the ECHR by Domestic Courts?" In *The Interpretation of International Law by Domestic Courts: Uniformity, diversity, Convergence*, edited by Helmut Philipp Aust and Georg Nolte, 175–97. Oxford: Oxford University Press.

Donald, Alice, and Philip Leach. 2016. *Parliaments and the European Court of Human Rights.* Oxford: Oxford University Press.

Dothan, Shai. 2016. *Reputation and Judicial Tactics. A Theory of National and International Courts.* New York: Cambridge University Press.

Dothan, Shai. 2018. "International Courts Improve Public Deliberation". *Michigan Journal of International Law* 39 (2): 217–40.

Dunoff, Jeffrey L., and Mark A. Pollack. 2018. "International Judicial Practices: Opening the Black Box of International Courts". *Michigan Journal of International Law* 40 (1): 47–114.

Emmert, Frank. 2012. "The Implementation of the European Convention on Human Rights and Fundamental Freedoms in New Member States of the Council of Europe – Conclusions Drawn and Lessons Learned" In *The European Convention on Human Rights and Fundamental Freedoms in Central and Eastern Europe*, edited by Leonard M. Hammer and Frank Emmert, 597–645. Hague and Portland, OR: Eleven International Publishing.

Fariss, Christopher J. 2014. "Respect for Human Rights Has Improved over Time: Modeling the Changing Standard of Accountability". *American Political Science Review* 108 (02): 297–318.

Fariss, Christopher J. 2018. "The Changing Standard of Accountability and the Positive Relationship between Human Rights Treaty Ratification and Compliance". *British Journal of Political Science* 48 (1): 239–71.

Fariss, Christopher J. 2019. "Yes, Human Rights Practices Are Improving Over Time". *The American Political Science Review; Washington* 113 (3): 868–81.

Garlicki, Lech. 2008. "Cooperation of Courts: The Role of Supranational Jurisdictions in Europe". *International Journal of Constitutional Law* 6 (3-4): 509–30.

Garoupa, Nuno, and Tom Ginsburg. 2017. *Judicial Reputation: A Comparative Theory.* Chicago, IL: University of Chicago Press.

Gerards, Janneke, and Joseph Fleuren, eds. 2014. *Implementation of the European Convention on Human Rights and of the Judgments of the ECtHR in National Case-Law: A Comparative Analysis.* Cambridge: Intersentia.

Gibson, James L. 1983. "From Simplicity to Complexity: The Development of Theory in the Study of Judicial Behavior". *Political Behavior* 5 (1): 7–49.

Goldstein, Judith, ed. 2001. *Legalization and World Politics.* Cambridge, MA: MIT Press.

Guzman, Andrew T. 2008. "International Tribunals: A Rational Choice Analysis". *University of Pennsylvania Law Review* 157: 171–236.

Hafner-Burton, Emilie M., and Kiyoteru Tsutsui. 2005. "Human Rights in a Globalizing World: The Paradox of Empty Promises". *American Journal of Sociology* 110 (5): 1373–411.

Hathaway, Oona A. 2001. "Do Human Rights Treaties Make a Difference?". *Yale Law Journal* 111: 1935–2042.

Hathaway, Oona A., and Scott J. Shapiro. 2011. "Outcasting: Enforcement in Domestic and International Law". *The Yale Law Journal* 121 (2): 252–349.

Helfer, Laurence R. 2014. "The Effectiveness of International Adjudicators". In *The Oxford Handbook of International Adjudication*, edited by Cesare Romano, Karen Alter, and Yuval Shany, 464–82. Oxford: Oxford University Press.

Helfer, Laurence R., and Anne-Marie Slaughter. 1997. "Toward a Theory of Effective Supranational Adjudication". *The Yale Law Journal* 107 (2): 273–391.

Helfer, Laurence R., and Erik Voeten. 2014. "International Courts as Agents of Legal Change: Evidence from LGBT Rights in Europe". *International Organization* 68 (1): 77–110.

Henkin, Louis. 1979. *How Nations Behave: Law and Foreign Policy.* 2nd edition. New York: Columbia University Press.

Heyns, Christof, and Frans Viljoen. 2002. *The Impact of the United Nations Human Rights Treaties on the Domestic Level.* Hague: Kluwer Law International.

Hillebrecht, Courtney. 2009. "Rethinking Compliance: The Challenges and Prospects of Measuring Compliance with International Human Rights Tribunals". *Journal of Human Rights Practice* 1 (3): 362–79.

Hillebrecht, Courtney. 2012. "The Domestic Mechanisms of Compliance with International Human Rights Law: Case Studies from the Inter-American Human Rights System". *Human Rights Quarterly* 34 (4): 959–85.

Hillebrecht, Courtney. 2014a. *Domestic Politics and International Human Rights Tribunals: The Problem of Compliance*. New York: Cambridge University Press.

Hillebrecht, Courtney. 2014b. "The Power of Human Rights Tribunals: Compliance with the European Court of Human Rights and Domestic Policy Change". *European Journal of International Relations* 20 (4): 1100–23.

Hillebrecht, Courtney. 2017. "Compliance: Actors, Context and Cuasel Processes". In *Research Handbook on the Politics of International Law*, edited by Wayne Sandholtz and Christopher A. Whytock, 27–54. Cheltenham: Edward Elgar Publishing.

Hirschl, Ran. 2007. *Towards Juristocracy: The Origins and Consequences of the New Constitutionalism*. Cambridge, MA: Harvard University Press.

Howse, Robert, and Ruti Teitel. 2010. "Beyond Compliance: Rethinking Why International Law Really Matters". *Global Policy* 1 (2): 127–36.

Huneeus, Alexandra. 2011. "Courts Resisting Courts: Lessons from the Inter-American Court's Struggle to Enforce Human Rights". *Cornell International Law Journal* 44 (3): 493–534.

Huneeus, Alexandra. 2014. "Compliance with Judgments and Decisions". In *The Oxford Handbook of International Adjudication*, edited by Cesare Romano, Karen Alter and Yuval Shany, 438–63. Oxford: Oxford University Press.

Janis, Mark W., Richard S. Kay, and Anthony W. Bradley. 2008. *European Human Rights Law: Text and Materials*. 3rd edition. Oxford and New York: Oxford University Press.

Kapiszewski, Diana, and Matthew M. Taylor. 2013. "Compliance: Conceptualizing, measuring, and Explaining Adherence to Judicial Rulings". *Law & Social Inquiry* 38 (3): 803–35.

Keller, Helen, and Cedric Marti. 2015. "Reconceptualizing Implementation: The Judicialization of the Execution of the European Court of Human Rights' Judgments". *European Journal of International Law* 26 (4): 829–50.

Keller, Helen, and Alec Stone Sweet, eds. 2008. *A Europe of Rights: The Impact of the ECHR on National Legal Systems*. Oxford and New York: Oxford University Press.

Keohane, Robert O., Andrew Moravcsik, and Anne-Marie Slaughter. 2000. "Legalized Dispute Resolution: Interstate and Transnational". *International Organization* 54 (3): 457–88.

King, Gary, Robert O. Keohane, and Sidney Verba. 1995. *Designing Social Inquiry: Scientific Inference in Qualitative Research*. Princeton, NJ: Princeton University Press.

Kingsbury, Benedict. 1997. "The Concept of Compliance as a Function of Competing Conceptions of International Law". *Michigan Journal of International Law* 19: 345–72.

Kosař, David, and Lucas Lixinski. 2015. "Domestic Judicial Design by International Human Rights Courts". *The American Journal of International Law* 109 (4): 713–60.

Kosař, David, and Jan Petrov. 2017. "The Architecture of the Strasbourg Systen if Human Rights: The Crucial Role of the Domestic Level and the Constitutional Courts in Particular". *Heidelberg Journal of International Law* 77 (3): 585–621.

Kosař, David, and Jan Petrov. 2018. "Determinants of Compliance Difficulties among "Good compliers": Implementation of International Human Rights Rulings in the Czech Republic". *European Journal of International Law* 29 (2): 397–425.

Krommendijk, Jasper. 2018. "National Parliaments: Obstacles or Aid to the Impact of International Human Rights Bodies?" In *International Courts and Domestic Politics*, edited by Marlene Wind, 227–61. Cambridge and New York: Cambridge University Press.

Kühn, Zdeněk. 2011. *The Judiciary in Central and Eastern Europe: Mechanical Jurisprudence in Transformation?* Leiden: Brill.

Kunz, Raffaela. 2019. "Judging International Judgments Anew? The Human Rights Courts Before Domestic Courts". *SSRN*, 7 June 2019. Accessed 21 August 2019. https://papers.ssrn.com/sol3/papers.cfm?abstract_id=3400666.

Lupu, Yonatan. 2013. "Best Evidence: The Role of Information in Domestic Judicial Enforcement of International Human Rights Agreements". *International Organization* 67 (03): 469–503.

Madsen, Mikael Rask, Pola Cebulak, and Micha Wiebusch. 2018. "Backlash against International Courts: Explaining the Forms and Patterns of Resistance to International Courts". *International Journal of Law in Context* 14 (2): 197–220.

Mälksoo, Lauri. 2016. "Russia's Constitutional Court Defies the European Court of Human Rights: Constitutional Court of the Russian Federation Judgment of 14 July 2015, No 21-ĐY/2015". *European Constitutional Law Review* 12 (2): 377–95.

Martin, Lisa L. 2013. "Against Compliance". In *Interdisciplinary Perspectives on International Law and International Relations: The State of the Art*, edited by Jeffrey L. Dunoff and Mark A. Pollack, 591–610. Cambridge: Cambridge University Press.

Moravcsik, Andrew. 2000. "The Origins of Human Rights Regimes: Democratic Delegation in Postwar Europe". *International Organization* 54 (2): 217–52.

Motoc, Iulia, and Ineta Ziemele. 2016. *The Impact of the ECHR on Democratic Change in Central and Eastern Europe: Judicial Perspectives.* Cambridge: Cambridge University Press.

Nollkaemper, André. 2012. "The Role of National Courts in Inducing Compliance with International and European Law: A Comparison". In *Compliance and the Enforcement of EU Law*, edited by Marise Cremona, 157–93. Oxford: Oxford University Press.

Oppong, Richard Frimpong, and Angela M. Barreto. 2017. "Enforcement". In *Research Handbook on International Courts and Tribunals*, edited by William Schabas and Shannonbrooke Murphy, 273–98. Cheltenham: Edward Elgar Publishing.

Popelier, Patricia, Sarah Lambrecht, and Koen Lemmens, eds. 2016. *Criticism of the European Court of Human Rights: Shifting the Convention System: Counter-Dynamics at the National and EU Level.* Cambridge: Intersentia.

Raustiala, Kal, and Anne-Marie Slaughter. 2002. "International law, International Relations and Compliance". In *Handbook of International Relations*, edited by Walter Carlsnaes, Thomas Risse and Beth A. Simmons, 538–58. London: SAGE Publications.

Roberts, Anthea. 2011. "Comparative International Law? The Role of National Courts in Creating and Enforcing International Law". *The International and Comparative Law Quarterly* 60 (1): 57–92.

Romano, Cesare, Karen J. Alter, and Yuval Shany. 2014a. "Mapping International Adjudicative bodies, The Issues and Players". In *The Oxford Handbook of International Adjudication*, edited by Cesare Romano, Karen J. Alter and Yuval Shany, 3–26. Oxford: Oxford University Press.

Romano, Cesare, Karen J. Alter, and Yuval Shany, eds. 2014b. *The Oxford Handbook of International Adjudication.* Oxford: Oxford University Press.

Romano, Cesare P.R. 2006. "The Shift from the Consensual to the Compulsory Paradigm in International Adjudication: Elements for a Theory of Consent". *International Law and Politics* 39 (2006): 791–872.

Rosenberg, Gerald N. 2008. *The Hollow Hope: Can Courts Bring about Social Change?* 2nd edition. Chicago, IL: University of Chicago Press.

Sandholtz, Wayne, Yining Bei, and Kayla Caldwell. 2018. "Backlash and International Human Rights Courts". In *Contracting Human Rights: Crisis, accountability, and Opportunity*, edited by Alison Brysk and Michael Stohl, 159–78. Cheltenham: Edward Elgar.

Schreuer, Christoph H. 1974. "The Authority of International Judicial Practice in Domestic Courts". *The International and Comparative Law Quarterly* 23 (4): 681–708.

Schreuer, Christoph H. 1975. "The Implementation of International Judicial Decisions by Domestic Courts". *The International and Comparative Law Quarterly* 24 (2): 153–83.

Shany, Yuval. 2009. "National Courts as International Actors: Jurisdictional Implications". *Federalismi*, no. 15. Accessed 12 July 2019. www.federalismi.it/ApplOpenFilePDF.cfm?artid=13810&dpath=document&dfile=29072009111203.pdf&content=National+courts+as+international+actors:+jurisdictional+implications+-+dottrina+-+dottrina+-+.

Shany, Yuval. 2012. "Assessing the Effectiveness of International Courts: A Goal-Based Approach". *The American Journal of International Law* 106 (2): 225–70.

Shapiro, Martin M. 1986. *Courts: A Comparative and Political Analysis.* Chicago, IL: University of Chicago Press.

Simmons, Beth A. 2009. *Mobilizing for Human Rights: International Law in Domestic Politics.* Cambridge and New York: Cambridge University Press.

Slaughter, Anne-Marie. 2003. "A Global Community of Courts". *Harvard International Law Journal* 44 (1): 191–219.

Slaughter, Anne-Marie, and William Burke-White. 2006. "The Future of International Law Is Domestic (Or, The European Way of Law)". *Harvard International Law Journal* 47 (2): 327–52.

Smekal, Hubert, and ŠipulováKatarína. 2014. "DH V Czech Republic Six Years Later: On the Power of an International Human Rights Court to Push through Systemic Change". *Netherlands Quarterly of Human Rights* 32 (3): 288–321.

Soley, Ximena, and Silvia Steininger. 2018. "Parting Ways or Lashing Back? withdrawals, Backlash and the Inter-American Court of Human Rights". *International Journal of Law in Context* 14 (02): 237–57.

Spano, Robert. 2015. "The European Court of Human Rights and National Courts: A Constructive Conversation or A Dialogue of Disrespect?" *Nordic Journal of Human Rights* 33 (1): 1–10.

Squatrito, Theresa. 2018. "Measurement and Methods: Opportunities for Future Research". In *The Performance of International Courts and Tribunals*, edited by Theresa Squatrito, Oran R. Young, Andreas Follesdal, and Geir Ulfstein, 373–405. Cambridge: Cambridge University Press.

Squatrito, Theresa, Oran R. Young, Andreas Follesdal, and Geir Ulfstein, eds. 2018. *The Performance of International Courts and Tribunals.* Cambridge: Cambridge University Press.

Staton, Jeffrey K., and Will H. Moore. 2011. "Judicial Power in Domestic and International Politics". *International Organization* 65 (03): 553–87.

Stone Sweet, Alec, and Thomas L. Brunell. 2013. "Trustee Courts and the Judicialization of International Regimes: The Politics of Majoritarian Activism in the European Convention on Human Rights, The European union, and The World Trade Organization". *Journal of Law and Courts* 1 (1): 61–88.

Sumption, Jonathan. 2019. "Human Rights and Wrongs". Reith Lectures, BBC Radio 4. Accessed 4 September 2019. http://downloads.bbc.co.uk/radio4/reith2019/Reith_2019_Sumption_lecture_3.pdf.

Terris, Daniel, Cesare Romano, and Leigh Swigart. 2007. *The International Judge: An Introduction to the Men and Women Who Decide the World's Cases.* Oxford and New York: Oxford University Press.

Tomuschat, Christian. 2010. "The Effects of the Judgments of the European Court of Human Rights according to the German Constitutional Court". *German Law Journal* 11 (5): 513–26.

Trachtman, Joel P. 2010. "International Law and Domestic Political Coalitions: The Grand Theory of Compliance with International Law". *Chicago Journal of International Law* 11 (1): 127–58.

Tzanakopoulos, Antonios. 2011. "Domestic Courts in International Law: The International Judicial Function of National Courts". *Loyola of Los Angeles International and Comparative Law Review* 34: 133–68.

Tzanakopoulos, Antonios, and Christian J. Tams. 2013. "Introduction: Domestic Courts as Agents of Development of International Law". *Leiden Journal of International Law* 26 (03): 531–40.

Vallinder, Torbjörn. 1995. "When the Courts Go Marching". In *The Global Expansion of Judicial Power*, edited by Chester Neal Tate and Torbjörn Vallinder, 13–26. New York: New York University Press.

Vanberg, Georg. 2010. "Establishing and Maintaining Judicial Independence" In *The Oxford Handbook of Law and Politics*, edited by Keith E. Whittington, R. Daniel Kelemen and Gregory A. Caldeira, 99–118. Oxford: Oxford University Press.

von Bogdandy, Armin, and Ingo Venzke. 2013. "On the Functions of International Courts: An Appraisal in Light of Their Burgeoning Public Authority". *Leiden Journal of International Law* 26 (1): 49–72.

von Stein, Jana. 2013. "The Engines of Compliance". In *Interdisciplinary Perspectives on International Law and International Relations: The State of the Art*, edited by Jeffrey L. Dunoff and Mark A. Pollack, 477–501. Cambridge: Cambridge University Press.

Waltz, Kenneth N. 2001. *Man, The state, and War: A Theoretical Analysis.* New York: Columbia University Press.

Wind, Marlene. 2016. "Do Scandinavians Care about International Law? A Study of Scandinavian Judges' Citation Practice to International Law and Courts". *Nordic Journal of International Law* 85 (4): 281–302.

Ziemele, Ineta. 2016. "Conclusions". In *The Impact of the ECHR on Democratic Change in Central and Eastern Europe: Judicial Perspectives*, edited by Iulia Motoc and Ineta Ziemele, 491–502. Cambridge: Cambridge University Press.

Part II

Judicial treatment of Strasbourg case law

A case study on Czechia

4 Research design

How to study judicial implementation: A prologue to the case study on Czechia

Case law analysis lies at the heart of legal scholarship (Posner 1993). Every day, both scholars and practitioners engage with legal language in decisions of courts and other public bodies which abounds with peculiar, sometimes quite technical phrases. Yet, until very recently, our comprehension of courts' case law built only on a rather low number of the most important rulings. The massive stock of data (i.e., court rulings) was almost impossible to analyze both due to their unavailability and exceptionally high demands on time and financial costs. Legal research still relies on traditional methods of analysis and views new trends with suspicion.[1] The failure to spread new techniques, especially automated text analysis, in the legal research reflected on considerable gaps existing in the otherwise voluminous research on interaction between domestic and international courts.

While it is widely acknowledged that international courts' case law is reflected by domestic courts, we do not know how exactly and in what proportion. Legal papers have typically built on a rather low number of the most important rulings and overlooked the big picture of the ordinary but most frequent rulings. We therefore do not know much about how and how often the domestic courts use international case law in daily practice.

The European Court of Human Rights (ECtHR or Strasbourg Court) is no exception as it still depends to a large extent on the cooperation of domestic courts, which are vital for the execution of its rulings. Several noteworthy questions were raised by standing research. Are domestic courts functioning as allies of the ECtHR?[2] How do they treat Strasbourg Court case law? Do domestic courts engage in judicial dialogue with Strasbourg? If so, in what form? Why, or in what instances, do courts refer to ECtHR? How did the reference patterns evolve in time? However straightforward these questions may read, we still lack clear answers.

Recent enormous developments in technology significantly improved accessibility to the data, the process of data collection, coding, and analysis (King 2011). The automated reference recognition has remarkably developed in legal informatics. It promises to reduce costs of reading enormous collections of rulings and explore the so-far largely unknown territory of courts' decision-making. Yet, the systematic tracing of references has only slowly started making its way to the study of interactions between national and international levels; it typically remains confined inside boundaries of one legal system, national or international (Liu et al. 2014; Kríž et al. 2014; Wind 2016; Harašta and Šavelka 2017), and unlike our project does not try to connect the two levels. Moreover, the use of the automated reference recognition has not massively spread further to the general legal research (Epstein, Friedman, and Stone 2015).

We utilize these developments to enrich traditional legal research methods and examine in our project the core research question: how domestic courts treat the ECtHR's case law. However, we also argue that due to the complexity and uniqueness of the legal language, the automated methods need careful validation because many false positives and negatives can occur. We therefore employ a three-level framework, which utilizes both manual and automated methods of data collection and coding, and quantitative and qualitative methods of analysis. While we use automated analysis to decode domestic rulings encompassing references to Strasbourg case law, we complement this by a hand-coding of the role the references play in the text of the ruling, whether the courts actively engage with the ECtHR's case law or merely acknowledge its existence, using it only as a supporting, ornamental argument. We are further interested in whether references amount to following the Strasbourg case law, distinguishing from it, or whether domestic courts sometimes openly reject Strasbourg rulings.[3] Thus, while our work relies not only on classical legal analysis of the most important rulings but also builds on automated text analysis, which allows us to see the frontage of the judicial treatment of Strasbourg case law, we complement the macro-level automated data analysis with a hand-coding of how in fact domestic courts treat the case law. It could be said that the meso level uncovers the interior of the judicial treatment while the micro level, an in-depth analysis of judicial treatment in particular areas (micro level) adds important knowledge on the overall atmosphere in the "judicial treatment house". We find this rich mix of methods of data collection, coding, and analysis to be the most promising way of acquiring knowledge about the phenomenon under study.[4]

Accordingly, this chapter is a prequel to the case study of the implementation of Strasbourg rulings by the Czech apex courts. However, it also aspires to introduce a framework for any systemic research on the use of the international case law by domestic courts. The chapter first defines the scope of the case study (judicial treatment of the ECtHR's case law) and the research design (Section 4.1). Then, we present fundamentals of our three-level framework which advances the research on how often and how domestic courts treat and implement the ECtHR's case law (4.2). Section 4.3 presents in detail the methodology of the project, specifically the data collection and coding with a contribution of automated methods. Finally, Section 4.4 points to the challenges and potential problems when conducting research based on our three-level framework.

4.1 Research scope: A three-level approach to the study of judicial treatment of the ECtHR's case law

We have already noted above that the growing importance of courts, including the international courts, is widely acknowledged. Both domestic and international courts can benefit from their co-existence. Domestic courts may use citations of the international case law to support their own reasoning while reminding executive and legislative branches that they themselves agreed to and ratified the international treaty establishing the international court. Vice versa, international courts to a large extent depend on the cooperation of domestic courts, especially those standing on the top of the judicial hierarchy. Apex courts unify domestic jurisprudence and may help with domestication of the international case law through frequently referring to it.

This book focuses on the use of the ECtHR's case law by Czech apex courts – the Constitutional Court (CC), the Supreme Court (SC), and the Supreme Administrative Court (SAC). We assume that when courts use the existing case law,[5] then they cite it, and references to the Strasbourg Court case law indicate that domestic judges feel the urge to engage with the ECtHR's rulings. A reference does not automatically mean judicial compliance (in the sense of conformity, see below); for example, in cases when domestic judges explicitly oppose the ECtHR's ruling. But even such a reference provides an important hint that domestic judges take the Strasbourg case law seriously, because they consider it important to expressly acknowledge their opposition against the direction of ECtHR case law.

When domestic courts approvingly refer to ECtHR case law, then they contribute to compliance with it. As we explained in Chapter 3, compliance is usually understood as a state of conformity of practice or policy with legal norms (Kingsbury 1998).[6] It has been widely argued that domestic courts belong to the most important compliance partners of international courts (Roberts 2011; Nollkaemper 2012; Gerards and Fleuren 2014). Frequent references to the international case law indicate its domestication by national judges and subsequently higher compliance. Thus, references by domestic courts help in building legitimacy of international courts and their case law (Wind 2016).

Drawing on our analysis in Chapters 2 and 3, we argue that in order to understand the role of domestic courts in fostering the overall compliance with ECtHR case law, we must move *beyond* the usual narrow understanding of compliance. We introduce a concept of "judicial treatment", and implement it with a use of a mix of quantitative and qualitative methods such as descriptive statistics (frequencies and crosstabs) and traditional legal analysis (rich description of rulings in context).

In contrast to the narrow concept of judicial compliance, a judicial treatment builds on a much broader understanding and points at comprehensive domestic application of all principles delivered by the ECtHR. As stressed in Chapters 1, 2, and 8, the cooperation of domestic courts is indispensable for the Strasbourg Court. The European Convention on Human Rights (ECHR or Convention) comes to life via its domestic application. The broader comprehension helps us get a little bit closer to understanding of this interaction.

We believe that the broad concept of judicial treatment is better for systemic research of ECtHR case law's impact on the domestic judicial practice because it oversteps the limitation of compliance focusing solely on adverse rulings against the home country. Broad understanding enables us to include all mutual interactions in the case law of both the domestic and international level and thus more comprehensively examine domestic judicial treatment of the Strasbourg Court case law.

The broad understanding of judicial treatment should also allow us to answer our core research question "How do domestic courts use the ECtHR's case law?" and the following subquestions:

1. Do domestic courts engage with the ECtHR, and why?
2. In what instances do domestic courts refer to the ECtHR?
3. How did the patterns of how domestic courts treat ECtHR case law evolve in time, under the influence of various historical, legal, and social factors?
4. Are domestic apex courts functioning as allies for the ECtHR?

In order to understand the domestic judicial treatment of Strasbourg case law, we must first identify the set of domestic rulings which use it. Then, we can focus on the extent of the use of the Strasbourg case law – i.e., the frequency of references to international rulings in domestic judgments and decisions and its development over time. This basic descriptive statistical exercise is important for a rough mapping of the terrain, but it does not tell us much about how the ECtHR's rulings are used by domestic judges. Specifically, we are interested in significance of the Strasbourg case law (i.e., is it important for deciding domestic rulings?), to what extent domestic judges follow their Strasbourg colleagues, how extensively they consider ECtHR case law, and how carefully they refer to it. We employ a dynamic perspective, which means that we are interested in developments in all these categories over time. We are looking both for overarching patterns and the most salient cases, examining the influence of various historical (emergence of new top court), political (transition, entry into the European Union), and social factors (personal changes at apex courts). In order to capture all these developments, we implement a three-level approach.

First, the macro-level analysis encompasses all references that domestic apex courts have ever made to the ECtHR's case law. The macro level asks how much courts refer over time to the ECtHR's case law. We provide the answer through measuring development in yearly frequencies of domestic apex courts' references to the ECtHR's case law. In other words, we record the number of references (as well as number of rulings with references) and compare it against the population of all rulings of respective apex courts in order to have a rough idea of how much the ECtHR's ruling is used and how the frequency develops in time.

The automated text analysis allows us to instruct computer programs on how to detect the use of certain words and phrases in texts. It replaces human hand-coding, but still needs some human involvement. While computers can learn clustering either being supervised by humans or not, the validation of the results requires precise and often time-consuming human involvement (Grimmer and Stewart 2013). As Grimmer and Stewart (2013, 270) point out, all automated methods, due to the complexity of the language, and particularly so of legal reasoning, are based on incorrect models of language. The following sections therefore introduce our model and validation process in detail (see more in Section 4.3)

Second, after the quantitative macro-level analysis of all domestic apex courts' rulings referring to ECtHR case law, only a stratified sample of a few hundred rulings which work with a reference to ECtHR case law in the reasoning is more closely examined. This meso-level analysis is crucial to understand the typical mode of use of the ECtHR's case law and its significance. How do domestic courts treat the ECtHR's case law? Do the domestic courts follow the ECtHR's case law? Do they engage with it? Or do they just acknowledge it? Do they follow Strasbourg case law, or do they frequently resort to distinguishing, or even refusal? Is the ECtHR's case law important for the outcome of the case, or is it a mere ornament and the case would have been decided in the same way even in the absence of the reference to the ECtHR's case law? Our meso-level analysis relies on close reading by humans as coding requires expert understanding of judicial interpretation (see Table 4.1 and Section 4.3.2).

Finally, qualitative micro-level analysis discusses a few carefully selected important rulings and jurisprudential areas. Based on the knowledge gained from the macro- and meso-level analyses, as well as on insider knowledge of the system, we identify both typical and atypical features of referencing to the ECtHR's case law, and evaluate more far-reaching consequences of the ECtHR's case law in domestic judicial practice (see Table 4.1 and Section 4.3.3). The micro-level analysis focuses on the most significant jurisprudential areas from the viewpoint of the ECtHR's influence. Focusing on these areas promises to uncover the details of different ways domestic courts treat the ECtHR's case law, especially in cases where the treatment goes beyond merely supportive use. In other words, these areas offer the greatest chance to explore what we call "engagement" with the Strasbourg case law; i.e., not only its acknowledgment by the means of a reference, but also its substantive use with further repercussions for domestic law. This allows us to complement quantitative and qualitative methods with doctrinal analysis and provide a holistic picture of the life of ECtHR case law before the Czech courts.

4.2 Data collection and coding

As noted above, the cooperation of domestic courts is indispensable for international judicial bodies. International human rights norms come to life by their domestic application. In order to understand the domestic judicial

Table 4.1 Three-level approach to judicial treatment: How do domestic courts treat Strasbourg Court case law?

Level	*Main question*	*Sampling*	*Coding*	*Analysis*
Macro	**How much do the apex courts refer to ECtHR case law?** What are the most cited ECtHR cases?	All rulings of Czech apex courts including references to ECtHR case law in reasoning	Automated with manual validation	Descriptive statistics (frequencies and crosstabs)
Meso	**How do the apex courts use ECtHR case law?** What is its significance for deciding domestic cases? Do domestic judges follow ECtHR case law? How detailed is the engagement of domestic judges with ECtHR case law? How carefully do domestic judges cite ECtHR case law? How does the ECtHR case law affect domestic judicial reasoning?	Stratified sampling based on the macro-level sample	Hand-coding based on the detailed codebook	Descriptive statistics (frequencies and crosstabs)
Micro	**What are the hidden consequences of the use of the ECtHR case law for domestic legal practice?**	Purposive sampling		Contextually rich legal case studies
	Significant importance of ECtHR case law for selected fields (e.g., discrimination)			Includes normative assessment of the citation (obsolete citation, "fig leaf" citation, etc.)
	Adoption of techniques used by the ECtHR by domestic courts (e.g., proportionality test)			Zeroes in on strategic citations (gate-keeping, etc.)

Source: authors.

treatment of the Strasbourg case law, we must first identify the set of domestic rulings which use it. Then, we can focus on the extent of the use of the ECtHR case law – i.e., the frequency of references to ECtHR rulings in domestic judgments and decisions and its development over time.

Most of the existing studies treat references as relevant arguments and reasoning sources. Such a pre-understanding fails to capture the real practice of domestic courts. A large chunk of references appears in other parts of rulings than reasoning (in the narrative part, the part summarizing the facts of the case and arguments raised by parties to proceedings, or in dissents). These references do not have the capacity to influence the core dispute underlying the case. When examining judicial implementation, it is vital to filter out those references which do not appear in substantive reasoning. However, even filtering the references and narrowing the set of analyzed rulings to those where the reference to the ECtHR was made in the domestic court's reasoning does not tell us much about the impact of the ECtHR's case law on the result of the case.

To tackle this problem, we developed a funnel-like filtering mechanism (Figure 4.1), which (1) cleaned our dataset of references which have not appeared in the court's substantive reasoning, and (2) further categorized references due to their impact on the result of the case.

In order to capture these different levels and understandings of judicial treatment, we divided our research into three levels: (1) the macro level that focuses on general patterns present in domestic case law; (2) the meso level, which digs deeper and inquires on the impact of references on the substance of domestic disputes; and finally, (3) the micro-level analysis that provides an in-depth qualitative analysis of individual rulings. The following section not only serves as an overview of problems related to automated coding, but also offers a guidebook for future research.

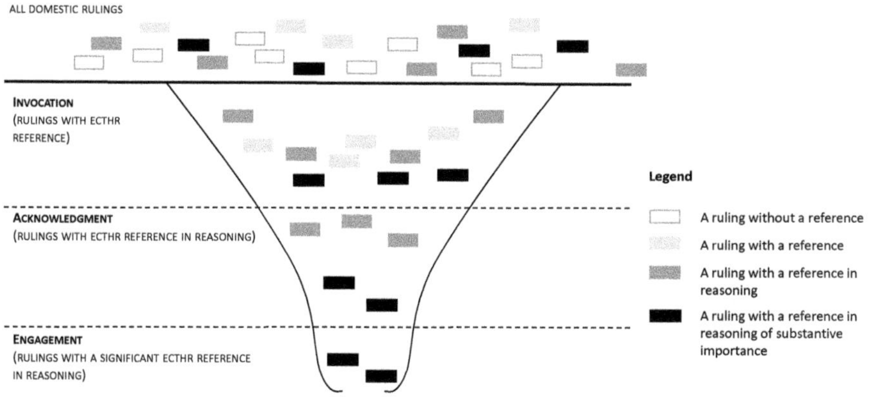

Figure 4.1 Visualization of filtering/reduction of the unit of analysis.
Source: authors.

4.3 In search of the data

One of the reasons why there is no comprehensive research on the use of references to ECtHR case law by domestic courts dwells, undoubtedly, in the accessibility of the data. In many jurisdictions, the access to case law of lower courts is virtually non-existent; some courts do not have online databases, and if they do, they usually do not cover older rulings. Although these courts do have their own archives, obtaining actual case files and their processing is highly costly. In most European countries, the situation is a little less troublesome when it comes to apex courts (as is also the case of Czechia). Yet, some difficulties remain.

As previously mentioned, our research project builds on an assumption of apex courts functioning as allies, promoting the domestic implementation and compliance with the ECtHR's case law. A proxy for measuring this implementation is a reference to the ECtHR's case law; i.e., citation of respective rulings delivered by the ECtHR (for more on the composition of the reference see below). First, we therefore had to collect the whole datasets of rulings delivered by top three Czech apex courts, the CC, the SC, and the SAC). All three databases are publicly accessible. Nevertheless, not all of these databases allow a user-friendly download of metadata. We also realized that some courts do not publish some of the rulings online.[7] We had to implement data scraping for some metadata in case of the CC and the SAC (in order to get information on the subject area, date, file numbers, judge rapporteur, etc.). The CC's dataset lacked file numbers of rulings in their identification, so we had to proceed with automatically obtaining the file numbers from the text of the rulings. Lastly, all obtained documents have been converted to a plain-text format, which allows for a smoother custom processing in the R program. We used a simple BVA (BioVisionAlexandria) program for the conversion. In further pre-processing of the files we removed punctuation and unnecessary white space, and we converted the character encoding to UTF-8, all using the R package *tau*.

For the CC, our dataset encompasses 60,403 rulings delivered between 1 January 1993 and 31 December 2015. For the SC we collected 84,374 rulings delivered between 1 January 1993 and 31 December 2015. The case law of the SAC covers a shorter period, from 1 January 2003 to 31 December 2015, as the court was established only in 2003. This dataset covers 39,477 rulings in total.

After obtaining the domestic datasets, we devoted similar attention to the ECtHR's case law. We scraped the online HUDOC database[8] for all decisions and judgments delivered by the Strasbourg Court and its predecessor (European Commission for Human Rights), together with metadata identifying the title of the rulings (name of the party to the proceedings), date of issuing, ECHR body which issued the ruling, subject area, result of the case (violation/non-violation), respective Convention rights, and adverse country. We scraped these data using the R package *jsonlite*. This phase resulted in the creation of a list of the ECtHR's rulings which could have potentially appeared as a reference in domestic apex courts' rulings. Only after the cleaning of the dataset could we proceed with tracing these references on a macro level.

4.3.1 Macro-level analysis: Gotta catch them all

As previously mentioned, the macro level of our analysis aims to uncover very broad patterns in which domestic apex courts refer to the ECtHR's case law. The macro-level analysis therefore concentrates on the overall development of domestic judicial treatment of the ECtHR's case law: how much, which domestic courts, and to which ECtHR rulings they refer. Embeddedness of the macro-level analysis in time also allows us to examine broad correlations with political and historical changes.

One of the crucial issues was therefore to establish the population for our research. As it is virtually impossible to identify the cases of non-application (i.e., a ruling where a domestic court should have or could have referred to the ECtHR case law,[9] but did not do so), we eliminated all cases where the courts did not refer to the ECtHR case law, and focused only on rulings with a reference to the ECtHR case law.

The core puzzle of the macro-level part of the research was how to tease out the information on the presence of a reference in the text of the ruling automatically. Similarly to the ECtHR, the Czech apex courts also face the crisis of an overflowing number of petitions. Since 1993,[10] the top three courts combined issued 180,000-plus rulings. It would be impossible to code such an amount of case law manually. Therefore, we decided to use an automated text analysis consisting of a three-step process. First, we defined "a reference to ECtHR case law" and identified its components (see below). Second, we wrote an R program searching for these components in the rulings using *grep* functions from the *base* package. Third, for the rulings with at least one reference found, we ran a separate R program splitting the text into logical sections in order to be able to determine in which part of the domestic ruling the reference was raised. Each one of these steps was manually validated.

As illustrated in Figure 4.2, our first step was to identify constituents of a reference to the ECtHR's case law; i.e., indicators that particular set of words represent a reference. For this purpose, we constructed an R algorithm based on several gazetteers.

Having data scraped the HUDOC database, we derived a list of all the ECtHR's ruling file numbers and consequently had an R program search for the presence of these file numbers in domestic rulings using the pattern-matching function in the R *base* package. If we found the respective file number, the program extracted a small paragraph of text surrounding the reference, which allowed us to validate the results. This first stage left us with many false positives. Typically, shorter ECtHR rulings' file numbers coincided with file numbers of rulings issued by domestic courts, particularly so in the case of the CC. Eventually, we eliminated all false positives with further amendments of the algorithm after several rounds of

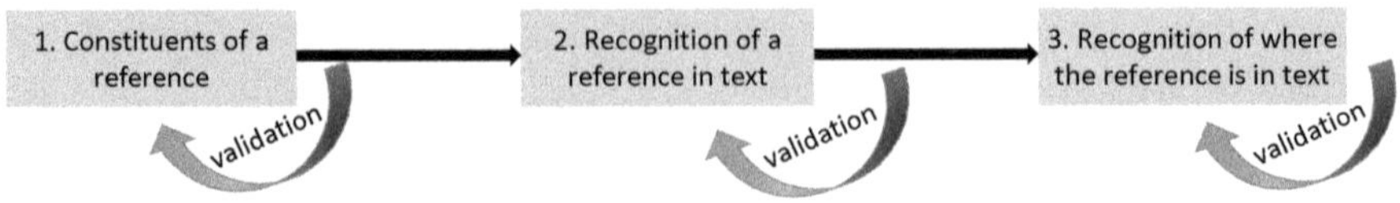

Figure 4.2 Process of automated recognition of references.
Source: authors.

manual validation. During this first phase, we also validated eventual false negatives (on a random sample of 200 rulings), checking whether rulings where the algorithm did not report any reference indeed did not encompass one.

Nevertheless, using the ECtHR's file number is only one way in which domestic courts refer to its case law and, both from our first validation and from practical experience, we knew that Czech apex courts are not particularly consistent in using the file numbers. We therefore amended the constituents of a reference as encompassing either the file number or a name of the party to the proceedings (Table 4.2). A word of caution should be raised here, however. Some ECtHR rulings are better known by popular titles rather than names of the parties to the proceedings (e.g., *Skoullos family*)[11] and some names are translated differently into Czech (e.g., *Handölsdalen Sami Village*,[12] in Czech referred to as "*Sámská vesnice Handölsdalen*"). We therefore derived a list of popular titles and Czech translations of all ECtHR rulings and added it to the respective titles in our algorithm. Yet, given the particularly high number and length of the text of rulings we had to proceed, adding the extensive list of names and popular titles into our algorithm for all domestic rulings would lead to extremely lengthy and time-consuming processing. Therefore, we opted to start with a presumption that every time a domestic court refers to a particular ECtHR ruling, it also mentions the ECtHR itself. In other words, we first searched for all references to the "ECtHR" and its Czech variations (Table 4.2) and then for the ruling titles and names in the vicinity of 1,000 characters surrounding the general reference to the ECtHR. Those results, which did not match with any file number or any name of the party/title of the ruling, were deleted as void general references.[13]

Table 4.2 Constituents of a reference

General reference to ECtHR	ESLP[1]
	Evrop* soud*[2]
Reference to a ruling	File number
	Name of the party to the proceedings

Source: authors.

1 ESLP is a Czech acronym for the ECtHR [*Evropský soud pro lidská práva*].
2 Evrop* soud* stands for the "European Court" in Czech (*Evropský soud*). The asterisks were used because of declinations in the Czech language.

During the process of validation, we had to amend our algorithm several times in order to capture various acronyms, typos, or incorrect terms. The most tedious part of the analysis was a validation of whether the found reference was not in fact a reference to the Court of Justice of the European Union (often referred to by Czech courts only as a "European Court") or if the file number did not match with some other domestic authority file number. Nevertheless, after the second phase, we managed to interactively assign the broad references to the ECtHR to individual respective ECtHR file numbers.

The final step of the macro-level dataset-building consisted of recognizing the part of the domestic ruling in which the reference appeared, in order to eliminate references outside of domestic courts' own reasoning. In order to do so, we had to identify phrases distinguishing the start of the court's own reasoning. This differed for every single apex court. As a result, based on the repeated manual validation of results, we created three separate list of "splitting terms" (i.e., terms which distinguished reasoning from other parts of rulings) for each individual court. The trickiest validation proved to be for the CC, which sometimes starts the ruling with a "headnote" (the core argument from the reasoning), then proceeds with facts and claims of the parties, then lengthy reasoning, and, finally, dissenting opinions of judges. Only references appearing in the headnote and reasoning constitute a reference in terms of judicial treatment in our understanding. Nevertheless, we had to incorporate several splitting words to break CC's rulings into more parts. The validation was manual, and we repeatedly checked the results in samples, adding new rules and amending rules which proved faulty in false-positives checks, until we managed to successfully divide all rulings without more than a handful of mistakes.

After this last stage, we validated the results via a third person who checked the presence of found references, the list of most common references (compared to the ECtHR's rulings known as important from legal practice), the rulings without a reference, etc., searching for potential false positives.

The macro-level analysis also allowed us to prepare samples for the meso level of analysis, which focuses on a more nuanced analysis of *how* domestic courts use the references in their reasoning (Table 4.3).

Table 4.3 Populations for our macro- and meso-level analyses

Population	*SAC*	*SC*	*CC*
All rulings 1993[1]–2015	***39,477***	***84,374***	***60,403***
MACRO level			
Rulings	1,913	1,309	4,184
References	5,894	7,122	11,977
MESO level			
Rulings	1,594	1,080	3,908
References	4,344	4,161	10,399

Source: authors.

1 2003–2015 for the SAC, which was established only in 2003.

4.3.2 Meso-level analysis: Gotta catch the representative sample

For the purposes of the meso-level analysis, we went one step further and instead of a mere occurrence of references examined *the mode of their use*. The meso level therefore concentrates on questions of *how* domestic courts use references to the ECtHR and whether the count of references actually translates to implementation. As previously mentioned, in the last step of the macro-level analysis, we reduced the original population of references by eliminating references in the narrative parts or dissenting opinions of domestic rulings. From the remaining rulings, we selected samples of few hundred rulings for each Czech apex court, in which we, with the help of a team of coders, manually coded the *form* and the *quality* of the reference, and *its impact* on the dispute at the heart of the case.

This means that apart from looking at the formal characteristics of references (Does the reference contain a direct quote? Does the reference refer to a particular paragraph of the ECtHR's ruling? Did the court use the full file number, a name of the party, etc.? Was the reference accompanied by a literature review?), we reviewed also *how* and *why* the apex court referred to the ECtHR's case law. We asked whether domestic courts used references only to support the reasoning based in domestic provisions, or to substantively change existing domestic practice; and whether the apex courts' use of the reference conforms to the ECtHR's reasoning or, on the contrary, whether domestic courts refer to the ECtHR's ruling only to refuse its implementation. Accordingly, the meso-level analysis proceeded based on a detailed and elaborated codebook (Table 4.4).

If we were to return to the reduction funnel (Figure 4.1), the aim of the meso-level analysis was to get to the narrowest part of the funnel and learn which references do indeed have a substantive impact on domestic rulings. The clipping from the codebook (Table 4.4) therefore captures the most important categories coded manually for every ruling in the meso-level sample:

A. How is the ECtHR's ruling followed in a domestic judgment or decision: i.e., whether the apex court followed (and confirmed) the ECtHR's finding, distinguished that the case at hand and the raised legal question is different from the ECtHR's ruling (therefore, the ECtHR's ruling cannot be applied), or directly refused to implement the ECtHR's ruling on the domestic case at hand.
B. The influence of the ECtHR's ruling on a domestic judgment or decision: i.e., whether the apex courts use references as a mere ornament (supporting influence of a reference), or substantively change the result of the case.
C. The technique of the use of the reference: Here, only in case the reference is of substantive relevance, we presume that apex courts can use it either to invalidate a domestic legal norm (this holds for a constitutional court, while using the narrative of the strength and primacy of international obligations), assign the ECtHR's ruling primacy without invalidating any legal norm,

Table 4.4 Meso-level reference coding – clipping from the codebook

How the domestic court follows the ECtHR ruling	1 Following	2 Distinguishing	3 Refusing		
Influence of the ECtHR ruling on domestic decision	1 Supportive	2 Substantive			
How the ECtHR ruling is used	1 Invalidation of a domestic legal norm	2 Direct application	3 Conforming interpret-ation of the domestic legal norm	4 Filling the gap in domestic law	5 Confirmation ("Blessing") of domestic law
Level of the detail of the reference	1 Generic reference	2 Reference to a specific ECtHR ruling	3 Reference to a specific part of the IHRB ruling		

Source: authors.

interpret the domestic legal provisions in conformity to the referred ruling, use the reference to the ECtHR ruling to fill in the gaps in domestic legislation, or to confirm ("bless") the content of the domestic law.

The full codebook is attached in the Appendix.

However, we should raise a few caveats regarding the sampling method implemented in our meso level of analysis. We already noted that in order to code the references manually, we used stratified samples capturing various importance of rulings inside apex courts' case law. The consideration underlining this decision reflected the over-representation of procedural, unpublished decisions in the case law of apex courts which have lower probability of encompassing a reference substantively influencing the result of the case. Each sample therefore captures certain percentages of published and unpublished decisions and judgments, corresponding to the composition of these categories in respective years (Figure 4.3).

4.3.3 Micro-level analysis: Gotta catch the important ones

In the micro-level analysis, we use the in-depth qualitative analysis to address some of the issues uncovered in the previous section. We concentrate on

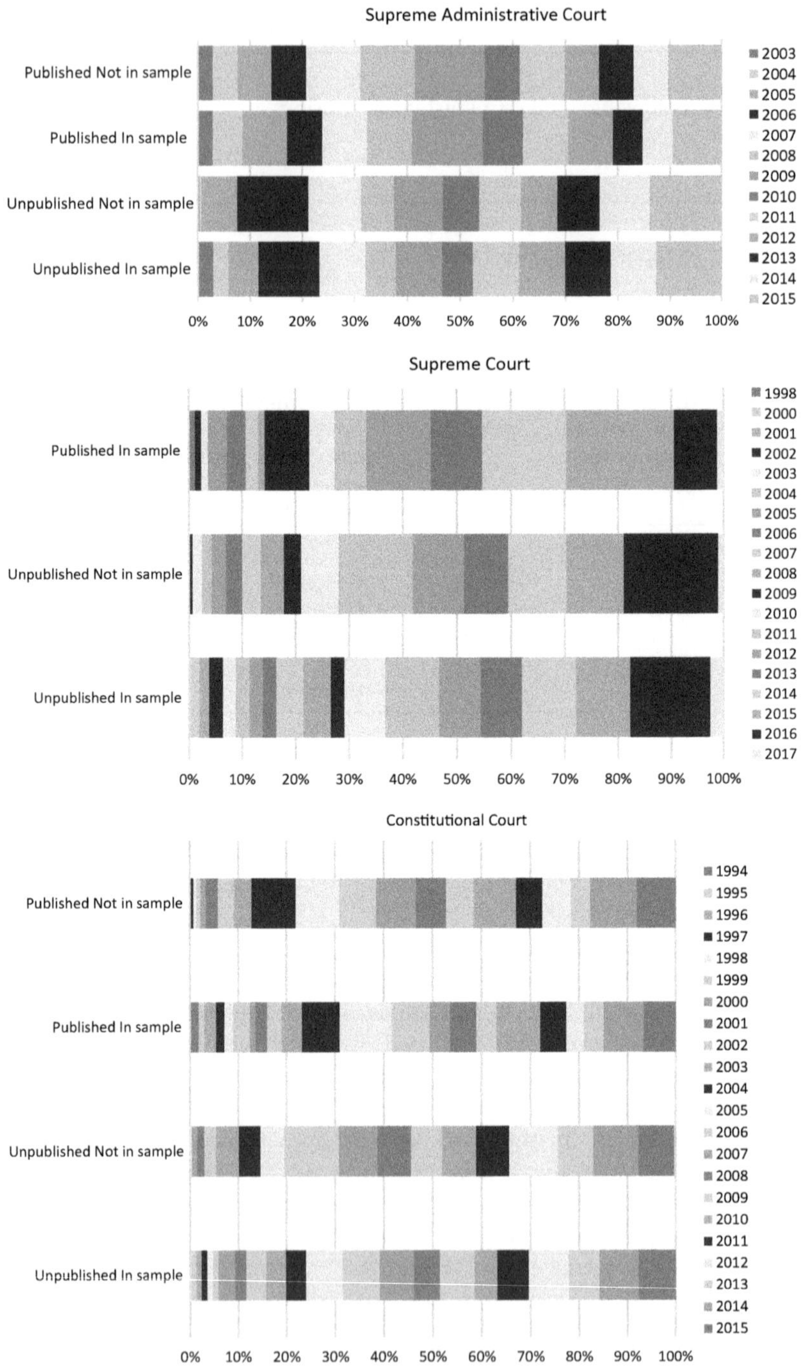

Figure 4.3 Clipping from the stratification of samples.
Source: authors.

selected Convention rights, where the judicial treatment of ECtHR case law significantly changed the existing domestic legal practice. Close examination of individual rulings should enhance our knowledge of the system, especially in the rulings which are exceptional in some sense. We explore both rulings where domestic apex courts pushed through systemic changes by following the Strasbourg ruling, as well as rulings where they directly distinguished or refused to implement the rulings. We search for reasons the domestic courts refused to abide with the ECtHR's findings. It is important to add that we work with explicit wordings of the courts. In other words, we examine what domestic courts say they are doing with the case law, not compare it with what they actually do with the case law.

The selection of analyzed jurisprudential areas was guided by secondary literature and insider knowledge of the Czech judicial system. Contrasts in the implementation of Article 5(5) ECHR by the SC and the CC stirred rich academic discussion on the limits of ECHR interpretation (Kosař and Petrov 2018; Kühn 2018). Controversies and challenges stemming from the unstable Strasbourg jurisprudence on the *ne bis in idem* principle and Article 4 of the Protocol No. 7 are reflected also by foreign academia (Trechsel 2005; van Bockel 2010; Gerards and Glas 2017). In case of the SAC, there is a broad consensus about the role of Article 6 ECHR's impact on administrative law, and about the significance of Article 11 ECHR for the domestic law of assembly and association (Molek 2014; Pospíšil and Týč 2016). Similarly, freedom of expression and Article 10 are recognized for the far-reaching impact on the CC's proportionality test (Molek and Jäger 2007; Pospíšil and Týč 2016).

4.4 Research challenges and potential inaccuracies

There are several caveats which need to be raised in relation to research of this complexity. We identified four possibly problematic factors, challenging the research aim and the results: (1) reduction of the research scope on the apex courts, (2) a reference to the ECtHR case law as a relevant indicator of judicial implementation, (3) the problem of silent (indirect) references, and (4) identification of cases of non-compliance or non-application.

First, in our case study, we decided to analyze the case law of apex courts, disregarding the lower courts. Lower courts play a similarly important part in bringing the ECtHR's case law into practice. Nevertheless, the top courts are typically seen as key actors and main players in judicial treatment, as they are generally better equipped to keep track of foreign legal sources and, with their reach to lower echelons of the judiciary, be a respective partner for the ECtHR. Especially so in the Czech context where the CC oversees protection of human rights and other two apex courts are responsible for unifying the case law of domestic courts. Taking into consideration the overwhelming case load at lower instances, language disposition of lower courts' judges, lack of legal clerks, or limited resources, we expect the lower courts to mostly follow how apex courts interpret ECtHR judgments.

We therefore believe that the apex courts function as allies of the ECtHR. They transmit the respective information and good practices in two directions: towards lower domestic courts, and towards other state actors and bodies.

Furthermore, in Czechia, similarly to many other countries (Wind 2016), obtaining databases of lower courts' rulings is virtually impossible. Apart from the data being heavily protected, lower courts have rarely developed own online databases. Most typically, lower courts store only written files, which makes any sort of research highly difficult. That being said, it would undoubtedly be interesting for future research to probe into the lower courts' case law and their comprehension of the ECtHR's case law, particularly so due to different personal characteristics of judges sitting at the courts (education, profile, academic background), or material factors influencing the performance of courts (presence of analytical units, assistants to judges, etc.).

The three chosen apex courts cover the three distinct jurisdictions present in the Czech system: general (civil and criminal) jurisdiction, represented by the SC; administrative, represented by the SAC; and the constitutional jurisdiction, represented by the CC.[14]

Second, some readers might wonder whether references to the ECtHR's case law are indeed a relevant indicator for assessing the role of apex courts in judicial implementation of ECtHR case law (Fishman 2013). Two considerations are needed here:

1. As previously mentioned, the sole number of references hardly equals any measurement of their impact and the importance the courts assign to the ECtHR's case law. Being conscious of the fact that not all references are of equal importance, we tackled this issue through the incorporation of the qualitative content analysis on the meso and micro level, looking deeper into how exactly the courts use references, in what instances, their position in the reasoning, and their influence on the result of the case.
2. Some references remain unattributed. Courts might often comply with the ECtHR's opinions without explicitly referring to its case law, either consciously, when trying to avoid controversies potentially caused by adhering to an opinion of an international body in politically and socially salient rulings (Rytter and Wind 2011), or unconsciously, mostly when quoting and referring to a plethora of consistent domestic law. However, as we already explained, our research builds on courts acknowledging openly how they treat Strasbourg rulings, and we do not confront these claims.

Third, it often appears at apex courts that once the court delivers a very detailed, well-reasoned ruling referring to the ECtHR's case law and pioneering a new line of jurisprudence, future similar rulings refer only to this domestic pioneering ruling and omit the baseline ECtHR case law which originally inspired the domestic court. We are convinced, however, that the mere decision of a judge to include or disregard the reference to the ECtHR's case law has a certain symbolic meaning and value and repercussion for the ECtHR's legitimacy as perceived by domestic judges. The future research might, however, attempt to build on our results and address the "silent references" through the network analysis, looking at indirect references to these very important pioneer rulings transmitting the ECtHR's case law into the domestic jurisprudence for the very first time. In this book, we pose a research question about how domestic courts use the ECtHR's case law, which to a large extent justifies our reduction of explicit references. Furthermore, we are complementing the search of references to the ECtHR's case law with a range of keywords capturing any case law concerning the Strasbourg Court itself, and compare the results with the usage of the Convention provisions (see Chapters 5–7).

Lastly, we might argue that without including the cases of non-application and no-referred non-compliance – i.e., the rulings where the apex courts should have referred but did not, and where they did not comply with the ECtHR reasoning without referring to ECtHR case law – our analysis paints only an incomplete picture. Nevertheless, we built our research on a pre-understanding that only direct, explicit references are a valid indicator of the position of domestic courts towards the ECtHR's case law. The purpose of the reference in the ruling is to strengthen the persuasive authority of the court's reasoning. In order to add another layer of legitimacy for its claims and findings, judges refer to rulings of those domestic and international bodies which they consider legitimate and authoritative (Lupu and Voeten 2012, 438). References therefore hold a strategic place in judicial reasoning and judges enhance the prestige of other institutions by incorporating references to their case law (Helfer and Slaughter 1997).

In other words, reference to ECtHR matters as a proxy for relationships between domestic courts and the ECtHR, although the mere number of references does not tell us much about the quality of this relationship. The inclusion of a meso- and micro-level analysis addresses this caveat and attempts therefore to shed light on a more nuanced position of domestic courts towards the ECtHR's opinions indicated in its case law.

Notes

1 Dyevre (2015) speculates that this might be a result of legal technical jargon which is not as conducive for automated content analysis, and also raises greater concerns for the process of validation. For more on suitability of legal language for application of methods using algorithms, see Hildebrandt (2018).
2 That is, courts helping the ECtHR to transmit certain ideas (Kosař and Lixinski 2015; Kosař and Petrov 2017).
3 A detailed description of our mode of work and rules for hand-coding on the meso level can be find in the attached codebook.
4 Mixed methods are believed to offset the weaknesses of both quantitative and qualitative research (Creswell and Clark 2018, 12).
5 For more details, see Section 4.4.
6 However, understanding of the term "compliance" remains quite divided (Hillebrecht 2017).

7 Sometimes by omission, sometimes intentionally; e.g., purely technical decisions, some decisions on recognition of foreign decisions and judgments.
8 www.hudoc.echr.coe.int.
9 We use the general term "ECtHR case law" even if sometimes the courts refer only to the ECtHR (or Strasbourg Court) without any further specification. It is obvious that when referring, the case law of the ECtHR is being meant, not the ECtHR as such.
10 2003 for the Supreme Administrative Court.
11 ECtHR, *Skoullos family v. Turkey*, no. 55819/00, judgment of 1 June 2010.
12 ECtHR, *Handölsdalen Sami Village and Others v. Sweden*, no. 39013/04, judgment of 30 March 2010.
13 It is quite common practice with Czech courts to refer to international bodies in very general terms ("as follows also from the case law of the European Court"). Nevertheless, we did not consider such broad references as adding to the concept of judicial compliance as they did not, in fact, refer to a particular opinion or requirement of the ECtHR.
14 For more information on the Czech judiciary, see Bobek (2006).

References

Bobek, Michal. 2006. "An Introduction to the Czech Legal System and Legal Resources Online". *GlobaLex*, August 2006. Accessed 28 July 2019. www.nyulawglobal.org/globalex/Czech_Republic.html#_2.4._The_Judiciary.

Creswell, John W., and Vicki L. Plano Clark. 2018. *Designing and Conducting Mixed Methods Research*. 3rd edition. Thousand Oaks, CA: Sage.

Dyevre, Arthur. 2015. "The Promise and Pitfalls of Automated Text-Scaling Techniques for the Analysis of Judicial Opinions". *SSRN* 3 July 2015. https://papers.ssrn.com/sol3/papers.cfm?abstract_id=2626370.

Epstein, Lee, Friedman, Barry and Stone Geoffrey R. 2015. "Testing the Constitution". *New York University Law Review* 90 (4): 1001–40.

Fishman, Joshua B. 2013. "Reuniting 'is' and 'ought' in Empirical Legal Scholarship". *University of Pennsylvania Law Review* 162: 117–68.

Gerards, Janneke, and Joseph Fleuren, eds. 2014. *Implementation of the European Convention on Human Rights and of the Judgments of the ECtHR in National Case Law*. Cambridge: Intersentia.

Gerards, Janneke, and Lize R. Glas. 2017. "Access to Justice in the European Convention on Human Rights System". *Netherlands Quarterly of Human Rights* 35 (1): 11–30.

Grimmer, Justin, and Brandon M. Stewart. 2013. "Text as Data: The Promise and Pitfalls of Automatic Content Analysis Methods for Political Texts". *Political Analysis* 21 (3): 267–97.

Harašta, Jakub, and Jaromír Šavelka. 2017. "Toward Linking Heterogenous References in Czech Court Decisions to Content". In *Legal Knowledge and Information System*, edited by Adam Wyner and Giovanni Casini, 177–82. Amsterdam: IOS Press.

Helfer, Laurence R., and Anne-Marie Slaughter. 1997. "Toward a Theory of Effective Supranational Adjudication". *Yale Law Journal* 107 (2): 273–391.

Hildebrandt, Mireille. 2018. "Law as Computation in the Era of Artificial Legal Intelligence: Speaking Law to the Power of Statistics". *University of Toronto Law Journal* 68 (supplement 1): 12–35.

Hillebrecht, Courtney. 2017. "Compliance: Actors, Context and Causal Processes". In *Research Handbook on the Politics of International Law*, edited by Wayne Sandholtz and Christopher A. Whytock, 27–54. Cheltenham: Edward Elgar Publishing.

King, Gary. 2011. "Ensuring the Data-Rich Future of the Social Sciences". *Science* 331 (6018): 719–21.

Kingsbury, Benedict. 1998. "The Concept of Compliance as a Function of Competing Conceptions of International Law". *Michigan Journal of International Law* 19 (2): 345–72.

Kosař, David, and Lucas Lixinski. 2015. "Domestic Judicial Design by International Human Rights Courts". *The American Journal of International Law* 109 (4): 713–60.

Kosař, David, and Jan Petrov. 2017. "The Architecture of the Strasbourg System of Human Rights: The Crucial Role of the Domestic Level and the Constitutional Courts in Particular". *Heidelberg Journal of International Law* 77: 585–621.

Kosař, David, and Jan Petrov. 2018. "Determinants of Compliance Difficulties among 'good Compliers': Implementation of International Human Rights Rulings in the Czech Republic". *The European Journal of International Law* 29 (2): 397–425.

Kríž, Vincent, Barbora Hladká, Jan Dědek, and Martin Nečaský. 2014. "Statistical Recognition of References in Czech Court Decisions" In *Human-Inspired Computing and Its Applications*, edited by Alexander Gelbukh, Félix Castro Espinoza and Sofía N. Galicia-Haro, 51–61. Cham: Springer.

Kühn, Zdeněk. 2018. "Case Law and Precedent in Continental and Anglo-American Law". In *Binding Effect of Judicial Decisions – National and International Perspectives*, edited by Pavel Šámal, Guido Raimondi, and Koen Lenaerts, 31–48. Prague: Wolters Kluwer – Supreme Court.

Liu, John S., Hsiao-Hui Chen, Mei Hsiu-Ching Ho, and Yo-Chen Li. 2014. "Citations with Different Levels of Relevancy: Tracing the Main Paths of Legal Opinions". *Journal of the Association for Information Science and Technology* 65 (12): 2479–88.

Lupu, Yonatan, and Erik Voeten. 2012. "Precedent in International Courts: A Network Analysis of Case Citations by the European Court of Human Rights". *British Journal of Political Science* 42 (2): 413–39.

Molek, Pavel. 2014. *Politická Práva [Political Rights]*. Prague: Wolters Kluwer.

Molek, Pavel, and Petr Jäger. 2007. *Svoboda Projevu: Demokracie, Rovnost a svoboda Slova [Freedom of Expression: Democracy, Equality and Freedom of Speech]*. Prague: Wolters Kluwer.

Nollkaemper, André. 2012. "The Role of National Courts in Inducing Compliance with International and European Law – A Comparison". In *Compliance and the Enforcement of EU Law*, edited by Marise Cremona, 157–93. Oxford: Oxford University Press.

Posner, Richard A. 1993. *The Problems of Jurisprudence*. Cambridge, MA: Harvard University Press.

Pospíšil, Ivo, and Vladimír Týč, eds. 2016. *Mezinárodní Lidskoprávní Závazky Postkomunistických Zemí: Případy České Republiky a Slovenska [International Human Rights Obligations of Post-communist Countries: Examples of the Czech Republic and Slovakia]*. Prague: Leges.

Roberts, Anthea. 2011. "Comparative International Law? the Role of National Court in Creating and Enforcing International Law". *International and Comparative Law Quarterly* 60: 57–96.

Rytter, Jens E., and Marlene Wind. 2011. "In Need of Juristocracy? the Silence of Denmark in the Development of European Legal Norms". *International Journal of Constitutional Law* 9 (2): 470–504.

Trechsel, Stefan. 2005. *Human Rights in Criminal Proceedings*. New York: Oxford University Press.

van Bockel, Bas. 2010. *The Ne Bis in Idem Principle in EU Law*. Alphen aan de Rijn: Kluwer law Ineternational.

Wind, Marlene. 2016. "Do Scandinavians Care about International Law? A Study of Scandinavian Judges' Citation Practice to International Law and Courts". *Nordic Journal of International Law* 85 (4): 281–302.

5 The Supreme Court

The story of a (post)communist Cinderella

In contrast to the two other Czech apex courts, established in the atmosphere of the democratic transition,[1] the starting line of the Supreme Court (SC) was drawn far back. In 1993, after the establishment of independent Czechia, the SC simply took over the competences of its former federal and communist predecessors. The strong post-communist legacy made it rather difficult for the former flagship of socialist textual positivism (Kühn 2011) to catch up with new trends of international human rights law.

Undoubtedly, the SC is an institution with a complicated heritage. Not only did it fail to undergo a substantive personal change after the 1989 Velvet Revolution, but it was also deeply burdened by its legacy as the sole top judicial authority. During the communist era, the SC enjoyed the position of the highest court, with the final word (albeit supervised by the General Prosecutor who reported directly to the leadership of the Communist Party) in questions of legal interpretation. The expectations following such a legacy made it rather difficult for SC judges to suddenly accept the superior position of the Constitutional Court (CC) and the European Court of Human Rights (ECtHR or Strasbourg Court). To make things even more difficult, the ECtHR prefers a very different approach, pushing for a purposive interpretation embedded in the principles of the rule of law.

It is often suggested that European Convention on Human Rights (ECHR or Convention) was a novelty for the SC, which has more or less ignored, or at best cherry-picked, international norms for the past 40 years. Nevertheless, if we were to look further back into history, the first SC established in 1919[2] was no novice in the application of foreign and comparative law, especially due to its links to the Austrian judiciary (Němčická 1930, 130, quoted in Mikeš 2012, 21). Moreover, the interwar SC accepted the direct effect of ratified international treaties as early as 1925 (Mikeš 2012).[3]

However, World War II and the communist *coup d'état* in February 1948 changed this approach significantly. The SC, composed of lay judges selected and heavily screened by the Communist Party, abandoned the previous tradition and introduced into its case law many elements of totalitarianism (Motejl 2009). The textual and very formal interpretation became one of the core tactics of the SC, which assumed the role of the state and the guardian of socialist legality.

This was reflected also in the communist SC's position towards international human rights treaties. Czechia became a member party to the International Covenant on Civil and Political Rights (ICCPR) in 1976. Nevertheless, the SC continuously refused to acknowledge the primacy or the direct effect of the Covenant. If the party evoked the ICCPR and respective human rights, the SC typically explained that although the ICCPR creates an obligation for Czechoslovakia, such obligation binds only administrative authorities.[4] International human rights treaties, putting more emphasis on individuals and setting out obligations of the state towards individuals, did not align with the vision of the communist SC.

Since 1993, the SC has undergone many challenges. The cohabitation with two other domestic apex courts[5] and two European courts (the ECtHR and the Court of Justice of the European Union, or CJEU) having arguably been among the biggest ones. The slowly evaporating communist spirit and legacy puts the SC at a double crossroads. It represents both the general v. constitutional, and the old v. new judiciary cleavage. The focus on human rights does not come to the SC naturally (in contrast to, for example, the CC), nor does subordinance to other judicial authorities. Nevertheless, the different spirit also makes the SC an interesting study on how unreformed communist judiciaries adapt to the gradual internationalization of law and how (and under what conditions) they internalize the use and implementation of the Strasbourg case law.

The aim of this chapter is to analyze the development of the SC's position towards the case law of the ECtHR. We start with a macro-level analysis searching for general patterns of the use of ECtHR case law, then proceed with the meso-level, examining the influence of ECtHR references on the SC's reasoning, and finally move to a micro-level study of individual cases and deeper context illustrating and explaining the development and shifts in the SC's position towards the ECtHR. We argue that the SC slowly shifted its position towards the ECtHR due to external pushes. While in the past its use of the case law was arbitrary and selective, nowadays it slowly moves to the position of active complier.

5.1 Looking from above: The macro-level analysis

The following section explores general patterns in the SC's judicial treatment of the Strasbourg case law and analyzes their development in time. It zeroes in on the broader trends and compares them with personal and jurisdictional changes at the SC. The macro-level analysis asks how often and with what intensity the SC refers to ECtHR case law, how (and why) its practice evolved, and what are the most cited ECtHR rulings.

5.1.1 The overview of general trends

The SC of independent Czechia was established in 1993. Nevertheless, the set of its competences evolved only gradually. Most importantly, the extraordinary appeal in civil matters was introduced in 1996. Taken together with the lack of any online database in the early 1990s, this explains why the first identified reference to ECtHR case law reaches only to the year 1998. In the period relevant for our analysis, 1998–2015, the SC delivered 100,314 rulings altogether. In these, it referred to 723 different ECtHR rulings, in 708 of its own decisions and judgments, bringing the overall number of references to 1,624 (i.e., our population). Figure 5.1 shows the development of the use of these references over time (including the comparison between all individual ECtHR references and SC rulings including at least one reference).

As we can clearly see, during the 1990s the SC generally neglected ECtHR case law, with the exception of a single judgment[6] dealing with the rules of a fair trial and the admissibility of evidence. The case addressed the question of which conditions allow for e-mail and phone interception, reaching the conclusion that an employer cannot justify the interception of the employee's correspondence without her knowledge by suggesting that this correspondence relates to the employer's (or public) interest. The SC based its reasoning on Article 13 of the Czech Charter of fundamental rights and freedoms (the protection of private life), concluding that the provision is well in line with the Strasbourg case law. It is worth noting that references to the cases *Kopp v. Switzerland*,[7] *Halford v. the United Kingdom*,[8] and *A. v. France*[9] appearing in the judgment originated from the then-existing Czech legal journals (publishing the Czech translations and commentaries on the ECtHR's new cases)[10] and commentary by Jan Čapek (Čapek 1995a, 71; 1995b). Instead of referring directly to the ECtHR, the Court referred to these secondary sources.

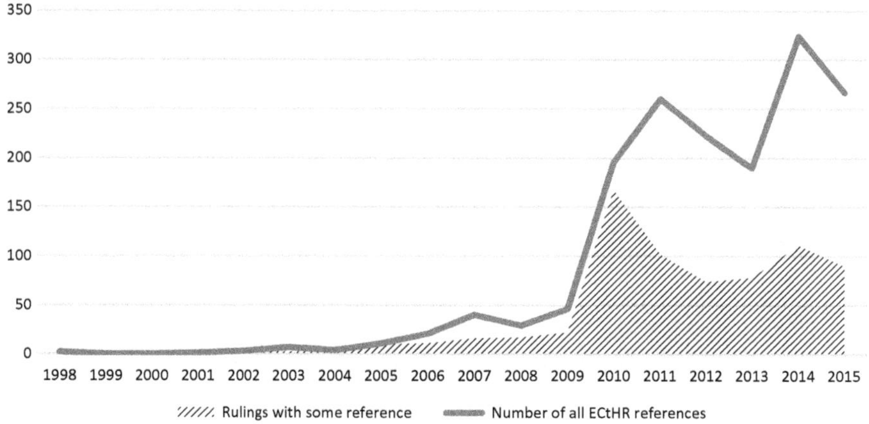

Figure 5.1 The use of the ECtHR's references over time (any placement).
Source: authors.

The huge breaking point in the SC's reluctance to "adopt" the Strasbourg Court case law and consider it a source of law comparable to domestic provisions and jurisprudence came only 10 years later, around 2010.

Figure 5.2 portrays the most precise picture, showing that the steep increase in the use of references did not result from a sudden increase in the Court's overall caseload. Furthermore, we can also see that compared to the Supreme Administrative Court (SAC) and CC, the proportion of the rulings including references to ECtHR case law remains overall very limited (never actually reaching the 5 percent limit).

The comparison might be, however, a bit misleading. We need to take into account that some areas of the SC's jurisdiction overlap with the Convention only very loosely (especially commercial law), and some legal questions were not initially covered by ECtHR case law (a good example might be the question of the position and rights of minority shareholders during a squeeze-out, the problem of storing DNA samples, etc.). Still, the presence of references to the ECtHR in areas well covered by Strasbourg case law, such as the protection of private life or in criminal law, was rare and found its place in the SC's reasoning only very slowly. This corresponds with a recurring narrative that the SC's judges were initially very reluctant to use the ECHR (just as any other international human rights treaty) as a legitimate source of law and did not perceive the Strasbourg Court as a potential ally.[11]

The sharp increase of the use of references occurred only in 2010, which correlates with the introduction of new legislation on state liability and immaterial damages, and with a SC Grand Chamber judgment on the direct

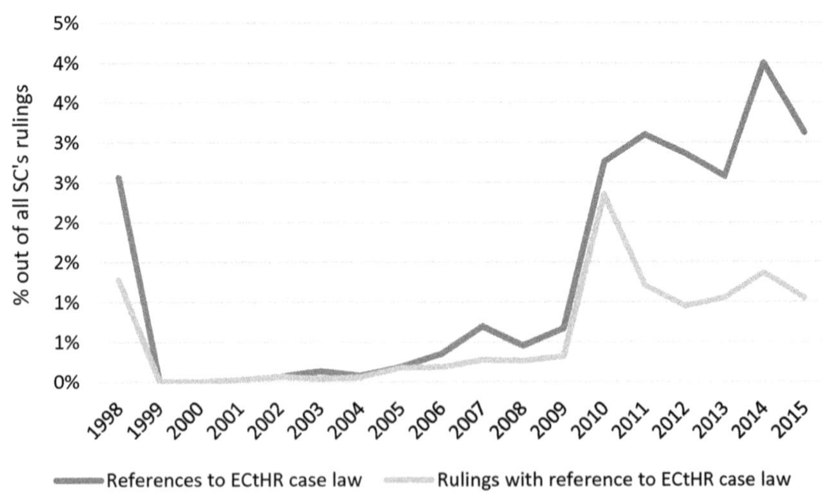

Figure 5.2 The use of the ECtHR's references over time compared to all case law of the SC.

Source: authors.

application of Article 5(5) ECHR awarding immaterial damage for unjust detention, which occurred before the entry of the above-mentioned legal amendment into force.[12] Up until this moment, the approach of the SC's judges towards the Convention was split, with only one panel recognizing the primacy and a direct effect of the Convention. We provide a more detailed analysis of the Grand Chamber judgment and its influence on the next line of SC case law in the micro-level analysis (Section 5.3).

However, several other important events preceded the breakthrough judgment. First, at the end of 2005, the President of the SC established a new analytical department. The department was meant to advise the judges on the application of European Union (EU) law, but gradually it covered all sources of international law and offered background analyses, consultations, and, most importantly, translation of the ECtHR's case law.

This period of time coincided with two other events: first, a boom of various workshops and trainings for judges on the application of international and EU law. We might even suggest that obligations stemming from membership in the EU led to an overall increase of knowledge, understanding, and openness towards international law as such. This correlates with generally more accessible information on the ECtHR finally published in the Czech language – most notably the Czech commentary on the Convention (Kmec et al. 2012). Second, the composition of the SC started to change. Although it still consisted exclusively of career judges, the new generation included judges who were much better educated in international law, and benefited from experience from various research stays at foreign universities. Many of the young new judges coming to the SC in 2010s have been keen on building their profiles as international law experts. Hence, the conservative wing of SC, which had been refusing to use the international human rights law on principle, became more challenged, and judges with a more neutral stance started getting more information on the existence of new ECtHR jurisprudence.

Another general comment relates to "the source" of references and SC judges' knowledge of Strasbourg case law. As we previously suggested, one of the biggest challenges of the research on references is the fact that not every single citation of ECtHR case law necessarily equals the use of the reference as a part of the reasoning. We therefore identified which references are present in narrative parts – i.e., parts summarizing the arguments of parties to the proceedings and courts deciding in lower instances – and which references the SC uses in its own substantive reasoning. Surprisingly, the SC has an extremely high proportion of references present only in the narrative part (the darker area of Figure 5.3). A large proportion of these are decisions delivered by the Criminal Division in extradition cases, which are known for a different style of legal language. In contrast to other SC rulings, these decisions typically do not contain a lengthy reasoning. On the contrary, the majority of a typical extradition decision consists of a mere recapitulation of lower courts' findings or reports of the Minister of Justice. The SC then briefly concludes whether these ought to be considered as valid. With limited space devoted to its own

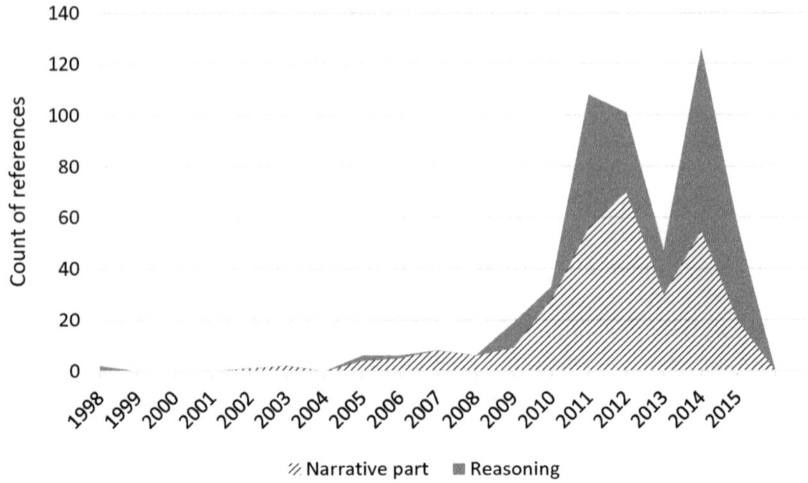

Figure 5.3 The use of ECtHR references over time: Narrative part v. reasoning.
Source: authors.

reasoning, the nested references of other parties to the proceedings then implicitly form the SC's arguments, although our automated text recognition did not manage to identify it as such. In other words, we expect that these references, occurring via a reference to the summary of lower courts, still implicitly belong and form the SC's own reasoning.

To some extent, the division between narrative parts and reasoning might therefore be misleading. However, in the case of the SC, it is an excellent indicator of who acted as the agenda setter bringing the ECtHR's case law into the SC's focus. The huge disproportion of references only in narrative parts suggests the hypothesis that it was often other public bodies and advocates who slowly pushed for the more frequent use of the Strasbourg Court's case law and brought it into the SC's attention.

Figure 5.3 furthermore demonstrates that the standard of referencing is changing. Since 2013, we can witness a prevailing use of references in reasonings of SC's rulings. Two factors, the establishment of the Analytical Department and changes on the SC's judicial board, no doubt played an important role in this development. The SC eventually shifted from "forced" treatment of ECtHR case law (under the influence and supervision of the Governmental Agent before the ECtHR, CC, or parties to the proceedings), to the facilitator of the judicial implementation inside the Czech judiciary. Since 2013, the SC transformed part of its Collection, which now publishes the specialized addendum "Collection of the most important ECtHR's rulings". Four times a year, a group of SC judges representing all relevant panels, together with the SC president, Analytical Department, and Governmental

Agent, meet to discuss which of the newly published Strasbourg rulings have the biggest relevance for the Czech civil and criminal law. Subsequently, these selected judgments are translated into Czech, published in the Collection, and distributed among Czech judges.

In order to understand the treatment of ECtHR case law, it is also critical to acknowledge the importance which SC assigns to its own rulings. The SC classifies its rulings into five categories according to their impact and importance. Typically, the panel and in particular the judge rapporteur decide on the ruling's categorization, depending on how much impact and publicity she wishes for the ruling. The category A stands for decisions and judgments proposed for publication in the Collection (which makes them binding on all subjects in Czechia). This category has the furthest impact on the case law of district and regional Czech courts. Category B includes other very important rulings not meant for publication in the Collection. Category C contains other rulings of a substantive character, Category D covers decisions on enforcement that are not covered by Category A or B, and finally Category E refers to decisions of a purely procedural character.

Figure 5.4 demonstrates the dispersion of rulings containing a reference among these categories. The Category A rulings – i.e., all decisions and judgments proposed for a publication in a Collection – are expected to contain many references for at least two reasons. First, these rulings are the SC's flagship for ordinary courts. Second, between 2012 and 2015, the internal Analytical Department oversaw the use of relevant international law in all rulings meant for publication in the Collection.[13] The biggest proportion of references

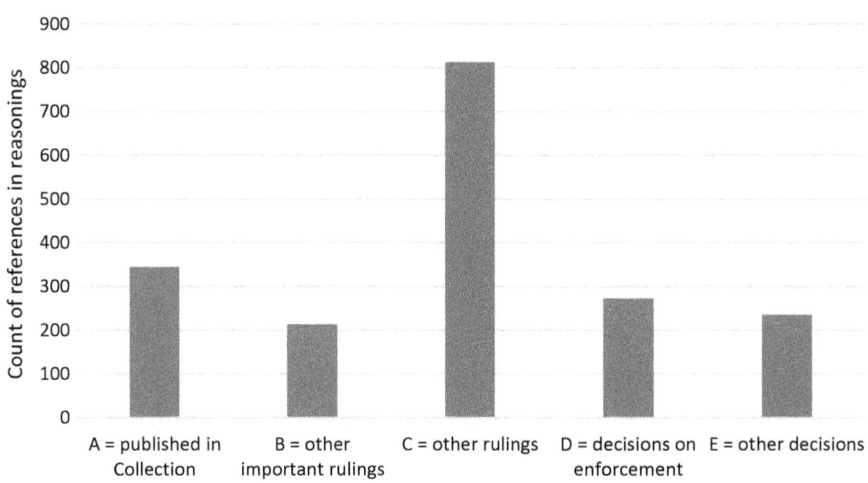

Figure 5.4 References in reasonings of SC rulings according to how the SC categorizes the importance of rulings.

Source: authors.

appearing in Category C (other substantive rulings which the SC judges do not find important enough to publish in the Collection) prompts various explanations. Perhaps the scope of cases involving the ECtHR's rulings does not coincide with those areas which are of the utmost interest for Czech courts (at least according to SC judges). Another explanation would be that the conservative majority of the SC does not find the rulings referring to the Strasbourg Court of particular importance, or does not deem them worth noticing. This finding seems to also align with insider gossip that often, when facing strong conservative opposition, SC judges pushed for a use of ECtHR case law outside of the whole SC's attention.

Figure 5.5 depicts those SC rulings which referred to the Convention (the dark gray line) compared to cases citing the ECtHR's case law. The application of the Convention is clearly prevalent over references to the ECtHR's case law, which, in contrast to the SAC (see Chapter 6), never gained dominance or even approached the frequency of the use of the Convention. The trend offers several interpretations. Either the SC judges have far better knowledge of the Convention than the Strasbourg case law, or they simply do not feel an urgent need to explicitly support the arguments and interpretations of the Convention with Strasbourg case law.

5.1.2 Going beyond compliance

The main idea behind our analysis is that the influence of ECtHR case law surpasses the mere implementation of adverse judgments against the respective state (in our case the Czech Republic). It is therefore necessary to look at the

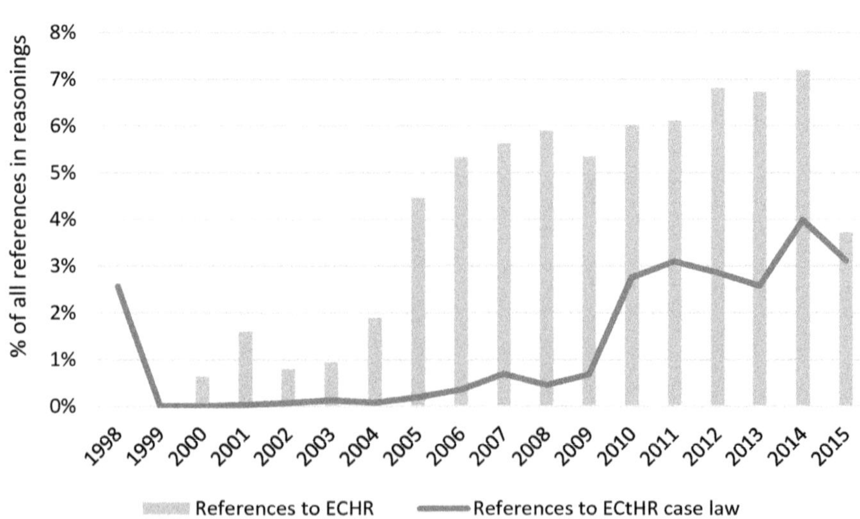

Figure 5.5 References to the Convention v. references to ECtHR case law.
Source: authors.

ECtHR holistically and analyze the judicial treatment of the Strasbourg case law in general, irrespective of the respondent state.

If we were to look at the ratio between references to adverse judgments against Czechia (directly binding for Czech authorities) and rulings against other Council of Europe member states, the results are surprising. Overall, 76.26 percent of references used by the SC refer to adverse judgments and decisions against countries other than Czechia. On the contrary, only a small fraction of the SC's rulings refer solely to Strasbourg rulings against Czechia (23.74 percent). Figure 5.6 shows that until the breakthrough in 2011, the SC did not care all that much about cases directly targeting Czechia. The very first references concerned more general principles developed by the ECtHR. On the contrary, once the practice of using ECtHR references increased, the proportion of Czech cases among all used references rose comparatively (in contrast to the SAC). The "Czech" adverse cases are clearly the most cited ones (23.74 percent; i.e., 420 times), followed by Italy (8.99 percent; i.e., 159 times).

Figure 5.6 therefore suggests several conclusions. First, at the very beginning, while the SC's treatment of ECtHR case law was still hesitant, the references were pushed forward by a few pioneer judges who referred mostly to general principles developed in Strasbourg, complementing the creative use and interpretation of the Convention. While the acceptance of the authority and legitimacy of the ECtHR eventually spread through various panels of the SC (mostly with the help of new judges more interested in international law and the Grand Chamber's confirmation of the direct effect of the Convention), the emphasis put on Czech adverse cases and findings directly targeting Czechia remained relatively high.

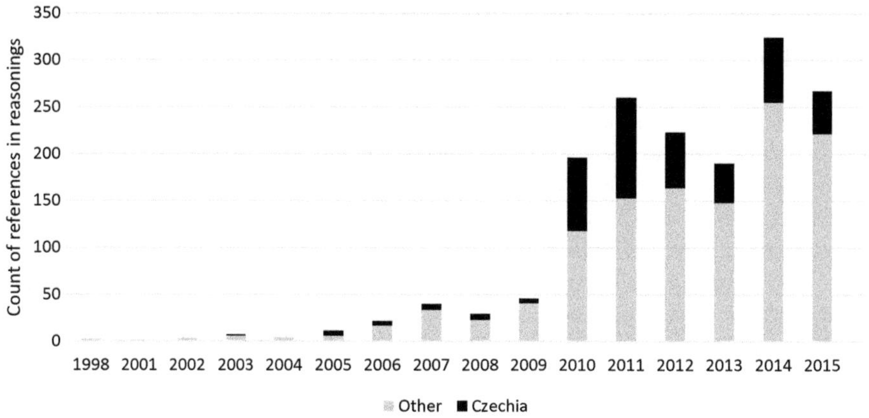

Figure 5.6 References to cases against Czechia v. other states.
Source: authors.

Although a number of the SC judges might still be more willing to accept the compliance in a narrow sense – i.e., to implement the ECtHR's findings explicitly related to the Czech legal order rather than to accept the more general role of the Strasbourg Court as an authoritative interpreter – the deeper level of the analysis shows how important it is to study the interactions of domestic courts with the whole case law of the ECtHR in order to understand the judicial treatment.

A brief notion should be raised here also on behalf of the meso-level analysis. The exploration of the precision of references showed that the level of detail is gradually increasing while the number of generic references is falling. However, when judges do refer to Czech cases, the level of detail in their reference is higher (often referring to a particular point or paragraph in the ruling). This seemingly clear tendency raises the question of what this means for their compliance. Perhaps we can argue that judges feel more restricted with the ECtHR's argumentation and wording in Czech cases directly related to Czech legal norms, while they enjoy a little bit more freedom of interpretation when using references to "foreign" adverse rulings. This might, however, also follow from the fact that rulings against Czechia are translated into Czech and concern Czech legal norms. The SC judges then better understand both the ECtHR reasoning and the overall context, which allows them a deeper analysis of a referred ruling.

Similarly, when we explored the amount of the space devoted to various references in the SC's rulings, the distribution of references was roughly equal. In 49.25 percent of cases the SC included a brief and short reference, in 44.78 percent of cases a more elaborate reference. We did not find any significant difference between the space devoted to references based on their origin (i.e., the respondent Council of Europe country). It is also interesting to mention that we found a tendency to devote more and more space to ECtHR case law in the text of the SC's rulings over time. This supports our cherry-picking hypothesis that the SC initially referred sparingly to the ECtHR. We argue that this comes down to very few judges with good knowledge of international human rights law being present at the Court shortly after the accession to the Council of Europe, or feeling the need to support their justification and reasoning by the ECtHR only in rare cases. For a long time, the SC almost exclusively referred to the right of a fair trial (Article 6), and then later to freedom of expression (Article 10), protection of property in restitution cases (Article 1 of the Protocol No. 1), and to detention (Article 5). Slowly, with an increasing diversity, the SC also adopted a more receptive approach towards the Convention and Strasbourg Court case law. But, interestingly, the tendency to use only very brief references to case law related to Article 6 persists (see Figures 5.8 and 5.9). This might result from the fact that majority of Article 6 references briefly appear as a marginal procedural reason for the admissibility of an extraordinary appeal to the SC.

The last comment on the relevance of differences between treatment of Czech and other ECtHR cases relates to the meso-level study of references of substantive or supporting relevance. We found little difference in references of substantive influence; i.e., references with biggest impact on the result of the courts' reasoning.[14] This is in stark contrast to the findings of older Czech scholarship, which suggested that the SC refused the normative power of those ECtHR rulings, where Czechia was not a party to proceedings (Kühn 2005). However, the SC's use of rulings against Czechia compared to rulings issued against other Council of Europe countries differs significantly when it comes to the implemented legal technique. If the SC inserts a reference to a Czech adverse ruling with substantive influence on the case result, it predominantly implements two techniques, either a direct application or a conform interpretation (see more in Section 5.2). This aligns with our intuitive expectation following from the strength of obligation put on the SC by the ECtHR. The SC treats the Strasbourg Court rulings against Czechia as a direct source of legal norms and does not hesitate to give them application preference over domestic legal norms, if these are in conflict with ECtHR findings. Such a treatment of ECtHR case law against other states is still less common.

5.1.3 References as an indicator of the Supreme Court's relationship to the Convention

Next, we looked more deeply into the character of references. Figure 5.7 reports that a surprisingly large difference exists between the references to cases where the ECtHR found or did not find a violation of the Convention. The SC refers to Strasbourg case law with an established violation more than three times as often (1,284 references; i.e., 76.5 percent) as to cases where no violation has been found (348 references; i.e., 21.3 percent). This is not surprising, however, as the ECtHR develops most of the principles pushing the interpretation of the Convention further and filling in the gaps in those cases where it finds a violation. The distribution, however, also points to limits of domestic judicial treatment of Strasbourg case law. Figure 5.7 allows us to hypothesize that visibility of rulings, as in cases of rulings finding a violation, plays a crucial part in the extent to which domestic courts know and use Strasbourg case law.

We already noted several instances that indicate that development of the SC's use of references to Strasbourg Court case law might also depend on the overall area of human rights protection guaranteed by the Convention and on the particular focus of the ECtHR on certain rights. Not all areas of the SC's jurisdiction cover human rights issues. The Convention is therefore most commonly applied in the area of criminal law and criminal proceedings (Articles 2, 3, 5 ECHR; Article 4 of the Protocol No. 7), fair trial, and, predominantly, the length of proceedings (Article 6), and protection of private life (Article 8, personal integrity rights, family life, etc.).

We checked whether these areas correspond to the scope of the ECtHR's rulings usually referred to by the SC. Figure 5.8 captures the different areas of human rights protection in which the SC most often relies on the ECtHR. The intuitive expectation that Article 6 will dominate, as it crosses the jurisdiction of both SC divisions and targets conditions of the admissibility of criminal and civil

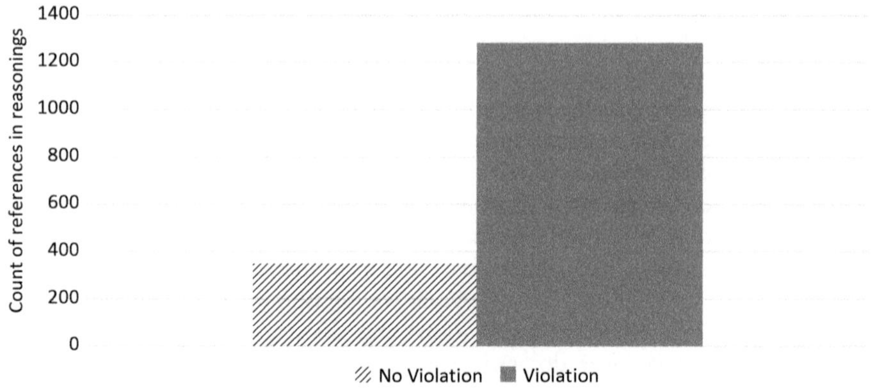

Figure 5.7 References to case law where the ECtHR found or did not find a violation.
Source: authors.

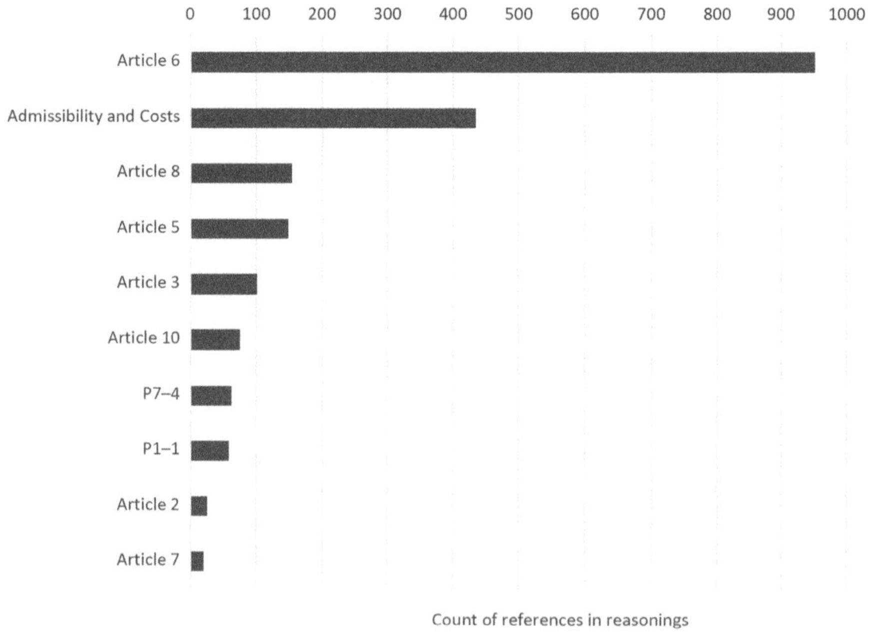

Figure 5.8 Articles of the Convention related to SC references.
Source: authors.

extraordinary appeal, was supported. The *ne bis in idem* principle (Article 4 of the Protocol No. 7), and protection of property (Article 1 of the Protocol No. 1, in relation to post-communist restitutions in particular), albeit being on the bottom of the list, are very important for the SC.

Figure 5.9 builds on previous findings and captures the development in the use of individual articles in time. The sparklines capturing the use of various Convention articles over time suggest the progress of the SC from narrow to vibrant use of the Convention and related case law. At the beginning of the examined period, the SC relied mostly on ECtHR rulings offering a general interpretation of the Convention and its position and scope, and jurisdiction of the ECtHR as such, as well as questions of fair trial and admissibility of extraordinary appeals (Article 6). Eventually, the scope expanded significantly into other areas. Although Article 6 still represents the biggest proportion of references, the diversity of cited rulings is definitely more vibrant.

Figure 5.10 appropriately complements this finding by capturing the areas of the SC's decision-making that most often contain a reference to ECtHR case law. While in the previous section we examined the character of the ECtHR's original rulings referred to by the SC, this figure helps us dig deeper into the character of rulings with references. Similarly to the previous section, it is important to bear in mind that some rulings relate to more than one area of legal regulation. We categorized them according to those fields of law that corresponded best to sections using references.

State liability cases clearly prevail over other areas, which again supports our hypothesis that the breaking point for the SC has been the Grand Chamber ruling on the application of Article 5(5) in cases of immaterial damages and compensation from the state (Kosař and Petrov 2018). We will therefore revisit this case in more detail in the micro-level part of the analysis. In needs to be pointed out, however, that the column "fair trial and impartiality (of judges)" covers only those cases that were solely of a procedural character; obviously, the reach of Article 6 is broader and references to cases related to Article 6 might also appear in substantive rulings of the SC, hence the discrepancy between the areas.

Lastly, these findings are further supported by the last figure of macro-level analysis, which illustrates the ECtHR rulings most frequently referred to by the SC (Figure 5.11). The most cited judgment, *Apicella v. Italy*,[15] addressed applicants who inherited previously expropriated land and disputed the amount of compensation for expropriation. The applicants argued before the ECtHR that Italian courts awarded them only a derisory amount of compensation in exceedingly long proceedings. The *Apicella* judgment is heavily referred to both in rulings addressing state liability (referred to also in cases dealing with property restitution within transitional justice issues), and rulings concerning the length of proceedings (similarly, *Eckle v. Germany*[16]). The *Zolotukhin* judgment[17] on the other hand extends into the activity of the Criminal Division and addresses a set of rulings on the *ne bis in idem* principle (Article 4 of the Protocol No. 7).

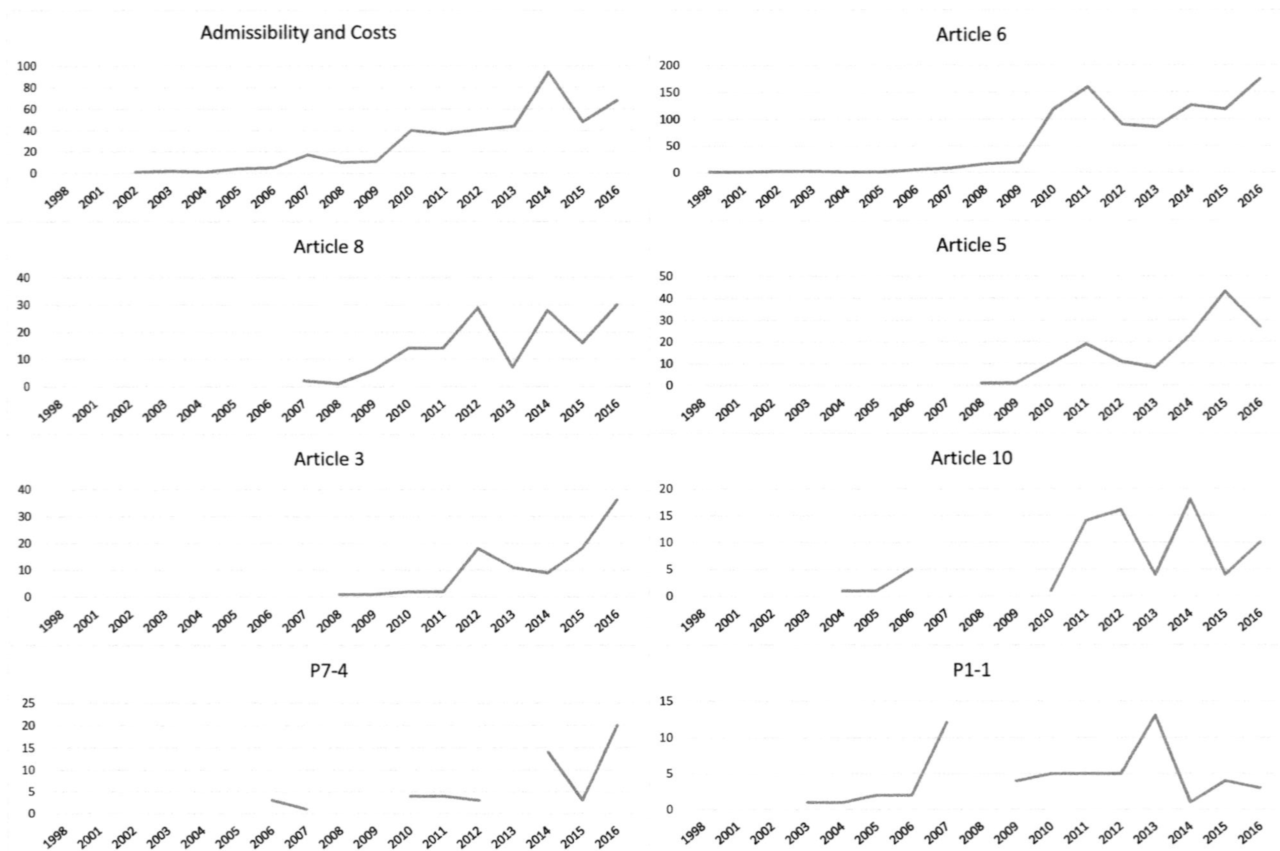

Figure 5.9 Convention articles related to references – development over time.
Source: authors.

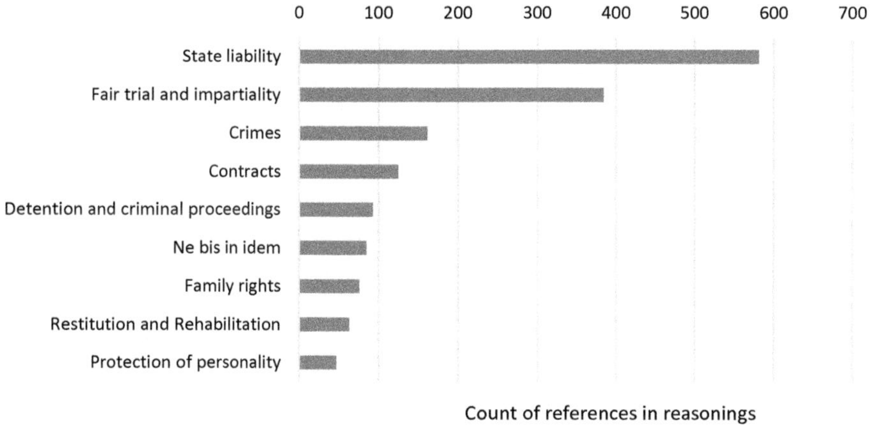

Figure 5.10 Areas of SC decision-making with most frequent references to the ECtHR.

Source: authors.

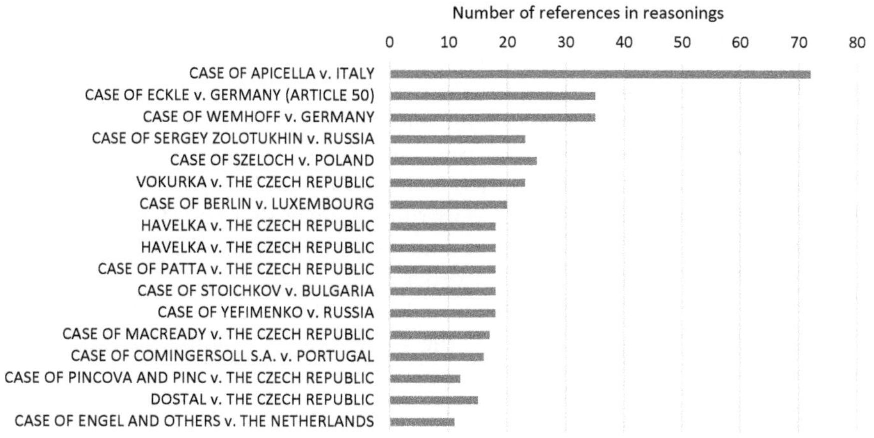

Figure 5.11 ECtHR cases most frequently referred to in a reasoning.

Source: authors.

5.1.4 *Instead of a conclusion: Building new hypotheses*

We started this analysis with a suggestion that the Czech Supreme Court illustrates the transformation of communist judicial authority and its stance towards the ECtHR (as well as other international human rights bodies in general). It therefore has the potential to tell us more about how to advance judicial implementation in transforming countries. The SC has a very progressive trend of including references to Strasbourg Court into its reasonings, with breaking points surrounding various external nudges and incentives, such as judicial training or establishment of analytical units focusing on international law. We propose the hypothesis that personnel policies are very important. As older judges often remain conservative and reluctant, we expect them to be more willing to refer to cases against Czechia than to the rest of the ECtHR case law. However, they become more willing to apply the Strasbourg Court findings once these are (a) confirmed by other domestic courts (i.e., references to domestic rulings instead of direct references to the ECtHR); (b) translated and commented on by domestic scholarship: Language, lectures, and education matter a lot. Finally, "agenda setters" – i.e., actors who push the SC to treat and address ECtHR case law – are often other actors. Parties to the proceedings and their attorneys invoke Strasbourg case law more frequently than some SC judges. We argue that similar findings are relevant for the general approach of post-communist courts towards international human rights bodies.

5.2 Meso-level analysis: Learning to understand the Supreme Court

The previous data and remarks suggest that the SC's relationship to the Strasbourg Court is still a complicated one. The aim of this section is to look beyond the general jurisprudential doctrines, as well as beyond the mere number of references to the Strasbourg Court, and examine the day-to-day use of the ECtHR's case law in the SC's decision-making. Judicial treatment of ECtHR case law in its narrowest meaning still offers domestic judges plenty of possibilities for how to work with the Strasbourg Court ruling. Inclusion of a reference into the text does not automatically mean that court implements the ECtHR's arguments (see Chapter 4 or Petrov 2019). In order to understand the effects of judicial treatment of Strasbourg Court rulings, we have to dig deeper and ask how the SC uses the ECtHR's case law, what is the significance and influence of ECtHR references on domestic cases, and in how much detail SC judges engage with ECtHR rulings. The meso-level analysis of a new hand-coded dataset of a little over 200 SC[18] rulings reveals the basic patterns and sheds light on the presented puzzle.

The introductory macro-level section revealed an increasing trend of the use of ECtHR references. The question stands, however, to what extent the mere numbers correspond to the SC's position towards ECtHR jurisprudence. The literature identified various positions that domestic courts may hold towards international bodies, pointing more and more frequently to domestic courts rebelling against some controversial judgments pushing for broader legislative or societal change (Madsen, Cebulak, and Wiebusch 2018).

The SC's inclination towards a formalistic view of law, deeply engaged with procedural rules and formal purity, intuitively does not bode well for the more purposive approach of human rights courts, especially the ECtHR. We therefore explored the SC's position towards the dynamic ECtHR. Using the content analysis of a sample of SC rulings with a reference to ECtHR case law, we found that the SC follows the ECtHR's reasoning in an overwhelming 93.75 percent of its rulings.[19] Moreover, we did not find any example of the SC openly rebelling against the ECtHR and refusing to follow the rulings of the Strasbourg Court. What is even more surprising, Figure 5.12 shows that the striking inclination to follow the ECtHR is not a recent phenomenon. On the contrary, it seems that rulings in which the SC did not follow an ECtHR ruling appear only in more recent history. Overall, these findings confirm the generally positive reflection of the approach of Czech judiciary towards the Strasbourg Court case law (Majerčík 2016).

While the SC has never openly refused to follow the Strasbourg Court's rulings, it has been using the tactic of "distinguishing" the case at hand from the ECtHR's finding in two situations. First, the SC distinguished cases regarding the compensations for the undue length of proceedings. The claimants typically argued that the length of their proceedings had breached Article 6 ECHR (right to a fair trial) as the ECtHR had previously found the very same period of time amounting to an unfair trial. The SC explained that the length on its own is an arbitrary category and the ECtHR does not prescribe the domestic courts to deliver a ruling within a specific time. This means that the broader context, behavior of parties to the proceedings, structural questions, etc., need to be taken into consideration when reviewing the length of proceedings. For example, in ruling No. 30 Cdo 1987/2014,[21] the claimant referred to *Apicella v. Italy* and *Golha v. the Czech Republic*,[22] interpreting the Strasbourg rulings to a finding that compensatory proceedings might take seven months, but 11 is too much and leads to a breach of Article 6.

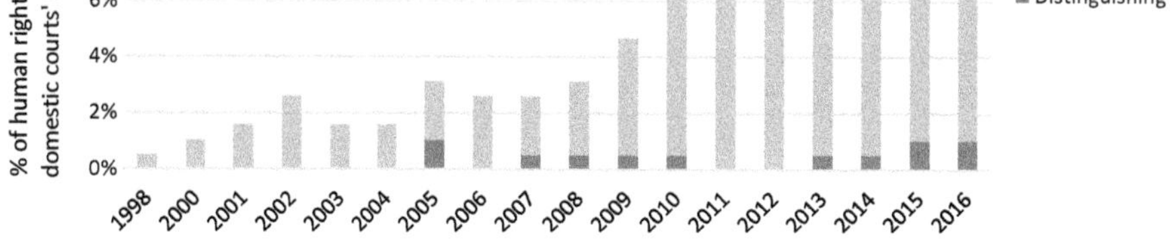

Figure 5.12 SC following the reasoning of the ECtHR's rulings.[20]
Source: authors.

The SC pointed out that a specific Italian legislative norm, one which allows Italian courts only four months to deliver a ruling, needs to be taken into account. Such a legislative requirement cannot automatically be translated into compensatory proceedings in Czechia. Furthermore, the SC also pointed out that while the referred cases addressed the length of proceedings in a single instance, in the case at hand, three different courts had repeatedly delivered their rulings. The SC therefore distinguished the factual and legal situation at hand and explained why it could not implement the ECtHR rulings.[23]

The second area where the SC typically uses the "distinguishing" technique is tax regulation and compensation. In case of tax regulation, the SC refused the claims attempting to apply Convention rules and the ECtHR's judgments on tax regulation, which, apart from very specific cases, stands outside of the Convention application.[24] Similarly, claimants also unsuccessfully attempted to use Article 5(5) on cases where the violation of their rights was not caused by one of the reasons defined in Article 5 as required by its Paragraph 5. This all might suggest that with gradually learning how to work with international human rights case law, the SC is becoming more precise. On the other hand, the references in narrative parts of rulings show us that while the applicants are raising more references in their extraordinary appeals, these are still often quite misplaced.

Although we did not find any example of the SC explicitly refusing the ECtHR's ruling, it does not mean that SC judges always necessarily agree with the Strasbourg Court.[25] Nevertheless, they opt for different strategies than direct confrontation, most often choosing to simply ignore the existence of the Strasbourg case law. Moreover, we suggest that the SC uses "the distinguishing practice" in order to camouflage its disagreement with the ECtHR. Instead of openly refusing to apply the ECtHR's findings, the SC tries its best to either shift the interpretation of the relevant ECtHR's ruling or to find the smallest difference in the facts of the case, which would justify the distinguishing practice. While the SC mostly follows rulings issued against Czechia, interestingly, there is one particularly sensitive and controversial case when the SC justified its refusal of the Strasbourg Court finding in a Czechia-adverse case by a distinguishing tactic. In judgment No. 30 Cdo 4277/2010[26] the SC dealt with extraordinary appeal of a Roma applicant who requested immaterial damage for his enrolment in a special school for children with mental disabilities back in the 1980s. The judgment reflects on the famous *D.H. v. Czech Republic* case,[27] the only adverse judgment in which Czechia failed to achieve compliance for more than 11 years (Smekal and Šipulová 2014). We analyze this peculiar case more closely in Chapter 8.

Another very important question, one which helps us to better understand the position of the SC towards the ECtHR as well as the effect of the Strasbourg case law on the domestic judicial level, is what impact the ECtHR rulings have on those SC judgments and decisions that include references. We identified two major levels of influence. The first level, supporting, is when the SC acknowledges the existence of the Strasbourg case law and uses a reference as further legitimation of its conclusion. The second, substantive influence, is present in rulings where the ECtHR case law plays a leading role in the conclusion and result of domestic proceedings.

Figure 5.13 demonstrates the occurrence of both forms of influence. While the supporting form of references is clearly prevalent (the dark gray line), the differences in annual trends are not particularly large. Both supporting and substantive influence are gradually increasing in frequency of use, although the gap between both types of effects is also becoming larger. This suggests that while in the late 1990s the use of references to ECtHR case law was rare, the SC cherry-picked references only to those rulings that helped it push through certain findings and principles not clearly following from domestic norms and jurisprudence.

Nowadays, although the SC still predominantly decides on the basis of domestic law and the CC's jurisprudence, the use of ECtHR case law has become standard for the SC. The ornamental role of references (Bobek and Kosař 2010), however, should not be underestimated. There are several instances where the SC uses an ECtHR reference to explain the essence of a respective human right and its embeddedness in international human rights law sources. Beyond this demonstrative use of the case law, references are often used to add to the overall legitimacy, transparency, and persuasiveness of the reasoning.

We should make one more remark here regarding the supporting use of ECtHR case law. There are some specific instances where the SC chose a "nested reference to ECtHR". Instead of building its reasoning around the Strasbourg Court ruling, it attached only a supporting role to the ECtHR, and

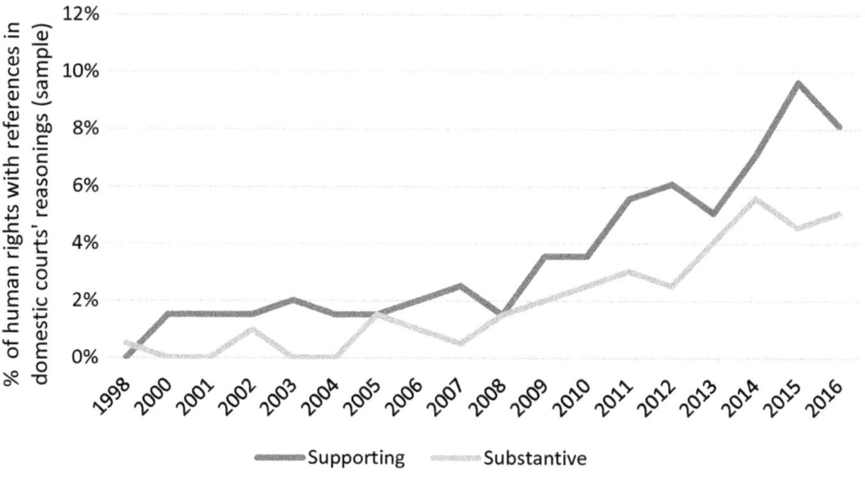

Figure 5.13 Influence of the ECtHR reference on the result of the case.
Source: authors.

referred to its own previous and consolidated case law, which had already discussed at length and adopted the findings and principles delivered by the ECtHR.[28] Overall, however, the distribution of references with substantive and supporting influence is surprising and negates the negative portrayal of the SC's position towards the ECHR and international law in general (Kühn 2009; Motejl 2009).

In the macro-level section, we described the Convention articles as well as the fields of law (Figures 5.9 and 5.10 above) where the SC uses references to ECtHR case law most frequently. The manual coding on the meso level delivered very similar results. Indeed, most of the references relate to Articles 6 (fair trial), 5 (right to liberty and security), and 8 (private life) ECHR. Articles 6 and 5 closely correlate, as the majority of their use relates to the length of proceedings and the length and lawfulness of the detention.[29] Article 6 furthermore partly covers conditions for admissibility of extraordinary appeal (review of proceedings held by courts deciding in first and second instance), which explains its frequent appearance. Not all Strasbourg rulings related to Article 6 are followed, however. In a part of case law, the SC distinguishes the factual findings from facts and conditions underlining the ECtHR's rulings, claiming they are inapplicable.[30]

Another frequently applied provision, Article 8 (right to respect private and family life), cuts across several areas under SC jurisdiction, such as the protection of personal rights and dignity, libel, defamatory disputes, protection of home searches, or interceptions, and compensation for conditions in prisons that disrespect the private lives of prisoners. The frequent occurrence of references to ECtHR case law interpreting Article 8 therefore corresponds to the composition of the SC's jurisdiction, as well as scholarly reflection of the impact of Article 8 on the protection of employees in Czechia (Štefko 2012).

Approximately one-third of references related to Article 6 substantively formed the outcome of the SC's reasoning, while with Articles 5 and 8 the substantive influence prevails. Even more surprisingly, when using case law related to Article 4 of the Protocol No. 7 (*ne bis in idem* principle), the SC almost exclusively grants the references substantive influence.

One slightly surprising occurrence is the particularly low representation of the prohibition of discrimination (Article 14), right to life (Article 2), and prohibition of torture (Article 3). Similarly to the Czech Constitutional Court, the SC long disagreed with the ECtHR and took a different approach to the interpretation of indirect discrimination.[31] The situation eventually changed under the influence of the EU law. The principles of indirect discrimination penetrate the SC's case law through the EU law and jurisprudence of the CJEU, especially in the areas of working conditions and private life. Introduction of the EU Charter of Fundamental Rights and the transposition of several EU directives related to discrimination pushed the SC to change its understanding of indirect discrimination. The EU law now takes clear precedents over references to the ECtHR and Convention, as it offers the Czech courts more detailed guidance on the application of principles.

When we return to those references, which substantively influence the result of the case at hand and play a leading role in the SC's reasoning, we are also interested in the legal techniques that the SC uses when working with the ECtHR's rulings. Figure 5.14 shows categories of *how the reference is used*, which we introduced in Chapter 4. Obviously, due to the legal competences of the SC, the very first category, invalidation of a legal norm, is missing, as only the CC has the competence of concrete judicial review. The remaining categories were identified as present.

Perhaps the most influential and interesting from a conceptual point of view is the primacy – i.e., the direct application – of principles in the ECtHR's case law, which sets aside national legal provision or previous practice of Czech courts. The SC applied the principle of primacy to approximately 4.2 percent of its references, most notably in the last decade (2008 on). The majority of these references relate to compensatory proceedings, either for the violation of a procedural branch of the right to life[32] or unjust detention.[33]

One more notion should be raised when discussing this technique. On principle, the direct application of an international norm might be in conflict with the CC's *Euro-amendment* judgment.[34] In this judgment, the CC constitutionalized the Convention, by which it attempted to cement its position as a sole reviewer of domestic norms and international human rights provisions and push the general judiciary to refer all such cases to it. Nevertheless, the judgment is not strictly followed by the SC, as doing so would, according to the SC, essentially only prolong the proceedings (Filip 2002; Kühn and Kysela 2002; Pospíšil 2016; Svobodová 2017). Although, all in all, very few SC rulings

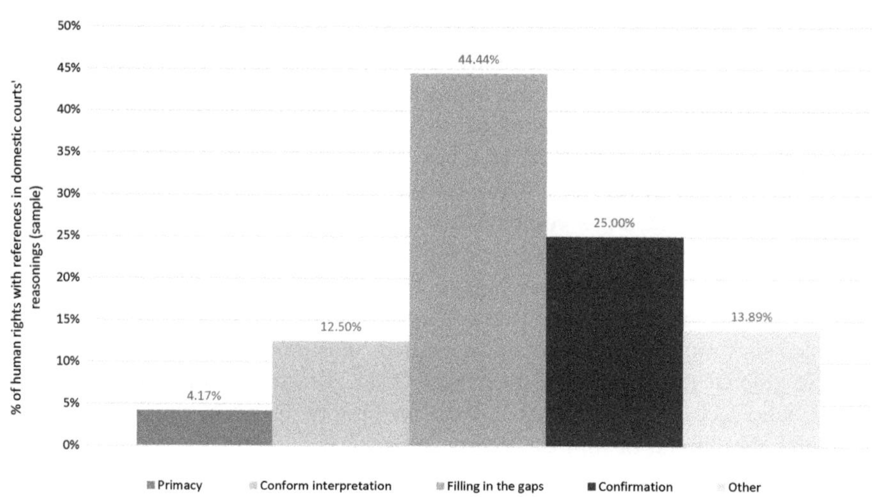

Figure 5.14 Legal techniques employed when using ECtHR case law substantively.
Source: authors.

employ the strategy of a direct effect, this technique still led to some of the most interesting and breakthrough cases in its jurisprudence, which we will explain in more detail in the micro-level analysis.

Conforming interpretation – i.e., harmonious interpretation – is a legal technique that has been employed by the SC perhaps for the longest time. Substantively, its strength and effect towards domestic legal norms is of a similar intensity to a direct application, as the Court often shifts the established decision practice and opts for an interpretation that is in harmony with the Convention and principles derived by the Strasbourg Court. This category represents around 12.5 percent of the substantively used ECtHR references. Despite a comparatively low number, the SC significantly modified the interpretation of the Insolvency Act[35] and committed the Czech courts to follow conditions on when to initiate insolvency proceedings according to the ECtHR judgment *E v. the Czech Republic.*[36] In contrast, the SC rarely applies the ECtHR case law directly. Some of the few exceptions appeared in ground-breaking cases where individual SC judges intentionally used the Convention and ECtHR to push through a substantive change in the domestic legal provisions. Some of the few examples can be found in the area of property restitutions or rehabilitations of unjustly detained individuals; we return to these cases in Section 5.3.

The most frequently used technique is "filling in the gaps"; i.e., clarification of domestic norms either where they did not cover a new social situation or overlooked a certain aspect. Here, the SC typically draws inspiration from various tests of violation developed by the ECtHR, particularly in the justification of a violation of private life and freedom of speech. This category represents 44.5 percent of all substantively used references and demonstrates how well the new principles developed by the ECtHR are already embedded in the SC's reasoning. It is this technique which illustrates the subsidiarity in the character of the ECtHR's reasoning and principles the best and therefore deserves more attention also in the micro level of our analysis.

Confirmation is another technique that has been employed from the very beginning of the use of ECtHR case law. It holds to 25 percent and primarily covers cases in which the SC confirmed that the status quo of the Czech legal norms and jurisprudence is compatible with the ECtHR's interpretation of the Convention and there is no violation of the Convention rights. It is quite surprising that his category has the second highest representation (although the SAC, for example, reaches an even higher number) and is used almost twice as often as, for example, conform interpretation. This perhaps illustrates the best internalization and the gradual rising perception of the ECtHR as a legitimate actor by the SC judges, who feel the need to refer to the Strasbourg Court in those cases which delineate the limits of human rights protection. Given the sparing use of substantive techniques in the 1990s and early 2000s, this technique has been gaining dominance, especially in recent years. This correlates with the SC finding its voice and confidence in the implementation of Convention. On one hand, the SC uses the invocation of ECtHR references to demonstrate the borders of human rights protection, while on the other, it fosters its argument that the existing practice and case law do not violate human rights. The ECtHR reference can then also serve as another layer of legitimacy argument in case of the constitutional review of the SC's rulings (Kratochvíl 2019).

Finally, the category "Other" (13.9 percent) relates mostly to those cases where the SC distinguished the case at hand from the ECtHR's ruling referred by one of the parties to proceedings. The majority of these cases relate to the length of proceedings, where the SC refused a simplified implementation of ECtHR findings. Typically, claimants approached the SC with references to various ECtHR rulings, arguing that Article 6 as interpreted by Strasbourg Court sets a concrete time limit to the due length of proceedings. The SC refused such a simplified implementation of ECtHR rulings and stressed that conditions on the length of proceedings developed by Strasbourg Court have to be considered in the overall context and complexity of the case. The length of proceedings has to be evaluated in every individual case. The SC therefore distinguished respective proceedings from ECtHR cases, stressing that the number of months spent by court proceedings is not on its own a sufficient condition.

5.3 From meso to micro level: From compliance to judicial war on interpretation

The meso-level analysis revealed the major patterns of using the case law of the ECtHR in the reasoning of the SC. On a meso level, it seems that the SC almost always follows ECtHR case law, predominantly using the references to adjust or add something new to existing domestic legal norms. Only recently has a more frequent use of the references as a "blessing" argument, confirming the compliance of the Czech law and domestic general courts' reasoning with the ECtHR, started to prevail. We already suggested that initially the SC used the tactic of cherry-picking the references in those instances when it wanted to overcome the existing case law and doctrinal approaches. The micro-level question then stands as to what were the motives behind the spare but ground-breaking rulings implementing ECtHR case law.

This section therefore zeroes in on those areas which were most significantly affected by the Strasbourg Court's case law. It contextualizes the crucial SC's rulings and attempts to uncover its motives when pushing forward a specific conclusion. In order to shed more light on the most important patterns identified in the meso-level analysis, the micro-level analysis examines those areas of the SC's case law that were most substantially challenged due to the ECtHR rulings. In particular, two explosive issues, the direct use of Article 5 and the blessing argument with Article 4 of the Protocol No. 7, are explored in more detail. The micro level shows strategic choices adopted by the SC and searches for agents of change in the old, conservative, and only slowly reforming judicial institution.

5.3.1 Article 5: Courts in a war over how direct the application should be

Although references to Strasbourg case law interpreting Article 5 do not represent the numeral majority of the SC's work with ECtHR rulings, they surely introduced some of the most controversial changes in the Czech legal order, both in judicial and subsequently legal sphere. As previously mentioned, references related to Article 5[37] represent some of the most strategic cases where the SC judges over-ruled existing legislative norms, and even the CC's practice, through the direct application of Convention provisions and the ECtHR's rulings.

5.3.1.1 Immaterial damage for detention: Substituting the legislator

At the beginning of the 1990s, the SC held a rather conservative and pessimistic (perhaps also condescending) view of the ECtHR case law and international human rights norms in general. Judges who suddenly had to take into account not only the authoritative position of the CC, but also various international judicial bodies, struggled with the loss of their authoritative voice. All the more, the ECtHR as well as the CC attempted to push the SC to consider fundamental rights and principles, a whole new world for a previously extremely formalistic institution. The compliance of the SC was therefore hard-born. It took the Court over 18 years to confirm the supremacy and direct effect of the Convention as the international human rights treaty.[38]

The breakthrough case, a judgment of the Grand Chamber of the Civil and Commercial Division,[39] rose from a claim of an appellant demanding the state pay compensation for the immaterial damage which he suffered due to an unjust detention. The appellant, accused of extortion, was put into detention in October 2000, found guilty by the district court in April 2001, and sentenced to 3.5 years in prison. The convicting ruling was later quashed by the CC, yet the appellant was once again taken into a custody in February 2002. In 2005, the courts acquitted the appellant and considered awarding him compensation for immaterial damage in line with Article 31a, Paragraphs 1 and 2 of the State Liability Act.[40] Nevertheless, provision Article 31a was introduced into the Act only in 2006 and allowed for retroactive consideration only for those claims that arose from maladministration (decision of administrative authorities delivered belatedly). In other words, the immaterial damages according to State Liability Act did not cover the case of the appellant, whose detention happened several years before the introduction of the respective provision into the Act. After failing at lower instances, the case finally reached the SC, where it was originally assigned to one of its most rigid and conservative panels. Yet before the panel managed to settle the case and refuse the claim on the basis of retroactivity, a different panel adopted a conflicting conclusion in a factually similar case, finding that irrespective of domestic provisions, the right to compensation for immaterial damage is also contained in the Convention and that immaterial damage can be awarded through the direct application of Article 5(5). As the conservative panel wished to overrule this finding, which stepped outside of most SC panels' comfort zone, the case had to be presented to the SC's Grand Chamber, which, surprisingly, adopted a very pro-international human rights law approach.

The Grand Chamber first used the leverage of the CC's case law, which had already confirmed the direct applicability of Article 5(5) in the Czech legal order.[41] Referring also to the case law of the ECtHR,[42] the Grand Chamber confirmed the existence of the immaterial damage claim within the scope of the Convention and confirmed the obligation of every domestic court to comply, and, in case of a conflict with domestic provisions, to apply Article 5(5) directly.[43] The line of the Grand Chamber arguments began with the CC, the ECtHR's rulings against Czechia, and a plethora of other ECtHR rulings[44] explaining the conditions which establish the claim to immaterial damage under Article 5. Finally, the SC also supported its new interpretation of immaterial damage claims with literature, particularly the Czech commentary on the Convention (Hubálková 2003).

Although the SC first started its arguments with references to the CC, the CC's rulings serve as a mere introduction to and preparation for the big argument: the direct effect of Article 5(5) as interpreted by the Strasbourg Court. From a factual point of view, the judgment of the Grant Chamber had limited impact. The 2006 amendment of the State Liability Act already introduced immaterial damages into its wording, and retroactive, controversial cases were bound to eventually disappear (Kosař and Petrov 2018). Yet, the conclusion of the Grand Chamber had tremendous impact on the overall jurisprudence of the SC. The deed was done. The SC, by an internally binding ruling of its own Grand Chamber, acknowledged that some Convention provisions, as well as principles delivered by the ECtHR, are directly applicable. That was the point of no return. Conservative members of the Court could not go back to pretending that the international human rights law is of no relevance to the SC.

It is worth mentioning that the composition of the panels played a huge role in delivering this finding. The Grand Chamber ruling was assigned to the President of the Court, Iva Brožová, who previously served as a constitutional judge and who faced huge opposition from the conservative camp of the SC judges in her attempts to introduce a constitutional focus and constitutional principles into the SC's decision-making. Moreover, the Grand Chamber ruling drew heavily from analyses of its relatively newly established Analytical Department.

5.3.1.2 The immaterial damage of communist political prisoners: Constraining the Constitutional Court

The Grand Chamber ruling was, however, only a mild example of the potential resting in the Article 5. The real explosive case came only later and threw the SC into a years-long judicial battle with the CC. A relatively large number of cases in which the domestic courts struggled with awarding immaterial damages related to communist crimes and rehabilitation of political prisoners of the 1950s;[45] i.e., the most repressive era of Czechoslovak communism. Many political prisoners, or prisoners of conscience, were people who refused compulsory military service, mostly based on religious reasons. The criminal convictions of these political prisoners were overturned by Czech military courts immediately after the Velvet Revolution, first only by changing the rulings so no punishment was rendered, and later, around 2007, by quashing and invalidating any sort of conviction. Nevertheless, similarly to the previous situation, the rehabilitation Act did not cover compensation for immaterial damage caused by an illegal decision.

The core of the dispute between the Supreme and Constitutional court turned out to be the temporal application of the Convention. While the SC claimed that the damages as such occurred in the 1950s, and therefore they could not justify the application of the Convention, which became binding on the Czech Republic only from 18 March 1992 when the Czech Republic ratified the Convention,[46] the CC, on the contrary, advocated the retroactive use of the Convention principles.[47]

The dispute between the courts took several years to resolve (Hadamčík 2015). The CC did not agree, and quashed down rulings of the SC as "foozling" and "failing to recognize which legal norm should be applied", or "resigning on its role to find justice and unify decision-making practice of Czech courts".[48] While in the very first rulings, the SC settled on a mere interpretation of the Convention article, the quarrel with the CC challenged the SC to work with ECtHR case law in a more detailed and nuanced way. The CC directly bound the SC with its opinion that Article 5(5) should be directly applied to compensate for immaterial damage caused by unjust decisions of the communist era.

Yet the SC refused such an interpretation of the Convention[49] and used the ECtHR case law to demonstrate that the Convention could not establish a material claim for damages suffered by an individual before its ratification,[50] as any other interpretation of the *ratione temporis* would go against the intent of Article 1 ECHR and violate established ECtHR case law.[51] Furthermore, the SC pointed out that compensation is a political choice of the democratically elected legislature and courts should not arbitrarily substitute and amend such a decision by an extreme interpretation of Czech international human rights commitments.[52] In light of the SC argumentation and ECtHR case law, the CC eventually changed its line of reasoning and stated that the crimes of communism against political prisoners should be interpreted as if the violation ceased only once the Act on the judicial habilitation was adopted by the Parliament; i.e., after the Czech Republic committed to the Convention.[53] The Plenary of the CC even admitted that by an overreaching interpretation of the Convention, it had created an unjust dual-tracked situation which could foster the legitimate expectations of petitioners (Kühn 2018).

Both above-mentioned instances of the use of references to ECtHR case law relate to immaterial damage and the liability of a state; i.e., a sensitive political question related directly to the state budget. The examples point to two findings about the SC's compliance with the ECtHR:

1. In the first case, the SC used the direct-effect technique to shift the political line, substituted for the legislature, and put forward individual rights. Moreover, Article 5(5) offered a platform to change the position towards the Convention and its effect inside the Court itself.
2. In the second case, the SC adopted a more constrained interpretation and refused to bind the legislature further than the international and domestic legal commitments of the Czech Republic went.

Such an approach corresponds with the self-constrained role of the apex court, which should not push the domestic legislation beyond the explicit commitments stemming from international human rights treaties. The SC used the ECtHR case law to show that the Convention cannot be applied outside of the *ratione temporis* and attempted, on the other hand, to constrain the over-arching interpretation of the CC, which substituted for the legislature. It therefore seems that the SC is willing to substitute domestic legal provisions with international human rights commitments and comply directly with the ECtHR, but it is also very careful about not going beyond the minimal and necessary conditions and obligations set by the Strasbourg Court on domestic authorities.

5.3.2 *Article 4 of the Protocol No. 7: Playing hide-and-seek with the ECtHR*

Another contested area concerns the *ne bis in idem* principle and the ECtHR case law related to Article 4 of the Protocol No. 7 to the Convention. The domestic courts were not in an easy position when it came to complying with the Strasbourg Court take on the *ne bis in idem* principle, as the ECtHR changed and shifted its interpretation and requirements placed on member states' courts four times. Although the *ne bis in idem* principle is an inherent part of the Czech legal order, the issue arose whether to interpret it as prohibiting the duality in the *bis* (identified crime) or the *idem* (facts) aspect. Between 1995 and 2001, the Strasbourg Court issued three major rulings – *Gradinger v. Austria*,[54] *Oliveria v. Switzerland*,[55] and *Franz Fischer v. Austria*[56] – slowly changing the interpretation of the principle from the duality of the committed act, irrespective of the criminal classification, to the duality of crime, and back (Trechsel 2005; van Bockel 2010; Gerards and Glas 2017). The conflicting case law obviously called for unification. This came in the famous *Zolotukhin* judgment, which took a step back to the original practice applied in *Gradinger*. *Zolotukhin* was perhaps the closest to the original standpoint of the Czech criminal legal theory, as well as to the approach of the Criminal Division of the SC.

Nevertheless, the *Zolotukhin* judgment also opened up a new can of worms by raising the question of the concurrence of an administrative offence and a crime. The SC first issued a breakthrough judgment on this topic in 2004,[57] when it concluded that the *ne bis in idem* principle could potentially cover such a concurrence, using a harmonious interpretation of the criminal procedural code with Article 4 of the Protocol No. 7 and its interpretation in all three of the above-mentioned ECtHR cases. Interestingly, even before the unification of the ECtHR's views by *Zolotukhin*, the SC concluded that the settled case law clearly suggests that the *ne bis in idem* principle is not limited to criminal proceedings. The SC therefore first inclined to the duality of the *bis* element, finding that criminal prosecution for the act which was already subjected to proceedings as an administrative offence violates the *ne bis in idem* principle as interpreted by the ECtHR.[58]

The judgment was widely criticized by both practitioners and scholars as misinterpreting the ECtHR case law.[59] The SC, however, remained predominantly open to the idea that, in some cases, a concurrence of criminal and administrative proceedings may contradict the *ne bis in idem* principle, referring to other ECtHR judgments. It accepted the autonomous interpretation of the criminal limb of Article 6 ECHR offered by the ECtHR. It also repeatedly reminded that those states that disagreed with such a broad understanding of the *ne bis in idem* principle entered reservations to the Protocol No. 7. As this was not the case of the Czech Republic, Article 4 and its interpretation by the ECtHR remained binding for the Czech courts.[60] Afterwards, the SC used the *Zolotukhin* reference repeatedly, reinterpreting and introducing the principles and test of *ne bis in idem* into the Czech legal order.[61]

The next judgment of the ECtHR on the *ne bis in idem* principle steered the Czech discussion on compliance even more. In the *Lucky Dev* judgment,[62] the ECtHR stretched the *ne bis in idem* principle to the concurrence of tax proceedings and criminal offences. The *Lucky Dev* judgment led to repeated seminars and workshops and internal discussions among the SC judges, as well as to attempts to consolidate the approach together with the SAC. Traditionally, both Czech legal scholarship and the SC case law considered the *ne bis in idem* to be a principle that guided only criminal proceedings, and not tax proceedings before administrative authorities. *Lucky Dev* challenged this approach. Eventually, both apex courts respected the ECtHR findings,[63] consulting together on how to proceed with the line of argumentation. The SC finally found a harmonious interpretation of the *Lucky Dev* results with provisions of Czech law, although we might argue that the attempt to use the conforming harmonious interpretation stretched the domestic jurisprudence and theory very far.

Problems with the implementation of the *ne bis in idem* principle also continued outside the time scope of our analysis. It is worth mentioning that the conflicting case law of the ECtHR and the changing interpretation of the principle raised doubts among the SC judges and became a source of criticism and challenges towards the Strasbourg Court. Many criminal judges started pointing out more coherent and better reasoned interpretations of the principle existing in the Czech law and older jurisprudence of the SC. In January 2017, the Criminal Division of the SC decided a similar case on the duality of tax and criminal sanction in the Grand Chamber, reflecting both the latest case law of the ECtHR and the Czech Supreme Administrative Court concerning the same legal question.[64]

In particular, the Grand Chamber unified the practice with a conform interpretation of domestic provisions with the newest ECtHR Grand Chamber judgment, *A and B v. Norway*,[65] in which the ECtHR clarified the principles which should be used to analyze the character of the tax sanction and the character of the crime. The Strasbourg Court stressed the test of material and time scope of the crime: (1) whether the tax sanctions were of a criminal character, (2) whether the prosecuted crime was the same as the one sanctioned by tax, (3) whether there is a material and time relation between the tax and the criminal proceedings (i.e., whether it constituted one reaction of the state towards the petitioners' actions). The SC first explained the facts of the *A and B v. Norway* judgment in detail and then proceeded with the application of the ECtHR's test on the case at hand, implementing the same finding. If the duality of proceedings (the *bis* element) was legitimate and predictable for claimants who did not suffer inference into their rights due to this duality, the principle of *ne bis in idem* was not violated.

We should also mention that the seemingly fluent and non-problematic compliance with the ECtHR's findings (the SC usually interpreted the ECtHR's case law as stable and constant, although this was hardly true), was complicated by different interpretations of the *ne bis in idem* question by the ECtHR and the CJEU (van Bockel 2010, 2017). The *ne bis in idem* became a part of the CJEU's focus, especially after the introduction of the EU Charter of Fundamental Rights into the primary law by the 2009 Lisbon Treaty.[66]

Playing hide-and-seek with two European courts that continuously shift the boundaries of the *ne bis in idem* principle, the SC had to repeatedly change its position.[67] Although not always agreeing with the ECtHR, it always managed to comply, using a harmonious interpretation, very promptly. The leading judge in delivering the *ne bis in idem* judgments was the current President of the SC Pavel Šámal, a professor of criminal law and a leading figure in Czech criminal law theory.

5.4 Conclusion

The Czech Supreme Court illustrates the transformation of communist judicial authority and its stance towards the Convention and the ECtHR. Initially, the SC started from a very different position than the younger SAC or the CC. Compared to them, the SC lived through the Velvet Revolution as an almost untouched institution, composed of judges trained in communist formalism. The change of regime in 1989 and the subsequent entry into the Council of Europe therefore brought very new challenges for the SC's style of work and reasoning.

Its story tells us more about how to push forward judicial use of the ECtHR case law (and hence foster judicial compliance) in transitioning countries. Although the SC had a rather slow, laid-back start in the 1990s, it eventually caught up with the ECtHR and uses its case law rather frequently. The breaking points in the treatment of the ECtHR typically followed after some external nudges; i.e., coming outside the SC itself. One of the most important impulses was the gradual change of the SC judicial bench. The appointment of new judges coming from the CC slowly but steadily introduced human rights language to at least some rulings and internal judges' discussions. Two court presidents in a row, Eliška Wagnerová (1998–2001) and Iva Brožová (2001–2015), entered the SC from the former position of CC judges (Blisa and Kosař 2018). The Analytical Department established in 2005 helped to speed up the learning curve of sitting SC judges through internal trainings. Moreover, it also serves as a safety check on the international-law-oriented rulings published in the Collection. Furthermore, delegation of judges from the SC to international organizations proved to be of importance. SC judge Robert Fremr, current Vice-president of the International Criminal Court, maintains a very close contact with his former Criminal Division colleagues who regularly visit international judicial institutions and are exposed to discussions on new international case law. Similarly, newly appointed younger judges, coming to the SC with international education and good language skills, proved to be more inclined to apply the Convention and ECtHR rulings. In this respect, we found that SC panels with the youngest judges are the most active when it comes to referring to the ECtHR.

Older judges, on the contrary, remain reluctant. They are willing to apply the ECtHR's findings only once these are (a) confirmed and re-interpreted by domestic courts as fitted for the Czech legal audience (references to domestic judgments rather than to ECtHR), (b) translated and commented on by domestic scholarship (language, lectures, and education matter a lot), and (c) when the ECtHR's case law is extensively raised by the parties to the proceedings, even though some SC panels still sometimes fail to address the ECtHR arguments brought by parties.

When it comes to the overall trends in the SC's use of references to the ECtHR, we can observe two conflicting results. On one hand, it seems that the SC still rather often opts for a cherry-picking approach, referring to the ECtHR when it needs creative inspiration and when the ECtHR's reasoning fits its position (although the tendency seems to be gradually disappearing with confirmation and filling-the-holes techniques prevailing). The differences between substantive and ornamental use of references is not as profound as with other Czech apex courts. Yet, on the other hand, quite a large proportion of substantive references is represented by confirmation of the Czech practice in cases where the SC does not find a violation of Convention rights. This suggests that the ECtHR is becoming entrenched as a legitimate authority, even though the process of penetration of ECtHR case law to day-to-day decision-making practice took more than a decade.

So, what lessons can we derive based on the SC experience for other jurisdictions transitioning and acceding to international human rights regimes? The changes happen only gradually, when supported by various nudges coming from different institutions. National actors, the CC in particular, but also the activity of the Government Agent representing Czechia before the ECtHR, matter a lot. The Government Agent in Czechia was a particularly active actor, keeping close contacts with apex courts judges, promoting the ECtHR case law workshops and trainings, and organizing various round tables. The change on the judicial bench is crucial; but so is accessibility of information: Spreading the knowledge of the ECtHR and its case law, in terms of both translations and access online, proved to be of utmost importance. Various university or judicial academy training sessions on the ECtHR also helped to diffuse information on the domestic level. This brings us to repeat Madsen, Cebulak, and Wiebusch (2018) claim on the need to distinguish between different forms of courts' resistance to international bodies. With the SC, representing the old conservative judicial institution, it shows that the resistance due to the lack of knowledge and information on the ECtHR proved to be most dangerous and harmful in terms of the SC's attitude towards the Strasbourg. The good news is, however, that this type of resistance can be quite easily overcome through better interaction, accessibility of case law, and a promotion of knowledge about the ECtHR.

Notes

1 The Supreme Administrative Court was established only in 2003. Nevertheless, the personal choices as well as approach to legal principles reflect the narrative of the "new court", unburdened by a communist legacy.

2 By an Act of November 1918. Interestingly, contrary to the current position of the SC and Supreme Administrative Court, it was the first Czechoslovak Supreme Court that freely implemented and applied international law, while the Supreme Administrative Court of the first republic refused the direct application of any international treaties (Mikeš 2012).

3 Supreme Court of Czechoslovakia, no. R I 488/25, judgement of 16 July 1925.

4 SC, no. Skno 1/94, decision of 31 August 1994.

5 The SC nowadays decides on civil, commercial, and criminal matters in proceedings on extraordinary appeal, nullity, or renewal of proceedings. Up until 2002, its jurisdiction also covered administrative matters.

6 No. 21 Cdo 1009/98, judgment of 21 October 1998, later published as R 39/1999.

7 ECtHR, *Kopp v. Switzerland*, no. 23224/94, judgment of 25 March 1998.

8 ECtHR, *Halford v. the United Kingdom*, no. 20605/92, judgment of 25 June 1997.

9 ECtHR, *A. v. France*, no. 14838/89, judgment of 23 November 1993.

10 *Přehled rozsudků Evropského soudu pro lidská práva [Review of European Court of Human Rights rulings]*, 2/1998.

11 Interview with an SC judge, 11 December 2018 and 18 December 2018. Interestingly, at the beginning of the 2010s, the SC judges who specialized in international human rights law and the Strasbourg human rights system were alienated within the Court.

12 SC [GC], no 31 Cdo 3916/2008, judgment of 11 May 2011.

13 The Collection of Rulings and Opinions of the Supreme Court; i.e., the most important rulings are issued by the SC annually.
14 The substantive influence of references in other than Czech cases is marginally lower by approximately 5 percent.
15 ECtHR [GC], *Apicella v. Italy*, no. 64890/01, judgment of 29 March 2006.
16 ECtHR, *Eckle v. Germany*, no. 8130/78, judgment of 15 July 1982.
17 ECtHR [GC], *Zolotukhin v. Russia*, no. 14939/03, judgment of 10 February 2009.
18 It is worth reminding the reader that the meso analysis uses individual rights as the units. For details on methodology, see Chapter 4.
19 Results based on the analysis of our sample. All meso-level figures analyze only references in reasonings of SC rulings.
20 The meso-level figure is constructed out of the sample, not the whole population of rulings.
21 SC decision of 17 December 2014.
22 ECtHR, *Golha v. the Czech Republic*, no. 7051/06, judgment of 26 May 2011.
23 See also ruling no. 3 Tdo 260/2007, decision of 21 March 2007, or no. 30 Cdo 24/2016, judgment of 20 December 2016.
24 For example, no. 30 Cdo 5172/2015, decision of 18 May 2016.
25 Interview with a former SC judge, 4 January 2019.
26 SC judgment of 13 December 2012.
27 ECtHR [GC], *D.H. and Others v. the Czech Republic*, no. 57325/00, judgment of 13 November 2007.
28 One example is Judgment no. 29 Cdo 2012/2010 of 31 May 2012 (maladministration during insolvency proceedings) in which the SC referred to its older case law (R 58/2011), which had already cited ECtHR jurisprudence.
29 See, for example, no. 5 Tdo 326/2014, decision of 24 September 2014; no. 30 Cdo 3964/2010, judgment of 31 August 2011; no. Tpjn 300/2016, opinion of 26 October 2016; etc.
30 See, for example, no. 30 Cdo 1290/2014, judgment of 16 September 2015, or no. 3 Tdo 260/2007, judgment of 21 March 2007.
31 Most famously in case *D.H. and Others v. the Czech Republic*. See also Smekal and Šipulová 2014.
32 SC, no. 28 Cdo 2789/2012, judgment of 9 January 2013.
33 Direct application of Article 5 § 5 in SC judgment no. 30 Cdo 2357/2010 of 11 January 2012.
34 CC, no. Pl. ÚS 36/01, judgment of 25 June 2002.
35 Act No. 328/1991 Coll.
36 ECtHR, *E v. the Czech Republic*, no. 49962/92, judgment of 5 July 2005.
37 Detention and particularly compensation for unjust detention, Article 5(5).
38 SC [GC], no. 31 Cdo 3916/2008, judgment of 11 May 2011. See also Section 5.2.
39 SC [GC], no. 31 Cdo 3916/2008, judgment of 11 May 2011.
40 Act No. 82/1998 Coll., on the liability of the state for damage caused by a decision of a public authority or maladministration.
41 CC, no. IV. ÚS 162/04, decision of 25 May 2005.
42 See *Smatana v. the Czech Republic*, no. 18642/04, judgment of 27 September 2007; *Crabtree v. the Czech Republic*, no. 41116/04, judgment of 25 February 2010; *Žirovnický v. the Czech Republic*, no. 23661/03, judgment of 30 September 2010.
43 It is worth noting that such an important first conclusion contains only a very broad and generic reference to ECtHR case law, without mentioning a particular case.
44 For example, *Wassink v. Netherlands*, no. 12535/86, judgment of 27 September 1990.
45 Act No. 119/1990 Coll. on the judicial rehabilitation.
46 See, for example, no. 30 Cdo 1614/2009, judgment of 8 September 2010.

47 The CC's argumentation eventually shifted, arguing that the Convention articles are not applied retroactively, but the claim to damages emerged not with unlawful conduct, but with the rehabilitation act of the 1990s which found the imprisonment to be in violation of the fundamental rights and principles of the new democratic Constitution. See, for example, no. I. ÚS 3438/11, judgment of 23 May 2012.
48 CC, no. I. ÚS 3438/11, judgment of 23 May 2012.
49 SC, no. 30 Cdo 2916/2012, judgment of 29 May 2013.
50 SC, no. 30 Cdo 1770/2012, judgment of 24 April 2013; no. 30 Cdo 1663/2012, judgment of 12 June 2013.
51 The SC referred to both ECtHR case law (*Blečić v. Croatia*, no. 59532/00, judgment of 8 March 2006, § 70; *Šilih v. Slovenia*, no. 71463/01, judgment of 9 April 2009, § 140; *Varnava and Others v. Turkey*, nos. 16064/90; 16065/90; 16066/90; 16068/90; 16069/90; 16070/90; 16071/90; 16072/90 and 16073/90, judgment of 18 September 2009, § 130; *Kopecký v. Slovakia*, no. 44912/98, judgment of 28 September 2004, § 38; *Bořánková v. the Czech Republic,* no. 41486/98, judgment of 7 January 2003) and academic literature.
52 It is worth noting that the legislature did consider the possibility of retroactively awarding immaterial damages, introduced only in 2006, for the past violations caused by unlawful decisions of public authorities. The Act 82/1992 includes a sentence allowing retroactive compensation for immaterial damage caused by maladministration. (The amendment was a follow-up to the SC decisions; for example, no. 2 Cdon 804/96 of 24 June 1999 and no. 25 Cdo 38/2000, of 8 February 2001). Nevertheless, the legislature did not cover damages caused by unlawful decisions, but merely referred to the Convention, Article 5 as a guideline for evaluating the length of proceedings (see also no. 30 Cdo 1337/2010, judgment of 20 October 2010).
53 CC [Plenary], no. Pl. ÚS-st 39/14, judgment of 25 November 2014.
54 ECtHR, *Gradinger v. Austria*, no. 15963/90, judgment of 23 October 1995.
55 ECtHR, *Oliveria v. Switzerland*, no. 25711/94, judgment of 30 July 1998.
56 ECtHR, *Franz Fischer v. Austria*, no. 27569/02, judgment of 29 May 2001.
57 SC, no. 11 Tdo 738/2003, judgment of 22 July 2004.
58 SC, no. 11 Tdo 738/2003, judgment of 22 July 2004.
59 See Gřivna and Sekvard (2005, 98) and Růžička and Polák (2005, 12).
60 SC, no. 5 Tdo 1399/2007, decision of 12 December 2007.
61 SC, no. 6 Tdo 1478/2009, decision of 27 May 2010.
62 ECtHR, *Lucky Dev v. Sweden*, no. 7356/10, judgment of 27 November 2014.
63 SAC [GC], no. 4 Afs 210/2014-2057, decision of 24 November 2015; SC [GC], no. 15 Tdo 832/2016, decision of 4 January 2017.
64 SC [GC], no. 15 Tdo 832/2016, decision of 4 January 2017.
65 *A and B v. Norway* [GC], nos. 24130/11 and 29758/11, judgment of 15 November 2016.
66 Back in 2013, the CJEU [GC] issued a ground-breaking ruling *Åkerberg Fransson* (no. C-617/10, judgment of 26 February 2013) stating the obligation of EU member states to prosecute tax offences, either through tax proceedings or criminal proceedings. Even more importantly, the CJEU introduced a three-step test for the national courts to consider whether the proceedings and sanctions have criminal character (legal qualification, the character of the offence, and the strength of the sanction). Later on, this had to be amended after another shift in the ECtHR's approach (*A and B v. Norway*: the concurrence is not against *ne bis in idem*, if there is enough linkage between material and time of both proceedings).
67 Lastly in another Grand Chamber decision, no. 15 Tdo 832/2016 of 4 January 2017.

References

Blažková, Kristina. 2016. "Právo na efektivní vyšetřování: dochází na třetím ústavním soudu k výrazné změně v koncepci ochrany základních práv? [Right to an Effective Investigation: Is the Approach to Constitutional Rights by the Third Constitutional Court Changing significantly?]" *Jurisprudence* 2016 (5): 3–14.

Blisa, Adam, and David Kosař. 2018. "Court Presidents: The Missing Piece in the Puzzle of Judicial Governance". *German Law Journal* 19 (7): 2031–76.

Bobek, Michal, and David Kosař. 2010. "The Application of European Union Law and the Law of the European Convention of Human Rights in the Czech Republic and Slovakia: An Overview". In *The National Judicial Treatment of the ECHR and EU Laws. A Comparative Constitutional Perspective*, edited by Giuseppe Martinico and Oreste Pollicino, 117–50. Groningen: Europa Law Publishing.

Čapek, Jan. 1995a. *Evropský soud a Evropská komise pro lidská práva [The European Court and European Commission for Human Rights]*. Prague: Linde.

Čapek, Jan. 1995b. "Z rozhodnutí Evropského soudu a Evropské komise pro lidská práva/ Ochrana soukromého a rodinného života, obydlí a korespondence/- část VII [From the Case Law of the European Court and European Commission for Human Rights/The Protection of Private and Family life, Home and correspondence/Part VII]." *Právní Praxe* 1995 (7): 430–32.

Filip, Jan. 2002. "Nález Č. 403/2002 Sb. jako rukavice hozená ústavodárci ÚS [Judgment No. 403/2002 Coll. As a Challenge for the legislator]." *Právní zpravodaj* 2002 (11): 11–24.

Gerards, Janneke, and Lize R. Glas. 2017. "Access to Justice in the European Convention on Human Rights System". *Netherlands Quarterly of Human Rights* 35 (1): 11–30.

Gřivna, Tomáš, and Ondřej Sekvard. 2005. "Nový pohled Nejvyššího soudu na zásade ne bis in idem? [A New View of the Supreme Court on the Ne bis in Idem Principle?]" *Právní Fórum* 2005 (3): 98–103.

Hadamčík, Lukáš. 2015. "Náhrada nemajetkové újmy osob věžněných v době nesvobody [The Compensation of Immaterial Damages for the Persons Imprisoned during the Age of Communism]." *Právní rozhledy* 23 (6): 214–18.

Hubálková, Eva. 2003. *Evropská úmluva o lidských právech a Česká republika [European Convention on Human Rights and the Czech Republic]*. Prague: Linde.

Kmec, Jiří, David Kosař, Jan Kratochvíl, and Michal Bobek, eds. 2012. *Evropská úmluva o lidských právech: komentář [European Convention on Human Rights: A Commentary]*. Prague: C.H. Beck.

Kosař, David, and Jan Petrov. 2018. "Determinants of Compliance Difficulties among 'good Compliers': Implementation of International Human Rights Rulings in the Czech Republic". *The European Journal of International Law* 29 (2): 397–425.

Kratochvíl, Jan. 2019. "Subsidiarity of Human Rights in Practice: The Relationship between the Constitutional Court and Lower Courts in Czechia". *Netherlands Quarterly of Human Rights* 37 (1): 69–84.

Kühn, Zdeněk. 2005. "K otázce závaznosti rozhodnutí Evropského soudu pro lidská práva pro domácí soudnictví [On the Binding Effect of ECtHR Case Law on Domestic Judiciary]." *Právní Rozhledy* 13 (1): 1–7.

Kühn, Zdeněk. 2009. "Socialistická justice [Socialist Judiciary]." In *Komunistické právo v Československu: kapitoly z dějin bezpráví [Communist Law in Czechoslovakia: Chapters from the History of Injustice]*, edited by Vojtěch Šimíček, Pavel Molek and Michal Bobek, 822–47. Brno: Masaryk University.

Kühn, Zdeněk. 2011. *The Judiciary in Central and Eastern Europe: Mechanical Jurisprudence in Transformation?* Leiden: Martinus Nijhoff Publishers.

Kühn, Zdeněk. 2018. "Case Law and Precedent in Continental and Anglo-American Law." In *Binding Effect of Judicial Decisions – National and International Perspectives*, edited by Pavel Šámal, Guido Raimondi, and Koen Lenaerts, 31–48. Prague: Wolters Kluwer – Supreme Court.

Kühn, Zdeněk, and Jan Kysela. 2002. "Euronovela Ústavy ve světle překvapivého nálezu Ústavního soudu č. 403/2002 Sb [Euro-amendment of the Czech Constitution in Light of a Surprising Constitutional Court's Judgment No. 403/2002]". *Soudní rozhledy* 2002 (12): 421.

Madsen, Mikael Rask, Pola Cebulak, and Micha Wiebusch. 2018. "Resistance to International Courts". *International Journal of Law in Context* 14 (Special Issue 2): 193–96.

Majerčík, Lubomír. 2016. "Czech Republic: Strasbourg Court Undisputed." In *Criticism of the European Court of Human Rights*, edited by Patricia Popelier, Sarah Lambrecht, and Koen Lemmens, 131–52. Cambridge: Intersentia.

Mikeš, Petr. 2012. *Aplikace mezinárodního práva v právním řádu ČR pohledem teorie a soudní praxe [Application of International Law in Legal Order of the Czech Republic from the Point of View of Theory and Practice]*. Prague: Wolters Kluwer.

Motejl, Otakar. 2009. Soudnictví a jeho správa [Judiciary and Its administration]." In *Komunistické právo v Československu: kapitoly z dějin bezpráví [Communist Law in Czechoslovakia: Chapters from the History of Injustice]*, edited by Vojtěch Šimíček, Pavel Molek, and Michal Bobek, 813–21. Brno: Masaryk University.

Němčická, Božena. 1930. O poměru mezinárodního a vnitrostátního právního řádu v teorii a judikatuře Československých soudů [On Relationship of International and Domestic Legal Orders in Theory and Case Law of the Czechoslovak Courts]." In *Ročenka University Komenského za studijní rok 1928-1929 [Yearbook of the Comenius University1928-1929]*, edited by Albert Pražák, 130–31. Bratislava: Comenius University.

Petrov, Jan. 2019. "Vnitrostátní soudy a způsoby argumentace judikaturou ESLP [Domestic Courts and Methods of Argumentation with the ECtHR's Law]." *Právník* 158 (2): 163–81.

Pospíšil, Ivo. 2016. Lidskoprávní smluvy v českém ústavním pořádku a judikatuře Ústavního soudu ČR: mezi „chudokrevnou" exkluzivitou a zdravým „glajchšaltováním"? Několik poznámek na margo proběhlých diskusí [Human Right Treaties in the Czech Constitutional Legal Order and in the Constitutional Court's Case law]." In *Mezinárodní lidskoprávní závazky postkomunistických zemí: případy České republiky a Slovenska [International Human Rights Obligations of Post-communist Countries: Examples of the Czech Republic and Slovakia]*, edited by Ivo Pospíšil and Vladimír Týč, 100–09. Prague: Leges.

Růžička, Miroslav, and Polák. Přemysl. 2005. Nad jedním rozhodnutím Nejvyššího soudu týkajícím se problematiky ne bis in idem z hlediska jeho aspektů mezinárodních a vnitrostátních [On the Decision of the Supreme Court Related to the Ne Bis in Idem from the Point of View of Its International and Domestic Aspects]." *Státní zastupitelství* 2005 (6): 2–16.

Smekal, Hubert, and Katarína Šipulová. 2014. "*DH v. Czech Republic* Six Years Later: On the Power of an International Human Rights Court to Push through Systemic Change". *Netherlands Quarterly of Human Rights* 32 (3): 288–321.

Štefko, Martin. 2012. "Ochrana soukromí zaměstnanců ve světle čl. 8 Úmluvy o ochraně lidských práv a základních svobod [Employee's Privacy Protection in Light of the Article 8 ECHR]." *Jurisprudence* 2012 (7-8): 17.

Svobodová, Magdaléna. 2017. "Listina základních práv EU v judikatuře Ústavního soudu ČR [Charter of Fundamental Rights of the EU in the Czech Constitutional Court's Case Law]." *Právní rozhledy* 2017 (23-24): 823–28.

Trechsel, Stefan. 2005. *Human Rights in Criminal Proceedings*. New York: Oxford University Press.

van Bockel, Bas. 2010. *The ne bis in Idem Principle in EU Law*. Alphen aan de Rijn: Kluwer law Ineternational.

Van Bockel, Bas. 2017. "The Single Supervisory Mechanism Regulation: Questions of *Ne Bis in Idem* and Implications for the Further Integration of the System of Fundamental Rights Protection in the EU." *Maastricht Journal of European and Comparative Law* 24 (2): 194–216.

6 The Supreme Administrative Court

A new kid on the block

Expectations about the Supreme Administrative Court's (SAC) treatment of the European Court of Human Rights' (ECtHR or Strasbourg Court) case law are puzzling. On the one hand, the SAC deals with some areas of law that are not too closely related to the European Convention on Human Rights (ECHR or Convention). Although the Strasbourg Court has touched upon areas such as social security or construction law, it is incomparable with the ECtHR's impact on criminal law, for instance.[1] Moreover, only a handful of the Czech cases before the Strasbourg Court have been concerned with administrative law.[2] For those reasons, one could expect the SAC to have fewer incentives to engage with the ECtHR's case law. On the other hand, the SAC's history rather speaks in favor of expecting frequent invocation and thorough treatment of the Strasbourg case law. First, the establishment of the new system of administrative courts in 2003, including the SAC, was closely related to compliance of the Czech system with Article 6 ECHR.[3] Also, the SAC is a relatively young institution staffed with judges coming from different backgrounds, including several younger experts in European Union (EU) law, international law, and comparative constitutional law. Since the existing research suggests that the personal composition of a court crucially affects its treatment of foreign sources of law (Bobek 2013, 153; Kosař and Petrov 2017; Vyhnánek 2017), one could expect the SAC to work more often and more thoroughly with the Strasbourg case law. Indeed, the SAC has ascribed significant normative force to the ECtHR's case law (Kadlec and Petrov 2017).

However, the aim of this chapter is to look beyond the general jurisprudential doctrines and examine the day-to-day use of the ECtHR's case law in the SAC's decision-making. The combination of the three levels of analysis should provide a detailed picture of the role of the Strasbourg judgments and decisions in the SAC's case law. We begin with the macro-level analysis, which offers a basic quantitative overview of the SAC's use of the ECtHR's case law. The chapter then continues with meso- and micro-level analyses that study a sample of cases in a more thorough way and thereby further explain and contextualize the developments concerning the treatment of Strasbourg jurisprudence.

6.1 Macro-level analysis

The existing scholarship evaluates the position of the SAC towards international human rights obligations as rather favorable (Molek 2013, 405). In fact, the SAC has engaged with various human rights treaties ever since its establishment (Petrov and Šipulová 2016, 188). Figure 6.1 supports these findings also with respect to the frequency of references to the ECtHR and its case law. As the SAC has been functioning only since 2003, we faced both a shorter life-span and a smaller dataset of rulings. In the observed period (2003–2015), the SAC delivered 39,477 rulings. Out of these, it referred to the ECtHR in 1,913 rulings, using a total of 5,894 references to individual rulings of the Strasbourg Court.[4] Figure 6.1 shows that the SAC started referring to the ECtHR quite soon after its establishment. The reference occurrence curve has been generally increasing, with a slight decline in years 2006–2007 and 2010, and has been steeper ever since. The declines might have been caused by several factors, most importantly by the overall volume of rulings issued by the SAC.

Figure 6.2 depicts the referencing trends in relation to the volume of all the rulings delivered by the SAC in the respective year. It offers a more precise picture and confirms that, overall, the use of the references to the ECtHR's case law has been rising when controlling for the growing number of issued rulings.

Nevertheless, a simple count of references can be misleading for the purpose of analyzing domestic courts' engagement with the Strasbourg case law. The presence of a reference in the ruling does not tell us much about its use and function in the ruling. In some instances, a reference might appear only in the narrative part[5] without being reflected by the court in its reasoning. Therefore, in order to get as precise numerical results as possible, we coded every single found

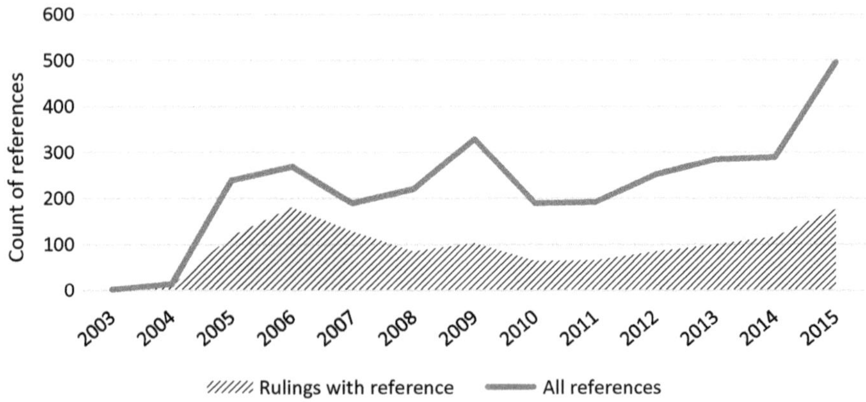

Figure 6.1 Use of ECtHR references over time by the SAC.
Source: authors.

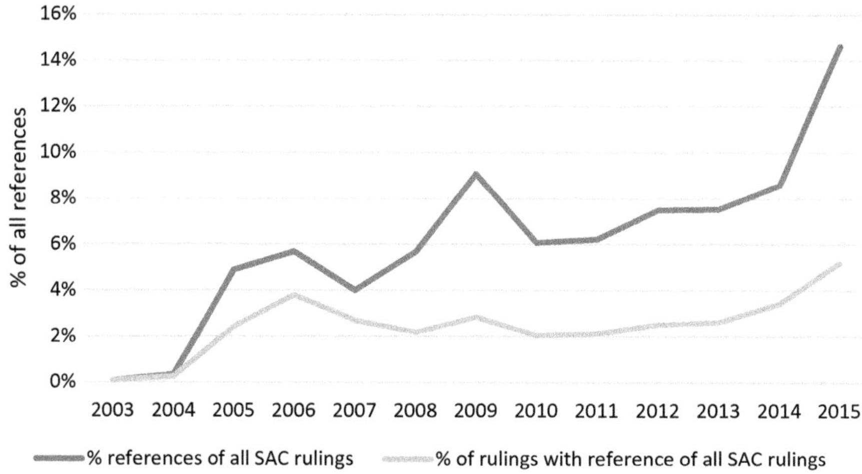

Figure 6.2 Use of ECtHR references over time compared to all case law of the SAC.
Source: authors.

reference according to its position in the narrative part or reasoning part of the respective domestic decision. Figure 6.3 reports interesting results. At the very beginning of the SAC's functioning many references to the ECtHR's case law occurred in the narrative parts. An example illuminating this is the use of the Strasbourg Court's decision in *O.B. Heller*[6] – surprisingly one of the most

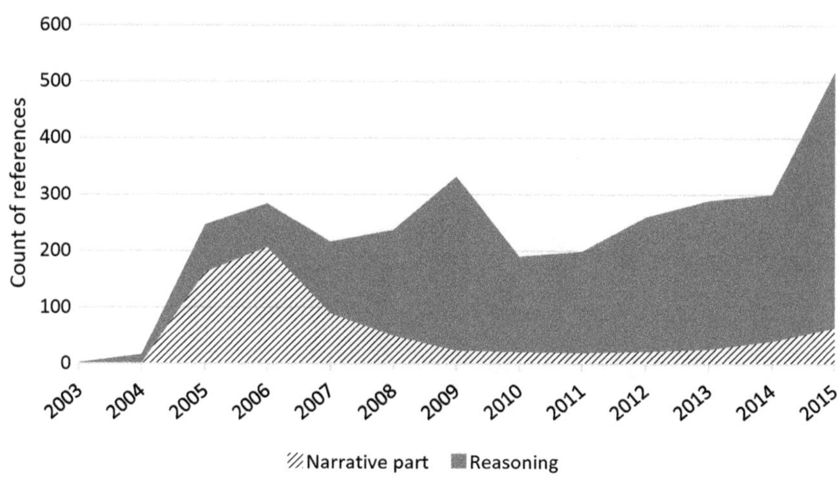

Figure 6.3 References to the ECtHR in different parts of domestic rulings.
Source: authors.

frequently cited Strasbourg rulings in the SAC's case law (see Figure 6.7). In *O.B. Heller*, the ECtHR somewhat confirmed the practice of the Czech customs authorities who, as parties to the proceedings, started invoking this decision extensively for their defense before the SAC.[7] However, the general trend changed around 2007–2008 with references in the SAC's own reasoning becoming dominant, which suggests a gradual habitualization and domestication of the ECtHR's case law – an idea we further explore in the micro-level analysis.

Another important factor for the effectiveness of the ECHR system is whether domestic courts refer only to the adverse rulings against their own countries or take into account case law against other countries too. Figure 6.4 shows that the SAC refers to both types of Strasbourg judgments and decisions; however, it refers much more often to the ECtHR's judgments adopted with respect to other countries. The Czech cases are cited less frequently. One apparent reason is that there have not been that many Czech cases before the Strasbourg Court, and, moreover, few of them have concerned administrative law. In addition, this trend suggests that the SAC consults the Strasbourg case law to find out about the general principles of ECHR law, rather than only about the part addressing the violations of the Convention by Czechia. This points to our initial conceptualization of domestic courts as diffusers and filters vis-à-vis the Strasbourg Court. The SAC's use of the entire body of the Strasbourg case law (rather than only the Czech rulings) increases its "filtering" capacity. Thereby, the SAC is more likely to "catch" the eventual ECHR violations and the problematic aspects in domestic legal provisions and check their compliance with the Convention as interpreted by the ECtHR before the case even makes it to Strasbourg. This indication is further explored in the meso- and micro-level analyses below.

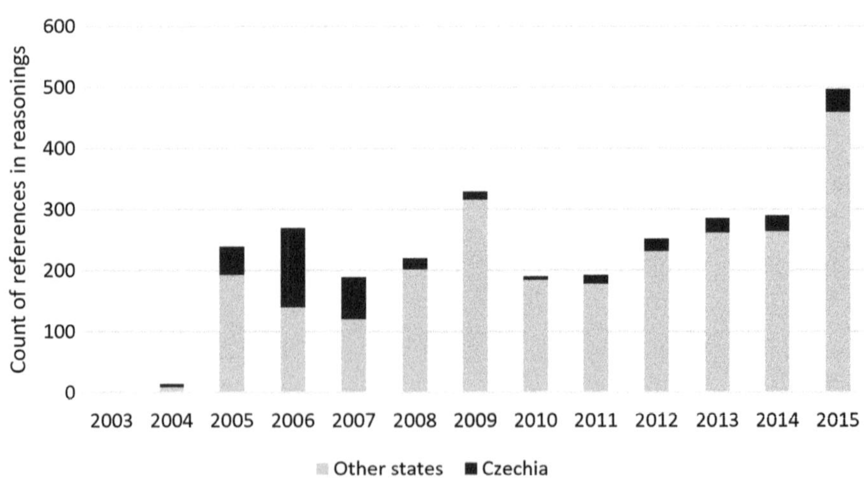

Figure 6.4 References to the ECtHR's rulings against Czechia and other states.
Source: authors.

Some differences exist between the references to the Strasbourg rulings declaring violation of the Convention on the one hand and those finding no violation on the other hand. The SAC refers to rulings with a declared violation almost twice as often as it does to rulings where no violation was found (Figure 6.5). This is understandable since most of the instances of pushing the interpretation of the Convention further are developed by the ECtHR in rulings where it finds a violation.

Going beyond the violation/non-violation dichotomy, the macro-level analysis allows us to dig deeper and show which areas of the ECtHR's case law were most frequently touched upon by the SAC. Figure 6.6 captures different areas of human rights protection in which the SAC most often relies on the ECtHR. To make the portrayal more comprehensible, the figure shows only those articles which were referred to by the SAC more than 50 times.

Most of the areas are expectable. Article 6 ECHR addresses various structural and procedural issues concerning the domestic judiciary and hence can be invoked in many situations. Moreover, the micro-level analysis explains how and why Article 6 ECHR has gained a prominent position in the litigation before Czech administrative courts. The frequent reference to Article 8 ECHR jurisprudence of the Strasbourg Court might seem surprising at first sight since the typical disputes concerning Article 8 ECHR (such as defamation or family law) fall within the jurisdiction of civil courts. However, the ECtHR has extended the scope and reach of Article 8 ECHR significantly. As a result, Article 8 ECHR jurisprudence is very complex and also addresses administrative legal issues such as environmental pollution, and family bonds as an obstacle to expulsion of migrants (Moreham 2008; Thym 2008). The meso-level analysis

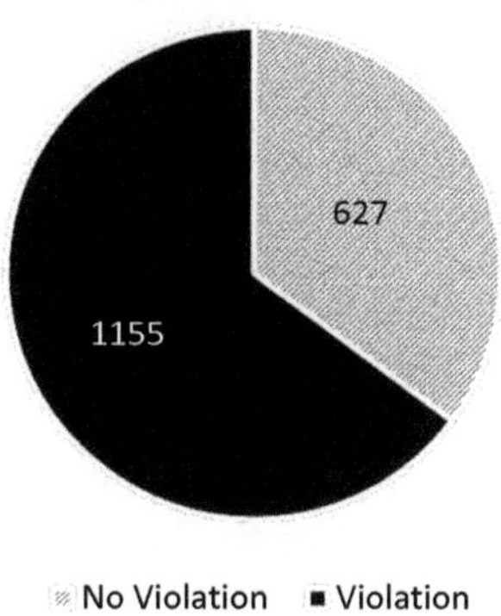

Figure 6.5 Reference to the ECtHR's case law declaring violation v. no violation of the ECHR.

Source: authors.

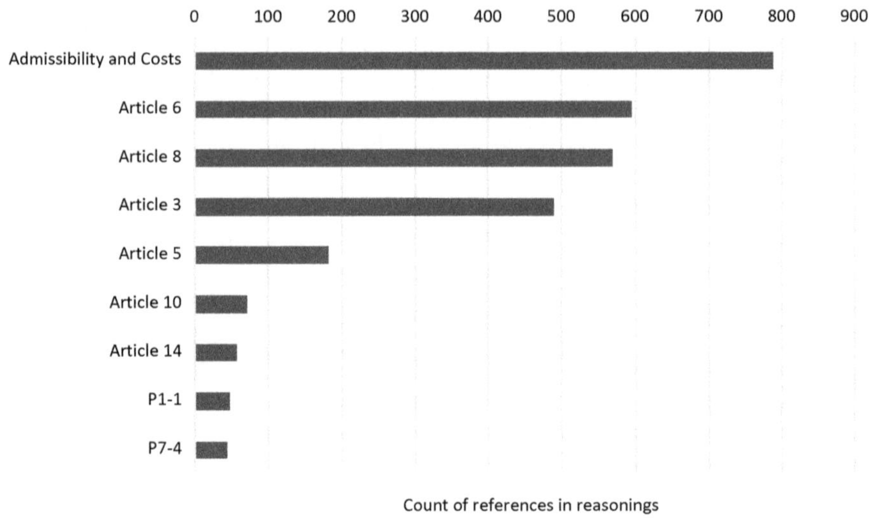

Figure 6.6 Articles of the Convention related to the SAC's references.
Source: authors.

explains how the SAC used Article 8 ECHR jurisprudence in greater detail. The rather frequent use of Articles 3 and 5 ECHR case law is logical and, as the meso-level analysis confirms, expectable with respect to the SAC's jurisdiction in immigration law matters. The main reasons are that the Strasbourg Court uses Article 3 ECHR as the basis for the *non-refoulement* principle (Greenman 2015) and that Article 5(1)(f) explicitly addresses detention with a view to deportation or extradition.

Besides the ECHR areas, the automated macro-level analysis also identified which judgments and decisions of the ECtHR have been the most frequently cited by the SAC in its reasoning (Figure 6.7). We only list the rulings here and contextualize their frequent quotation in the meso- and micro-level analyses. At this point we will only address the front runner: the ECtHR's *Van de Hurk* judgment.[8] Since Article 6 ECHR quickly domesticated in the litigation before the Czech administrative courts (see below), the litigants have often claimed that lower administrative courts violated their duty to give sufficient reasons for their decision. In response, the SAC has often invoked the *Van de Hurk* judgment, arguing that Article 6(1) ECHR "obliges courts to give reasons for their decisions, but cannot be understood as requiring a detailed answer to every argument".[9]

The macro-level analysis has identified fundamental aspects of the SAC's use of the ECtHR's case law, such as the frequency of references and development over time, as well as the basic characteristics of the cited Strasbourg rulings. At the same time, however, several issues remain unanswered. So far, we do not know whether the SAC follows the Strasbourg Court's conclusions, how it

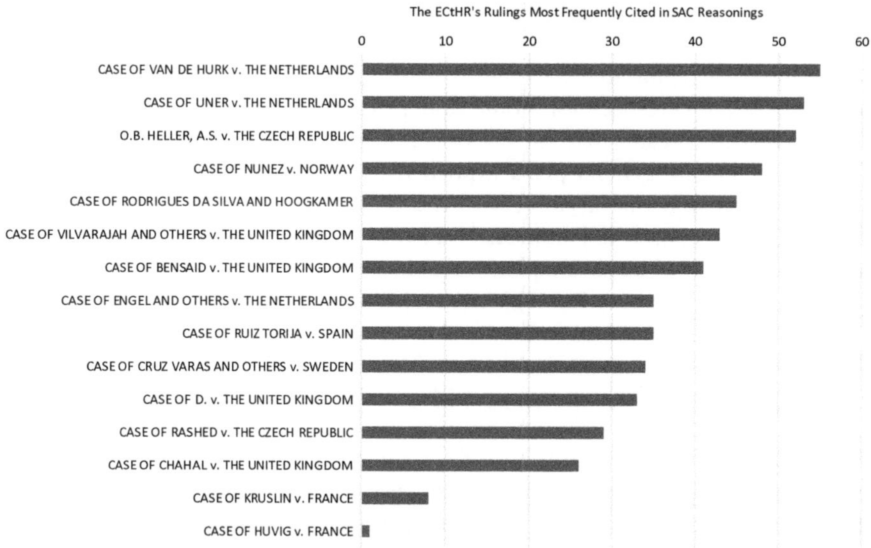

Figure 6.7 Most frequently cited ECtHR rulings in the SAC's reasonings.
Source: authors.

engages with the ECtHR's case law, and what influence the Strasbourg jurisprudence actually has on the SAC's reasoning. Moreover, some results of the macro-level analysis beg for more detailed explanation. Accordingly, the subsequent part looks beyond the number of references to the Strasbourg Court and asks deeper questions about the role of references to the ECtHR's case law in the SAC's judicial reasoning. The meso-level analysis of a new hand-coded dataset of nearly 300 rulings of the SAC[10] reveals the basic patterns and sheds more light on the puzzle presented earlier.

6.2 Meso-level analysis

Going back to the great debates about the role of national courts in enforcement of international law (see Chapter 2), results of the meso-level analysis suggest that the SAC is quite a reliable partner in giving effect to the ECtHR's pronouncements, rather than a disobedient or evasive actor. The SAC has followed the Strasbourg Court's conclusions nearly all the time (95.7 percent).[11] This finding corresponds with the general perception of the SAC as an actor positively inclined to human rights, international, and foreign law (Bobek 2013, 165; Molek 2013, 405). No case of explicit and admitted rejection of the ECtHR's conclusions appeared in the analyzed sample. However, we get back to this category later since we found some exceptional cases of non-following of the Strasbourg Court in the micro-level analysis.

The remaining 4.3 percent are instances in which the SAC distinguished the cases at hand from the ECtHR's case law. Sometimes the SAC resorts to distinguishing based on facts. For example, in an environmental law case, the SAC refused the applicability of the ECtHR's rulings concerning environmental pollution and the respect for home and private life.[12] Whereas the ECtHR's case concerned already existing nuisance, there was no such nuisance in the SAC's case, merely general plans expressed in a conceptual document. Hence, the SAC concluded that arguing with the ECtHR's rulings in the given case is like comparing apples and oranges.[13] However, when using the technique of distinguishing, the most frequent are instances where the SAC uses the domestic legal differences for explaining why the ECtHR's case law is irrelevant for the given dispute. For instance, the SAC distinguished its case from the ECtHR's *Öllinger v. Austria* judgment[14] since the Austrian law – unlike the Czech legal order – did not recognize the a priori ban of multiple assemblies at one place.[15]

Overall, when distinguishing cases from the ECtHR's rulings, the SAC usually just briefly explains why the Strasbourg case law does not apply at all to the present case rather than employing sophisticated techniques of distinguishing typical for common law judicial reasoning. The subsequent micro-level analysis explains that this is often a result of litigants' efforts to stretch the ECtHR's case law beyond its original scope.

The macro-level analysis suggested that the use of the Strasbourg jurisprudence by the SAC is rather uneven across various ECHR provisions. The sample used for the meso-level analysis is in line with the macro-level results, with Articles 6, 8, and 3 ECHR jurisprudence being the most often quoted respectively. The meso-level analysis allows us to better understand these trends.

As noted above, the frequency of invoking Article 6 ECHR case law on fair trial rights is expectable since procedural issues can emerge in all cases. Moreover, the SAC has been rather permissive as to the scope of application of Article 6 ECHR. Several times, the SAC stated that the criminal prong of Article 6 ECHR applies to *all* administrative offences.[16] At the same time, it stressed the Article 6 ECHR guarantees in administrative cases falling within the civil limb of Article 6 ECHR,[17] and was able to react to the changing Strasbourg case law on the applicability of Article 6 ECHR on disputes of civil servants.[18] Indeed, Article 6 ECHR case law of the Strasbourg Court has played a very complex role in the SAC's case law. As further argued in the micro-level analysis, Article 6 case law led to many changes in proceedings before administrative bodies and administrative courts and, ultimately, to the emergence of an "Article 6 mindset" and quite a broad internalization of Article 6 case law within the administrative law community.[19]

The second most frequently invoked provision is Article 8 ECHR. There have been several privacy law cases before the SAC where Article 8 ECHR case law played an important role.[20] Yet, Article 8 ECHR case law is most often cited in cases concerning the expulsion of foreigners. In such cases, the SAC uses Article 8 case law of the ECtHR as a framework for assessing whether an expulsion amounts to violation of the right to family life.[21] This explains why the macro-level analysis revealed the ECtHR's *Üner* judgment[22] as one of the most frequently cited Strasbourg rulings. In *Üner*, the Strasbourg Court provided guidance on assessing interferences with private and family life in the context of expulsion and deportation. Other frequently invoked provisions like Article 3 and Article 5 ECHR were most often referred to in the context of refugee law too; mainly with respect to the *non-refoulement* principle and detention of asylum seekers respectively.[23] This explains the very frequent use of the *Vilvarajah*[24] and *Cruz Varas*[25] judgments by the SAC (see Figure 6.7), which have addressed the factors for assessing the real risk of being subjected to torture or to inhumane or degrading treatment or punishment in the extradition or deportation context.[26]

The meso-level sample also supports the macro-level result suggesting that the SAC does not seem to make any great differences as to the normative force of the Strasbourg rulings directly addressed to Czechia and to other countries.[27] Often, such rulings are cited together without necessarily placing the "Czech rulings" higher than the rest. Apparently, the SAC has a rather strong sense of the *res interpretata* effect of the Strasbourg case law. We are not aware of any rulings in which the SAC refused to take an ECtHR judgment into account just because Czechia was not party to the proceedings before the Strasbourg Court.[28]

One of the crucial questions of the meso-level analysis is what influence the ECtHR's case law has on the SAC's reasoning. The existing scholarship analyzing other countries suggests that the influence is most often only supporting (Sadurski 2009, 442–43). The case of the SAC supports this thesis. In 68 percent of the rulings, the SAC uses the ECtHR's case law as a supporting or auxiliary argument in its reasoning. Although a Strasbourg reference sometimes plays a merely ornamental role (Sadurski 2009, 442; Bobek and Kosař 2010), even supporting use of the ECtHR's case law is important for the domestic level of the ECHR system. Supporting use of the Strasbourg case law increases the frequency of the ECtHR's occurrence in domestic jurisprudence. Thereby, it contributes to raising awareness of the Strasbourg Court's existence and its significance for administrative law and legal discourse (Sadurski 2009, 442). It also leads to broader dissemination of the ECtHR's case law, since supporting use implies that the SAC takes the Strasbourg rulings into account even if it is not strictly necessary.

Beyond the merely ornamental use, two patterns of supporting use of the ECtHR's case law are recognizable in the practice of the SAC. First, the SAC sometimes cites the Strasbourg case law to describe the general background of the given fundamental right. For example, in a case concerning the judicial review of a decision by which a child was not admitted to kindergarten, the SAC referred to *the Belgian linguistic case*[29] and explained the fundamental features of the right to education. However, the key legal question was subsequently decided predominantly on the basis of national law.[30] Second, the ECtHR reference is often used as an additional justification of the SAC's conclusion based on the domestic law. The SAC thereby shows that its reasoning is acceptable, or even necessary, from the point of view of ECHR law too.[31] Such use of the Strasbourg case law also shows that a domestic judge sees the ECtHR's case law as something to be consulted before adopting a final legal conclusion.

The lower number of instances of the ECtHR's substantive influence is logical. The SAC often deals with detailed provisions of the Czech administrative law and is also guided by its own case law and the case law of the Constitutional Court (CC). Still, cases of substantive influence of the ECtHR do occur. In fact, the Strasbourg jurisprudence played a substantive role in the SAC's reasoning in 32 percent of examined rulings.

Strasbourg case law concerning Articles 3, 5, 6, 8, 11 ECHR, Article 1 of the Protocol No. 1, and Article 4 of the Protocol No. 7 most frequently showed substantive influence (see Figure 6.8). As already suggested, some of these provisions are directly linked to certain aspects of administrative law, such as immigration. What all of these provisions have in common is that the ECtHR's jurisprudence offers some additional and more developed guidance compared to the Czech law, including the CC's case law (Petrov and Šipulová 2016, 161–63). Article 5 ECHR case law exemplifies this. It is broader and includes more specific guarantees than the protection of the right to liberty in the Czech Bill of Rights (Langášek 2012, 229–30). Importantly for the area of administrative law, the ECHR explicitly addresses detention in an immigration context and the ECtHR thus developed more detailed guidance in this area.[32] For instance, in 2011 the SAC stated that according to the ECtHR's case law a foreigner cannot be detained if it is already clear during the detention proceedings that the purpose of the detention (expulsion, in this case) cannot be met. Consequently, the SAC held that the administrative bodies have to address the eventual obstacles to expulsion of foreigners already at the moment of deciding about their detention.[33]

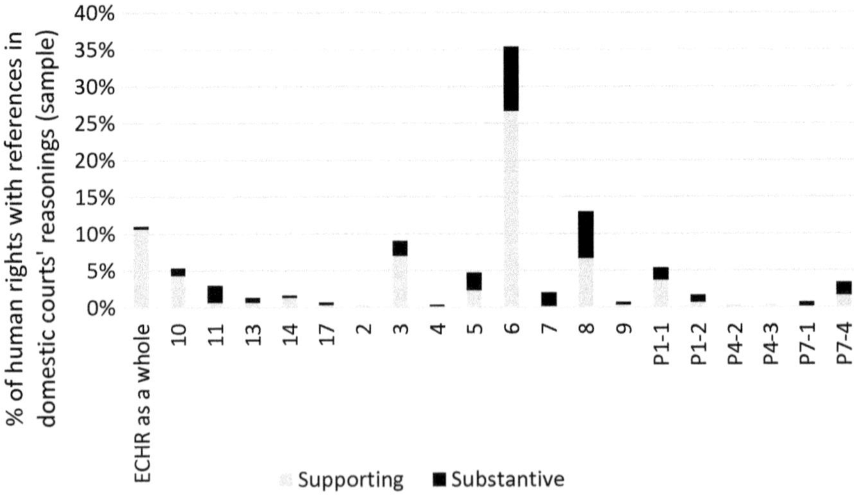

Figure 6.8 Substantive and supporting influence according to ECHR provisions.[34]
Source: authors.

Sometimes, especially in the immigration law context, there is a synergic effect of the ECtHR's case law and EU law. These two sources usually reinforce each other. However, since the EU legislation and the Court of Justice of the European Union's case law concerning immigration are becoming more and more detailed, several cases suggest that the EU law provides greater guidance and, therefore, the ECtHR's case law sometimes plays only a secondary role with respect to the EU law reasoning.[35]

Getting back to the substantive influence of the ECtHR's case law, how exactly does the SAC use the Strasbourg rulings when it grants them substantive influence? Only very rarely does the SAC use the ECtHR's rulings to set aside conflicting statutory law and apply the ECHR directly. Although such an approach is foreseen by Article 10 of the Constitution, the CC effectively "rewrote" this provision and held that in case of a conflict between statutory law and a human rights treaty, courts have to refer the case to the CC.[36]

Nevertheless, the SAC rebelled against this conclusion of the CC. In 2007, the SAC was deciding on the complaint of a former civil servant claiming service allowance (a type of social security allowance). The first-instance court dismissed the motion since statutory law excluded such disputes from judicial review. The SAC took a different stance and found the exclusion contrary to Article 6(1) ECHR. The SAC analyzed the development of the ECtHR's case law concerning the applicability of Article 6 ECHR on cases of civil servants. It was led by the criteria developed by the Strasbourg Court[37] and concluded that the case in hand concerned "civil rights and obligation", which made Article 6 ECHR applicable. Therefore, the complainant had a right to have the dispute reviewed by an independent tribunal; the SAC concluded there was a breach of the ECHR. Importantly, the SAC criticized the CC's interpretation of Article 10 of the Constitution and applied the ECHR directly. Therefore, the SAC deduced the competence of administrative courts to review such disputes directly from Article 6(1) ECHR.[38] The SAC used a detailed analysis of the ECtHR's case law to justify this extraordinary move and showed its preparedness to protect ECHR rights directly, even without activating the CC.

Another technique of substantive influence – ECHR-harmonious re-interpretation of domestic statutory provisions – is not so frequent either.[39] Still, the SAC has used this technique in several remarkable rulings, for instance to widely construe the statutory provisions allowing judicial review of administrative decisions,[40] or to extend the number of errors in administrative decisions that courts must review *ex officio*.[41]

Much more often, the SAC uses the ECtHR's case law to clarify or supplement the Czech legal regulation, often in the form of formulating some additional requirements or by introducing an ECtHR-inspired test or criteria. In such cases, the SAC goes beyond the re-interpretation of a particular statutory provision. Rather than influencing which interpretation of a statutory provision the SAC chooses, the ECtHR's case law is used to deduce the standards that are used to assess the case, pretty much independently of the original statutory provision. Particular provisions of domestic law stay in the background and the

ECtHR's case law provides a more detailed framework for review. The SAC has used this technique most extensively with respect to the right of assembly and association (Article 11 ECHR). In this area, the use of the Strasbourg case law by the SAC led to the creation of standards supplementing and specifying rather brief statutory law. Since this technique is essential from the point of view of subsidiarity in the ECHR system, we analyze this area in detail below in the micro-level analysis.

Nevertheless, the most frequent technique of substantive influence was using the Strasbourg case law to confirm the status quo of domestic law and legal practice. At first sight, this may seem rather paradoxical. International human rights law is usually seen as a tool for challenging the status quo and advancing domestic rights protection. However, the SAC also makes use of the ECtHR's case law when confirming the current situation. The Strasbourg rulings are not only used to push the human rights protection further, but also to demonstrate where its borders are. Given the SAC's reputation as a pro-human-rights court, in order to maintain its legitimacy in the eyes of some audiences it is important for the SAC to be persuasive when arguing that a restriction of a right in question is justified. In this context, the Strasbourg case law can provide both the guidance for assessing such restrictions and a powerful argument for showing that the status quo does not violate human rights. Besides persuading the litigants or non-governmental organizations, invoking the ECtHR's case law is also useful with regard to the eventual review of the SAC's ruling by the CC or the ECtHR itself.[42]

A typical area where the SAC uses the Strasbourg case law to confirm the status quo is the expulsion of migrants. As already mentioned, litigants often argue that their expulsion will violate their right to family life (Article 8 ECHR). The executive authorities and administrative courts are rather strict in this respect. On many occasions, the SAC has confirmed their practice and used the ECtHR's case law to explain why Article 8 ECHR does not preclude the complainant's expulsion in the given case.[43] In fact, this approach amounted to a somewhat standardized approach. In many rulings, the SAC uses virtually the same paragraph to explain why Article 8 ECHR is not an obstacle to expulsion.[44]

6.3 Micro-level analysis

The meso-level analysis revealed the major patterns of using the case law of the ECtHR in the reasoning of the SAC. In short, the SAC predominantly follows the ECtHR's conclusions and mostly uses them as an auxiliary argument in its reasoning. However, there are important instances when the ECtHR's case law played a more important role in the SAC's argumentation and even led to significant changes to the domestic law.

Combining these findings with the micro-level analysis can tell us even more. This section zeroes in on some of the areas significantly affected by the Strasbourg case law. It contextualizes and explains the logic beyond reasoning with the ECtHR's case law, which is important for learning broader lessons from the Czech case. In order to shed more light on the most important patterns identified in the meso-level analysis and on the "diffusing" and "filtering" roles of the SAC, the micro-level analysis examines some of the most "Strasbourgized" areas of the SAC's case law. In particular, treatment of the most frequently referred Article 6 ECHR case law is analyzed, as well as the use of Article 11 ECHR case law since the share of substantive uses was much higher than of supporting references. The micro-level examination of using the Article 6 and 11 ECHR case law by the SAC reveals two main interrelated conclusions about the substantive references to the Strasbourg case law. First, the ECtHR's case law is used as a legitimacy resource when changing the status quo, but also when justifying rights restrictions. Second, the Strasbourg jurisprudence is used as a crucial guideline, especially when addressing novel issues.

6.3.1 "Article 6 mindset": Extending procedural rights in administrative law

Czech law distinguishes between criminal law and administrative criminal law. The latter is usually concerned with illegal acts that are socially less harmful than crimes per se. Administrative offences[45] are first enforced by administrative (executive) bodies whose decisions are generally reviewable by administrative courts. Although it might not seem to be a prime human rights issue, judicial review of administrative offences and its ECHR dimension were crucial for the emergence and design of the contemporary system of administrative judiciary in Czechia. In 2001, the CC decided that the then-existing system of administrative judiciary was unconstitutional and completely derogated the respective statutory regulation. The CC held that the system violated Article 6(1) ECHR as interpreted by the Strasbourg Court. Specifically, the lack of administrative courts' full jurisdiction over "civil rights and obligations" and "criminal charges" violated the right to a fair trial. The CC emphasized the criminal prong of Article 6(1) ECHR and concluded that according to the Strasbourg jurisprudence many acts labelled as administrative offences in the Czech law amounted to "criminal charges" as understood by the ECtHR and therefore were supposed to meet the requirements of Article 6(1).[46] The CC's intervention facilitated the adoption of a new law that aimed to comply with the CC's and the ECtHR's pronouncements (Svoboda 2012). The new system of administrative judiciary headed by the newly established SAC began operating in 2003.

With this background, the SAC has had quite a clear vision of judicial cultivation of the public administration system. Among other topics, the SAC made compliance with fair trial rights (Article 6 ECHR), especially in the area of administrative offences, one of its priorities. The SAC substantially recreated the law of administrative offences, and administrative procedure more generally, by supplementing sometimes brief and incomplete legislation with judge-made requirements, often based on Article 6 ECHR and the ECtHR's jurisprudence.

In several cases this amounted to refining procedural guarantees even in proceedings before administrative courts. However, the area of administrative offences later gave rise to rulings less attuned to following the Strasbourg Court's conclusions too. Hence, the development of the SAC's treatment of the ECtHR's case law in administrative offences cases can be divided to several overlapping stages.

At first, the SAC made use of the legitimizing function of the ECtHR's case law in justifying its interventions into the decision-making of administrative (executive) bodies. Since the origins of the existing system of administrative judiciary are linked to the ECHR dimensions of administrative criminal law, the SAC – as a new actor having to build its authority – often used references to the EC(t)HR to bolster the persuasiveness of its interventions vis-à-vis the executive and the lower courts and explain the rationale of the new system. Most often, this included a reference to the principle of full jurisdiction enshrined in the ECtHR's Article 6 jurisprudence. The SAC would emphasize that the new system and the principle of full jurisdiction require the administrative judges to "review the correctness and completeness of the findings of administrative bodies independently and on their own".[47]

Very soon, the SAC started extending the procedural rights of parties of administrative proceedings, especially of persons accused of administrative offences. The instrument was the extension of domestic criminal law guarantees on administrative offences based on analogy. The vehicle making this possible was Article 6(1) ECHR and the ECtHR's case law. In an early decision, the SAC held that the principle of retroactivity of lighter penalty is applicable to administrative offences too, although statutory law says so only with respect to crimes. More importantly, the SAC made a general conclusion that all the Article 6 ECHR guarantees have to be met with respect to administrative offences.[48]

The general inclusion of administrative offences under the category of "criminal charges" as understood by Article 6(1) ECHR opened the door to further extension of procedural rights. As a result, the SAC created numerous judge-made guarantees for suspects in the area of administrative criminal law based on the analogy with criminal law guarantees. This led to considerable refinement of rather crude and often incomplete statutory law in this area.[49] The ECtHR's case law has often formed the basis for the rights extension. More specifically, the Strasbourg jurisprudence often provided the basic mindset for the SAC's reasoning rather than detailed guidelines. The main point was that the domestic distinction between criminal and administrative criminal law is not a final stop for determining the scope of parties' human rights guarantees. Article 6 ECHR jurisprudence was used as a platform for elevating administrative offences to a higher level of protection. In fact, the extension of procedural rights in administrative (criminal) procedure was often not a result of mere compliance with the ECtHR's case law. Frequently, the SAC resorted to its own elaboration of what fundamental ECHR principles imply in the context of the Czech administrative criminal law. The resulting guarantees have often been much more detailed than those enshrined in the ECtHR's case law, and sometimes they have gone beyond what the Strasbourg Court explicitly requires.

To illustrate this pattern, we summarize a few examples. In an early ruling, the SAC stated that Article 6(1) ECHR and the related case law of the ECtHR require an exception from a domestic legal principle that the parties themselves delimit the subject matter of the proceedings before administrative courts. Since administrative offences amount to "criminal charges" in the ECHR sense, the administrative courts must *ex officio* take account of the extinction of liability for the offence due to the expiration of prescription period – even if the party did not make such a claim – as is the case in criminal law. Only then will a uniform procedure for all "criminal charges" be retained.[50] In a structurally similar fashion, the SAC also extended the applicability of criminal law doctrine of continuing offence on administrative criminal law. The starting point for doing so was again the "Article 6 mindset".[51] From a formal point of view, the references to the ECtHR's case law were often merely generic or at least not particularly detailed in many rulings of the early phase. Yet, a more detailed analysis of the Strasbourg jurisprudence soon became a standard, as for instance in a ruling from 2006, where the SAC stressed that the rights of defense enshrined in Article 6(3) ECHR must also be respected in the administrative criminal procedure.[52]

The SAC's rulings mentioned so far show how the "Article 6 mindset" allowed and facilitated the extension of procedural rights of individuals in administrative proceedings and proceedings before administrative courts. Nevertheless, this phenomena had further repercussions. Article 6 ECHR showed itself to be a powerful instrument capable of transferring an administrative-law issue to the level of international legal argumentation and securing a better position for the individuals disputing decisions of administrative bodies. The parties and their legal representatives soon realized the convenience of Article 6 ECHR, started invoking the provision and the ECtHR's case law on a regular basis, and argued for stretching the procedural rights even further. As a result, Article 6 ECHR to a large extent became a part of the standard "language" of litigation before administrative courts. In some areas, especially driving offences, this practice has even gone too far. Some litigants have taken advantage of the new mindset characterized by sensitivity towards procedural rights and have tried to obstruct the procedure and avoid conviction by abusing their procedural rights.

The increased activity of the litigants and more frequent invocation of Article 6 ECHR marked a new phase in the development of the SAC's treatment of the ECtHR's case law. The SAC had to face the challenge of squaring the extension of procedural rights with the factual requirements on the functionality of public administration. Thus, the SAC had to specify and eventually narrow down the scope of some of the ECHR-inspired procedural guarantees. On a general level, in a 2014 judgment the SAC made clear that it is not necessary that all the guarantees of Article 6 ECHR have to be met in the proceedings before administrative bodies; it is usually sufficient if the subsequent review proceedings before administrative courts fulfil those requirements.[53]

Most of the mentioned procedural guarantees did not directly implement the ECtHR's pronouncements, but rather built on them and fine-tuned the domestic law in line with them or even went beyond them. Thus, the practice of specifying or narrowing down the guarantees would not lead to clashes with the Strasbourg Court or even non-compliance with its rulings. However, this phase brought about a new pattern of using the ECtHR's case law in the SAC's reasoning. The frequency of citing the ECtHR's case law to justify the status quo and to argue why restrictions of some rights are justified increased.

Sometimes, the necessity to narrow down the ECHR-related guarantees was a result of the development of the ECtHR's case law as such. The mentioned extension of procedural rights was mainly based on Article 6 ECHR. Applicability of Article 6 ECHR, however, has broader repercussions for applicability of other ECHR provisions, for instance Article 4 of the Protocol No. 7 (*non bis in idem* principle).[54] In particular, the combination of the ECtHR's and the SAC's broad reading of Article 6 ECHR with developments in interpretation of the *non bis in idem* principle proved to be a problem for the SAC.

Regarding the ECtHR's part, in *Zolotukhin* the Strasbourg Court aimed to unify its case law on the principle of *non bis in idem* (Article 4 of the Protocol No. 7 to ECHR), in particular the notion of the same offence (*idem*). The ECtHR concluded that the approach based on the legal characterization of the two offences is too restrictive and that Article 4 of Protocol No. 7 must be understood as "prohibiting the prosecution or trial of a second 'offence' in so far as it arises from identical facts or facts which are substantially the same" (*idem factum* approach).[55] The combination of the *idem factum* approach and the extensive interpretation of "criminal charges" in Article 6 ECHR was shown to cause difficulties in jurisdictions with a dual system of criminal and administrative sanctions or plurality of administrative sanctions for certain acts.[56]

The SAC faced the latter issue in 2012 in a case that gave rise to an outstanding ruling in which the SAC refused to follow the Strasbourg Court's conclusions in *Zolotukhin*. The facts of the case were simple. The Czech Environmental Inspectorate (CEI)[57] inspected the municipality Kralice nad Oslavou with respect to waste disposal on premises owned by the municipality. CEI found violations of several environmental laws and started separate administrative proceedings in the field of water protection, waste management, and protection of nature. CEI found the municipality guilty in all these proceedings and imposed three separate fines. The municipality subsequently started litigation before administrative courts, claiming that CEI had violated the *non bis in idem* principle. In the last instance, the SAC rejected the claims of the municipality. The SAC engaged thoroughly with the ECtHR's case law. First, it applied the *Engel* criteria[58] to the given offences and concluded that Article 4 of the Protocol No. 7 was applicable to the case. Subsequently, the SAC analyzed the development of the Strasbourg Court's case law on the *idem* element of the *non bis in idem* principle and summarized the ECtHR's conclusions in *Zolotukhin*. Nevertheless, the SAC refused the *idem factum* conception adopted by the ECtHR and instead adhered to an approach that takes the legal qualification of an action as decisive (*de iure* approach).[59]

The main reason for departing from the ECtHR's case law was the SAC's concern about the proper functioning of the public administration and administrative criminal law. The SAC mentioned that a regular feature of some systems of administrative criminal law (including the Czech system) is that different administrative bodies have material jurisdiction over different offences. Thus, it is only the *de iure* approach that makes it possible to punish an offender for all the harmful consequences of one action. On the other hand, according to the SAC, the *idem factum* approach would only allow the fastest administrative body to punish the perpetrator for just one consequence of the act. The remaining proceedings addressing other consequences of the same act would have to be halted. Such a situation is even more critical regarding the consequences of acts that are punishable by criminal law and other consequences that are punishable by administrative criminal law. Then, the *idem factum* approach could result in replacing the administrative law tools with increasing criminal repression. According to the SAC, the ECtHR judges hardly intended such a development.[60] For all these reasons, the SAC found it necessary to reject the ECtHR's approach to the *non bis in idem* principle as adopted in *Zolotukhin*. The SAC repeated this approach in several subsequent rulings without clearly indicating a departure from *Zolotukhin*.[61]

The rejection of *Zolotukhin* did not start any large-scale revolt against the ECtHR though. Some of the SAC's concerns were resolved due to the ECtHR's judgment in *A and B v. Norway*, which revisited the issue of *non bis in idem* in the context of multiple combined proceedings, and to some extent mitigated the consequences of *Zolotukhin* by relaxing the interpretation of the *bis* element.[62] The SAC seems to have quickly embraced the ECtHR's conclusions adopted in *A and B*.[63]

Notwithstanding the (partial) rejection of *Zolotukhin*, the SAC continued applying the ECtHR's case law and in several cases kept on extending the procedural guarantees in administrative proceedings based on Article 6 ECHR. The most important recent rulings concern the qualification as "criminal charges" of measures that had previously been perceived as regulatory rather than criminal measures: the penalty-points system for driving offences and penalty payment (*penále*) in tax law. Established case law of the SAC did not consider these two measures to be "criminal charges" in the sense of the ECHR but rather mere administrative measures. Nonetheless, two three-judge panels of the SAC initiated the proceedings before the Grand Chamber of the SAC[64] in order to overturn this opinion and apply the ECHR guarantees on those two measures.

In both cases, the Grand Chamber sided with the smaller panels and concluded – nearly exclusively on the basis of the ECtHR's case law – that the measures amount to penalties in the sense of the ECHR and, therefore the

ECHR guarantees must extend to them.[65] Although both rulings implied major changes in the case law, the penalty payment in tax law was received as less controversial since the Strasbourg case law was quite clear.[66] The case of the penalty-points system for driving offences was controversial even among the judges of the Grand Chamber. In fact, the dispute was about the interpretation of the ECtHR's judgment in *Malige v. France*.[67] The SAC's majority concluded that the Strasbourg Court's conclusions in *Malige* imply that the points system should be treated as a "criminal penalty" in the sense of the ECHR, with all its implications. Yet, two dissenting judges read the ECtHR's judgment in *Malige* much more narrowly and expressed concerns about the implications of the majority's opinion for the legal practice. According to the dissenters, *ratio decidendi* in *Malige* did not address the nature of the entire points system for driving offences but merely rejected the possibility of excluding penalty points from judicial review. The dissenting judges thus concluded that the ascription of points for driving offences does not amount to "criminal penalty".[68]

To summarize the uses of Article 6 ECHR judgments in the SAC's case law (on administrative offences), it first served as a useful legitimacy resource for explaining and justifying the new system for the judicial review of administrative acts. Soon, Article 6 ECHR jurisprudence was used by the SAC as a platform for achieving changes in the administrative procedure, especially concerning administrative criminal law. The ECtHR's case law was used as a platform allowing the extension of procedural rights of parties of administrative proceedings. Such a progressive invocation of Article 6 case law led to the creation of "Article 6 mindset" – the fundamental postulates of Article 6 procedural protection spread throughout the administrative law community. Attorneys, especially, started referring to ECtHR's Article 6 case law in order to gain advantage for their clients. Sometimes these attempts went too far. Hence, the SAC – having in mind not only the procedural rights of individuals but also concerns about the functioning of the public administration system – had to specify and sometimes refine the scope of the procedural guarantees (co-)based on Article 6 ECHR. Accordingly, the use of the ECtHR's case law to justify restrictions of (procedural) rights increased. The peak of this pattern was the SAC's rejection of some of the Strasbourg Court's conclusions in *Zolotukhin*. Although this was an extraordinary case of disobedience vis-à-vis the ECtHR, the latter ruling did not damage the relations between the two courts and the SAC kept on following the Strasbourg jurisprudence on the right to fair trial.

6.3.2 ECtHR case law as a guideline: Article 11 ECHR

Slightly different patterns of the ECtHR's substantive impact on the SAC's case law emerged in the area of Article 11 ECHR. By the time the SAC was established, the CC had already produced a considerable body of case law providing some guidelines for the interpretation of many constitutional rights. Still, there were some provisions of the Bill of Rights only rarely invoked in litigation before the CC. Freedom of assembly and association was one of them

(Kosař 2014, 499). Nevertheless, the SAC faced several hard cases concerning the freedom of assembly and association. As the CC's case law did not provide too much lead, the SAC found inspiration in the ECtHR's case law. This section looks more closely at two areas: the dissolution of political parties and freedom of assembly.

The SAC has jurisdiction over deciding the government's motions for suspending the operation of or dissolving political parties. In 2008 and 2009, the government filed two motions proposing the dissolution of the Workers' Party (*Dělnická strana*) – a far-right party that, according to the government, showed significant undemocratic signs related to its cooperation with an ultranationalist movement.[69] The first judgment of the SAC (hereinafter "DS I") attracted less media attention than the second, but was extremely important from the legal point of view, since it introduced the whole framework for deciding dissolution disputes. Until then, vast majority of cases concerning the dissolution of political parties dealt with the failure of smaller parties to comply with administrative obligations. However, in DS I the SAC dealt with a major case concerning the freedom of association, freedom of expression, and the doctrine of militant democracy.

In the absence of developed domestic case law, the SAC found the greatest guidance in the jurisprudence of the ECtHR. The SAC analyzed in detail the Strasbourg Court's case law on dissolution of political parties and stated that domestic law must be interpreted in line with it.[70] The first part of the reasoning recapitulates relevant ECtHR case law and deduces an overall framework for dissolution of political parties in the name of militant democracy.[71] In a nutshell, the SAC invoked the doctrine of militant democracy, but emphasized the significance of political pluralism and freedom of association in political parties for the democratic society. Hence, the judges stated that a party can be dissolved only under very strict conditions. Convincing and compelling reasons for dissolution have to be given, requirements of necessity and proportionality have to be met, and the risk to democracy must be imminent.[72] Also, the undemocratic operations have to be imputable to the party as such; they cannot be mere excesses of particular individuals.[73] Subsequently, the SAC applied those standards, heavily inspired by the ECtHR's rulings, to the case at hand. It concluded that the government failed to meet the burden of proof of fulfilling all the conditions. The first motion was therefore rejected.

Several months later, the government filed a second motion proposing dissolution of the Workers' Party. This time the motion was more detailed and reacted to the ECtHR-inspired framework adopted in DS I. After concluding that the court was not barred from deciding the case due to the obstacle of *res judicata*, the SAC examined the motion for dissolution. It built on the framework created in DS I[74] and updated the references to the ECtHR's case law when it cited jurisprudential developments at the ECtHR level since DS I.[75] Based on this updated framework, the SAC examined the manifesto of the Workers' Party, the party's symbols, its relation to ultranationalist groups, and concrete acts of the party and its foremen. This time, the SAC concluded that the Workers' Party's political manifesto and its operations were in "sharp contradiction with the concept of a democratic state based on the rule of law".[76] Since all the listed conditions were met, the SAC decided to dissolve the Workers' Party.

The Workers' Party subsequently sought review of the SAC's ruling at the CC. The CC, however, dismissed the Workers' Party complaint as manifestly ill-founded. The CC's decision was very brief and accepted both the SAC's framework and conclusions.[77] The SAC also used the ECtHR's case law to assess the decision of the Ministry of Interior to dissolve the Communist Youth Union (*Komunistický svaz mládeže*) – an association of young people claiming communist ideology – stressing that the public authorities failed to thoroughly assess the necessity of such a measure.[78] Thus, in this area it was the SAC who synthetized the ECtHR's jurisprudence on dissolution of political parties and other associations and introduced those important EC(t)HR standards into the Czech legal practice, thereby fulfilling a major "diffusing" role of domestic courts.[79]

Another area where the SAC used the ECtHR's case law as a major guideline is the freedom of assembly. In the 1990s and early 2000s, there was not much litigation concerning freedom of assembly and thus the respective jurisprudence remained rather underdeveloped. This changed around 2007–2008 when cases posing key legal questions concerning freedom of assembly made their way to the SAC. Since the post-1989 regulation of the freedom of assembly in Czechia has been very liberal,[80] cases concerning complicated and novel issues about the scope of freedom of assembly and conflicts with other rights appeared in the SAC's docket. The SAC again used the ECtHR's case law as a sort of guideline providing basic principles for dealing with such rights collisions.[81]

The first group of cases concerned assemblies convened by extremist groups and the employment of the militant democracy doctrine. Going far beyond the statutory text, the SAC stated that under certain conditions the administrative bodies may take into account not only the declared purpose of the assembly but also its real objective. If the real objective conflicts with fundamental principles of democracy and human rights, the administrative body can ban such an assembly. In order to support such conclusions, the SAC cited the ECtHR's case law on Article 17 ECHR, which prohibits any abuse of rights.[82] In a follow-up case, however, the SAC made clear that the conditions for using this option are very strict and the administrative body carries a strict burden of proof with respect to the real purpose of the assembly.[83] In another case, the SAC reviewed dissolution of an assembly that, according to the administrative authority, departed from a declared purpose and in fact led to promotion of fundamental rights violations. To examine the proportionality of the dissolution, the SAC used the test introduced by the ECtHR.[84] Referring extensively to the Strasbourg rulings, the SAC concluded that the dissolution fell within permissible restrictions of the freedom of assembly and that freedom of assembly does not protect the convener of an assembly promoting racist opinions.[85]

In addition, the ECtHR's case law served as a model in freedom of assembly cases not concerning militant democracy. It served as guidance for balancing freedom of assembly with the rights of children to not be exposed to shocking and drastic photographs,[86] or for dealing with less traditional types of assemblies such as sit-in protests[87] or assemblies organized to block other assemblies.[88] Hence, it can be summarized that the SAC used the guiding role of the Strasbourg case law especially in cases posing novel questions unaddressed by the domestic jurisprudence or difficult cases of fundamental rights collisions.

6.4 Conclusions

The three-level analysis of the SAC's treatment of the ECtHR's case law shows a bigger picture of how the SAC uses the Strasbourg jurisprudence in its reasoning and the effects it has on domestic law. At the same time, it allows us to draw more general conclusions about the SAC's role in the domestic level of the ECHR system.

First, the SAC's performance is positive from the point of view of the subsidiarity principle.[89] Rather frequent invocation of the ECtHR's case law, the following of the ECtHR's conclusions in nearly all the cases, and the high significance de facto ascribed to the *res interpretata* effect of Strasbourg rulings are the three key features positively affecting the SAC's subsidiarity roles. As a result, the SAC's performance goes beyond mere compliance with the Strasbourg judgments and brings about more than contributing to the case-specific effectiveness of the ECtHR (see generally Helfer 2014, 467). The SAC's treatment of the ECtHR's case law contributes to increasing the *erga omnes* effectiveness of the Strasbourg Court. Taking the ECtHR's conclusions seriously and applying them to the domestic reality of administrative law have resulted in the SAC's strong "diffusing" and "filtering" role vis-à-vis the ECtHR. The SAC has many times served as an autonomous domestic introducer of the ECtHR's standards. Hence, in the area of administrative law, the CC is not the only important "partner" of the Strasbourg Court (Petrov 2018a). The SAC's partnership is crucial since the SAC has developed closer communication channels with some actors than the CC, particularly with the lower administrative courts, administrative bodies, and the administrative law community as such.

However, the SAC seems to be more active than merely transmitting the ECtHR's pronouncements to the domestic realm. Especially in certain areas, the SAC works quite creatively with the Strasbourg jurisprudence. The above-mentioned case law on administrative procedure and Article 6 ECHR exemplifies this. The ECtHR's rulings did not always directly answer the question at stake. Still, the SAC was able to distill the general principles of the Strasbourg rulings and apply them on the particularities of the Czech administrative law. In this respect, the SAC has contributed to the domestic development of ECHR rights. Although it did not lead to a fully fledged judicial dialogue and responses from the Strasbourg Court, such practice is very important for the protection and development of ECHR rights. The SAC's case law shows that domestic courts can contribute to the development of the ECHR not only by challenging the abstract interpretations of certain ECHR provisions,[90] but also by adjusting them to the domestic context and by filling the sometimes vague pronouncements of the ECtHR with concrete content informed by the domestic context.

Yet, there seem to be some qualifications to the narrative of the SAC as the ECtHR's faithful partner. The SAC has a reputation of a pro-human-rights court. However, it also shows a great concern for the proper and effective functioning of the public administration system in Czechia.[91] As a result, it sometimes reads the Convention rights rather narrowly,[92] or exceptionally even refuses to follow the ECtHR's interpretations.[93] Although these are untypical cases, they may nevertheless be related to the differences between the SAC (a domestic administrative court) and the ECtHR (an international human rights court). Protection of individual rights is an important aspect of the SAC's quest to cultivate the public administration; however, it is not its only goal. Unlike the ECtHR, the SAC hears complaints by the administrative bodies too. Overall, it seems that the SAC's vision is not only about limiting the executive and giving the public administration authorities fundamental rights lessons, but also about providing a framework enabling and guiding their action. This does not suggest that the Strasbourg Court does not pay any attention to other values than human rights. It only says that structurally the SAC is more often exposed to the views of the domestic administrative bodies, which may affect its approach to some legal issues and may explain some less enthusiastic uses of the ECtHR's judgments such as *Zolotukhin*.

Second, the three-level analysis also sheds more light on the use of the ECtHR's case law as a legitimacy resource. Our findings are in line with the existing scholarship, which argues that the Strasbourg jurisprudence is used by domestic courts as an authority-augmenting tool or even as a shield against opposing actors (Procházka 2002, 218; Sadurski 2009, 438; Bobek and Kosař 2010, 138; Garlicki and Kondak 2016, 329). Using the Article 6 ECHR case law as a platform for achieving further changes of administrative criminal law and presenting them in the context of the very rationale of the new system of administrative judiciary is a typical example. Nevertheless, the meso- and micro-level analysis also show that the SAC also refers to the Strasbourg jurisprudence to legitimize the status quo and point out the proportionality of rights limitations. This does not suggest that the SAC misuses the ECtHR's case law. Rather, it shows that the Strasbourg rulings on proportionality of rights limitations can serve not only as an instrument for changing the status quo, but also as a tool motivating critical examination of the existing practice and eventually confirming it.[94]

Third, the study of the SAC's treatment of the ECtHR's case law also provides insights for the human rights "handbook" (Ziemele 2016, 498) and the "transformative guidance" (Çali, Koch, and Bruch 2013, 981) function of the Strasbourg rulings for new democracies. The meso-level analysis shows that the auxiliary use of the ECtHR's rulings to support the domestic court's own conclusions is very frequent. In such cases, the "handbook" is often used for *ex post* double-checking that the domestic court's conclusion is appropriate. However, in some cases the ECtHR's case law gains a greater significance for the *process* of coming to the conclusion. This chapter argues that the ECtHR's case law often guides the SAC's reasoning when it is confronted with novel issues unanswered by domestic legal materials. As a result, combined reading of the meso- and micro-analysis suggests that the guiding function of the Strasbourg case law is most significant when it offers some additional or more detailed guidance on assessing the new issues in comparison to the domestic sources of law (especially the CC's case law).

Despite all the positive conclusions, our analysis confirms the previous conclusions by Bobek and Kosař (2010), who pointed out some flaws in the formal treatment of the ECtHR's case law. Generic citations or excessive anonymization of the ECtHR's rulings, which both make the reasoning with the Strasbourg case law less transparent and less persuasive, do appear in the SAC's rulings. Exceptionally, there was even some confusion between the ECtHR and the Court of Justice in individual rulings.[95] Yet, it is fair to say that the majority of those issues date back to the earlier days of the SAC. The number of such flaws decreases with time. Several developments concerning the accessibility and awareness of the Strasbourg case law can explain it. The first is the mainstreaming of ECHR law. International human rights law with a primary focus on EC(t)HR law has become a part of legal education (Kilian, Pospíšil, and Smekal 2016). Hence, younger judges and law clerks[96] often enrich the SAC in this expertise. In addition to changes in legal education, accessibility of information on the ECtHR's case law in Czech seems to be crucial. Publishing the most detailed commentary to the ECHR in the Czech language in 2012 has arguably been crucial in this context (Kmec et al. 2012). Also, the Office of the Government Agent for the representation before the ECtHR has made considerable efforts to disseminate information on the Strasbourg rulings in Czech.[97] Next, the work of the SAC's Analytical Department, which is addressed in greater detail in Chapter 9, affects the treatment of the ECtHR's case law (Bobek 2013, 168). Finally, the ECtHR itself has been working on making its case law more accessible and comprehensible.[98]

In sum, the SAC seems to be quite an active and reliable partner and ally of the ECtHR. The question is whether this trend will continue. After all, the liberal-democratic consensus in the region has been shaking and the resentment against international human rights law and institutions has been a part of the story (Petrov 2018b). There are – so far rather isolated – signs that the SAC will not necessarily accept the ECtHR's progressive minority rights jurisprudence. In May 2019 – i.e., only after the period covered by our dataset – the SAC rejected the Strasbourg Court's conclusions in the context of LGBTI rights. The complainant – a transgender person – sought a change of personal identification number so that (s)he was not identified as a male anymore. The administrative bodies rejected such an application since the Czech law made it conditional on sex change understood as surgery disabling reproductive functions and transforming the genitalia. The complainant argued before the SAC that such a requirement is unconstitutional and violates the ECHR – in *A.P., Garçon and Nicot*, the ECtHR held that refusing a change in civil status on the grounds of failing to undergo a surgical treatment leading to sterilization amounts to violation of Article 8 ECHR.[99] The SAC acknowledged that the Strasbourg case law functions as an essential guideline for application of domestic law, but stressed that its precedential effects are not unlimited and that principled judicial dialogue contesting the ECtHR's conclusions is acceptable.[100] The SAC refused to follow the Strasbourg judgment and argued that the strictly binary account of sex prevailing in the Czech society prevents the court from complying with the ECtHR's ruling by challenging the status quo based on the requirement of surgical treatment and sterilization.[101] Thus, this time the rejection of the ECtHR's case law seemed to be somewhat bolder. It was based on a different position in "culture wars" and on voicing the (alleged) local resentment against loosening the concept of sex, rather than on mere concerns about the functioning of public administration as in previous cases. As of now, it is hard to judge whether this ruling marks the end of one era and a beginning of further disputes between the SAC and the ECtHR. So far, it is only one ruling by a small chamber of the SAC,[102] and it provides rather few arguments (besides the prevailing social view argument) and lacks a thorough engagement with the ECtHR's legal reasoning. All in all, only the future will show if the ruling turns out to be a game-changer or merely an isolated departure from the SAC's standard friendly approach towards the Strasbourg Court.

Notes

1 Especially if one considers the Czech cases in Strasbourg. The vast majority has dealt with the length of judicial proceedings in criminal and civil law cases, then with procedural issues of criminal law, family law issues, squeeze-out, and restitution of property. See, for example, the country profile of Czechia available at www.echr.coe.int/Documents/CP_Czech_Republic_ENG.pdf.

2 In this chapter, *administrative law* is understood broadly as all areas in the jurisdiction of the SAC, including tax law, social security, asylum, environment, dissolution of political parties, and electoral disputes.

3 See below.

4 This means a sum of references to different individual ECtHR rulings found in all SAC rulings. A repeated reference to the same ECtHR ruling was not counted.

5 A part of a judicial decision which merely recapitulates the procedural development of the case and the claims of the parties to the proceedings.

6 ECtHR, *O.B. Heller, a. s. v. the Czech Republic*, nos. 55631/00 and 55728/00, judgment of 9 November 2004.

7 See, for example, SAC, no. 8 Afs 133/2006-106, judgment of 6 November 2007; and no. 7 Afs 29/2006–68, judgment of 13 April 2006.

8 ECtHR, *Van de Hurk v. the Netherlands*, no. 16034/90, judgment of 19 April 1994.

9 Ibid., § 61. See, for example, SAC, no. 7 Azs 6/2013-105, judgment of 11 July 2013; no. 9 Afs 5/2010–81, judgment of 15 July 2010; no. 6 Ads 1/2011-433, judgment of 31 August 2011.
10 For details on methodology, see Chapter 4.
11 But recall that the meso-level analysis only takes into account what the courts say they do, which is not necessarily the same as what they actually do.
12 For example, ECtHR, *López Ostra v. Spain*, no. 16798/90, judgment of 9 December 1994.
13 SAC, no. 1 Ao 7/2011-526, judgment of 21 June 2012, § 114.
14 ECtHR, *Öllinger v. Austria*, no. 76900/01, judgment of 29 June 2006.
15 SAC, no. 2 As 60/2013–26, judgment of 29 November 2013.
16 For example, SAC, no. 5 Afs 33/2010–55, judgment of 15 July 2010.
17 For example, SAC, no. 1 As 42/2005–62, judgment of 21 June 2006.
18 SAC, no. 6 As 55/2006–96, judgment of 11 July 2007.
19 See the micro-level analysis for further details. Emergence of the "Article 6 mindset" does not mean that all administrative lawyers became ECHR experts. Rather, it suggests that the SAC's case law contributed to a certain degree of "domestication" of Article 6 ECHR, which has been seen as an important source of fundamental principles of administrative procedure. Of course, not all officials of administrative bodies gained expertise in Article 6 ECHR overnight; however, the repeated invocation of Article 6 case law by the SAC contributed to much higher awareness about the EC(t)HR's existence and their relevance for administrative law.
20 For example, SAC, no. 1 As 113/2012-133, judgment of 25 February 2015.
21 See, for example, SAC, no. 1 Azs 160/2014–37, judgment of 4 March 2015.
22 ECtHR, *Üner v. the Netherlands*, no. 46410/99, judgment of 18 October 2006.
23 See, for example, SAC, no. 6 As 48/2013–33, judgment of 26 July 2013 (on Article 3 ECHR); and no. 5 Azs 13/2013–30, judgment of 17 September 2013 (on Article 5 ECHR).
24 ECtHR, *Vilvarajah and Others v. the United Kingdom*, nos. 13163/87; 13164/87; 13165/87; 13447/87 and 13448/87, judgment of 30 October 1991.
25 ECtHR, *Cruz Varas and Others v. Sweden*, no. 15576/89, judgment of 20 March 1991.
26 See, for example, SAC, no. 2 Azs 52/2015–52, decision of 27 May 2015. Interestingly, in the past the SAC criticized the use of *Vilvarajah* by the administrative authorities as outdated – see SAC, no. 2 Azs 7/2010-100, judgment of 19 March 2010, § 30.
27 An exception in which the SAC found a difference between judgments against Czechia and other countries is linked to a very specific situation of activating the SAC's Grand Chamber (see Kadlec and Petrov 2017).
28 Unlike the Supreme Court, which stated so in its earlier case law (see Kühn 2005).
29 ECtHR [Plenary], *Case "relating to certain aspects of the laws on the use of languages in education in Belgium"*, nos. 1474/62; 1677/62; 1691/62; 1769/63; 1994/63 and 2126/64, judgment of 9 February 1967.
30 SAC, no. 1 As 53/2011-109, judgment of 27 July 2011.
31 For example, SAC, no. 1 As 78/2014–41, judgment of 13 August 2014; no. 4 Afs 216/2014–32, judgment of 28 January 2015, § 18; no. 1 Azs 36/2006–71, judgment of 25 July 2007.
32 For example, ECtHR [GC], *Saadi v. UK*, no. 13229/03, judgment of 29 January 2008.
33 SAC, no. 7 As 79/2010-150, decision of 23 November 2011, §§ 22–4. The SAC used the ECtHR's case law in combination with EU law in order to justify this conclusion. Other examples concerning Article 5(1)(f) ECHR include SAC, no. 5 Azs 13/2013–30, judgment of 17 September 2013; no. 7 As 97/2012–26, judgment of 4 September 2012.
34 Figure 6.8 is based on our meso-level sample.

35 For example, SAC, no. 5 Azs 13/2013–30, judgment of 17 September 2013; no. 9 As 111/2012–34, judgment of 1 November 2012; no. 7 Azs 11/2015–32, judgment of 19 February 2015.

36 CC, no. Pl. ÚS 36/01, judgment of 25 June 2002.

37 ECtHR, *Pellegrin v. France*, no. 28541/95, judgment of 8 December 1999; and *Vilho Eskelinen and Others v. Finland* [GC], no. 63235/00, judgment of 19 April 2007.

38 SAC, no. 6 As 55/2006–96, judgment of 11 July 2007.

39 Recall that the category of ECHR-harmonious reinterpretation of domestic statutes is construed rather narrowly for the purposes of meso-level analysis – see Chapter 4.

40 SAC, no. 1 Afs 86/2004-54, judgment of 26 October 2005.

41 SAC, no. 3 As 57/2004–39, judgment of 15 December 2005.

42 Kratochvíl (2019) showed that application of human rights provisions by lower courts in Czechia implies a lower chance that the CC will find a violation.

43 However, on several occasions the SAC used the ECtHR's case law for the benefit of the individual. More specifically, the SAC quashes the decisions of executive bodies and lower courts if they fail to take into account the criteria developed in the Strasbourg jurisprudence on expulsion and family life. See, for example, SAC, no. 5 Azs 6/2015–31, judgment of 16 April 2015.

44 The approach introduced probably in the SAC's judgment no. 8 As 118/2012–45 of 5 March 2013, has been reiterated ever since. See, for example, SAC, no. 1 Azs 160/2014-37, judgment of 4 March 2015; no. 9 Azs 49/2014–27, judgment of 26 March 2014; no. 10 Azs 53/2015–28, judgment of 28 May 2015.

45 Czech legal doctrine breaks down administrative offences into three categories: minor offences (*přestupky*), disciplinary offences (*disciplinární delikty*), and other administrative offences (*jiné správní delikty*). The aim of this chapter is not to provide a doctrinal analysis of these categories; hence, details are left aside. If this chapter speaks about administrative offences, it mostly addresses minor offences, which form the largest group most often addressed in the SAC's case law.

46 CC, no. Pl. ÚS 16/99, judgment of 27 June 2001.

47 SAC, no. 1 As 32/2006–99, judgment of 28 March 2007; see also SAC, no. 3 As 57/2004–39, judgment of 15 December 2005. A similar pattern can be found in the SAC's early case law on the civil prong of Article 6(1) ECHR – see, for example, SAC, no. 1 As 42/2005–62, judgment of 21 June 2006.

48 SAC, no. 6 A 126/2002–27, judgment of 27 October 2004.

49 The statutory regulation of administrative offences from 1990 was long seen as unsatisfactory. However, new legislation was adopted only recently.

50 SAC, no. 3 As 57/2004–39, judgment of 15 December 2005.

51 SAC, no. 8 As 29/2007–121, judgment of 31 May 2007.

52 SAC, no. 4 As 2/2005–62, judgment of 20 January 2006. The SAC illuminated the basic mindset with references to classic rulings such as *Engel and Others v. the Netherlands* ([Plenary], nos. 5100/71; 5101/71; 5102/71; 5354/72 and 5370/72, judgment of 8 June 1976) or *Özturk v. Germany* (no. 8544/79, judgment of 21 February 1984) and then explained some details with references to *Lutz v. Germany* (no. 9912/82, judgment of 25 August 1987) and *Garyfallou AEBE v. Greece* (no. 18996/91, judgment of 24 September 1997) and *Bendenoun v. France* (no. 12547/86, judgment of 24 February 1994). In addition the SAC also cited *Lauko v. Slovakia* (no. 26138/95, judgment of 2 September 1998) and *Kadubec v. Slovakia* (no. 27061/95, judgment of 2 September 1998) since the Slovak legal order still displays many similarities with the Czech one, which might grant some additional authority to the SAC's argument.

53 SAC, no. 4 As 120/2014–21, judgment of 24 July 2014, § 26.

54 For example, SAC, no. 1 As 202/2014–28, judgment of 4 December 2014, § 17.

55 ECtHR [GC], *Zolotukhin v. Russia*, no. 14939/03, judgment of 10 February 2009, § 82.
56 See the arguments of several governments intervening in ECtHR [GC], *A and B v. Norway*, nos. 24130/11 and 29758/11, judgment of 15 November 2016, §§ 87–100.
57 CEI is an executive body mainly charged with supervising the enforcement of environmental legislation.
58 In *Engel v. Netherlands* the ECtHR listed criteria for deciding whether an offence amounts to a "criminal charge" in the sense of Article 6 ECHR.
59 SAC, no. 1 As 125/2011-163, judgment of 11 January 2012, § 30.
60 *Id.*, § 32.
61 SAC, no. 1 As 202/2014–28, judgment of 4 December 2014, § 18; no. 6 As 106/2014-25, judgment of 3 June 2015, § 19; no. 8 As 124/2017–51, judgment of 21 March 2018, § 20.
62 ECtHR [GC], *A and B v. Norway*, nos. 24130/11 and 29758/11, judgment of 15 November 2016. For the argument on factual rewriting of *Zolotukhin*, see the dissenting opinion of judge Pinto de Albuquerque, §§ 50–9.
63 See SAC, no. 6 As 163/2016-39, judgment of 13 December 2016, § 25.
64 The Grand Chamber (typically) consists of seven judges and is charged with unification of the SAC's case law (Kadlec 2019).
65 SAC [GC], no. 4 Afs 210/2014–57, decision of 24 November 2015 (tax law penalty payment); SAC [GC], no. 6 As 114/2014–55, decision of 30 September 2015.
66 The ECtHR's case law was emphasized as the main reason for the change by the SAC's President even in the press release – see www.nssoud.cz/Nejvyssi-spravni-soud-rozhodl-o-povaze-danoveho-penale/art/2281.
67 In *Malige*, the ECtHR held that "although the deduction of points has a preventive character, it also has a punitive and deterrent character and is accordingly similar to a secondary penalty. The fact that Parliament intended to dissociate the sanction of deducting points from the other penalties imposed by the criminal courts cannot change the nature of the measure". ECtHR, *Malige v. France*, no. 27812/95, judgment of 23 September 1998, § 39.
68 Dissenting opinion, SAC [GC], no. 6 As 114/2014–55, decision of 30 September 2015.
69 SAC, no. Pst 1/2008–66, judgment of 4 March 2009, § 3; no. Pst 1/2009-348, judgment of 17 February 2010, part I.
70 DS I, § 107.
71 SAC summarized the framework in § 68 and § 106 of DS I judgment.
72 DS I, §§ 49–51.
73 DS I, § 52.
74 SAC, no. Pst 1/2009-348, judgment of 17 February 2010, § 228 (hereinafter DS II).
75 DS II, § 233. The SAC referred specifically to ECtHR, *Herri Batasuna and Batasuna v. Spain*, nos. 25803/04 and 25817/04, judgment of 30 June 2009.
76 DS II, § 632.
77 CC, no. Pl. ÚS 13/10, decision of 27 May 2010.
78 SAC, no. 7 As 29/2008-104, judgment of 8 August 2009. Later, this ECtHR-inspired approach was also applied in the case of the Sudeten-German Association (*Sudetoněmecké krajanské sdružení*), see SAC, no. 8 As 67/2014–69, judgment of 3 March 2015, § 25.
79 See Chapter 1.
80 SAC, no. 8 As 51/2007–67, judgment of 5 November 2007.
81 In some cases, however, the Strasbourg inspiration was not exclusive; case law of German courts was also invoked. See, for example, SAC, no. 8 As 51/2007–67, judgment of 5 November 2007.
82 In this case, the declared purpose was a "protest against participation of the Czech military on the occupation of Iraq". Nevertheless, based mainly on the route of the

march (proximity to the historic Prague Jewish Town), personal history of the convener, and date of the march, the administrative body concluded that the real purpose of the assembly was related to the anniversary of the *Kristallnacht* – a 1938 pogrom against the Jewish population in the Nazi Germany.

83 SAC, no. 8 As 7/2008-116, judgment of 31 August 2009.

84 SAC, no. 5 As 25/2009–83, judgment of 25 February 2010, §§ 40–5.

85 SAC, no. 5 As 25/2009–83, judgment of 25 February 2010.

86 The assembly protesting against abortion in close proximity to a school included photographs of dead fetuses along photos of people killed during pogroms and genocides. See SAC, no. 2 As 104/2012–35, judgment of 30 October 2012; or no. 5 As 112/2014–33, judgement of 7 November 2014.

87 SAC, no. 6 As 255/2014–42, judgment of 25 May 2015, §§ 23–24; no. 6 As 256/2016–79, judgment of 1 March 2017, § 31. In the latter decision, however, the SAC concluded that the conditions for granting squatters protection of Article 11 ECHR had not been met, see § 34.

88 SAC, no. 2 As 60/2013–26, judgment of 29 November 2013. In this case, the SAC referred to *Öllinger v. Austria*, but in the end distinguished its case from the ECtHR's judgment on the basis of relevant differences between Czech and Austrian law.

89 On subsidiarity, see Chapter 1.

90 Like in the famous *Horncastle* saga (ECtHR, *Horncastle and Others v. the United Kingdom*, no. 4184/10, judgment of 16 December 2014).

91 Besides the cited rulings, see also SAC's 2004 decision: "The application of general constitutional and international law requirements on the administrative offence proceedings shall not entail such interpretation of the procedural provisions that would – in its consequences – de facto exclude any effective penalization". SAC, no. 2 As 3/2004–70, judgment of 22 April 2004.

92 See, for example, the *Regner* case, which addressed withholding of information on the grounds of national security in the context of Article 6 ECHR. Although the SAC's approach was later confirmed by the ECtHR, there were critical voices questioning it. See a dissenting opinion in ECtHR [GC], *Regner v. the Czech Republic*, no. 35289/11, judgment of 19 September 2017, and Preziosi (2017).

93 SAC, no. 1 As 125/2011-163, judgment of 11 January 2012, § 30 (rejecting the *idem factum* approach adopted in Zolotukhin).

94 Besides the examples cited above, see also SAC, no. 6 As 167/2015–37, judgment of 2 December 2015 (confirming the consistency of pre-election silence period with the freedom of speech).

95 See SAC, no. 5 Afs 185/2004–85, judgment of 23 September 2005; no. 5 Afs 178/2006–81, judgment of 23 February 2007.

96 Law clerks at the SAC are quite often recruited from among recent law school graduates or young lawyers with a short amount of professional experience.

97 For example, establishing the Czech database of the Strasbourg case law available at eslp.justice.cz, publishing quarterly newsletter informing about the recent ECtHR judgments, organizing seminars for domestic judges addressing recent case law of the ECtHR, and creating the Committee of Experts for the Execution of the ECtHR judgments and Implementation of the Convention.

98 See, for example, the HUDOC database, fact sheets, guides on interpretation of ECHR, legal summaries of major rulings, more translations etc.

99 ECtHR, *A.P., Garçon a Nicot v. France*, nos. 79885/12; 52471/13 and 52596/13, judgment of 6 April 2017.

100 § 63–5.

101 SAC, no. 2 As 199/2018–37, judgment of 30 May 2019.

102 Thus, it can be later overturned by the SAC's Grand Chamber (if another SAC chamber disagrees with this ruling in a future case) or by the CC (if the litigants file a constitutional complaint, as can be expected).

References

Bobek, Michal. 2013. *Comparative Reasoning in European Supreme Courts.* Oxford: Oxford University Press.

Bobek, Michal, and David Kosař. 2010. "The Application of European Union Law and the Law of the European Convention of Human Rights in the Czech Republic and Slovakia: An Overview". In *The National Judicial Treatment of the ECHR and EU Laws. A Comparative Constitutional Perspective*, edited by Giuseppe Martinico and Oreste Pollicino, 117–50. Groningen: Europa Law Publishing.

Çali, Başak, Anne Koch, and Nicola Bruch. 2013. "The Legitimacy of Human Rights Courts: A Grounded Interpretivist Analysis of the European Court of Human Rights". *Human Rights Quarterly* 35 (4): 955–84.

Garlicki, Lech, and Ireneusz Kondak. 2016. "Poland". In *The Impact of the ECHR on Democratic Change in Central and Eastern Europe*, edited by Iulia Motoc and Ineta Ziemele, 305–29. Cambridge: Cambridge University Press.

Greenman, Kathryn. 2015. "A Castle Built on Sand? Article 3 ECHR and the Source of Risk in Non-Refoulement Obligations in International Law". *International Journal of Refugee Law* 27 (2): 264–96.

Helfer, Laurence R. 2014. "The Effectiveness of International Adjudicators". In *Oxford Handbook of International Adjudication*, edited by Karen J. Alter, Cesare Romano and Yuval Shany, 464–82. New York: Oxford University Press.

Kadlec, Ondřej. 2019. *Role velkých senátů v rozhodování vrcholných soudů České republiky [The Role of Grand Chambers in the Decision Making of the Czech Apex Courts].* Prague: Wolters Kluwer (forthcoming).

Kadlec, Ondřej, and Jan Petrov. 2017. "Rozšířený senát NSS: Judikatura ESLP jako zákaz vjezdu na křižovatce právních názorů [The Grand Chamber of the Supreme Administrative Court: ECtHR's Case Law as a No-entry Sign at the Crossroads of Legal solutions]." *Soudní rozhledy* 23 (1): 2–7.

Kilian, Petr, Ivo Pospíšil, and Hubert Smekal. 2016. "International Human Rights in Czech Legal Education". *International and Comparative Law Review* 16 (2): 87–98.

Kmec, Jiří, David Kosař, Jan Kratochvíl, and Michal Bobek, eds. 2012. *Evropská úmluva o lidských právech: komentář [European Convention on Human Rights: A Commentary].* Prague: C.H. Beck.

Kosař, David. 2014. "Politická práva [Political Rights]". In *Ústavní právo: Casebook [Constitutional Law: Casebook]*, edited by David Kosař et al., 475–513. Prague: Wolters Kluwer.

Kosař, David, and Jan Petrov. 2017. "The Architecture of the Strasbourg System of Human Rights: The Crucial Role of the Domestic Level and the Constitutional Courts in Particular". *Heidelberg Journal of International Law* 77: 585–621.

Kratochvíl, Jan. 2019. "Subsidiarity of Human Rights in Practice: The Relationship between the Constitutional Court and Lower Courts in Czechia". *Netherlands Quarterly of Human Rights* 37 (1): 69–84.

Kühn, Zdeněk. 2005. "K otázce závaznosti rozhodnutí Evropského soudu pro lidská práva pro domácí soudnictví [On Bindingness of ECtHR Case Law on Domestic Judiciary]." *Právní rozhledy* 13 (1): 1–7.

Langášek, Tomáš. 2012. "Čl. 8 (Osobní svoboda) [Art. 8 (Personal liberty)]". In *Listina základních práv a svobod: Komentář [Charter of Fundamental Rights and Freedoms: A Commentary]*, edited by Eliška Wagnerová et al., 217–59. Prague: Wolters Kluwer.

Molek, Pavel. 2013. "Judikatura ve správním právu [Case Law in Administrative law]". In *Judikatura a právní argumentace [Case Law and Legal Argumentation]*, edited by Michal Bobek, Zdeněk Kühn et al., 377–416. 2nd edition. Prague: Auditorium.

Moreham, Nicole A. 2008. "The Right to Respect for Private Life in the European Convention on Human Rights: A Re-examination". *European Human Rights Law Review* 10 (1): 44–79.

Petrov, Jan. 2018a. "Unpacking the Partnership: Typology of Constitutional Courts' Roles in Implementation of the European Court of Human Rights' Case Law". *European Constitutional Law Review* 14 (3): 499–531.

Petrov, Jan. 2018b. "The Populist Challenge to the European Court of Human Rights". *Jean Monnet Working Paper Series* 24 (3): 1–40.

Petrov, Jan, and Katarína Šipulová. 2016. "Mezinárodní lidskoprávní smlouvy v judikatuře obecných soudů: Nejvyšší soud a Nejvyšší správní soud [International Human Rights Treaties in case Law of the General Courts: The Supreme Court and Supreme Administrative court]". In *Mezinárodní lidskoprávní závazky postkomunistických zemí: případy České republiky a Slovenska [International Human Rights Obligations of Post-communist Countries: Examples of the Czech Republic and Slovakia]*, edited by Ivo Pospíšil and Vladimír Týč, 141–65. Prague: Leges.

Preziosi, Andrea. 2017. "Regner V. Czech Republic: Has the European Court of Human Rights Forgotten the Fair Trial Rights When National Security Is at Stake?" *Strasbourg Observers*. Accessed 5 June 2019. https://strasbourgobservers.com/2017/10/23/regner-v-czech-republic-has-the-european-court-of-human-rights-forgotten-the-fair-trial-rights-when-national-security-is-at-stake/.

Procházka, Radoslav. 2002. "Európsky dohovor o ľudských právach v slovenskom ústavnom poriadku [The ECHR in the Slovak Constitutional Order]." *Časopis pro právní vědu a praxi* 10 (3): 215–19.

Sadurski, Wojciech. 2009. "Partnering with Strasbourg: Constitutionalization of the European Court of Human Rights, the Accession of Central and East European States to the Council of Europe, and the Idea of Pilot Judgments". *Human Rights Law Review* 9 (4): 450–83.

Svoboda, Petr. 2012. "Vliv Evropské Úmluvy na české správní právo [The ECHR's Influence on Czech Administrative Law]." *Jurisprudence* 21 (7-8): 9–17.

Thym, Daniel. 2008. "Respect for Private and Family Life under Article 8 ECHR in Immigration Cases: A Human Right to Regularize Illegal Stay?" *International & Comparative Law Quarterly* 57 (1): 87–112.

Vyhnánek, Ladislav. 2017. "A Holistic View of the Czech Constitutional Court Approach to the ECtHR's Case Law". *Heidelberg Journal of International Law* 77 (3): 715–43.

Ziemele, Ineta. 2016. "Conclusions". In *The Impact of the ECHR on Democratic Change in Central and Eastern Europe*, edited by Iulia Motoc and Ineta Ziemele, 491–502. Oxford: Oxford University Press.

7 The Czech Constitutional Court

The Czech Constitutional Court (CC) was established in 1993. Drawing on the legacy of its 1991 federal predecessor,[1] it carried a symbolic reference to the Velvet Revolution and the democratic transition of Czechia. Like most post-communist constitutional courts (Grudzinska-Gros 1994; Teitel 2000), the CC represented a clean slate and a break with the previous regime both in terms of its personal composition and material focus. Compared to the rest of the Czech judiciary, the CC started with a bench composed of 15 justices coming mostly from the dissidents and revolutionary elite. Moreover, it swiftly abandoned the communist idea of legality, pushing forward a normative interpretation of the new Constitution and focusing predominantly on human rights of individuals. Nowadays, rulings on individual complaints represent the majority of the CC's activity. Apart from complaints, the CC decides on the interpretation of international treaties. It can preventively review their conformity with the constitutional order, and it reviews the constitutionality of legal acts and provisions, as well as acts of other constitutional actors (Kosař and Vyhnánek 2019).

Following our understanding of the role of domestic courts in the system of implementation of European Court of Human Rights (ECtHR or Strasbourg Court) case law, we started the empirical research with several general expectations. First, with regard to the specific task and jurisdiction of the CC (around 99 percent of the cases concern human rights protection),[2] we expected that the CC would be more receptive towards the Strasbourg case law than the general courts. As already hypothesized in the Introduction and Chapter 2, we perceived the CC to be the most important ally and intermediary for the ECtHR's communication with other domestic bodies (Kosař and Petrov 2017; Petrov 2018). Bobek and Kosař (2010, 178) have even coined the phrase "champion in the application of the ECHR [European Convention on Human Rights, or Convention]" with regard to the CC's attitude. In more specific terms, this translated into our expectation that the CC will use references to the ECtHR's rulings very frequently.

It is important to note that during the 26 years of its existence, the CC has gone through many changes. Many of those changes were exogenic in nature and not specific to the CC. These include the general development of the law in Czechia (including the preparation for and consequences of the Czechia's accession to the European Union) and the gradual change of the CC agenda (from the specific transitional problems to the more general legal problems arising in an established democratic state).

On the other hand, there has been some internal development as well. The most important factor in this regard is the change of the CC's personnel. As the term of office of a CC justice is ten years (Article 84[1] of the Constitution), there is an extensive change in personnel composition every ten years. In this text, we use the terms "first CC", "second CC" and "third CC" to refer to the composition of the CC in 1993–2003, 2003–2013, and 2013–present respectively. Even though the Czech Constitution does not demand that justices shall be appointed in waves, it is practically making the case. Fourteen justices of the CC were appointed in 1993 and one in 1994 and their terms (with some complications concerning resignations and new appointments that are not important for the purposes of this chapter) generally ended in 2003 and 2004, respectively. The second wave of appointments was not that smooth; therefore, the time between appointments of the first justice and the last justice of the second CC stretched to more than three years. The third wave of appointments then logically occurred between 2013 and 2015. Still, we can talk about compact generations of the CC (Kosař and Vyhnánek 2016, 187; 2019). Other important internal changes include the establishment of the Analytical Department or the gradual growth of the number of justices' legal assistants (Kosař and Vyhnánek 2019).

7.1 A helicopter view: General trends concerning the ECtHR case law references

In the examined period – i.e., 1993–2015 – the CC dealt with 61,582 rulings in which it made 6,012 individual references to 1,276 various Strasbourg Court rulings. The overall number of the CC's decisions and judgments containing a reference to the ECtHR was 2,674; i.e., approximately 4.3 percent of all rulings decided by the CC. The low percentage might seem surprising given the reputation of the CC[3] as a very pro-human-rights and internationalized (or Europeanized) court; however, it results from the internal structure of the CC's rulings. According to the CC's own statistical analysis,[4] the CC issues substantive judgments only in roughly 6.6 percent of all rulings; 56.3 percent of the petitions are dismissed as manifestly ill-founded, while the rest comprises – generally speaking – various procedural decisions.[5] References to ECtHR case law can therefore be realistically expected only in rulings substantively analyzing violation of human rights; i.e., in judgments and some of the more complex decisions that dismiss a petition as manifestly ill-founded.

Figure 7.1 captures the timeline of the use of both individual references (gray line) and the CC's rulings containing these references[6] (dark area). At the very beginning of the 1990s, the references to ECtHR case law were rare (two judgments in 1994, zero in 1995, and four in 1996). The very first pioneering rulings covered issues related to the freedom of expression (*Handyside v. the*

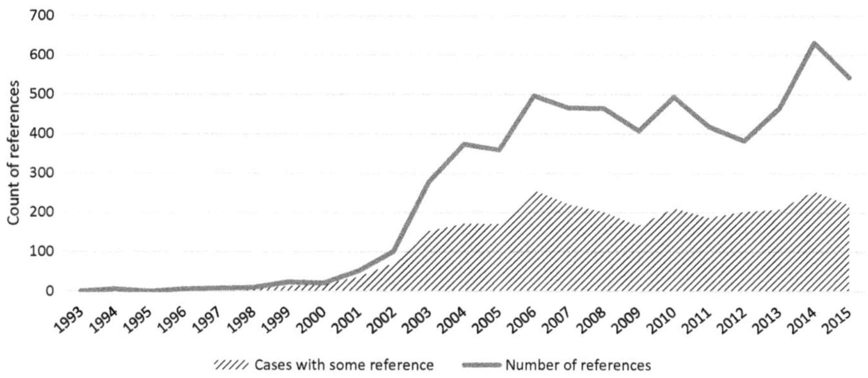

Figure 7.1 Development in the use of references to ECtHR case law (any placement).
Source: authors.

United Kingdom, *The* Sunday Times *v. the United Kingdom*, or the *Lingens v. Austria* case),[7] and fair trial conditions (*Windisch v. Austria*; *Schmautzer v. Austria*; *Le Compte, Van Leuven and De Meyre v. Belgium*).[8]

This suggests that similarly to both general courts, the CC found its way to ECtHR case law only slowly. After the rather "lean" 1990s – when the approach of the CC towards ECtHR case law was just developing – the number of references started to rise significantly in the early 2000s and especially around year 2003, which correlates *inter alia* with the switch from the "first" to the "second" CC. The second important rise took place in 2006, followed by significant decline in 2009 and 2012.[9] Nevertheless, the overall frequency of rulings containing a reference (dark area of Figure 7.1) remains more or less steady. This, however, means that around 2009 and 2012, the CC issued a series of rulings referring to the ECtHR and its case law, but only sparingly. We therefore examine these two points in time in a qualitative analysis of the character and significance of references.

Figure 7.2 offers a different perspective, capturing the proportion of references compared to the overall volume of rulings delivered by the CC. It gives us a more precise picture and confirms that the trend of the use of references does not depend on the overall development of the caseload. Nevertheless, the solid line confirms a significant drop in the number of references used per ruling in 2009 and 2012.

In this respect, Figure 7.3 captures an interesting development in terms of the placement of references in the structure of individual CC rulings. As explained elsewhere,[10] the simple count of references might be slightly misleading, as isolated references in the narrative part of rulings without a further reflection in the reasoning itself do not add to the judicial treatment or implementation of the Strasbourg case law.[11] For the purposes of this study, we therefore separated

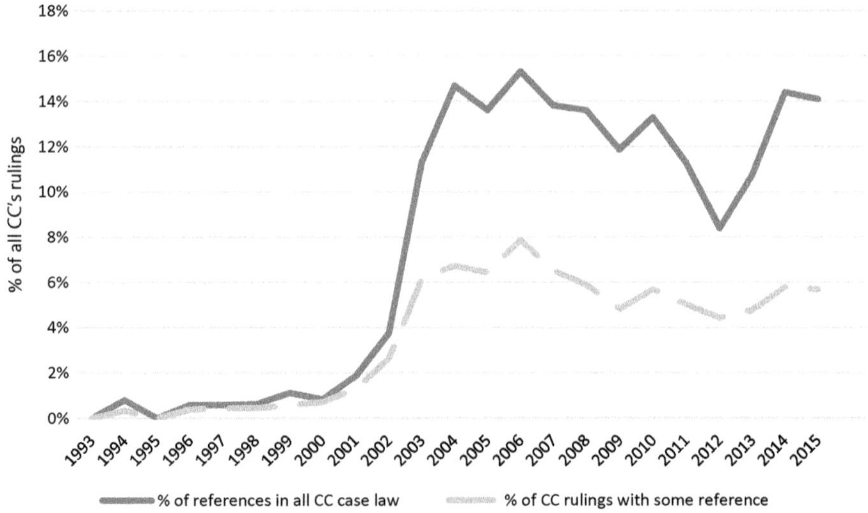

Figure 7.2 Development in the proportion of rulings with references to ECtHR case law.
Source: authors.

out those rulings that contain a reference only in the narrative part (dark gray area of the Figure 7.3) or a dissenting opinion (black area in Figure 7.3) without any reflection in the reasoning. It is worth contemplating whether the declines resulted from the character of the petitions reaching the CC or changes in the CC's attitude towards ECtHR based arguments.

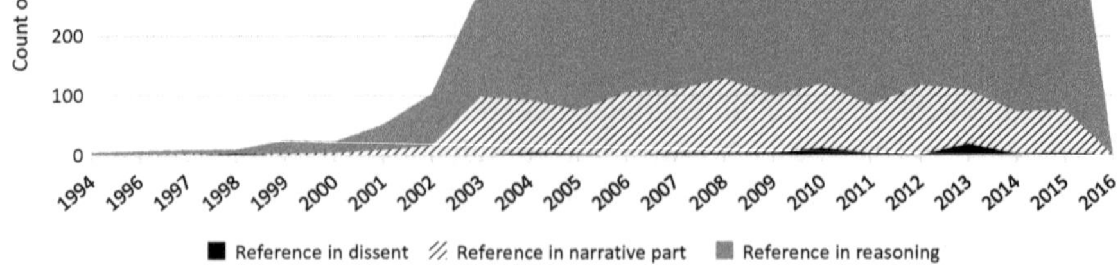

Figure 7.3 Development in the placement of references to ECtHR case law.
Source: authors.

In terms of our principal research question – i.e., whether the Czech top courts engage with the ECtHR case law and why (or why not) – it may thus be said that the CC engages with the Strasbourg case law very frequently but that this has not always been the case. Given our initial hypothesis, that a new and "human rights friendly" (as generally reflected by the expert community) institution will have a positive attitude towards the ECtHR case law and that it will engage with it significantly, the difference between the lean 1990s and the later years deserves a closer examination. As we have already mentioned elsewhere (Vyhnánek 2017, 726–30), there are several hypotheses on how to interpret the development of the timeline and the rise in use of the ECtHR case law by the CC after 2003.

First, the rapid growth might be explained by the aforementioned changes in the personnel composition of the CC. The year 2003 marked the end of the so-called "first CC" and justices of the "second CC" were appointed between 2003 and 2005 (Kosař and Vyhnánek 2016, 187–8; 2019). We have many reasons to believe that despite the relatively low number of references, the general perception of the first CC as a human-rights-friendly court still holds. There is an obvious difference between following and respecting the ECtHR case law in substantive terms (which roughly correlates to human rights friendliness) and an explicit reference to the ECtHR case law in the reasoning of a ruling. We should not forget that the first CC was comprised predominantly of older generations of lawyers who have been trained in the "classical Central European style". In this legal culture, explicit engagement with case law, including ECtHR case law, was not a prevalent method of drafting a reasoning. At the same time, it can be argued that the first generation of CC justices was relatively lacking in resources (such as accessible literature, assistants trained in international human rights law, or even computers equipped with databases) that would make the engagement with the ECtHR case law easier.

Second, the CC issued the *Euro-Amendment* judgment in 2002[12] and it might have been compelled to defend its position as a guardian of the ECHR by working with the ECtHR case law in a more extensive manner.

Third, one should also not forget the systemic changes on the part of the Strasbourg Court. In 1998, Protocol No. 11 replaced the original two-tier structure – the ECtHR and the Commission – and allowed individuals to access the ECtHR directly. Not only did this strengthen the position of the ECtHR, it was also accompanied by an increased number of rulings issued by the Strasbourg Court, which in turn might be reflected, with a certain lag, by the growing number of their citations.

The fourth set of explanations is connected to the aforementioned availability of resources. Relevant resources might include publications and databases containing information about ECtHR case law, legal assistants and advisors and their skills, or even something as prosaic as technical equipment. As regards the equipment, the growing use of computers with more sophisticated text editors that allow copy and paste and, obviously, the spread of the internet might at least partially explain the rise in the number of references in the early 2000s.[13]

At the same time, new publications concerning ECtHR case law became available in Czech. One of the groundbreaking publications was without doubt the Czech translation of *Case Law of the European Court of Human Rights* by Vincent Berger, which was published in 2003. Another important book that was published in 2003 was *The European Convention on Human Rights and the Czech Republic* by Eva Hubálková.

In the 1990s and early 2000s, each justice was appointed one and later two legal assistants. These were generally more experienced and older lawyers. Since September 2003, however, each justice has been entitled to three legal assistants. This enhanced the research potential of each "mini-team" – a justice and her three assistants. Moreover, it was not only the simple fact that each justice had more assistants, but it was also the skills of the new assistants that arguably played an important role (Kosař and Petrov 2017; Vyhnánek 2017). Between 2003 and 2013, the young graduates, who generally had better language skills and often studied abroad, gradually supplemented or replaced older lawyers.

As Kosař and Petrov (2017, 613) point out, analytical departments are an understudied and potentially significant factor. However, the CC's Analytical Department was established only in 2007; i.e., too late to be responsible for the increase in referrals between 2003 and 2006. This does not diminish in any way the significance of the Analytical Department, but the Department's role lies in the qualitative rather than quantitative realm. It informs the justices about developments in the ECtHR case law or, at the request of an individual justice, conducts specialized research in this area. By providing the justices with necessary information and thus making it easier, the Analytical Department can contribute to compliance, but it does not necessarily influence the frequency of references.

Additionally, the behavior of petitioners and especially their attorneys should be taken into account. The growing number of references by the CC and the newly available resources encouraged petitioners and their lawyers to rely on the case law of the ECtHR in their petitions, and the CC had to respond to such arguments. This interpretation also aligns with findings in Figure 7.3, which demonstrate a steep rise of ECtHR references occurring in the narrative parts of rulings from 2001 on.

Finally, we should not overlook a phenomenon that may be called "the snowball effect" (Vyhnánek 2017, 730). When the CC referred to the ECtHR case law, it simultaneously incorporated it in its own case law. The parts of reasoning in the CC's ruling that contained references were often copied – for various reasons[14] – in later rulings. Thus, by referring to itself or copying paragraphs from the reasoning of a previous ruling, the CC "indirectly" refers to ECtHR case law. The problem of the snowball effect is closely connected to the issue of entry points by which the ECtHR case law infiltrates the CC.

As suggested in the description of Figure 7.3, the drop in 2012 might be explained by a synergic effect of at least two factors. First, the structure of the docket in 2012 was unprecedented. As much as a quarter of the docket comprised near-identical similar petitions of companies[15] whose business model included suing in low-value cases and profiting from the awarded costs of the proceedings. A change in the case law of the general courts regarding the costs initiated this wave of petitions, which were dismissed with no need to use references to ECtHR case law. Furthermore, as a vast majority of justices were about to leave the Court in 2013, these justices generally aimed to issue a ruling in as many cases as possible and thus lower the number of cases in their respective dockets. Strategically, this may have led them towards deciding the "easy cases" first, while often leaving the more complicated cases (where references to ECtHR case law might have been appropriate relatively more often) to their successors.

To sum up, we are convinced that the shift in engagement with the ECtHR case law on the part of the CC was not connected to the domestic court's attitude (such as human rights attitude or international law attitude), but rather to a general style of work and the availability of resources. Thus, after a rather brief period of "lean years", the CC can be described as an institution that frequently engages with the ECtHR case law.

In the following section, we are looking at some specifics and common characteristics of CC rulings that refer to the Strasbourg Court and its case law. While the majority of references are contained in decisions (which is not surprising, as decisions, especially procedural decisions, represent the majority of the CC's decision-making activity and caseload), the proportion of references encompassed in judgments is fairly good. It is important in this regard that the CC does not have a clear policy on whether to substantively dismiss cases with a judgment or with a decision. This unclear practice causes some confusion and it probably distorts the results.

Figure 7.4 below gives us a more precise picture of the character of proceedings that rely on the Strasbourg Court's case law. The figure breaks down individual types of proceedings. Again, as expected, the overwhelming majority of references belong to rulings on individual complaints.

We also looked at who typically initiates petitions in rulings that later rely on the ECtHR case law: The composition of petitioners is very vibrant (Table 7.1). Moreover, the composition is becoming even more diversified over time, as cases are gradually brought before the CC by a wider range of actors.

We were interested to see if there are differences between individual justices when serving as rapporteurs and their usage of references to the ECtHR case law (Figure 7.5). Kateřina Šimáčková, followed by Eliška Wagnerová and Miloslav Výborný, clearly prevail in their rates of referring to the ECtHR case law.

At least in the case of Justices Wagnerová and Šimáčková, it corresponds well with their profiling as very pro-human-rights, liberal justices with a good understanding of international obligations and the ECtHR case law. At the same time, both Šimáčková and Wagnerová hold a PhD in constitutional law and have been involved in legal academia. This is an important factor, especially with regard to Kateřina Šimáčková, who has been a human rights and

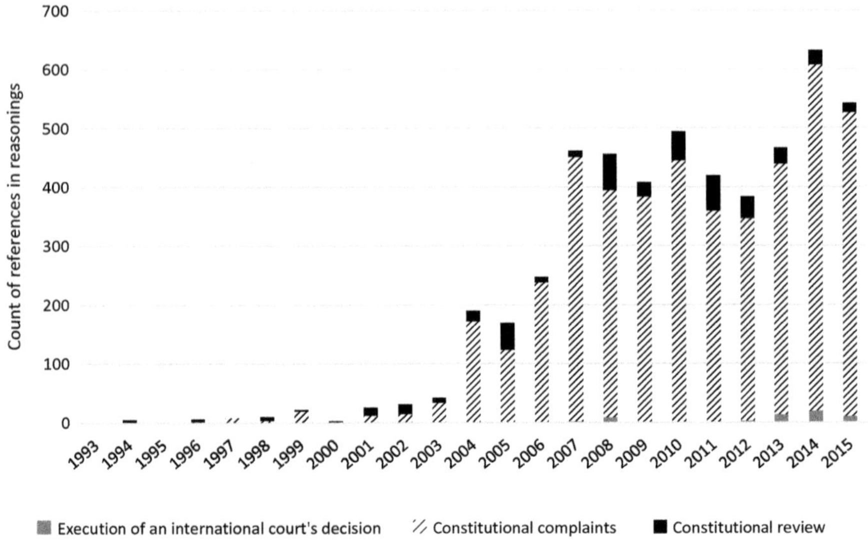

Figure 7.4 Development in the number of rulings containing a reference to ECtHR according to the type of proceedings.

Source: authors.

Table 7.1 Petitioners in the CC's proceedings

Petitioner	*Count of references in reasonings*	*%*
Ombudsman	6	0.1%
President	7	0.1%
Political party	10	0.2%
Ministry	14	0.3%
Municipality	67	1.3%
Senate of CC	75	1.5%
MPs/Senate	124	2.5%
General courts	174	3.5%
Legal person	590	11.7%
Natural person (human being)	3,970	79.9%

Source: authors.

constitutional law lecturer for more than 25 years and has been involved in the formation of many human rights and clinical education courses at Masaryk University in Brno. Furthermore, Justice Šimáčková has one of the highest proportions of references used when compared to the length of her mandate at

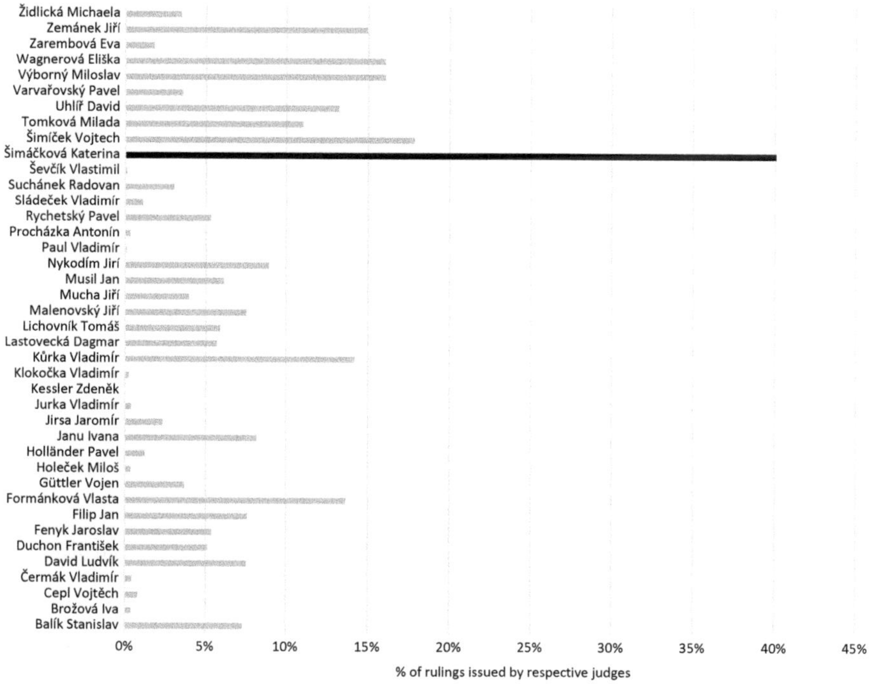

Figure 7.5 Use of references (in reasonings) by individual justices according to the number of issued rulings.

Source: authors.

the CC, which started only recently. Justice Vladimír Kůrka, who has also referred to ECtHR case law quite often, is an interesting case to examine more deeply: he started his career as a judge at the Supreme Court (SC), then was appointed as a CC justice, and returned back to the SC after the end of his mandate in 2015. His reassignment to the SC, where he was named President of the Civil and Commercial Division, could have caused some tension with his former SC colleagues, who were worried that Kůrka had changed his decision-making and views too much to fit in at the (rather conservative) SC.

The following figures move on to a better understanding of the character of those ECtHR rulings which the CC typically chooses as appropriate to refer to. First, we were looking at the differences in approach towards cases originating in Czechia (narrow compliance) compared to the rest of the Council of Europe (CoE) countries (wider compliance). Figure 7.6 demonstrates that while adverse cases against Czechia dominate the State of Origin category (1,374; the second most referred is Spain with 453, then France and Austria), overall the references to a broader spectrum of cases against other states dominate. Again, this is understandable and expected given the composition and structure of the

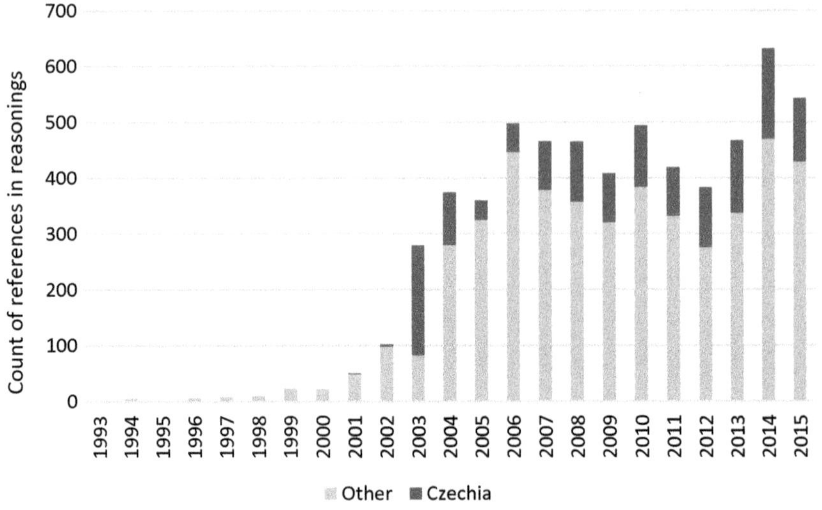

Figure 7.6 Development in the number of references to ECtHR rulings against Czechia v. other CoE states.

Source: authors.

ECtHR case law. On the other hand, the high number of references to ECtHR rulings against other states than Czechia demonstrates that the CC accepts the more general role of the ECtHR in the unification and creative interpretation of the Convention.[16] It seems that the CC does not limit itself to the very narrow understanding of compliance. In other words, the CC does not seem to distinguish (at least at the general level) between the legitimacy of references to ECtHR rulings against Czechia and other CoE states, and seems to use both categories in a similar manner. This phenomenon may be interpreted as yet additional support for the "loyal ally" narrative. By accepting the precedential normative force of the ECtHR case law (and not only the direct effect of rulings against Czechia), the CC functions not only as a passive complier, but also acts as a kind of "missionary" that spreads the ECtHR case law in the broadest sense.

Second, similarly to the other two apex courts, the majority of references relate to cases in which the ECtHR found a violation of the Convention. While partly understandable, as these cases probably also get more academic and political attention, the repeating trend is still worth some further examination (Figure 7.7).

However, the results regarding the scope of ECtHR rulings to which the CC typically refers are surprising. A huge part of the CC's caseload concerns human rights protection (especially in individual complaints proceedings), whereas the general courts have broader jurisdiction and many of their rulings do not

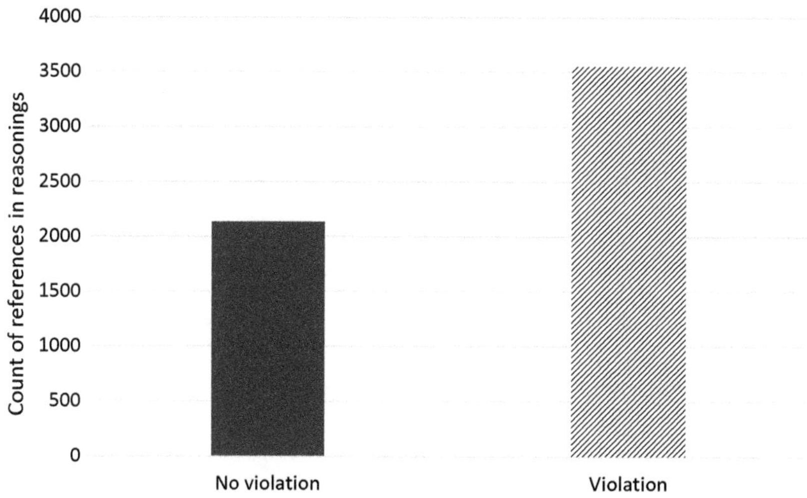

Figure 7.7 Number of references to ECtHR rulings that found a (non-)violation.
Source: authors.

involve a human rights dimension. Similarly to the SC and Supreme Administrative Court, Article 6 and the general criteria of admissibility prevail. Other important areas include detention (Article 5), protection of private and family life (Article 8), freedom of speech (Article 10), property and restitution rights (Article 1 of the Protocol No. 1), and prohibition of torture (Article 3, which in the Czech context relates most often to conditions in prisons).

When looking at the development in the use of references related to various Convention articles over time, the sparklines in Figure 7.8 demonstrate the gradual change of trends. In the 1990s, the CC, still inexperienced in the use of the Strasbourg case law, emphasized the general admissibility criteria and general principles explaining the scope and application of the Convention, and the jurisdiction of the ECtHR, as well as Articles 6 and 8. Currently, however, the CC is broadening the range of the Convention articles and respective case law and diving into different agendas. This might, to a certain degree, correspond to the shifting policy focus of the CC in various time periods. As previously mentioned, the 1990s were in fact dominated by transitional justice processes, fair trial issues, and conditions for an efficient and legitimate judiciary, while in the early 2000s the petitions and rulings shifted more towards social issues, or the conditions of the legislative process.

At the same time, however, the number of references to the ECtHR case law concerning Article 6 ECHR is not surprising for several reasons. First of all, Article 6 ECHR covers an extremely broad array of issues, including access to court, procedural rights (in both civil and criminal cases), independence and impartiality of the judiciary, quality of judicial reasoning, or the reasonable time

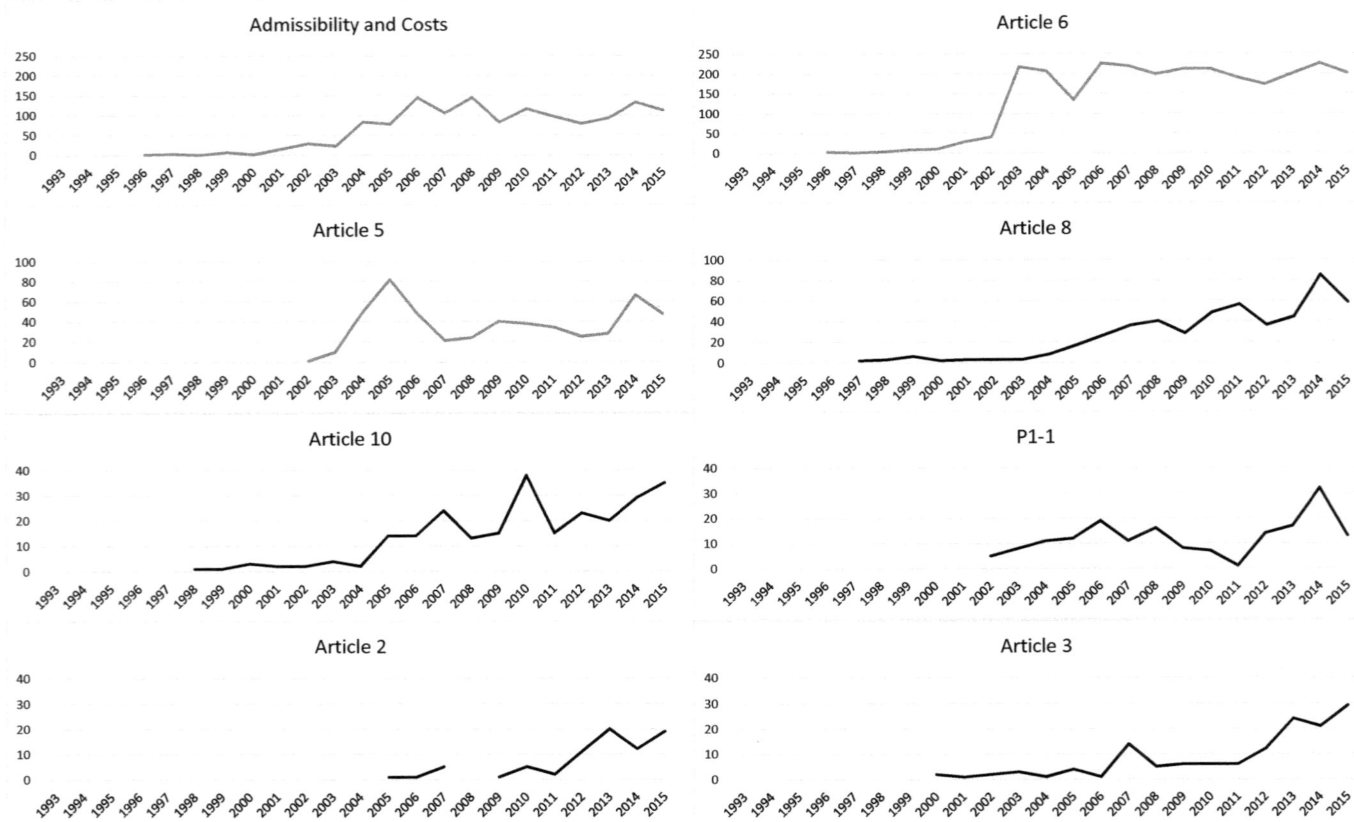

Figure 7.8 Development in the number of CC rulings referring to ECtHR rulings according to the Convention articles used.
Source: authors.

requirement. It is thus applicable in almost every case heard by the CC (especially in the constitutional complaint procedure), whereas the other ECHR provisions are quite specific and applicable only in a narrow set of cases. Second, the CC has a tendency to overuse the *fair trial* argument (even though this mainly applies to the domestic Article 36 of the Czech Charter), and this tendency might have spilled over to the references to Article 6 case law of the ECtHR. The rise in the number of Article 6 references around 2003 corresponds to the overall rise of references covered by Figure 7.1.

Figure 7.9 shows that – not surprisingly, given that Article 6 case law is used most often – the most frequent references to ECtHR case law concern some general principles stemming from Article 6 ECHR. For example, the most frequently cited case, the *García Ruiz v. Spain* judgment,[17] is typically referred to in cases where the complainant claims that an appellate court ruling's reasoning was inadequate. In such cases the CC refers to *García Ruiz* and holds that the appellate court can, in principle, simply take over the reasoning of the lower court and refer to it. In similar cases, the CC also often refers to the "runner-up", *Ruiz Torija v. Spain*,[18] to stress that the extent of a general court's reasoning may vary from case to case and that there is no general obligation to exhaustively reflect every objection made by the parties of the proceedings. The frequent use of such general references is quite logical as they can be used with regard to typical generic arguments that are raised by the complainants in hundreds of CC cases each year.

On the other hand, very specific references to rulings dealing with substantive questions (Articles 8 and 10 ECHR and Article 1 of the Protocol No. 1) can be

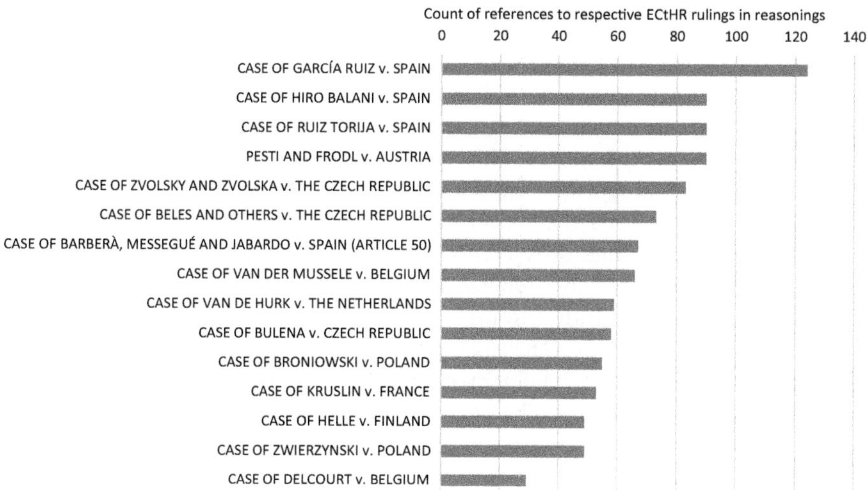

Figure 7.9 ECtHR rulings most frequently referred to in the reasoning.
Source: authors.

considered extremely important for the development of the CC doctrines, yet – as they are limited only to specific and less numerous cases – they could never have reached the top of the chart.

The macro-level analysis has identified fundamental aspects of the CC's use of the ECtHR case law, such as the frequency of references and development over time, as well as the basic characteristics of the cited Strasbourg Court rulings. At the same time, however, several issues remain unanswered. The count of references does not reflect how the CC actually treats the Strasbourg case law – which is the core question that we aim to answer in the following sections.

7.2 A closer look at the nature of the CC's engagement with ECtHR case law

As hinted above, the macro-level analysis has provided us with an understanding of some general trends concerning the treatment of ECtHR case law, but it obviously has its limits. Crucially, it does not deal with questions such as whether the CC follows the Strasbourg Court's conclusions, how it engages with the ECtHR case law, or what impact the ECtHR case law does have on the CC's reasoning. Moreover, some results of the macro-level analysis beg for more detailed explanation. Accordingly, the subsequent section looks beyond the number of references to the Strasbourg Court and asks deeper questions about the role of references to the ECtHR case law in the CC's reasoning. The meso-level analysis of a new hand-coded dataset of 336[19] rulings of the CC reveals the basic patterns and sheds more light on the puzzles that the macro-level analysis simply cannot solve.

7.2.1 The CC as a loyal ally?

As we have already noted, one of our key research questions was whether domestic apex courts function as allies for the ECtHR. The meso-level analysis seems to support the conclusion that this is exactly the case for the CC. Perhaps the most important indicator in this regard is the category dissecting whether the CC follows, distinguishes, or rejects ECtHR rulings. Our sample analysis finds that the CC follows the ECtHR's conclusions nearly all the time, as 343 out of 355 observed units of reference[20] have been coded as "following". This finding corresponds with the general perception of the CC as a human rights court with a positive attitude towards international and foreign law (Bobek and Kosař 2010; Majerčík 2016, 151–52). Previous literature suggests that systemic "behind-the-door" factors[21] help in communicating the ECtHR ideas to the CC (Pospíšil 2018, 213–15). The analyzed sample does not contain any case of explicit rejection of the ECtHR's conclusions and only in 13 cases in the sample did the CC distinguish from the ECtHR conclusions.

However, while the "loyal ally" interpretation is definitely a viable one, we cannot jump to it without a few caveats. First of all, it is naturally possible that an exceptional case of rejection might have escaped our sampling (as we are working with a sample and not the whole population). Perhaps even more importantly, our research (especially its macro and meso levels) only concerns rulings explicitly referring to an ECtHR judgment. It is then plausible to expect that cases of non-following (or even de facto rejection) exist where the CC did not refer to an ECtHR judgment, either because it was not aware of the applicable ECtHR case law, or because it wanted to hide its non-following.[22]

Distinguishing can be used as a functional alternative to outright rejection. A domestic court can significantly narrow the scope (factual distinguishing) or soften the impact (legal distinguishing) of an ECtHR ruling. However, the 12 cases of distinguishing (i.e., roughly 3.4 percent of the sample) are not an example of the CC trying to limit an "undesirable" impact of the ECtHR case law. Most cases of distinguishing are connected to the activity of the parties to the proceedings that refer to an ill-fitting ECtHR judgment while the CC rejects their argument by distinguishing the situation at hand from the context in which the ECtHR judgment was adopted.

7.2.2 Substantive impact of the ECtHR case law

Most of the references in our sample were used only as a supporting argument, while only roughly 18 percent of the references (65 out of 355 cases) had substantive impact. The category of substantive impact is defined as follows: the ECtHR case law has substantive impact *if the CC applies the norms stemming from ECtHR case law to the facts of the case under consideration.* Still, such an application (subsumption) has to be a meaningful one and not a mere ornament. Such subsumption had a significant impact on the reasoning of the CC (and its result), even though the ECtHR case law was *not always the only* significant normative factor.

In the "supporting use" category, several frequent patterns of references deserve a closer look. First of all, the CC often uses a reference to ECtHR case law in the opening section of its reasoning in order to highlight general principles governing the interpretation of a certain ECHR provision. These guiding principles usually have some traceable influence on the subsequent parts of the reasoning, but the decisive arguments lie elsewhere. A typical example of this pattern is the reference to *The Sunday Times v. the United Kingdom* in some freedom of expression cases that generally stress its importance in a democratic society.[23] Another broad category can be called the "ornamental reference" of "subsequent legitimation". Cases where the decisive arguments are constructed independently by the CC, which are then "embellished" by a laconic reference to an ECtHR ruling, fall into this category.

Even though the supporting references could be hastily dismissed as mere window dressing, we consider them quite significant from the point of the perceived legitimacy of the ECtHR. By referring to ECtHR case law even in situations when the domestic court "does not have to",[24] it further confirms that it (1) considers the case law of the ECtHR an important source of law, and (2) recognizes the legitimacy-enhancing influence of the ECtHR case law. In this sense we have reason to believe that the CC acts as an institution that internalizes the rules and principles stemming from the ECtHR case law to a great degree and then bona fide enforces those normative guidances in the domestic settings.

However, it is important to note that the practices concerning the use of the ECtHR case law are not uniform at the CC. On the contrary, it depends heavily on the particular judge rapporteur whether the ECtHR case law will be referred to at all in a particular ruling (Vyhnánek 2017) or for what purposes such references are included in the reasoning. Therefore, it is extremely important to look below the level of the "whole court" to properly understand the dynamics and nature of references to the ECtHR case law by the CC.

An interesting case in point is the difference between the treatment of ECtHR case law at the third CC by Justice Šimáčková and Justice Jan Musil[25] (acting as rapporteurs). When it comes to the period of the third CC (from 2013 onwards), both are among the justices who refer to the ECtHR rulings the most. But whereas in the case of Justice Musil the references were mostly used as a very general background for subsequent legal arguments or as ornaments[26] without a significant substantive impact,[27] Justice Šimáčková's references are very often substantive, quite novel,[28] and form the backbone of many of her important judgments. Justice Musil, in contrast, frequently refers to an ECtHR ruling just to legitimize the dismissal of a petition as manifestly ill-founded. For example, in four of his decisions,[29] Justice Musil referred to the ECtHR's ruling in the case *Orion-Břeclav, s.r.o. v. the Czech Republic*[30] using the same paragraph word for word concerning the need to balance the conflicting interests in cases where a financial burden is placed on an individual. In five decisions,[31] Justice Musil used the same paragraph containing a reference to *Bochan v. Ukraine*[32] to convey the message that the ECtHR does not serve as a court of fourth instance reviewing the finding of facts and legal conclusions reached by domestic courts.[33] In two other decisions, Justice Musil used the same reference and a slightly different wording to convey the same message.[34] A similar practice also appears in other sets of decisions.

Figure 7.10 then shows the development of the impact (substantive or supporting over time). We can observe significant rises at the respective starts of the "second" and "third" CCs. This might be explained by the new justices – who have to adapt to their new role as human rights guardians –looking for guidance in the ECtHR (as well as the CC) case law. Most of the newly appointed justices (including judges of general courts or attorneys) had not been previously confronted with the ECtHR case law or with the application of the ECHR in general. In other words, most of the justices have not applied ECtHR case law on a daily basis and human rights cases amounted only to a fraction of their respective agendas. Therefore, it is quite understandable that they are looking for an explicit guidance (in the form of ECtHR case law). Later on, references in routine "easy" cases might be dropped and a reference to an already established CC case law might be used instead, simply because of the perceived redundancy of further references to ECtHR case law.

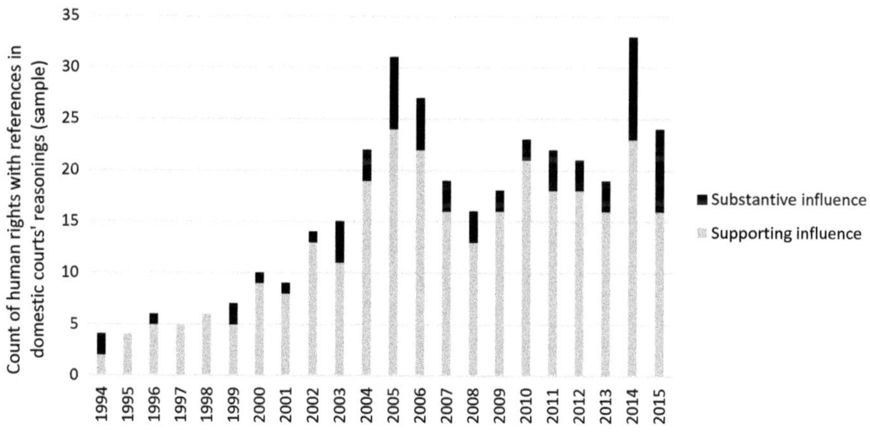

Figure 7.10 Substantive effect by year.
Source: authors.

References with a substantive impact can further be divided into several categories according to the "technique of application". As Figure 7.11 shows, the most frequent categories are Supplementing and Confirmation. The category Supplementing concerns rulings where the CC uses the ECtHR's case law to clarify or supplement the somewhat lacking Czech legal regulation, often by formulating some additional requirements or by introducing an ECtHR-inspired test or a set of criteria. It does not involve a simple re-interpretation of a single statutory provision (such cases would fall into the Interpretation category), but

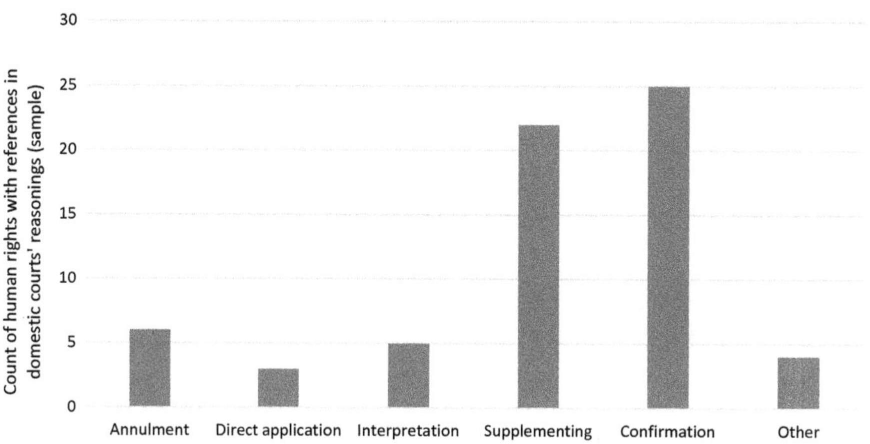

Figure 7.11 Technique of application.
Source: authors.

rather introduction of an additional normative layer to the Czech legal order that – paired with the existing law – changes the status quo. Both of the micro-level case studies can generally be included in this category.

Even more frequently, the CC uses substantive references to confirm the current status quo (confirmation). References in such cases can be seen as a legitimization tool by the CC. They can serve both to convince the parties to the proceedings and the broader public that the CC's ruling is consistent with the international human rights obligations, but also as a pre-emptive message to the ECtHR in the event that a complaint were to be filed in the Strasbourg Court.

The ratio of substantive/supporting references significantly varies according to the ECHR article concerned. As we have shown above (Figure 7.8), Article 6 references are by far the most numerous. At the same time, however, they are used predominantly in a supporting manner, while in cases of some other provisions, the ratio of supporting/substantive impact is more balanced. For example, the CC frequently uses references to ECtHR case law on Article 5 or Article 10 in a more sophisticated manner that contains subsumptions with decisive influence on its final ruling. This does not come as a complete surprise, since the nature of fair trial cases and substantive rights cases is – as a general rule – quite different. In "fair trial" cases, even though the ECtHR's Article 6 case law can always provide some guiding principles, the structure and content of domestic procedural law is usually very important for the CC's ruling. ECtHR rulings concerning specific substantive rights, on the other hand, are often analogically applied to the facts of the domestic case at hand. This is especially evident in cases whose outcome depends on balancing (or generally on proportionality testing) and the structure and wording of statutory law is not that relevant.

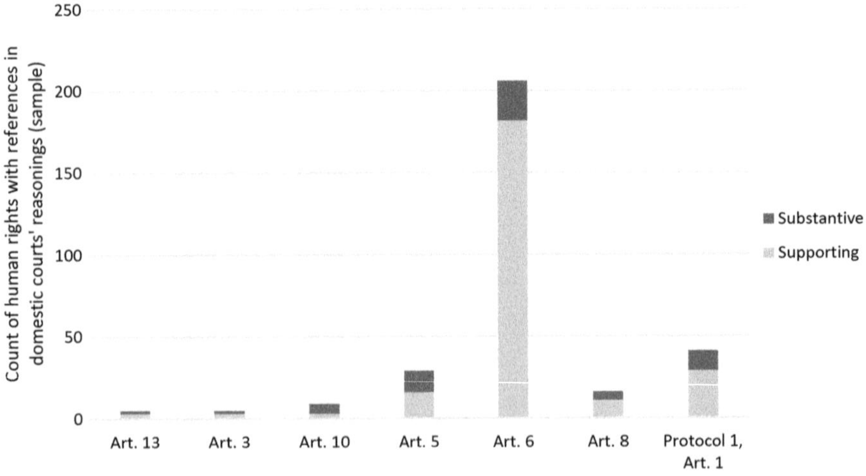

Figure 7.12 Ratio of substantive and supporting impact according to the ECHR article.[35]
Source: authors.

7.3 From numbers to case law: Case studies of the impact of ECtHR case law on the CC's jurisprudence

The meso-level analysis has shown some general patterns concerning the CC's use of the ECtHR case law. Several of those patterns deserve a closer look in this section – both to introduce a deeper analysis of both typical and important examples and also to highlight some "black swans" and problematic aspects that might have escaped our attention in the upper tiers of our research.

While it is true that – statistically speaking – the majority of the CC's references to the ECtHR case law can be described as having an auxiliary or supporting effect, the number of references to ECtHR case law with significant substantive effect or even with a decisive effect is by no means negligible. There are a number of broader areas in the CC's case law that have been shaped by ECtHR rulings. The effect of the ECtHR case law in these cases has not been limited to a "mere" determination of outcomes of individual CC cases, but it has also decisively influenced the concepts and methodology used by the CC.[36] The most important examples concern the structure of freedom of speech cases,[37] the general approach to proportionality testing (including the notion of "necessity in a democratic society"), concepts from Article 1 of the Protocol No. 1 case law (legitimate expectation), and many others. Some of these are analyzed below.

In particular, we will take a closer look at two specific areas of the CC's case law that have been thoroughly influenced and shaped by the ECtHR jurisprudence, namely (1) the case law concerning conflicts between freedom of speech and personality rights, and (2) case law concerning positive obligations of the state related to both right to life and prohibition of torture and inhuman and degrading treatment.

7.3.1 Freedom of expression cases

Even though we have stated above that the impact of ECtHR jurisprudence on the current state of the domestic case law has been significant in both of the micro-level case studies, the domestic context and the patterns of influence vastly differ. Therefore, before we turn our attention to the actual analysis of the CC's case law concerning freedom of expression and its conflicts with personality rights, we deem it important to highlight the most important contextual features.

First of all, the freedom of expression is regulated quite similarly by both the European Convention of Human Rights and the Czech Charter of Fundamental Rights and Freedoms. At the very least, despite some differences in the wording of Article 10 ECHR and Article 17 of the Czech Charter, it is possible to interpret them in a harmonic manner and neither of them offers prima facie more or less protection than the other.

Second, the CC case law in this area developed under conditions of "heavy judicial traffic" – defamation/personality rights cases have been occurring quite frequently before civil courts. Moreover, the civil law regulation of personality rights in the Czech (and Czechoslovak) legal order was much older than the CC itself. A significant part of the CC case law in the 2000s was formulated while the 1964 Civil Code was still in force. Therefore, by the time the CC issued its first rulings in these sorts of cases, there was already decades-old and reasonably settled case law of the civil courts. This settled case law often (even well into 2000s) relied on conclusions and concepts drawn by the SC in the 1970s, when the position of fundamental rights generally, and of freedom of speech in particular, was dramatically different from the current position. On the other hand, the heavy judicial traffic gave the CC ample opportunities to develop its case law, test it on various sets of factual backgrounds, and tweak it accordingly.

While there are now many significant and influential CC cases concerning the conflicts between freedom of expression and personality rights, we can highlight one pioneering case: *Rejžek v. Vondráčková.*[38] Before this judgment, the approach of the general courts towards the freedom of expression in civil law (i.e., in cases concerning personality rights and defamation cases) was rather restrictive. The *Vondráčková* ruling changed this status quo and it did so by borrowing two important concepts from the ECtHR case law.

The constitutional complaint was filed by a music critic (Mr. Rejžek) who was ordered by the general courts to apologize to a famous singer (Mrs. Vondráčková), because Mr. Rejžek wrote an article asserting that Mrs. Vondráčková owed her prominent position in Czech showbusiness to her pre-revolutionary[39] contact with mafiosos. The CC – unlike the general courts before – emphasized both the conceptual distinction between the "statement of facts" and a "value judgment" and the importance of the fact that Helena Vondráčková was a public figure. Both of these crucial distinctions have of course been borrowed from the rich ECtHR case law.

As regards the first point, the CC criticized the formalist approach of the lower courts who had tried to ascertain whether Vondráčková had some actual ties to people that could be described as "Mafiosos" (i.e., members of an organized crime group). The CC emphasized that general courts need to distinguish between value judgements and statements of fact. Consequently, it opted for a contextual reading of the music critic's statements[40] and considered them a typical example of value judgments. Consistent with the cited ECtHR case law (mainly *Lingens v. Austria*), the CC pointed out that value judgments cannot be proven as a matter of fact. At the same time, it stressed that the appropriateness of the interference with the personality rights can depend upon whether there exists a sufficient factual basis for the contested statement, since even a value judgment can be excessive if it lacks any factual basis whatsoever (relying on ECtHR judgments *De Haes and Gijsels v. Belgium*[41] and *Oberschlick v. Austria [No. 2]*[42]).

When deciding on the appropriateness of the critic's statement, it made use of the "public figure factor" and, based on *Lingens v. Austria*,[43] held that a famous and publicly active person (such as one of the most popular Czech singers) must tolerate more intensive interferences with her personality rights than the average person.

Turning away from the outcome of this individual case, it is of utmost importance that both of these factors/distinctions that the CC borrowed from the ECtHR case law (a statement of facts v. a value judgment and a public figure v. an "ordinary" person) became an integral part of the future CC freedom of expression case law.

The distinction between a statement of fact and a value judgement/opinion and the importance of contextual reading of a statement served as an important factor in a number of later cases, including the *Šlouf* case[44] concerning criticism of a close advisor of the former Prime Minister Miloš Zeman, and in the *Píchová* case[45] concerning criticism of a judge participating in some communist-era criminal trials with dissidents.

The public figure argument was further developed in a subsequent line of case law, including the *Čouka* case.[46] This particular case was based on an even more complete and detailed analysis of the ECtHR Article 10 case law[47] than the previous ones and concerned a citizen's criticism of an elected mayor. The key arguments of the ECtHR case law were adopted without any opposition at the CC level and they now form the backbone of the CC's case law.

This, however, does not mean that the CC's approach to such cases (as regards the structure of reasoning) is a precise copy of the ECtHR practice. Rather, the ECtHR approach was slightly developed and restructured over time. Perhaps most significantly, the CC merged and generalized the previous ECtHR and CC case law in the 2015 *Řápková v. Hůle* case[48] in order to formulate a simplified working formula for both itself and the general courts when deciding freedom of expression v. personality rights cases. More specifically, the CC put together a list of factors (though non-exhaustive) that must be taken into account when balancing freedom of expression against personality rights. It was perhaps the emphasis on the balancing test in the case law of the ECtHR (and the CC) that led it to formulate this "balancing checklist".[49] This list had not been explicitly formulated in the ECtHR case law, but the CC has assembled it based on its interpretation of various key ECtHR judgments. It can thus be considered a rephrasing of principles that stem from the ECtHR case law.

Specifically, the CC identified the following eight key balancing factors:

1. The nature of the statement (i.e., whether it is a statement of fact or a value judgment).
2. The content of the statement (e.g., whether it is a "political" or "commercial" expression).
3. The form of the statement (especially how expressive/vulgar the statement was).
4. The position of the criticized person (e.g., whether it is a public figure, mainly a politician or a figure otherwise known to the public – typically "celebrities").
5. Whether the statement (criticism) interferes with the private or public sphere of the criticized person.

6. The behavior of the criticized person (such as whether the criticism could be considered "provoked" by the criticized person's actions or speech).
7. The position of the author of the statement (e.g., whether it is a journalist, an expert in a particular area, an ordinary citizen, or a politician).
8. The time, place, and communication channel of the statement (e.g., whether it was an immediate reaction in an interview; a prepared, thought-over statement in a book; an advertisement on a billboard).

These ready-to-use factors have since been referred to in the subsequent CC case law[50] as well as in the case law of the lower courts. It cannot be claimed that this checklist would "replace" the ECtHR case law and remove the need to refer to it, but it has established itself as a useful heuristic tool that allows judges to structure the case effectively.

7.3.2 Positive obligations under Articles 2 and 3 ECHR (effective investigation)

The second micro-level case study concerns a significantly different issue. In the previous section, we have stressed that freedom of expression case law of the CC developed under conditions of heavy judicial traffic and that the communication between general courts and the CC involving cases with various factual backgrounds provided ample opportunity to develop and settle the Strasbourg-inspired case law.

The introduction of positive obligations under Articles 2 and 3 ECHR happened under different circumstances. First of all, ECtHR case law concerning positive obligations developed later than the Article 10 case law and for a while it was not part of "general Strasbourg knowledge" among Czech lawyers. But perhaps more importantly, the procedural context is incomparable. While the CC was used to hearing constitutional complaints in defamation cases and deciding them on the merits, there were no cases before the CC raising the problem of effective investigation to begin with. For at least two decades, established case law of the CC had stated that it is proper to dismiss (as manifestly ill-founded) petitions by individuals harmed by alleged criminal conduct asking for review of an investigation by the police and a state attorney, relying on the argument that there is no fundamental right to have another person punished.[51]

This approach was usually applied in cases falling outside the scope of Articles 2 and 3 ECHR, but some cases involved issues of life or ill-treatment as well.[52] These cases also illuminate one feature and limitation of our research, as they are typical "false negatives". Even though ECtHR case law concerning the effective investigation requirement could have and perhaps should have been referred to and dealt with in these CC rulings, both of them simply followed the aforementioned line of the CC's case law, without mentioning (and perhaps even without considering) a potential ECHR dimension. Systemically identifying such false negatives in the CC case law would be an extremely complicated task. Were it to be done, however, the results could somewhat disturb the image of the CC as a good pupil of the ECtHR.

The aforementioned Justice Šimáčková, relying on a detailed analysis of principles stemming from the ECtHR case law,[53] reversed this trend both as regards investigating threats to the right to life[54] and suspicions of ill-treatment.[55] These judgments stressed some of the basic principles of the ECtHR case law concerning effective investigation under Articles 2 and 3[56] (threshold for effective investigation, burden of proof, independence and impartiality of the investigation). Case law concerning effective investigation under Article 3 ECHR was further confirmed and developed by yet another judgment by the same CC chamber and the same judge rapporteur.[57]

Unlike the freedom of expression v. personality rights case law that has been adopted by all chambers of the CC and never seriously challenged, the fate of effective investigation case law is still to be determined. Still, on a general level (more as a question of principle than the real *ratio decidendi*), it has since been confirmed by one plenary judgment of the CC,[58] and the initial treatment of the effective investigation doctrine by other chambers also seems to be rather positive.[59]

One factor that could complicate the matter is that in effective investigation cases, the CC usually deals with petitions aimed directly at the conduct of the police and state attorneys, without the general courts acting as intermediaries. Such a setting is not the most effective; the relative willingness and capability of the general courts to accept the CC's case law in freedom of expression cases should be considered an important factor in its ultimate success.

Without the cooperation of the general courts and considering that this line of case law effectively introduced completely new concepts and standards to the Czech human rights case law, compliance with effective investigation of ECtHR case law faces some serious challenges. Still, proper statutory changes or changes at the level of internal (police) manuals and guidelines might help in surmounting these obstacles. This, however, is a complex systemic issue that goes well beyond the scope of the CC's powers.

7.4 Conclusion

Generally speaking, all of the levels of our analysis show the CC as an ally of the ECtHR that – with the above-explained exception of the 1990s – frequently engages with the ECtHR case law and whose attitude towards the ECtHR is quite positive and friendly. This conviction of ours is obviously not based primarily on the *number* of references to the ECtHR case law (even though this gives us a rough idea about the CC's attitude in general), but rather on a complex analysis of the nature of the references and on the qualitative analysis of selected areas of the CC human rights case law.

We consider it important that the CC does not stick to the bare minimum – i.e., only to direct compliance with the rulings against Czechia – but that it frequently engages with and follows (rather than rejects or distinguishes from) the rules and principles stemming from the ECtHR case law in the broad sense. The holistic assessment of all three levels of analysis lends itself to interpretation that the CC actually internalizes the ECtHR case law and considers it its normative duty to enforce it to the fullest extent.

Furthermore, as the micro-level analysis shows, the CC is not an entirely passive actor that simply waits for what the Strasbourg Court has to say. It does not hesitate to further develop the specific formulation of the ECtHR rules and principles in order make them more comprehensible in the domestic settings and easier to use for ordinary courts, such as in the analyzed case study of the freedom of speech cases.

Despite the overall positive attitude, it has to be noted, however, that the frequency and the nature of the CC's engagement with the ECtHR's rulings varies both across time and even between different CC justices sitting on the same bench. The availability of resources in the broadest sense, and the human rights friendliness of individual justices and their style of work, seem to be among the most important few factors that determine the nature and frequency of the engagement. Still, even considering these factors, the narrative of an ECtHR-friendly court that frequently and in good faith engages with the ECtHR case law is – in our opinion – correct.

Notes

1 The Federal Czechoslovak Constitutional Court had been established in 1991 as a completely new institution. Although the communist Constitution presumed the existence of a constitutional court, the respective provisions were never implemented in practice.

2 This figure can be deduced from the fact that the constitutional complaints procedure (around 99 percent of the cases; see the CC database NALUS at http://nalus.usoud.cz) by definition always concerns human rights.

3 And this applies even to the 1990s; i.e., the period in which judicial treatment of the ECtHR case law by the CC was rather scarce.

4 Yearly statistical data of the CC, the 2016 edition (capturing data until 31 December 2015).

5 A vast majority of those procedural decisions are issued pursuant to Article 43(1) of the Act on the Constitutional Court (182/1993 Coll.). According to this provision, the Court, enacted by the judge rapporteur, dismisses the petition if: (a) the petitioner fails to remediate defects in the petition by the designated deadline; (b) the petition was submitted after the deadline for its submission as laid down in this Statute; (c) the petition was submitted by a person who is clearly not authorized to submit it; (d) it is a petition over which the Court has no jurisdiction; or (e) the submitted petition is inadmissible, unless the Act provides otherwise.

6 The distinction between both categories is caused by the fact that a single ruling can include multiple references concerning separate legal questions.

7 ECtHR, *Handyside v. the United Kingdom*, no. 5493/72, judgment of 7 December 1976; *The Sunday Times v. United Kingdom*, no. 6538/74, judgment of 26 April 1979; *Lingens v. Austria*, no. 9815/82, judgment of 8 July 1986.

8 ECtHR, *Windisch v. Austria*, no. 12489/86, judgment of 28 June 1993; *Schmautzer v. Austria*, no. 15523/89, judgment of 23 October 1995; *Le Compte, Van Leuven and De Meyre v. Belgium*, nos. 6878/75 and 7238/75, judgment of 23 June 1981.

9 The decline in 2015 is caused by the fact that we obtained only part of the database for year 2015.

10 See Chapter 2.
11 See Chapter 4.
12 CC, no. Pl. ÚS 36/01 *Euro-Amendment*, judgment of 25 June 2002. In this judgement, the CC refused to acknowledge the effects of a constitutional amendment (the *Euro-Amendment*) which took away the CC's power to review conformity of domestic legislation with international human rights treaties (which had been previously explicitly entrenched in the Constitution). Arguing that such a change would "result in limiting an already achieved procedural level of protection for fundamental rights and freedoms", and thus be contrary to Article 9(2) of the Constitution, the CC continued to interpret the Constitution as if it was still allowed to review domestic legislation from the point of view of its conformity with international human rights treaties. This judgement has shown that the CC attaches a great importance to its position as a guardian of international human rights treaties.
13 This equipment was obviously introduced earlier at the CC, but the problem might well have been in the personnel who were not willing or able to use them properly.
14 The main reason is probably that the CC has a relatively high caseload and it has no formal filtering mechanism (Bobek 2009, 38). Therefore, it often has to deal with repetitive complaints (sometimes even in hundreds of cases), where "the copy and paste" technique of drafting makes sense.
15 Including more than 700 petitions by a single company that were dismissed as manifestly ill-founded in 2012.
16 See Chapter 1.
17 ECtHR, *García Ruiz v. Spain*, no. 30544/96, judgment of 21 January 1999.
18 ECtHR, *Ruiz Torija v. Spain*, no. 18390/91, judgment of 9 December 1994.
19 Whereas one ruling could have produced several units of analysis, if dealing with several independent ECHR problems (such as Article 6 issues and Article 8 issues being dealt with in the same ruling). See Appendix 1.
20 Meso-level analysis treats respective rights – i.e., Convention provision or a particular (sub)paragraph – as a unit of an analysis.
21 Such as communication between the CC and the Government Agent before the ECtHR.
22 The second case study in the micro-level section (see below) mentions several CC rulings that do not refer to the applicable ECtHR case law, even if it would be hasty to label them as non-following or rejection.
23 In our sample, CC, no. I. ÚS 526/98, judgment of 18 February 1999, for example, uses such a reference.
24 While we are aware that domestic courts do not have to refer to ECtHR case law as a rule, it is prudent to do so in situations when a particular ECtHR judgment has direct normative influence on the outcome of the domestic case.
25 With regard to Justice Musil, we again only take into account his work at the "third CC", where he worked with a different set group of assistants and referred to ECtHR case law much more than during his first term, Otherwise, Justices Šimáčková, Wagnerová and Výborný were the frontrunners (see Figure 7.5).
26 See Appendix 1.
27 This can be supported by the fact that only a fraction of Justice Musil's references can be found in "judgments", while a vast majority of references are used in (generally less important) decisions. Similarly, Justice Josef Fiala referred to the ECtHR case law in 48 cases, but only once in a judgment. Justice Fiala, however, is the newest addition to the CC, so it is perhaps better to wait before drawing conclusions.
28 See also the second case study in the micro-level section.
29 Decisions no. III. ÚS 3522/15 of 21 July 2016, no. III. ÚS 1305/14 of 16 October 2014, no. III. ÚS 306/14 of 15 May 2014 and no. III. ÚS 2837/12 of 20 February 2014.
30 No. 43783/98, judgment of 13 January 2014.

31 Decisions no. IV. ÚS 434/16 of 9 November 2016, no. III. ÚS 1033/15 of 8 October 2015, no. III. ÚS 693/15 of 17 September 2015, no. III. ÚS 541/15 of 3 September 2015 and no. III. ÚS 3913/14, decision of 1 July 2015.

32 ECtHR [GC], *Bochan v. Ukraine*, no. 22251/08, judgment 5 February 2015.

33 Namely: "[ECtHR] reiterates that, according to its long-standing and established case law, it is not for this Court to deal with alleged errors of law or fact committed by the national courts unless and in so far as they may have infringed rights and freedoms protected by the Convention."

34 Decisions no. IV. ÚS 2320/16 of 21 January 2017 and no. IV. ÚS 2308/16 of 14 December 2016.

35 Provisions with a negligible number of references and/or virtually no substantive impact references are omitted from this figure.

36 This does not mean, however, that the CC case law in these areas is a simple copy of the ECtHR templates – as we will see, even the conceptual framework of the ECtHR-inspired jurisprudence is not immune to developments and slight modifications.

37 For example, the difference between *value judgments* and *statements of facts.*

38 CC, no. I. ÚS 367/03 *Rejžek v. Vondráčková*, judgment of 15 March 2005.

39 This refers to the 1989 Velvet Revolution that ended the communist rule in Czechoslovakia.

40 Even doing this, it relied on an example from the ECtHR case law. The CC stressed that in evaluating the foundation of a value judgment, it is necessary to take into consideration the entire article, and not just the one or two sentences at issue as the ordinary courts had done, as well as the overall societal context in which a certain statement is made (making a reference to the ECtHR case *Feldek v. Slovakia* [no. 29032/95, judgment of 12 July 2001], revolving around the interpretation of the word "fascist" in an article).

41 *De Haes a Gijsels v. Belgium*, no. 19983/92, judgment of 24 February 1997.

42 *Oberschlick v. Austria (no. 2)*, no. 20834/92, judgment of 1 July 1997.

43 The CC also referred to the United States case law, but the normative value of a ECtHR judgment was of course much higher.

44 CC, no. IV. ÚS 146/04 *Šlouf*, judgement of 4 April 2005.

45 CC, no. IV. ÚS 23/05 *Píchová*, judgement of 17 July 2007.

46 CC, no. IV. ÚS 1511/13 *Čouka*, judgment of 20 May 2014.

47 No less than 11 ECtHR judgments have been referred to and applied to the facts of the domestic case.

48 CC, no. II. ÚS 2051/14 *Řápková v. Hůle*, judgment of 3 February 2015.

49 The CC uses a different version of a proportionality test (basically the German one) than the ECtHR.

50 As of 31 August 2019, the *Řápková v. Hůle* judgement has been referred to in 19 subsequent CC rulings, including rather important judgements; for example, in the *Šimůnek* case (no. I. ÚS 750/15, judgment of 19 January 2016) or the *Kydalka* case (no. I. ÚS 2617/15, judgment of 5 September 2015).

51 See, among dozens of others, the decision no. I. ÚS 1941/09, decision of 21 January 2010.

52 See, for example, decisions of the CC no. II.ÚS 2733/08 of 11 June 2009 and no. IV. ÚS 1921/09 of 17 September 2009 (both concerning investigation of a death of a person in a hospital).

53 Most of the ECtHR's judgments were referred to for the first time by the CC, including *Oğur v. Turkey* (no. 21594/93, judgment of 20 May 1999), *Makaratzis v. Greece* (no. 50385/99, judgment of 20 December 2004), and *Finogenov and Others v. Russia* (nos. 18299/03 and 27311/03, judgment of 20 December 2011).

54 CC, no. I. ÚS 1565/14, judgment of 2 March 2015 (case involving investigation of a life-threatening situation during birth).

55 CC, no. I. ÚS 860/15, judgment of 27 October 2015. This case involved an alleged mistreatment of an alien who was about to be deported and who was (while naked) handcuffed, teargassed, and allegedly beaten by the police. The CC held that the investigation was conducted with undue delay (especially interviewing the witnesses) and that the investigators were generally lax with regard to collecting evidence.
56 Quite interestingly, these judgements also included the effective investigation requirement under the scope of the corresponding domestic provisions (Articles 6 and 7 of the Czech Charter respectively).
57 CC, no. I. ÚS 1042/15, judgement of 24 May 2016.
58 See no. Pl. ÚS 32/16, judgement of 8 August 2017, §§ 62–5.
59 See no. II. ÚS 3626/13, judgement of 6 December 2015 and no. II. ÚS 3436/14, judgement of 19 January 2016, both concerning the investigation of human trafficking allegations.

References

Berger, Vincent. 2003. *Judikatura Evropského soudu pro lidská práva [Case Law of the European Court of Human Rights]*. Prague: IFEC.

Bobek, Michal. 2009. "Quantity or Quality? Re-Assessing the Role of Supreme Jurisdictions in Central Europe". *American Journal of Comparative Law* 57 (1): 33–65.

Bobek, Michal, and David Kosař. 2010. "The Application of European Union Law and the Law of the European Convention of Human Rights in the Czech Republic and Slovakia: An Overview". In *The National Judicial Treatment of the ECHR and EU Laws. A Comparative Constitutional Perspective*, edited by Giuseppe Martinico and Oreste Pollicino, 117–50. Groningen: Europa Law Publishing.

Grudzinska-Gros, Irena. 1994. *Constitutionalism in East Central Europe: Discussions in Warsaw, Budapest, Prague, Bratislava*. Bratislava: Czecho-Slovak Committee of European Cultural Foundation.

Hubálková, Eva. 2003. *Evropská úmluva o lidských právech a Česká republika [European Convention on Human Rights and the Czech Republic]*. Prague: Linde.

Kosař, David, and Ladislav Vyhnánek. 2016. "Senát a výběr soudců Ústavního soudu [The Senate and the Selection of the Constitutional Court's Justices]". In *Dvacet Let Senátu Parlamentu České Republiky V Souvislostech [20 Years of the Senate of the Parliament of the Czech Republic]*, edited by Jan Kysela, 187–210. Prague: Leges.

Kosař, David, and Ladislav Vyhnánek. 2019. "The Czech Constitutional Court". In *Constitutional Courts (Ius Publicum Europaeum Series)*, edited by von Bogdandy Armin. Oxford: Oxford University Press (forthcoming).

Kosař, David, and Jan Petrov. 2017. "The Architecture of the Strasbourg System of Human Rights: The Crucial Role of the Domestic Level and the Constitutional Courts in Particular". *Heidelberg Journal of International Law* 77: 585–621.

Majerčík, Ľubomír. 2016. "Czech Republic: Strasbourg Case Law Undisputed". In *Criticism of the European Court of Human Rights: Shifting the Convention System: Counter-dynamics at the National and EU Level*, edited by Patricia Popelier, Sarah Lambrecht and Koen Lemmens, 131–154. Cambridge: Intersentia.

Petrov, Jan. 2018. "Unpacking the Partnership: Typology of Constitutional Courts' Roles in Implementation of the European Court of Human Rights' Case Law". *European Constitutional Law Review* 14 (3): 499–531.

Pospíšil, Ivo. 2018. "Ústavní soud v systému implementace rozsudků ESLP: několik postřehů z praxe, aneb co se odehráva „behind" compliance [Constitutional Court in the System of the ECtHR's Case Law Implementation: What Is Happening 'behind' Compliance]". In *Beyond Compliance: Implementace rozhodnutí mezinárodních lidskoprávních těles na národní úrovni [Beyond Compliance: Domestic Judicial Implementation of the International Human Rights Case Law]*, edited by Hubert Smekal and Ladislav Vyhnánek, 221–228. Prague: Wolters Kluwer.

Teitel, Ruti G. 2000. *Transnational Justice*. New York: Oxford University Press.

Vyhnánek, Ladislav. 2017. "A Holistic View of the Czech Constitutional Court Approach to the ECtHR's Case Law". *Heidelberg Journal of International Law* 77 (3): 715–743.

8 Judicial treatment patterns

More complicated than they seem

Synthesis of the findings from individual chapters on the Czech apex courts helps to build a bigger picture of the domestic judicial treatment of European Court of Human Rights (ECtHR or Strasbourg Court) case law. We compare individual apex courts and assess to what extent the data fits the general image of each court. We must again bear in mind that all three Czech apex courts serve not only legally distinct purposes, but also have a distinct identity that builds upon their historical legacy and expectations associated with their founding. The Constitutional Court (CC) was built anew after the 1989 Velvet Revolution as a "downstream consolidator of democracy" (Ginsburg 2012, 729). It was given the mission of deciding constitutional review cases and individual complaints in order to protect rights stemming from the constitution. It was endowed with an ethos of the institution protecting a newly established liberal democratic regime (Procházka 2008; Bobek 2013, 172). In contrast, the post-1989 Supreme Court (SC) survived the shift from a communist to a liberal democratic regime and has remained at the top of the civil and criminal judicial hierarchy. The personal transition followed only gradually and its staff included many judges from the communist era (Kühn 2005, 2011; Bobek 2008, 2015; Kosař 2016). Finally, the Supreme Administrative Court (SAC) started functioning only in 2003 and from the beginning portrayed itself as a "Different Court". Such a label should indicate that it performs with greater dynamics corresponding to its composition, which also included a younger generation of lawyers and non-career judges. The SAC gained the reputation for easily absorbing foreign influences and entering into international judicial dialogues, especially with the Court of Justice of the European Union (Bobek 2013, 164–8; Bobek and Kosař 2010; Matczak, Bencze, and Kühn 2010; Molek 2013; Petrov and Šipulová 2016).

The following synthesis helps us see if and how the trends in the use of ECtHR case law spread between the three Czech apex courts. Either the apex courts operate autonomously, each of them resting in their own specific environment and (not particularly quickly) adopting external impulses, or the apex courts can be sensitive to the developments at other apex courts and adjust their behavior according to outside trends. Both scenarios of either institutional encapsulation or institutional spillover from one court to another are conceivable. Furthermore, we observe similarities and differences between the old (the SC) and new courts (the CC and the SAC), and between the ordinary apex courts (the SC and the SAC) and the specialized apex court (the CC).

8.1 Macro-level analysis

The macro-level analysis provides a helicopter view of the treatment of ECtHR case law by Czech apex courts.[1] First, in order to evaluate the degree of the ECtHR case law's penetration into national judicial practice, we wanted to know to what extent domestic apex courts use it. Having the overall picture of the development in the number of references enabled us to identify important points in time when the trend changed. We could then have zoomed in to trace potential causes of the shifts in the number of references.

Second, the macro-level question examined where references to ECtHR case law appear – whether in narrative parts of rulings, which merely sum up previous proceedings and argumentation of parties, or in reasoning parts, where courts build their argumentation to decide disputes. A huge disproportion between occurrences of references in the narrative and reasoning parts suggests that parties try to substantiate their cases with the authority of ECtHR case law, which, however, domestic courts do not then explicitly discuss. Put very roughly, observing where references occur provides us with some indication of who brings ECtHR case law to national courtrooms. Consequently, such an examination helps in shedding light on the level of awareness national courts have about Strasbourg case law. However, great caution is needed here before jumping to hasty conclusions. Without a detailed study of individual rulings (which goes against the logic of the macro-level study), one cannot be sure if a court inserted a reference to ECtHR case law on its own initiative, or did so only upon being alerted by a party to the case. As noted above, the information on where a reference appears provides us with some signal, particularly when big disproportions appear or when trends markedly change.

Finally, the macro-level analysis maps whether national courts focus on putting into practice rulings against their own home states, or if they go beyond the implementation of individual rulings and make use of ECtHR case law as a whole. Elaborating on this issue provides us with valuable information on the domestic judicial perception of the general applicability and binding nature of ECtHR case law. We uncover changes in trends and make informed guesses about the drivers of change.

More straightforwardly, the macro-level analysis focused on questions such as (1) how often do the apex courts use ECtHR case law, (2) in which part of rulings they do use it (if they use it more in the operative part, or only in the summary of facts and positions of parties), and (3) do the apex courts tend to use more ECtHR case law against the home state or rather rulings against other parties to the European Convention on Human Rights (ECHR or Convention).[2] We adopted a dynamic approach and observed how the trends develop over time.

One important caveat warrants attention. The three apex courts do not deal with the same type of cases. Their treatment of ECtHR case law thus can be predetermined by the nature of the disputes that the particular courts hear. The CC is very often directly concerned with complaints that explicitly claim a violation of human rights. Therefore, the case law of the ECtHR becomes a potential source for application here more frequently than before other apex courts. On the other hand, as ECtHR case law massively expanded after the turn of the millennium,[3] so did the breadth of covered areas and the number of rulings from which all the apex courts can draw inspiration. Consequently, because of ECtHR case law expansion in terms of both quantity and scope, the SC and the SAC faced spreading ECtHR case law into their primary fields of operation (civil and criminal law, and administrative law respectively).

One can expect two synchronic trends to be in action. First, judges will experience a learning curve stemming from the reorientation from the communist legal system to the legal order of a liberal democratic regime. They will look for guidance to the case law of the courts that they associate with a liberal democratic legal order. The ECtHR is especially convenient here because its case law embodies the human rights norms to which the newly democratic state legally subscribed via the ratification of the ECHR. Second, ECtHR case law will gradually expand into other areas of law. This expansion is arguably more pronounced in the case of administrative and civil law because the ECtHR case law has intervened in these areas of law much less in the past. The spread of ECtHR case law into the administrative agenda provides a particularly good example of the expansion of ECtHR case law because the administrative law was not originally an area into which the ECtHR was supposed to intervene.[4] Unlike other jurisdictions (Sumption 2011), Czechia has not experienced any opened public uproar over the ECtHR's judicial overreach (Majerčík 2016).

8.1.1 How often do apex courts refer?

Figure 8.1 shows a basic comparison among Czech apex courts as regards development in the number of rulings in which they refer to ECtHR case law. It is only a very crude measure, useful merely to demonstrate the overall picture, which shows some bumps along the road.[5] The development in the number of rulings containing a reference (or references, because one case can include more than one reference) to ECtHR case law is far from linear, yet we can observe some similarities among the courts. The curves jump up and down in the case of all courts, but while both the CC and the SC[6] started using references to ECtHR case law only slowly, the SAC's curve rose very steeply right after its establishment in 2003. The slower increase in the number of rulings with a reference to ECtHR case law in the case of both older courts was quite expectable for the following reasons. The CC started functioning in the early days of the newly democratic state and helped to entrench new legal order. The CC focused particularly on the application of the Czech Charter of Rights,

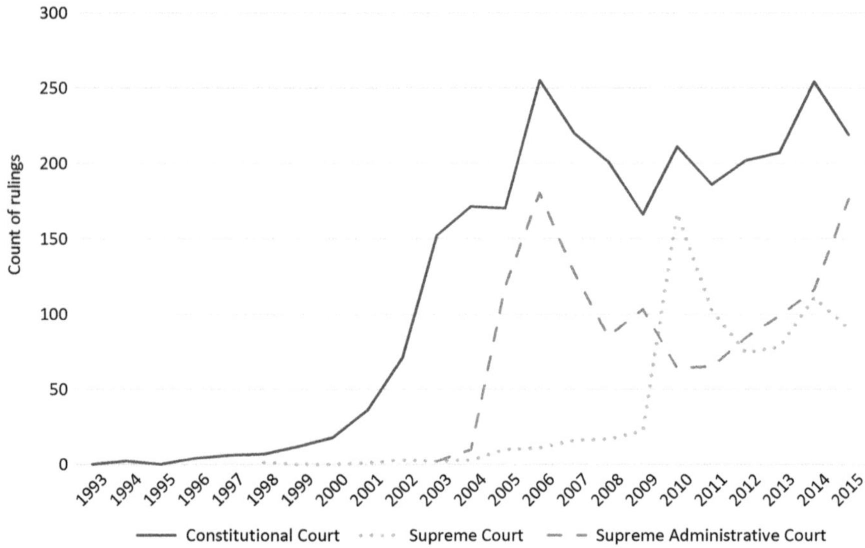

Figure 8.1 Number of apex courts' rulings referring to ECtHR case law.
Source: authors.

which needed to get recognition on the domestic political and legal scene, and hence it did not need the ECHR. The SC proved its conservative legal formalist reputation and started referring to ECtHR case law only with the Czech accession to the European Union (EU) in 2004.[7] Since then, its use of international case law has grown slowly but steadily, until it suddenly quantitatively sprang up in 2010.[8] The SC has one more peculiarity: compared to other apex courts, it frequently refers solely to the Convention without citing the ECtHR's interpretations of ECHR provisions.[9]

When comparing the "old" (the SC) and the "new" courts (the CC and the SAC) in terms of the number of rulings referring to ECtHR case law, one can especially notice the slow start of the SC. The institutional environment and a rather hostile mindset towards the use of international implants apparently projected itself into only sporadic references to the ECtHR rulings.[10] A quote from our interview with a SC judge provides a fitting illustration of the institutional mindset at the SC:

> When someone wanted to search for an inspiration in ECtHR case law and/ or interpret the law in a pro-human-rights, not strictly textualist, way, eye-brows were raised and there was a sigh of 'You are growing for Strasbourg!' (and it was definitely not meant as a compliment)[11]

The SC generally showed much more institutional allegiance to the CC, rather than to the ECtHR. Therefore, in earlier years, ECtHR case law made it to the SC, especially through the diffusing work done by the CC. The SC decided restitution disputes on properties nationalized by the communist regime, which oftentimes found their way back to the original owners in a very complicated way. When judges at one chamber directly used ECtHR case law, the rest of the SC perceived them as "freaks".[12] Other chambers at the SC have not debated ECtHR case law, and for lower courts such debates have been non-existent.[13] However, even the "old court" caught up in referring to ECtHR case law in the 2010s.

Comparison of the specialized CC and two ordinary apex courts shows that the CC recorded steadier performance over time than the SC and the SAC. Particularly the period of the "second CC" (from 2003 until 2013) did not witness twists as dramatic as in the case of the two other apex courts. When observing this and the following graphs, one has to bear in mind the context. In the 1990s, judges did not have access to Strasbourg case law due to a lack of materials, such as translations of rulings or books, handbooks, and commentaries in Czech;[14] poor command of foreign languages such as French or English; and very low employment of information technology in Czech judiciary. From the mid-2000s, things started to change rapidly and information on ECtHR case law became available as access to internet connections increased, computers were introduced into daily judicial work, and knowledge of foreign languages improved. More materials on the ECtHR in the Czech language have appeared as well, peaking in 2012 with a gargantuan authoritative commentary by leading Czech experts in the field of the ECHR (Kmec et al. 2012). The availability of information assists not only judges but also litigants, who began to refer to ECtHR case law much more, although sometimes in a rather naïve way. Once litigants started citing Strasbourg case law, the feedback loop kicked off, because courts were then pushed to familiarize themselves with the arguments used by parties.

The non-linear development in the number of references to ECtHR case law gives rise to the hypothesis of ECtHR referencing saturation. Once a domestic apex court reaches a certain level of usage of ECtHR case law, the gradual increase in the number of rulings that refer to the ECtHR judgments will halt. The apex courts may have found an optimal level of references to ECtHR judgments around which they oscillate, but they do not continue to steadily increase. Frank Emmert (2012, 600, 607–8) hypothesized that the number of references will grow as younger lawyers staff the apex courts and more literature covering ECtHR case law becomes available in domestic languages. These elements certainly help in embedding ECtHR case law more in the apex courts' practice, but it seems that this is only true until a certain threshold of references is achieved. After that moment, other variables come decisively into play. For example, when observing records of current Czech Constitutional Court judges (Vyhnánek 2017), the association between a number of references and their age does not emerge as particularly striking. On the one hand, one can find older justices among the most referring judges, and on the other hand, even representatives of the younger generation belong to the group of judges with the least number of rulings with references. Moreover, the sole number of rulings with references to ECtHR case law can be a very misleading indicator of engagement with the Strasbourg jurisprudence.[15] Looking at the data, it seems that the judge's area of specialization can be a better predictor of engagement with ECtHR case law than age. Additionally, drawing on the personal experiences of our team members with the working environment of the apex courts and on informal interviews with justices, the career paths of their law clerks play an important role.[16] Those clerks with professional experience from the Strasbourg Court or those who studied at Western European universities and took specialized courses in human rights know ECtHR case law better and engage with it almost automatically. Clerks' experiences then often translate into the high number of rulings with references. Finally, the number of clerks a judge has in her team conditions how deeply she can engage with the case. For example, constitutional judges had one full-time position for a clerk in 1990s, then two, and since 2003 they have had three full-time positions for clerks (Kosař and Petrov 2017; Vyhnánek 2017).[17]

As already mentioned, the mere count of references or rulings with references to ECtHR case law is a very basic measure and it does not tell us particularly much. The overview of the proportion of cases with an ECtHR reference in the whole caseload (see Figure 8.2) informs us better about the extent of engagement with ECtHR case law in the rulings of a particular court. Imagine a scenario in which both Court A and Court B reference the ECtHR in 100 cases, but Court A deals with 500 cases annually, while Court B deals with 5,000 cases – a simple count of the number of cases with references to ECtHR case law would not uncover any difference.

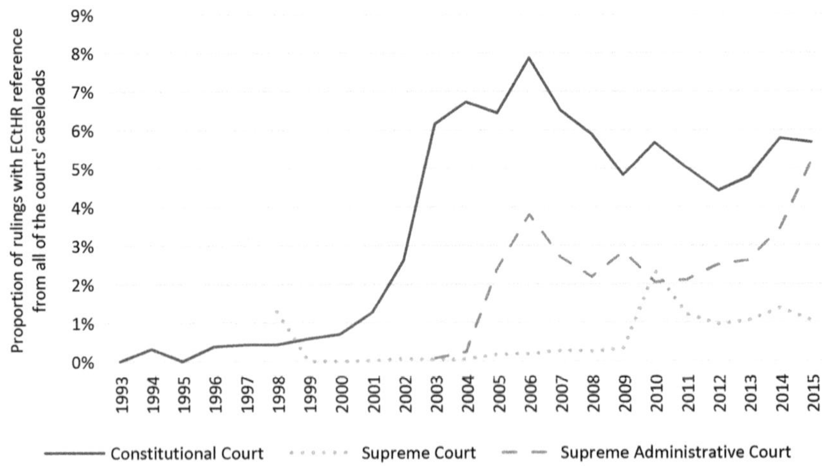

Figure 8.2 How often do apex courts refer to ECtHR case law?
Source: authors.

Even when controlling for the total caseload, the frequency with which individual apex courts refer to ECtHR case law remains virtually unchanged when compared to the previous figure. The data again confirms the basic expectation that the CC refers to ECtHR case law the most frequently, followed by the SAC and the SC. The data from the CC shows the importance of persons who sit at the Court. The composition of the Court totally changed in 2003 and 2013, as a consequence of (renewable) ten-year mandates of CC judges. The periods of 1993–2003 ("the first CC") and 2003–2013 ("the second CC") score very differently in terms of frequency of referring to ECtHR case law. While until 2002 the CC made a reference in only less than 2 percent of its rulings, between 2003 and 2013 the proportion of rulings with a reference did not drop under 4 percent. Therefore, the judges who entered the CC in 2003, and in the following years, were much more prone to cite ECtHR case law than their predecessors were.

8.1.2 Drivers of citation patterns

As discussed above and especially in individual chapters, the interplay of numerous factors on various levels can explain the development in the frequency of referring to ECtHR case law. First, on the ECtHR level, its case law massively expanded, both numerically and into new areas, hence covering more situations that can serve as guidance for domestic courts. The ECtHR generally acts strategically, seeking to show sensitivity towards states, but at the same time building, through its case law, support communities among domestic judges and civil society (Dothan 2013; Madsen 2015). Moreover, the ECtHR itself actively outreaches and tries to communicate its case law to domestic audiences and publishes various case law guides, admissibility guides, etc.

Second, on both the international and national level, judicial protection of human rights and corresponding general growth in importance of courts substantially increased in the 1990s. This trend even led to the widespread use of the label "judicialization of politics" (Tate and Vallinder 1995; Hirschl 2008; Alter 2014; Follesdal and Ulfstein 2018; Pin 2019).[18] Simultaneously, as hard borders in Europe progressively disappeared and communication channels developed and advanced, international ties between courts multiplied and domestic judges came into contact with foreign elements much more frequently than ever before (Claes and de Visser 2012). In addition to this, ECtHR case law has attracted progressively increasing scholarly attention. Commentaries in national languages are regularly being written and legal education increasingly involves courses on the ECHR regime, thus making the legal community as a whole more and more informed about the issue. Moreover, plentiful information is readily available on the internet, with current ECtHR rulings analyzed in the blogosphere, including specialized blogs on the ECtHR.[19]

Third, on the domestic level, apex courts have undergone various institutional innovations, which include the establishment of expert analytical units that inform and advise on news from foreign and international courts. To a varying extent, the apex courts have also received funds to acquire literature, or even build their own libraries. Czech law schools have started to include human rights courses in their curricula (Kilian, Pospíšil, and Smekal 2016), so consequently younger judges and law clerks who progressively staff the courts have more awareness about the issue than their predecessors. In parallel, Czechia had been preparing for the EU accession since the mid-1990s, including numerous seminars on EU law for judges, which helped in acquiring a generally more open approach to other legal systems than solely Czech. Importantly, court presidents and powerful judicial personalities with strong informal influence may impact how international law is perceived among the judicial ranks of a given court.

Finally, cooperation with other public administration bodies matters. Specifically, the activities of the Government Agent before the ECtHR Vít A. Schorm, who has held his position since 2002 and has since acquired a high reputation in issues of ECtHR case law, helped in spreading the ECtHR gospel. The Government Agent Office informs apex courts about ECtHR rulings against Czechia and more recently also about important judgments in general, and uses various soft measures, such as seminars, meetings, or the Collegium of Experts on ECtHR Judgments Execution (Schorm 2018), to make courts consider ECtHR case law.

What explains variation among domestic apex courts as regards their treatment of ECtHR case law? For a comprehensive analysis, one has to explore all levels. Even the international factors cannot be treated as a constant, because the ECtHR might have started to issue rulings in a specific domain only recently or rarely, but for the national court this very domain can generate a substantial portion of the disputes it deals with. Similarly, for outreach activities, the ECtHR may identify one court at the national level that it perceives to be the most important ally, and it may focus on networking with its judges comparatively more than with judges of other apex courts. However, most decisively, judges at apex courts and their working environment account for variations in the treatment of international case law.

When trying to understand elements influencing the frequency of referring to the ECtHR case law, the chapters of the book covering individual courts[20] pointed to the importance of the field the courts operate in, while particular attention has been paid to the establishment and activities of analytical units. The total caseload and the availability of manpower to assist judges in their work belong among other important variables of interest. According to our interviews with judges across the courts, all of them feel overburdened with cases. Their final decisions are products of a delicate compromise between the time and energy judges want to devote to cases, and the time and energy they can devote to cases given other dossiers waiting on their desks. There are 15 constitutional judges, over 30 supreme administrative judges, and around 70 supreme judges.

Arguably, the CC, with its constitutional review powers, represents the most prestigious institution out of the three courts. This is further supported by the fixed and rather low number of positions. Constitutional judges often belong among the most respected lawyers in the country. Accordingly, when constitutional judges organize open calls for the positions of law clerks, the call should attract highly qualified applicants having at least some knowledge of the ECHR regime and its judicial outputs. Moreover, CC clerks enjoy comparatively higher salaries and often work at the Court only part-time, which enables them to retain their academic (or other) positions while at the same time enjoying the reputational benefits of working at the top legal address deciding very important issues. This endows them with an opportunity to influence the interpretation of the law in the country. Law clerks at the CC have since its establishment thus included respected personalities, featuring highly positioned academics, former dissidents, and acclaimed lawyers. CC judges have very diverse career trajectories and include representatives of almost all legal professions (Vyhnánek and Jakubíček 2016). Academics, forming a large portion of the CC, have easy access to the most talented students from the law faculties who then sometimes fill their clerkships. On the contrary, the composition of the SC leans towards professional judges who lack close contacts with bright young legal minds. The SAC is, as regards its professional composition, somewhere in the middle between the Constitutional and Supreme courts.

Moreover, the content of the clerking work differs among the courts, which is connected to the presence of more senior people clerking at the CC. While constitutional law clerks were often expected to come up with a proposal on how to decide a dispute and with a sound legal reasoning, law clerks at both supreme courts have consisted of comparatively more junior staff who were not always vested with such complex tasks and sometimes acted more as analytical assistants to a judge than autonomous clerks.

The SAC also stands out as a prestigious address. Given the lower number of seats, newly renovated building, and its reputation as the "Different Court", the competition among applicants for clerkships should attract some of the most qualified young candidates. That arguably leaves the SC as the least prestigious place to work as a law clerk, both due to the high number of legal clerk positions (over 190) and work modus operandi. The overall number of law clerks lowers the prestige of the position and makes it more difficult for SC judges to attract the best lawyers. Moreover, it also took a substantial amount of time to teach SC judges how to cooperate with clerks. Finally, the CC and to a lesser extent the SAC directly deal with human rights issues, and therefore will attract lawyers already acquainted with ECtHR case law.[21]

Enough literature documents the non-trivial influence of law clerks on final judicial decisions;[22] therefore, it can be inferred that clerks with better knowledge of ECtHR case law contribute to higher reference rates by their judges. Our anecdotal evidence goes in line with these assumptions: the CC attracted people with direct experience from the Strasbourg Court for clerkships, and the same goes for the SAC. Comparatively, the SC remains a domestic top institution for young experts in civil, commercial, and criminal law who do not necessarily have much exposure to ECtHR case law.

To conclude, we suggest that the personnel composition of a court, including its president, leading personalities, judges, and their law clerks and analysts, decisively influences how often and how a given court treats international human rights case law.

8.1.3 In which rulings and parts of rulings do apex courts refer?

The apex courts issue various types of rulings, with judgments counting as the most important, so they are crucial for our further analysis. The other types of rulings include, for example, procedural decisions declaring that the court will not deal with the case substantively. Judgments are the most elaborated of all types of rulings and should include a persuasive argumentation to substantiate the findings. Yet, references to ECtHR case law also frequently appear in other types of rulings than judgments. For example, since the end of the 1990s, only around 30 percent of references to ECtHR case law annually appear in the CC's judgments.[23] The proportion of references to ECtHR case law oscillates more in the case of the SC, but a majority of references also appears in other types of decisions than judgments. It seems that the apex courts have become accustomed to inserting references into less important decisions almost automatically, in a copy-and-paste style.

Next, we zoom in on where references to ECtHR case law appear in the text of domestic rulings. It makes a difference if a court uses a reference in the reasoning, or if a reference appears only in the narrative part, which summarizes previous proceedings at lower courts or arguments of the parties or *amici curiae*. Unfortunately, no macro data can answer the question why judges use references or what made them use a reference – if it is their own knowledge or the arguments contained in the case docket, especially documents of the parties to the dispute. Still, detecting where references occur in rulings brings us interesting information on at least two counts. First, if references appear predominantly in the narrative part, and only seldom in the reasoning, we can infer that parties try to make arguments based on ECtHR case law, while the court regularly disregards them (or, at least, does not acknowledge them via references in the reasoning). Second, significant turns in the data imply that something happened in the way a court treats ECtHR case law. However, reading too much from these statistics might be risky, because the style of individual courts and judges when writing rulings differs too much. While some discuss all the sources that played a role when deciding the dispute at hand, others remain much more silent in this regard.

The three Czech apex courts slightly differ in the positioning of their citations. The CC holds a pretty constant high proportion of references in the reasoning, which oscillates around 80 percent. It indicates that when citing ECtHR case law, constitutional judges do so very often in the reasoning itself, not only in the narrative part. Similarly, the SAC locates the majority of ECtHR case law citations in reasonings.[24] On the contrary, we find comparatively far fewer ECtHR references in the SC's reasoning. Over the long term, the SC tended to refer more in the narrative part than the other apex courts. However, the trend shows a gradually increasing proportion of citations in reasonings by the SC as well, and it has slowly started to catch up. But overall, we can see a cleavage between the "new" and "old" courts (the CC and the SAC v. the SC). While the "new" courts refer overwhelmingly in reasoning, the "old" court quite often summarizes the past proceedings or arguments of parties without its own elaboration on ECtHR case law.

8.1.4 To which ECtHR rulings do apex courts refer?

After elaborating on the citation practices of domestic apex courts (who refers, how much, and where) and showing that it might be tricky to rely on a simple count of references,[25] we now turn to the question: Which ECtHR rulings do the apex courts refer to the most frequently? We were further interested in whether the apex courts refer more to ECtHR rulings against Czechia, or if they use the whole corpus of ECtHR case law indiscriminately, and how it changed over time. Such an examination sheds light on how judges perceive ECtHR rulings. Predominantly citing rulings against the home state indicates that domestic courts construe ECtHR case law as an *inter partes* affair and are familiar with those rulings in particular. Frequent references to ECtHR case law in general hints that domestic courts consider ECtHR relevant as a whole, beyond case law against their own state. ECtHR case law hence acquires the status of *res interpretata* (Kosař and Petrov 2017, 590–5). Finally, we tracked which articles of the Convention included in ECtHR rulings were most invoked by the domestic courts.

First, we were interested in examining the reasonings of the Czech apex courts to identify which ECtHR rulings are cited most often. We learned that legal scholars did not find the most famous ECtHR rulings among the top 15 most referred cases by the respective apex courts. Some of the most cited ECtHR rulings came as a surprise even to ECtHR experts, who did not expect lesser-known judgments to be used so frequently. This finding needs a bit of clarification. Maybe surprisingly, prominent ECtHR judgments[26] do not appear among the most cited cases, but the Czech apex courts still refer to important pieces of ECtHR case law, at least from the point of view of the ECtHR's self-categorization. Possibly, the apex courts cite rulings crucial to their specific sub-field, which can evade the radar of a generalist ECtHR pundit.

Quite interestingly, there has not been much overlap between the apex courts as regards the most cited ECtHR rulings. No ECtHR judgment has made it to the top 15 list of the most cited ECtHR judgments in reasonings of all three apex courts, and only three ECtHR judgments[27] appeared among the 15 most cited by two Czech apex courts. These findings suggest that the apex courts cherry-pick the ECtHR rulings that suit their needs, and not those that introduce some important general principles or ground-breaking verdicts.

The apex courts differ in the frequency of citations of top-cited ECtHR rulings against their home state. While the CC and the SAC referred to an ECtHR ruling against Czechia thrice and twice, respectively, the SC used a ruling against Czechia a full six times.

We used the ECtHR's own classification of its case law to assess whether Czech apex courts cite important cases or not. The ECtHR divides cases into four categories, from the "key cases" to categories 1, 2, and 3. The examination of the 15 top-cited ECtHR rulings in reasonings of Czech apex courts shows that the CC refers on average to the most important ECtHR rulings, followed by the SAC and the SC. The CC referred to a key ECtHR ruling six times while the remaining two apex courts referred three times each.[28] The CC, just like the SAC, used the ECtHR ruling of the lowest importance only once, while the SC did so five times. This finding also reinforces the claim that the SC's top-cited ECtHR rulings include judgments categorized as less important. Generally, this coincides with the SC's tendency to frequently cite ECtHR rulings against Czechia, which are important for domestic judicial practice, but not so much for the ECHR regime as a whole.

As regards the rights covered by the top 15 most cited ECtHR rulings by each apex court, the right to a fair trial prevails at all courts, but it clearly dominates only in the case of the CC. The other two apex courts have referred to varied ECtHR rulings, covering also the prohibition of torture (Article 3 ECHR), the right to liberty and security (Article 5 ECHR) and the right to respect for private and family life (Article 8 ECHR). Interestingly, the CC, compared to other apex courts, most often cites ECtHR rulings on the protection of property (Protocol No. 1 Article 1 ECHR), which are at the same time self-classified by the ECtHR as of key importance. This brief comparison suggests that the CC relies on ECtHR rulings that are considered important. In contrast, the SC focuses on rulings against Czechia (i.e., *inter partes* authority) and invokes ECtHR rulings of comparatively lower importance.

Second, we were eager to learn how frequently the apex courts cite rulings against Czechia. Above, we presented data only covering references to the 15 most cited ECtHR rulings; here we elaborate on all references to ECtHR case law in the rulings of the Czech apex courts. One can assume that courts will first be aware of ECtHR rulings against their home state. With passing time and increasing overall familiarity with the ECHR regime, the apex courts could also start referring more to ECtHR rulings against other countries. When citing cases against Czechia, the apex courts typically secure direct compliance with ECtHR rulings.[29] When citing cases against third states, the apex courts perform their diffusing role and contribute to broad compliance with the ECHR regime as such. Through these citations, lower national courts can learn about general ECtHR jurisprudence and help to prevent potential future complaints to the Strasbourg Court. Such a scenario takes time to materialize, as it takes several years to accumulate a body of case law against a new state in the ECHR regime; in the 1990s there were only a few ECtHR judgments against Czechia. The proportion of references to ECtHR rulings against

Czechia jumps up and down in the practice of all apex courts (Figure 8.3). In early years, it can be explained by a low number of rulings with a reference, while the later, comparatively smaller jumps might indicate that courts react to fresh ECtHR case law. The ECtHR delivers hundreds of new rulings annually, including a few against Czechia, which mostly deal with the right to a fair trial (Article 6); i.e., an issue frequently under review before the apex courts. The extraordinary turn in the proportion of cited Czech cases by the CC in the year 2003 calls for a closer elaboration. What otherwise would have been a quite gradual increase in the proportion of references to ECtHR rulings against Czechia suddenly spiked in 2003 and partially returned back into expected levels a year later. When digging deeper into what happened in 2003, we found that a great majority of the CC's rulings citing an ECtHR ruling against Czechia referred to the ECtHR judgments *Běleš*[30] and *Zvolský and Zvolská*,[31] which were both delivered on 12 November 2002 and concerned the issue of admissibility. Exploring the puzzle further, we found that four (out of 15) judges routinely included short references to *Běleš* and *Zvolský and Zvolská* judgments into their numerous procedural decisions, which rejected petitions. This copy-and-pasting exercise of a few judges lasted for a limited time until the problem was settled, but it greatly disrupted the trends in our macro data.

It thus seems that apex courts react to new ECtHR rulings against Czechia and frequently use them until the problem is solved and new petitions of this kind no longer appear before apex courts. The high proportion of references to ECtHR rulings against third states suggests that apex courts fulfil their general diffusing function and help to filter out petitions that would otherwise appear before the Strasbourg Court.

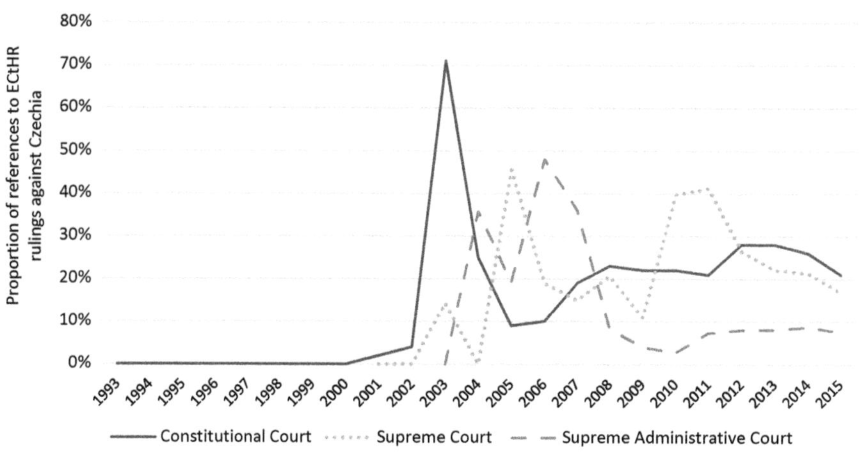

Figure 8.3 References to ECtHR rulings against Czechia v. against third states.
Source: authors.

Finally, we sought to find out which areas of human rights are the most frequently ruled on by apex courts using the ECtHR's interpretation of the Convention provisions. All three apex courts have cited ECtHR rulings dealing with Article 6 ECHR (right to a fair trial), with admissibility and costs cited the most. The apex courts thus follow the ECtHR practice because it rules the most frequently on rather technical issues of Article 6 as well. This comes as no surprise, because apex courts generally deal with fair trial and admissibility issues very often and, moreover, the ECtHR had many opportunities to issue rulings on cases coming from Czechia. Domestic courts can therefore rely on rich ECtHR case law in procedural issues that very frequently appear also in domestic judicial practice. Interestingly, the ECtHR case law does not always serve only as a tool for promoting fair trial rights of petitioners, but it can sometimes provide domestic courts with a helping hand to justify judicial practice against too demanding petitioners.[32]

The abundant Strasbourg Court case law on Article 6 sets up a convenient base for the diffusing function of apex courts, because oftentimes the problem has not lain in the legislation, but in the judicial practice. The apex courts have generally followed the ECtHR's instructions on admissibility of complaints to apex courts and on the necessary content of judicial decisions. Through invoking ECtHR case law, the apex courts assist in filtering out potential future complaints and guide lower domestic courts on how to write rulings.

In addition to the right to a fair trial, all of the apex courts most often made use of the ECtHR's interpretation of Articles 3, 5, 8, and 10; i.e., prohibition of torture and of inhuman or degrading treatment or punishment, and rights to liberty and security, private and family life, and freedom of expression.

8.2 Meso- and micro-level analysis

The macro-level analysis proves useful in showing overall trends. Nevertheless, a better understanding of the local judicial ecosystem is necessary to make some sense of what the numbers and graphs show. For example, two phenomena explain the 2012 drop in the proportion of the CC's use of ECtHR case law. First, the structure of the docket differed from "standard" years because approximately one-quarter of all rulings dealt with almost identical petitions,[33] all of which ended up as manifestly ill-founded and without any ECtHR reference. Second, the vast majority of constitutional justices finished their terms and wanted to clear their desks in order not to leave the CC with a reputation of non-performing judges with a big backlog. Therefore, they focused on easier cases, which formed a clear majority of the docket. Such petitions, quickly refused as manifestly ill-founded, do not require long rulings that carefully engage with ECtHR case law. This example nicely illustrates the usefulness of our three-level approach in which the macro-analysis identifies an unusual point in the data and a close familiarity with the issue then helps in providing the explanation.

Deeper knowledge of the environment at the apex courts enabled us, for example, to understand why only after many years did the SC start to catch up with the other two apex courts in their citation practices to ECtHR case law. The SC referred to the ECtHR very sparsely until 2010, which is explained by an overall mistrustful atmosphere towards international human rights law, including ECtHR case law. Moreover, those relatively few references were the product of only one chamber which comprised few pioneering judges who distinguished themselves from the hostile majority. Unlike the CC and the SAC, which were both newly built after the democratic transition, the SC's transformation in personnel, and especially in spirit, has taken much longer, and differences persist even now. The chasm stems also from the distinct perception of the *raison d'être* of each court. SC judges highly value the stability and clarity of the legal order and are not impressed by the sometimes erratic rulings of the CC, which, according to them, seek too much individual justice at the expense of a balanced legal order.[34] Yet, the SC recognized the authority of the CC much more than the authority of the ECtHR. SC judges have long not agreed on whether Strasbourg rulings were binding on national courts, and if yes, whether only those rulings against the home state, or ECtHR case law in general.[35]

In addition to the informed and more fine-grained look at macro trends, analyses of meso and micro levels answer other important questions that could not have been dealt with at the macro level. Unlike the automated coding of the population of references in macro-level analysis, the meso-level examination required closer engagement with the text of individual domestic apex court rulings and manual coding based on our codebook. We learned about the particulars of the apex courts' treatment of ECtHR case law, such as how important ECtHR rulings were for deciding domestic disputes, how they were used, and for what purpose, and to what extent the apex courts followed ECtHR case law. The individual micro-studies examined deliberately chosen legal areas where ECtHR case law played an especially important role in the development of domestic judicial practice, or, on the contrary, where apex courts experienced difficulties or even resisted when putting ECtHR rulings into practice.

The main message from the meso-level analysis is clear. The apex courts overwhelmingly follow ECtHR case law (in approximately 95 percent of rulings). Any open disagreement is exceptional and, moreover, does not mean explicit principled rebellion against the ECtHR. The ECtHR authority as such is undisputed; reservations arise only against rare particular rulings that are ill-suited to Czech conditions. Domestic courts ordinarily explain why they have not used ECtHR case law, albeit such "distinguishing" sometimes hides judges' disagreement with a Strasbourg ruling.[36] The apex courts refer to ECtHR rulings frequently in situations when such a reference is not needed for resolving the dispute at hand. This suggests that apex courts embraced their position as a part of the ECHR regime and use ECtHR case law routinely and without reservations. Yet, such a rosy picture does not fully reflect the richness of practice. Therefore, an informed micro-level analysis is needed to depict the complexity of the situation and to supplement the meso- and macro-level analyses. We move on to discuss the findings more in detail.

8.2.1 Meso-level analysis

References to ECtHR case law have different importance for resolving disputes. Some can play only a supportive role when they further endorse what has been decided based on other sources, especially domestic law. Other references can have substantive influence in deciding the dispute. All the apex courts use supporting references to ECtHR case law much more frequently than substantial ones (see Figure 8.4).[37] A pessimistic reading of this finding might downplay the importance of citations of ECtHR case law, which supposedly serve as mere ornaments for more important sources of law. Optimistic readers might point out that domestic apex judges routinized the use of references to ECtHR case law that firmly occupies their intellectual universe. Domestic courts resort to ECtHR references regularly, even in cases when they do not necessarily need to, which implies a profound level of the embeddedness of ECtHR case law. A closer look at the citation practice of domestic courts lends support to more optimistic reading, because citations of ECtHR case law which have a substantive effect on the reasonings of courts represent a not insignificant portion of all references.

Figure 8.4 Substantive v. supporting references.
Source: authors.

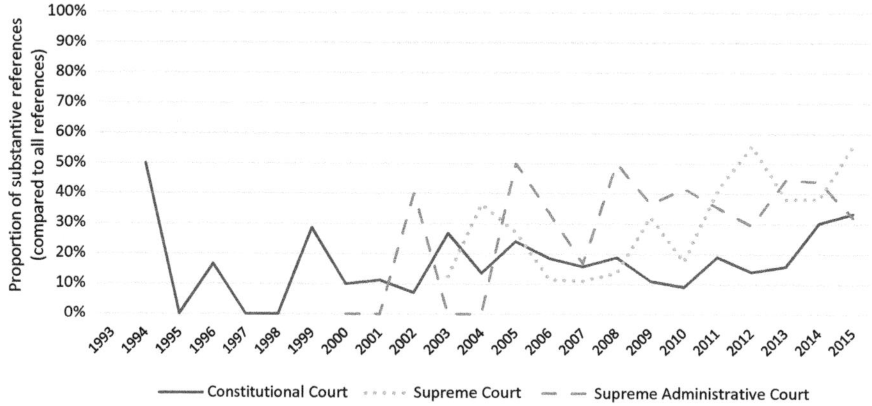

Figure 8.5 Substantive v. supporting references: development over time.
Source: authors.

In addition to mere ornamental citations, two patterns of supportive use of ECtHR case law emerged at all apex courts. First, domestic apex courts use Strasbourg case law to generally describe a given fundamental right and to identify its main features. Such use plays an important educational function, especially for lower courts and litigants. Second, ECtHR rulings provide additional justification to the domestic court's ruling based on national law. Hence, one cannot readily dismiss supporting references as unimportant. They found a firm ground in apex courts' reasoning and consequently permeate domestic legal discourse as a whole, because lower layers of court hierarchy can see that referring to ECtHR case law has become a new normal.

Figure 8.4 shows a differing approach between ordinary and special apex courts to references with a substantive influence. While ECtHR rulings substantively influence the CC's findings in only 18 percent of rulings in the sample (but the figure has been rising recently, as Figure 8.5 shows), for both the SC and the SAC, ECtHR case law plays a substantive role for the finding in 36 percent and 32 percent of references, respectively. The comparatively lower proportion of references with substantive influence stems from the CC's treatment of ECtHR case law on Article 6 ECHR (right to a fair trial). All of the apex courts deal with ECtHR case law on the right to a fair trial more than all of the other rights, but the CC cites it even more frequently than the two other courts. In addition, it is precisely Article 6 case law where supporting references generally clearly prevail over substantive references, yet in the case of the CC, the dominance of Article 6 plainly outweighs the SC and the SAC. In other words, the CC uses ECtHR case law on the right to a fair trial more often than the two ordinary apex courts and, moreover, the CC gives it supporting, rather than substantive, influence comparatively more often. When referring to ECtHR rulings covering a different right than a fair trial, the proportion between substantive and supporting influence is more balanced, or even diverted towards substantive influence.

Despite the quantitative prevalence of the supporting influence of references to ECtHR case law, the substantive references promise more interesting material to study. We can distinguish two purposes for the use of substantive references: defensive and offensive. Defensive references use ECtHR case law in order to defend the status quo. All apex courts resort to an ECtHR ruling in order to justify the restriction of a right. An apex court's substantive citation of ECtHR case law should persuade the petitioner that even the ECtHR would not find a violation of a fundamental right. One can also imagine the strategic use of citations by the Supreme or Supreme Administrative courts to appease the CC, or by all apex courts to appease other branches of power and the ECtHR itself by citing Strasbourg case law. The offensive use of substantive references relies on the citation of ECtHR case law in order to change domestic practice. One of the most spectacular uses of ECtHR rulings by Czech apex courts involved the SAC's reliance on ECtHR rulings in order to contravene the practice of the CC.[38] The SC has also mastered the strategic approach by cherry-picking ECtHR rulings, especially when it wants to overcome its own previous case law.

An important middle ground between defensive and offensive use of substantive references is represented by quite common instances when ECtHR case law serves to clarify or supplement a vague Czech legal regulation. In such cases, the apex courts build on ECtHR rulings when, for example, formulating additional requirements or introducing an ECtHR-inspired test or criteria. ECtHR case law thus contributes to the refinement of domestic practice.

In sum, and using terminology elaborated in Chapters 5, 6, and 7, all three apex courts resort the most often to two techniques: supplementing and confirmation. While two "new" courts, the CC and the SAC, confirm the status quo by citing ECtHR case law the most frequently, the "old" SC the most often "fills in the gaps" via Strasbourg case law when domestic norms either did not cover a new social situation or overlooked a certain aspect. In such scenarios, for example, a test developed by the ECtHR comes in handy.

Scholars studying the effectiveness of international courts' case law should pay particular attention to the offensive use of substantive references because here ECtHR rulings demonstrate their transformative potential at its fullest – if there was no ECtHR case law, there would probably not be such apex court rulings and related change in domestic practice. The CC, for example, borrowed two concepts from the ECtHR when developing its jurisprudence on freedom of expression and incorporated them into its own approach.[39] Adopting the ECtHR's approach as a building block for its own judicial contemplations also fares well for the SAC. When deciding on novel issues, SAC judges start with ECtHR rulings as guidelines and fine-tune them to fit local circumstances. For example, ECtHR case law played a significant role when the SAC developed important jurisprudence on the dissolution of political parties.[40] Even more profound Strasbourg impact was noticed in the right to a fair trial (Article 6) cases in which SAC judges adopted an "Article 6 mindset" and spread the ECtHR Article 6 jurisprudence outside its original criminal law boundaries to a much wider field of administrative offences.[41] Moreover, the SAC managed to react to the proliferating ECtHR Article 6 case law and adapted its approach accordingly. This indicates that (at least some) judges monitor recent developments in the Strasbourg Court and reflect them. Hence, they contribute to constant diffusion of Strasbourg case law among the domestic judiciary and consequently to the legal arena as a whole.[42]

All of the apex courts overwhelmingly follow ECtHR case law. The scant cases of non-following in the meso-level analysis fall under the category "distinguishing", which denotes situations when courts explain why they do not apply ECtHR case law. For example, the SC typically discusses why the situation at hand does not qualify as an unduly lengthy proceeding as understood by the ECtHR.[43] Such a phenomenon clearly shows the high level of embeddedness of ECtHR case law in domestic decision-making practice since the courts feel the need to explain why they have not used ECtHR case law. The apex courts often "distinguish" in response to the misplaced arguments of the parties that invoked ECtHR rulings, which were clearly not applicable to the dispute. Distinguishing is quite a tricky exercise because there is a thin line between situations when apex courts do not apply ECtHR case law justifiably and unjustifiably. For example, the SC occasionally uses distinguishing to camouflage potential non-following of ECtHR case law. In such cases, judges try to find even the smallest elements in which the situation at hand and the one dealt with in previous ECtHR rulings differ in order to declare that they cannot use ECtHR case law because it covers different scenarios.[44]

Finally, we also observed how precisely the apex courts refer to ECtHR case law and how the practice evolves. Expectedly, the precision of references increases over time. While in the 1990s it was not rare that the apex courts generally stated that "the ECtHR found that ..." without citing any particular ruling, nowadays full references with names of the parties, docket numbers, and even relevant paragraphs of ECtHR rulings appear in domestic rulings. Interestingly, while the SC follows the trend of more detailed citations, it does not always do so when ECtHR rulings on Article 6 ECHR are at play. In sum, we observe gradual cultivation of citation practices at domestic apex courts.

8.2.2 Micro-level analysis

The micro-level analysis zooms in on issues in which ECtHR case law played an especially important role. Moreover, it points also to remarkable instances of rare clashes between the Strasbourg Court and domestic courts. The meso-level analysis draws from a sample of the apex courts' rulings and cannot uncover all cases of non-following. Some interesting instances may slip through the sampling process. Therefore, a scholarly expertise building on close knowledge of domestic courts' case law helps in identifying those cases and especially in elaborating on reasons for non-compliance with ECtHR case law. Micro-level analyses in individual chapters thus also discuss when, why, and how small revolts against ECtHR case law happen. Most frequently, they come unwittingly when judges have not known about existing ECtHR rulings or have not used them in the way the ECtHR intended. Thanks to our inside knowledge, we have a suspicion that in rare cases judges willfully do not cite ECtHR case law because they do not agree with it. They typically prefer to hide their reservations against Strasbourg rulings rather than initiate an international judicial dialogue. Exceptionally, Czech apex courts voice their different opinion, as did, for example, the SAC when it opposed the ECtHR's overly ambitious *Zolotukhin* judgment.[45] The SAC took care to explain why the *Zolotukhin* judgment would disturb the proper functioning of the Czech public administration and thus should not be applied. The ECtHR subsequently modified its case law in *A and B v. Norway*[46] and the SAC judges happily switched back to their usual following mode.[47]

The tipping point for (non-)following differs among individual judges, whose approach towards Strasbourg case law ranges from a sense of an international hierarchy, with the ECtHR on the top, to a suspicion of any external elements.[48] Generally, the apex courts experiences difficulties with accommodating ECtHR case law when it does not go hand in hand with the perceived meaning of the existence of a given court. For example, even the ECtHR-friendly SAC turns to a narrow interpretation of ECtHR rulings when it feels that a more expansive reading would jeopardize the proper functioning of the public administration.[49] The SC reacts in the same way when it senses the risk of destabilization of the domestic legal order.[50] The ECtHR caused a stir at the CC with its *Pincová and Pinc*[51] judgment in a property restitution case, which arguably ignored the local specificity of the situation and, moreover, ruled differently than in previous comparable cases against Germany. Constitutional judges pushed the Czech government to bring the case before the ECtHR Grand Chamber, but the Ministry of Justice declined to make such a bold move. In reaction, the CC followed the ECtHR judgment, but only on a case-by-case basis and the law that gave rise to the violation of ECHR rights has not been quashed.[52]

Overall, the disagreements on the side of domestic apex courts are only partial, or in specific disputes, and do not openly and directly question the general authority of the ECtHR.

8.3 Synthesizing conclusion

Bringing the Convention and ECtHR case law into practice is a task for the entire state apparatus. Nevertheless, the attention of policy-makers has recently turned to national courts. The 2012 Brighton Declaration (High Level Conference on the Future of the European Court of Human Rights 2012) explicitly called on national courts to take into account the Convention and ECtHR case law and thus help to tackle the colossal ECtHR overload crisis. Complaints to international bodies are best avoided by compliance at home, and domestic courts should lead by example and follow ECtHR rulings in order to prevent the influx of new petitions pointing to problems already dealt with by the ECtHR.

Czechia belongs among countries that toe the line, and it does not send thousands of new applications to the Strasbourg Court every year (Kosař and Petrov 2018; von Staden 2018). It has its troubles with the length of proceedings and other Article 6 issues, but all in all, Czechia performs reasonably well, especially for a country with four decades' experience with a non-democratic regime. The only long-term stain on Czechia's reputation comes from the still unresolved issue of discrimination against Roma children in their right to education (*D.H. and Others*[53] – see Section 8.4).

We argue that the Czech apex courts have significantly contributed to the overall satisfactory picture in terms of compliance with the Convention and with its interpretation by the Strasbourg Court. We document development in the citation practices of ECtHR case law and identify reasons for their changes over time and for differences between the three apex courts.[54]

The example of the SAC demonstrates that even a court whose fields of judging are not necessarily always covered by ECtHR case law can quickly become active in citing the Strasbourg Court's rulings. The personal composition of the court matters. The SAC included the younger generation of lawyers who were familiar with the EU law, international law, and comparative constitutional law. Moreover, the smaller size of the SAC might have played some role as well. Similarly, as in case of the CC, which has only 15 judges and is the smallest out of the apex triad, the SAC with its roughly 30 judges can still meet collectively and discuss issues in the plenary sessions. The informal exchange of information and peer pressure can work in smaller-sized bodies much better than in the approximately 70-headed behemoth (the SC), where meaningful interactions are possible only in smaller formations.

Our three-level approach to the judicial treatment of ECtHR case law goes a step further from the usual study of compliance and effectiveness that tends to assess developments in relation to individual cases. We do not focus much on the question of whether a court complied with an ECtHR ruling in a given case, or to what extent an ECtHR ruling caused a change in a given practice. Instead, we seek to identify deeper structural movements brought about by the existence of an additional normative layer beyond the state. We bring new findings on how ECtHR case law becomes embedded in domestic judicial practice. Czech apex courts do not only cite rulings against Czechia to comply in individual cases, but also frequently draw inspiration and follow ECtHR rulings against other states.

Seeing that ECtHR case law matters, litigants resort to arguments made by the Strasbourg Court and push the apex courts to either apply ECtHR case law or explain why it does not apply to the situation at hand or not in the way the litigant intended. By using ECtHR case law, the apex courts send signals not only to the parties of the dispute but also to lower courts, which should follow their lead. Thus, by diffusing the information, the apex courts contribute to the lower courts' compliance with ECtHR case law.

The apex courts use citations of ECtHR case law predominantly to support their findings, and not as the main source of argumentation. This nevertheless suggests that judges perceive it to be important to manifest that their solution does not contravene Strasbourg jurisprudence. Supporting references again play an important signaling role to litigants, lower courts, other branches of power, and also to the ECtHR itself. In less frequent cases when ECtHR rulings have a substantive influence on the verdicts of domestic apex courts, domestic courts use Strasbourg case law to introduce new concepts or tools of interpretation, or to help answer questions that are difficult to answer with the use of domestic sources alone. In this sense, we document the direct effectiveness of ECtHR case law, but also identify those model situations in which ECtHR rulings decisively matter.

ECtHR rulings provide an especially important impetus when the issue is quite novel in the home state. In such cases, the apex courts eagerly investigate whether the Strasbourg Court has anything to say. For instance, ECtHR case law has been crucial in developing the framework for very sensitive issues such as the dissolution of political parties or banning extremist assemblies.[55] Similarly, ECtHR case law can provide an interpretation of concepts that then change domestic judicial practice. For example, this has happened in the CC's case law concerning the clash between a journalist's freedom of expression and a pop star's privacy.[56]

Czech apex courts belong among the faithful followers of ECtHR case law. Rare instances of non-following typically include situations in which apex courts explain why an ECtHR ruling is not applicable in the given dispute due to some social, political, or legal distinctions. Overt rebellion is close to non-existent. When explicit dissatisfaction with the domestic applicability of the principles developed by the ECtHR in the *Zolotukhin* judgment appeared,[57] the apex courts contentedly invited the ECtHR's subsequent reconsideration and readily followed its new case law. Occasionally, covert non-following may occur when domestic judges do not know or do not apply ECtHR case law properly. Alternatively, judges may know ECtHR case law but disagree with it. Then, instead of entering into a closely watched judicial dialogue with the Strasbourg Court via an opened substantiated disagreement expressed in a judgment, they opt for a covert rebellion and hope that no one will notice.

Each apex court lives in its own microcosm guided by different meanings of existence and varying historical experience that together structure the overall atmosphere in the court, which subsequently influences those who work at a given court. When trying to understand the domestic judicial treatment of international case law, it is not easy to paint a unified picture of Czechia, as three different stories occur simultaneously.

Our umbrella concept of the judicial treatment combines a macro-level "helicopter" analysis together with a more nuanced, yet still systematic, meso-level analysis and a profound, informed, micro-level analysis. It provides us with a better understanding of the phenomenon of the influence of international case law on domestic judicial practice than previously employed concepts of judicial compliance and effectiveness of international case law. The concept of judicial treatment examines what is happening, how, and why, and due to its complex three-level approach it paints a more accurate and richer picture of reality than competing concepts.

8.4 Beyond conclusion: *D.H. and Others v. the Czech Republic* – Lonely troublemaker

We conclude with a crosscutting micro-study of the single most known judgment ever delivered by an international court against Czechia. The case of discrimination against Roma children requires special attention because it has occupied all levels of the court hierarchy as well as the CC, not only in the original case but also in various follow-up procedures. The case illustrates that sometimes even good compliers are not able or willing to follow an ECtHR judgment. We describe the whole saga and identify conditions that worsen prospects for smooth and quick compliance.

Czechia takes pride in smooth execution of adverse ECtHR rulings,[58] which ranks it as a "good complier". However, one notable exception has persisted for a long time. The ECtHR Grand Chamber delivered a judgment in the case *D. H. and Others v. the Czech Republic* in 2007,[59] but even after more than a decade, the Committee of Ministers has not been satisfied with its domestic implementation and continues to deal with the case under the enhanced supervision regime.[60]

The *D.H.* ruling is considered, especially among anti-discrimination lawyers, one of the most important judgments the ECtHR has ever delivered. The ECtHR Grand Chamber, with a clear majority of 13 judges (against four dissenting), completely overturned a previous Chamber judgment.[61] This was, to the great disappointment of some members of the legal community, decided with an even more convincing 6:1 majority (Goodwin 2006). The Grand Chamber judgment also provoked split reactions. Dissenting opinions introduced the main opposing arguments. These were then followed by a critical discussion that was started by a comment by Michal Bobek, who is now an Advocate General at the Court of Justice of the EU, on the then-influential Czech legal blog *Jiné právo* (Bobek 2007). Both the ECtHR's handling of questionable data and its legal reasoning were criticized. The following quotation from the judgment probably stirred the most controversy:

> Lastly, since it has been established that the relevant legislation as applied in practice at the material time had a disproportionately prejudicial effect on the Roma community, the Court considers that the applicants as members of that community necessarily suffered the same discriminatory treatment. Accordingly, it does not need to examine their individual cases.[62]

It appears that one has only to show an affiliation with a minority that is negatively affected by a disputed practice and it is then automatically assumed that the person was inevitably discriminated against as well. The Court thus moved from assessing individual cases to assessing policies in general.

The Grand Chamber judgment critically evaluated the Czech practice that disproportionately placed Roma children into special schools for students with mental disabilities. Such a placement negatively influenced their later educational and job opportunities. The practice has long been tolerated by almost all segments of Czech society; even Roma parents have not strongly protested against placing their children into the special schools that carry with them a stigma of mental disability. Only with the internationally-induced legal action that ended up at the Strasbourg Court did the issue attract more domestic attention, and it began to be presented as a potential problem. The anti-discrimination camp comprised non-governmental organizations (NGOs) and the Office of the Public Defender of Rights (the Ombudsperson). There are many reasons why the Ministry of Education, as the public administration body responsible for resolving the problem, has not endorsed the fight against discrimination of Roma children in education for a long time. First, the Ministry faced other, more pressing challenges that directly impacted the majority population, such as issues of high school final exams, the introduction of university tuition fees, and the distribution of EU funds. Second, the fight against discrimination against the Roma has not found any noticeable support base inside the Ministry. Individual ministers have not made the issue a priority and lower-ranked staff, who could build sector expertise and push for change, have suffered from very high turnover in personnel. The agenda thus has not enjoyed support from a strong expert base at the Ministry. Third, the ministerial bureaucracy has been staffed mainly with people with more conservative approaches to education who view any anti-discrimination agenda with suspicion. Fourth, the Ministry operates in the wider context of broadly shared anti-Roma sentiments and a simultaneous conviction about the high quality of Czech special education. In an environment in which the Ministry remains largely inactive or promotes the status quo, the prospect for change in the fundamental structure of the educational system remains elusive (Smekal and Šipulová 2014).

The compliance camp, composed of NGOs and the Public Defender of Rights, has faced the unpleasant scenario of an unhelpful Ministry of Education and an overwhelmingly pro-status-quo group of actors who provide and use the education services. To simplify it slightly: Majority parents do not want their children to share classrooms with Roma children who might slow down the pace of the education process, while Roma parents do not hesitate to send their kids to special schools where they will not be bullied by the majority children. Teachers happily welcome classes without lively Roma children and headmasters like their schools to have a reputation as a non-Roma school. Special pedagogues and headmasters of special schools receive more money when they have more clients (i.e., Roma children). In such a deeply embedded pro-status-quo environment, either a strong push from the Ministry of Education or concerted external efforts that would make it clear that the current practice is unacceptable would be needed. The official international pressure from the Council of Europe has been channeled through the Ministry of Justice, specifically through the Government Agent before the ECtHR, which is nonetheless more of an expert than a political body. Despite the pressure from the United States and Norway and international NGOs, the Ministry of Foreign Affairs has never felt a need to intervene or to voice strong support for a change in practice, because the international shaming has arguably never become too intense. The ECtHR Grand Chamber judgment came after the Czech accession to the EU, and thus another possible strong external incentive was not available. The infringement procedure started by the European Commission in 2014 has somehow faded away (Smekal and Šipulová 2014).

Czechia began its compliance efforts only slowly, by renaming the special schools, which left the Committee of Ministers highly unimpressed. Any real breakthrough has not come for a long time, despite efforts of the NGOs and other members of the pro-compliance camp. Nevertheless, the Grand Chamber judgment had important hidden consequences. Respondents from NGOs and from the Ombudsperson's office mentioned in interviews that after the *D.H.* judgment, the people from the Ministry of Education had at least started to communicate with them. On the other hand, the debate quickly became highly polarized, with both parties having great difficulties in coming to any compromise. Both the status quo camp and the inclusion camp inhabited mutually exclusive worldview spaces. The situation became further convoluted with the emerging practice of segregating primary schools: When more Roma children began attending the same classes of one mainstream fundamental (primary or elemental) school, the non-Roma parents started to transfer their children to other schools (Smekal and Šipulová 2014).

The situation finally changed with the efforts of Social Democrat Kateřina Valachová, who became the Minister of Education in 2015 and made inclusive education one of her priorities. Dr. Valachová has long worked for the Office of the Public Defender of Rights and held several positions in public administration dealing with human rights. She supported the Inclusive Education Action Plan for 2016–2018, which was prepared prior to her coming to office. The 2016 amendment to the School Act included compulsory one-year attendance of pre-school classes, which was supposed to prepare all children for the fundamental school. Moreover, the amendment changed financing of special schooling and increased budgets for assistants for students with special needs. The reform provoked a backlash in the public space, with many harsh voices against inclusive education. It is also possible that this unpopular reform contributed to the poor result of the Social Democratic Party in the 2017 general election. It is too early to evaluate the effects of the reform, as comprehensive data is not available yet. From the data available, it follows that the share of Roma children outside of mainstream education is decreasing, albeit extremely slowly. Moreover, the above-mentioned occurrences of Roma-dominated fundamental schools raise eyebrows.

The issue of discrimination against the Roma in education is raised in parliamentary debates from time to time. The Government Agent's expert group for the execution of the ECtHR judgments discuss the development at their regular sessions[63] and the pressure also persists internationally. The issue has been repeatedly raised during the United Nations (UN) Universal Periodic Review process[64] and the UN High Commissioner for Human Rights addressed the Czech Minister of Foreign Affairs in a letter summing up the gravest problems of Czechia in the field of human rights, which also included discrimination against the Roma in education.[65] The executive and legislative branches responded by amending or adopting various action plans and by legislative changes. Only the 2016 School Act amendment seems to please the Committee of Ministers, which is considering concluding the supervision of the *D.H.* judgment execution in the near future. However, the problem of discrimination against Roma children persists more deeply within the society (Office of the Public Defender of Rights 2018), and even the Czech apex courts have not been of much help so far.

As our book focuses on judicial treatment of ECtHR rulings, the rest of this micro-level study covers the involvement of domestic judges in the implementation of the *D.H.* judgment. Based on the open-worded Grand Chamber *D.H.* judgment, one could expect an avalanche of legal actions from Roma students who frequented special schools. Nevertheless, Czech courts have not heard many such cases, which indicates a low level of knowledge of the judgment inside the Roma community and/or Roma distrust of public institutions. In those few cases with which the Czech courts were confronted, they manifested low levels of sympathy towards the concept of indirect discrimination as understood by the ECtHR. While ordinary courts, led by the SC, widely cited the *D.H.* judgment but have not availed of its spirit, the CC tried to engage with the ECtHR findings in much more depth. In the end, the complainants – the Roma who had studied in special schools in the more distant past – did not succeed. Conversely, in a recent Czech regional court judgment, the Roma students did succeed, but without a single mention of the ECtHR judgment. Nevertheless, it was apparent that the regional judge was familiar with the concept of anti-discrimination and its use. This simple example clearly shows how misleading a study of compliance can be when it relies solely on a simple citation count. The previous case included a number of *D.H.* citations, however, without taking its spirit into account, while the new case omitted any citations to the ECtHR case law, but adopted an approach in line with it.

Mr. J.S., of Roma origin, was born in 1978 and at the age of 2 was moved into temporary institutional care and then to a children's home. He was repeatedly checked on by the pedagogical-psychological advisory bureau, which recommended that his fundamental school education be postponed. Later, he was moved to a special school because he did not cope well with the fundamental school curriculum, had to repeat the first year, and his total IQ stood at 48. J.S. successfully finished secondary school in 2005. J.S. took legal action against Czechia for sending him to a special school; he perceived this as discrimination on the basis of ethnic origin, and he demanded a written apology and 500,000 Czech crowns. The first-instance court found in April 2009 that his transfer to the special school was lawful and justified due to his repeated psychological examinations, the postponement of his fundamental school attendance, his repeated school year, and his low IQ. Moreover, as J.S. had not lived in the Roma community since the age of 2, he was not culturally a part of the Roma community, and thus could not have been discriminated against for his Roma behavior. The applicant appealed and made an argument based on the *D.H.* judgment that in the case of a huge disproportion, there is no need to examine circumstances of individual cases because every member of the disadvantaged group is a victim of discrimination. The appeals court emphasized in its 2010 judgment that it respected the ECtHR's case law and acknowledged the vulnerable position of Roma people; nevertheless, it did not find a violation on the part of the Czech Republic because all the steps the Czech authorities took were justified and the presumption of discriminatory practice rebuttable. The complainant then appealed to the SC, alleging that the appeals court did not comprehend the concept of indirect discrimination. J.S. put forward that in the context of the negative sentiment of the majority towards the Roma, he was a priori discriminated against based on his ethnic origin at the first moment of contact with the educational system.[66] However, this potential lesson from the ECtHR *D.H.* judgment does not resonate well within the Czech judiciary.

In its 2012 judgment, the SC cited its earlier case law positing that ECtHR judgments do not have precedential power and bind only the parties of the particular dispute. Nevertheless, the SC judges argued that the ECtHR case law cannot be overlooked because the ECHR is a living instrument and the ECtHR case law does not only interpret the Convention, but also gives it new meaning. Therefore, if Czechia is to follow the ECHR, it has to conform to the ECtHR's case law. The SC then cited the ECtHR cases and made an absurd claim (not following from the Strasbourg case law) that in order to establish prima facie evidence of discrimination needed for shifting the burden of proof, it is necessary that at least 50 percent of special school students are Roma. As the proportion of Roma students in the total special school population was only 40 percent, the SC did not find anything worrisome in the statistics.[67] The SC requested additional evidence that the complainant had been discriminated against. Even if J.S. had brought such evidence, it sufficed to show that the decisive reason for sending J.S. to the special school was not his ethnic origin. The SC added that it was possible to refute the allegation that a transfer to the special school was motivated by the ethnic origin with the use of the proportionality test, specifically by showing guarantees preventing a situation when a child ended up in a special school without being mentally disabled. To sum up, the SC referred to the ECtHR case law, including that against its own home state, but did not follow its spirit. Instead, the SC cherry-picked some excerpts from the Strasbourg case law and applied its distorted version to the facts of the case to rule that no discrimination had occurred.

Finally, the complainant tried his fortune at the CC which, in its 2015 judgment, turned down his petition on the one hand, but on the other hand provided some criticism of the previous proceedings. The CC provided much more thoughtful elaboration and pointed to flaws in the SC's reasoning, including its work with statistics.[68] The CC distinguished the case of Mr. J. S. from *D.H. and Others* because, unlike the *D.H.* case, the procedure in the J. S. case included all the guarantees which safeguarded that his transfer to the special school was justified.[69] The CC made an effort to explain that J.S. had been treated differently than victims of discrimination in the *D.H.* case. Again, the CC did not accept the possible reading of the *D.H.* judgment that once a person showed that he was a member of a discriminated community, then he was automatically mistreated as well. But, unlike the SC, the CC put forward strong arguments to show that belonging to a Roma community has not played a role in placing a person at a special school.

The opposite scenario arose in the recent (2017) case before the first-instance court in Ostrava, the city in which the *D.H.* case originated: While the *D.H.* judgment was not cited, the Roma applicant was successful. The regional court ordered the fundamental school in Ostrava to send a written letter of apology to two Roma children who were not accepted there. The court nonetheless did not award any pecuniary damages, despite the requested sum of 50,000 Czech crowns (approx. 2,000 euros) to each. The school was caught by surprise when many Roma kids unexpectedly showed up in order to register for the first classes. The headmaster announced very late that, due to capacity reasons, the school could only admit 30 children. The applicants had to pass tests, of which the parents were not informed and evaluation was not transparent. Moreover, the headmaster stated in interviews that he thought that integration works best when only a limited number of Roma pupils sit in a class. All non-Roma applicants were admitted to the first year, as the limited capacity and the late introduction of the non-transparent test of maturity, which moreover did not have any basis in law, negatively affected only the Roma applicants. The judge in the case found the headmaster's approach to be directly discriminatory, motivated by fear of being labelled a "Roma school", which could lead to the departure of majority children. The pecuniary damages were not awarded because the school minimized the discriminatory interference with human dignity when the headmaster subsequently accepted both unsuccessful applicants (who nonetheless refused the offer after such a bad experience with the school).[70] Despite not formally citing the *D.H.* judgment, the local judge applied the concept of direct discrimination in favour of the Roma children and even used some numerical data in reaching his conclusions. Paradoxically, this judgment, without an explicit citation of the ECtHR's case law, contributed to compliance with the underlying norm (racial equality) more than the aforementioned SC judgment that heavily cited the *D.H.* judgment but did not follow its spirit.

Búzás (2018) points to the change in behavior that occurs when there is a strong international compliance pull and domestic violation push. States no longer openly violate a norm, but tend to evade it: they technically comply with international law, while continuing to violate its underlying norms. Such a characterization also suits the practice of the Czech apex courts well, or at least the SC, which invokes the ECtHR's *D.H.* judgment, but does so in a way that violates the underlying norm of anti-discrimination. Kosař and Petrov (2018) argue that in order to escape protracted compliance difficulties, events such as external shocks, synergic effects with the EU, and reframing the human rights issue, the EU could help with getting in line with the ECtHR case law. So far, the national judicial community has not committed itself to becoming a strong ECtHR compliance partner, which could destabilize the political and social pro-status-quo camp. The caution exhibited towards progressive, anti-discrimination norms persists across the Czech society, including judges at the apex courts. Moreover, the compliance exercise is not a one-way street: The persuasiveness of the international judgment to be complied with plays an important role, and the ECtHR here has not arguably helped as much as is needed. Czech apex courts remain hesitant towards embracing a potentially far-reaching Strasbourg interpretation and, rather, proceed either in a piecemeal fashion or opt for evasion when pretending compliance with dense referencing of the ECtHR case law, but practically going against its spirit.

Notes

1 See Chapter 4 for the description of the methodology used.
2 See the Introduction for the closer elaboration of the main research questions.
3 The ECtHR delivered 837 judgments in the first four decades of its existence (1959–1998), which is less than the ECtHR currently issues annually. In 1999, the ECtHR delivered 177 judgments, but only one year later there were a full 695 judgments. The number of judgments issued annually has not dipped under 700 since then. See European Court of Human Rights (2018, 4).
4 See Chapters 5 and 6 for more on the expansion of ECtHR case law to the domains of law which the SC and the SAC primarily deal with.
5 Our dataset includes both the number of rulings and number of references citing ECtHR case law. Here we present the number of domestic rulings, so that the reader gets an idea about the number of rulings in which citations of ECtHR case law appear. Study of references is important in other parts of our research; here, the overall picture would be distorted by domestic rulings in which a series of references appear in one parenthesis.
6 An important notice when reading graphs: For the SC, the data is available only from 1998, although the court itself came into existence on 1 January 1993 via transformation from the Federal Supreme Court. Generally, the data from 1990s is shaky because both the CC and the SC introduced their online databases only at the turn of the millennium. We hopefully managed to obtain the whole collection of both courts' rulings, but still, a bit of caution is advised when reading about the development in 1990s.
7 See Chapters 5 and 7 for a closer elaboration on the reasons behind the gradual increase in the use of ECtHR case law.
8 Chapter 5 elaborates more on interrelated reasons for a sharp increase in the number of references to ECtHR case law in 2010, which include gradually learning to work with foreign case law, changes in the personnel composition, a more active research unit, and the

SC's recognition of direct applicability of the Convention's provisions. In addition to these factors, we notice a change in the nature of rulings when we compare years 2009 and 2010. The year 2010 saw a huge increase in the number of the SC's judgments referring to ECtHR case law as opposed to the year 2009, when the SC cited Strasbourg rulings primarily in decisions. Moreover, many of the SC's rulings delivered in 2010 concerned compensation for the length of proceedings and relied directly on ECtHR judgments against the Czech Republic.

9 See Chapter 5.

10 An interview with a former SC judge, 5 December 2018, Brno.

11 An interview with a SC judge, 10 December 2018, Brno.

12 An interview with a former SC judge, 11 January 2019, Brno.

13 An interview with a former SC judge, 11 January 2019, Brno.

14 A translation of a short book on ECtHR case law in 1993 (Gomien 1993) and translations of excerpts from new ECtHR judgments (since 1998) were pioneering acts in 1990s as regards informing the public about the ECHR regime.

15 See especially Chapter 7 on the CC, which shows, for example, that one judge scored very highly in the number of rulings with references to ECtHR case law. That information surprised our author team because the judge did not have a particularly human-rights-friendly reputation. We took a deeper look at the record of the judge to find that a vast proportion of those references were just copied-and-pasted generic references without substantive importance for deciding the case.

16 The literature gradually acknowledges the increasing role of law clerks in the functioning of courts (see, for example, Rutledge 2007). Specifically in Czechia, the role of law clerks at the CC differs markedly depending on the judge. Some judges give their clerks considerable space for their own creativity, while other judges stringently instruct clerks on how they want to decide the cases (Papoušková 2019). Regardless of the kind of relationship a judge and a clerk have, a clerk can always bring to a judge's attention the existence of ECtHR case law that applies to the case at hand.

17 A full-time position does not necessarily mean that one person works full-time; a judge can employ, for example, two half-time clerks.

18 Recently, scholars have observed a backlash against international courts (Madsen, Cebulak, and Wiebusch 2018), but that does not change much for our analysis. First, our period under examination is much longer than the last few years. Second, the judicialization of politics persists, although some countries in some cases openly disagreed with some international courts.

19 See, for example, Strasbourg Observers (https://strasbourgobservers.com/) or ECHR Blog (http://echrblog.blogspot.com/).

20 Chapters 5, 6, and 7.

21 We describe general tendencies; highly knowledgeable ECtHR experts both among judges and their clerks sit also at the SC, but proportionately in smaller numbers than at the two remaining apex courts.

22 See, for example, Peppers and Zorn (2008) and Swanson and Wasby (2008).

23 In the case of the CC, we have to approach the distinction between judgments and other rulings with a grain of caution. The CC regularly uses decisions to reject the petition instead of deciding a case on merits. Consequently, the Court issues mainly granting judgments, while non-granting judgments appear rather seldom, because such petitions are solved as rejecting decisions (not judgments) (Papoušková 2018).

24 The SAC experienced an exceptional period in 2005–2006 when references in narrative parts clearly outweighed references in the reasoning. This is because a series of similar cases appeared before the Court and references in the narrative part repeatedly cited few ECtHR judgments (for example, *Huvig v. France*, no. 11105/04, judgment of 24 April 1990; *Kruslin v. France*, no. 11801/85, judgment of 24 April 1990; *Vilvarajah and Others v. the United Kingdom*, nos. 13163/87; 13164/87; 13165/87; 13447/

87 and 13448/87, judgment of 30 October 1991; *Cruz Varas and Others v. Sweden*, no. 15576/89, judgment of 20 March 1991).

25 For example, Marlene Wind (2016) builds on the number of references without further distinguishing among them.

26 From the ECtHR list of "landmark judgments" (www.coe.int/en/web/human-rights-convention/landmark-judgments), which consists of approximately 30 judgments, only *Broniowski v. Poland* ([GC], no. 31443/96, judgment of 22 June 2004) made it into the top 15 most cited cases by one of the Czech apex courts (the CC).

27 *Ruiz Torija v. Spain*, no. 18390/91, judgment of 9 December 1994; *Van de Hurk v. the Netherlands*, no. 16034/90, judgment of 19 April 1994; and *Kruslin v. France*, no. 11801/85, judgment of 24 April 1990.

28 To further substantiate that the CC refers the most to the most important ECtHR rulings, we computed the mean of the top 15 most cited ECtHR rulings by the respective courts. Category 3 (according to ECtHR self-categorization) was assigned 1 point, going through categories 2 and 1 (2 and 3 points respectively) up to 4 points for "key" ECtHR rulings. The CC's top 15 most cited ECtHR rulings scored 3.1 on average, while the SAC's score was 2.9 and the SC's was 2.4.

29 Only rarely do Czech apex courts openly oppose ECtHR rulings or explain why they will not use them.

30 ECtHR, *Běleš v. the Czech Republic*, no. 47273/99, judgment of 12 November 2002.

31 ECtHR, *Zvolský and Zvolská v. the Czech Republic*, no. 46129/99, 12 November 2002.

32 See, for example, the most frequently invoked ECtHR judgment by the SAC, *Van de Hurk v. the Netherlands*, which on one hand obliges courts to give reasons for their decisions, but on the other hand does not require them to provide a detailed answer to every argument. Domestic courts use *Van de Hurk* to justify their non-exhaustive responses to parties' claims.

33 The petitions were brought by companies whose business model included suing in low-value cases and profiting from the awarded costs of proceeding (see Chapter 7).

34 An interview with a SC judge, 10 December 2019, Brno; an interview with a judge who had a career both at the SC and the CC, 11 January 2019, Brno; an interview with a retired SC judge, 5 December 2018, Brno.

35 See Chapter 5 for details.

36 See especially the practice of the SC, described more in detail in Chapter 5.

37 See Chapter 4 for the description of the construction of the sample, which is not fully representative because the substantive references are overrepresented. However, it works well for the proportional comparisons among courts such as those presented in Figures 8.4 and 8.5.

38 See Chapter 6.2 for details.

39 See more in Chapter 7.3.1.

40 See Chapter 6.3.2.

41 See Chapter 6.3 for details.

42 See Chapter 1 for the concept of apex courts as "diffusers".

43 See Chapter 5.2 for details.

44 See Chapter 5.3 for details.

45 ECtHR [GC], *Zolotukhin v. Russia*, no. 14939/03, judgment of 10 February 2009.

46 ECtHR [GC], *A and B v. Norway*, nos. 24130/11 and 29758/11, judgment of 15 November 2016.

47 See Chapter 6.3.1.

48 An interview with a CC judge, 5 December 2018, Brno.

49 See Chapter 6.3.1.

50 An interview with a SC judge, 10 December 2019, Brno.

51 ECtHR, *Pincová and Pinc v. the Czech Republic*, no. 36548/97, judgment of 5 November 2002.

52 An interview with a former CC judge, 17 December 2018, Brno.
53 ECtHR [GC], *D.H. and Others v. the Czech Republic*, no. 57325/00, 13 November 2007.
54 It is important to bear in mind the dynamic character of the researched phenomena. Not only do domestic courts and political arenas change, but also the supply side has also undergone fundamental reforms that influenced interactions with national actors. The ECtHR became a permanent fully-fledged court with compulsory jurisdiction after Protocol No. 11 came into effect in 1998, and has since massively expanded its case law, which covers an ever-wider area of issues.
55 See Chapter 6.3.2.
56 See Chapter 7.3.1.
57 See Chapters 5.3.2 and 6.3.1.
58 As of 22 June 2018, the Czech Republic closed by final resolution 215 of 221 cases which were transmitted for supervision (Council of Europe: Committee of Ministers 2018, 1).
59 ECtHR [GC], *D.H. and Others v. the Czech Republic*, no. 57325/00, judgment of 13 November 2007.
60 The enhanced procedure applies when a case is of a specific nature; for example, when judgments require urgent individual measures; in case of pilot judgments; judgments disclosing major structural and/or complex problems; or in interstate cases (Council of Europe: Committee of Ministers 2010, § 10).
61 ECtHR, *D.H. and Others v. the Czech Republic*, no. 57325/00, judgment of 7 February 2006.
62 ECtHR [GC], *D.H. and Others v. the Czech Republic*, no. 57325/00, judgment of 13 November 2007, § 209.
63 See https://justice.cz/web/msp/kolegium-expertu-k-vykonu-rozsudku-eslp.
64 See the last review of Czechia in November 2017, whose compilation includes explicit mention of the *D.H.* judgment (Human Rights Council 2017, § 50).
65 The letter is available here: https://lib.ohchr.org/HRBodies/UPR/Documents/Session28/CZ/Czech_RepublicHCLetter.pdf.
66 SC, no. 30 Cdo 4277/2010-180 *J.S.*, judgement of 13 December 2012.
67 To document the bizarreness of the finding, one can imagine a situation of a 300-child, large minority, all of whom are sent to special schools with a total capacity of 1,000 children in a country with 1 million children. Despite the fact that all of the minority children attend special schools, the SC would probably not be concerned, because they represent only 30 percent of all the children at the special schools. Mistakenly, the SC was interested in the number of Roma children in special schools/the number of special schools' population, instead of a comparison of the number of Roma children in special schools/the total number of Roma children and the number of majority population children in special schools/the total number of majority children population; or, alternatively, a huge disproportion between the number of Roma children in special schools/number of special schools' children population and total number of Roma children/total number of children in population.
68 CC, no. III. ÚS 1136/13 *J.S.*, judgment of 12 August 2015, §§ 48–52.
69 CC, no. III. ÚS 1136/13 *J.S.*, judgment of 12 August 2015, § 60.
70 District Court Ostrava, no. 26 C 42/2016-124 *Z.Ž. and J.V. v. Základní škola Ostrava Muglinov*, judgment of 1 March 2017.

References

Alter, Karen J. 2014. *The New Terrain of International Law: Courts, Politics, Rights.* Princeton, NJ: Princeton University Press.

Bobek, Michal. 2007. "Ostravo, Ostravo …". *Jiné právo (blog)*, 14 November 2007. Accessed 16 July 2019. http://jinepravo.blogspot.com/2007/11/ostravo-ostravo.html.

Bobek, Michal. 2008. "The Fortress of Judicial Independence and the Mental Transitions of the Central European Judiciaries". *European Public Law* 14 (1): 99–123.

Bobek, Michal. 2013. *Comparative Reasoning in European Supreme Courts.* Oxford: Oxford University Press.

Bobek, Michal, ed. 2015. *Central European Judges under the European Influence: The Transformative Power of the EU Revisited.* Oxford and Portland, OR: Hart Publishing.

Bobek, Michal, and David Kosař. 2010. "The Application of European Union Law and the Law of the European Convention of Human Rights in the Czech Republic and Slovakia: An Overview". In *The National Judicial Treatment of the ECHR and EU Laws. A Comparative Constitutional Perspective*, edited by Giuseppe Martinico and Oreste Pollicino, 117–50. Groningen: Europa Law Publishing.

Búzás, Zoltán I. 2018. "Is the Good News about Law Compliance Good News about Norm Compliance? The Case of Racial Equality". *International Organization* 72 (2): 351–85.

Claes, Monica, and Maartje de Visser. 2012. "Are You Networked Yet: On Dialogues in European Judicial Networks". *Utrecht Law Review* 8 (2): 100–14.

Council of Europe: Committee of Ministers. 2010. "Supervision of the Execution of the Judgments and Decisions of the European Court of Human Rights: Implementation of the Interlaken Action Plan – Outstanding Issues Concerning the Practical Modalities of Implementation of the New Twin Track Supervision System". Accessed 9 August 2019. https://rm.coe.int/16804a3e07.

Council of Europe: Committee of Ministers. 2018. "Country Factsheet. Czech Republic". Accessed 9 August 2019. https://rm.coe.int/1680709744.

Dothan, Shai. 2013. "How International Courts Enhance Their Legitimacy". *Theoretical Inquiries in Law* 14 (2): 455–78.

Emmert, Frank. 2012. "The Implementation of the European Convention on Human Rights and Fundamental Freedoms in New Member States of the Council of Europe - Conclusions Drawn and Lessons Learned". In *The European Convention on Human Rights and Fundamental Freedoms in Central and Eastern Europe*, edited by Leonard M. Hammer and Frank Emmert, 597–645. Hague and Portland, OR: Eleven International Publishing.

European Court of Human Rights. 2018. "Overview 1959-2017". Accessed 9 August 2019. www.echr.coe.int/Documents/Overview_19592017_ENG.pdf.

Follesdal, Andreas, and Geir Ulfstein, eds. 2018. *The Judicialization of International Law: A Mixed Blessing?* Oxford and New York: Oxford University Press.

Ginsburg, Tom. 2012. "Courts and New Democracies: Recent Works". *Law & Social Inquiry* 37 (3): 720–42.

Gomien, Donna. 1993. *Stručná rukojeť Evropské úmluvy o lidských právech [Brief Handbook of the European Convention on Human Rights].* Prague: Council of Europe.

Goodwin, Morag. 2006. "D.H. And Others V. Czech Republic: A Major Set-Back for the Development of Non-Discrimination Norms in Europe". *German Law Journal* 7 (4): 421–31.

High Level Conference on the Future of the European Court of Human Rights. 2012. "Brighton Declaration". Accessed 9 August 2019. www.echr.coe.int/Documents/2012_Brighton_FinalDeclaration_ENG.pdf.

Hirschl, Ran. 2008. "The Judicialization of Mega-Politics and the Rise of Political Courts". *Annual Review of Political Science* 11 (1): 93–118.

Human Rights Council. 2017. "Compilation on Czechia". Accessed 9 August 2019. https://documents-dds-ny.un.org/doc/UNDOC/GEN/G17/257/14/PDF/G1725714.pdf?OpenElement.

Kilian, Petr, Ivo Pospíšil, and Hubert Smekal. 2016. "International Human Rights in Czech Legal Education". *International and Comparative Law Review* 16 (2): 87–98.

Kmec, Jiří, David Kosař, Jan Kratochvíl, and Michal Bobek. 2012. *Evropská úmluva o lidských právech: komentář [European Convention on Human Rights: A Commentary]*. Prague: C.H. Beck.

Kosař, David. 2016. *Perils of Judicial Self-Government in Transitional Societies*. Cambridge: Cambridge University Press.

Kosař, David, and Jan Petrov. 2017. "The Architecture of the Strasbourg System of Human Rights: The Crucial Role of the Domestic Level and the Constitutional Courts in Particular". *Heidelberg Journal of International Law* 77: 585–621.

Kosař, David, and Jan Petrov. 2018. "Determinants of Compliance Difficulties among 'good Compliers': Implementation of International Human Rights Rulings in the Czech Republic". *The European Journal of International Law* 29 (2): 397–425.

Kühn, Zdeněk. 2005. *Aplikace práva soudcem v éře středoevropského komunismu a transformace: Analýza příčin postkomunistické právní krize [An Application of Law by a Judge in Era of Central European Communism and Transformation: An Analysis of Causes of Post-Communist Legal Crisis]*. Prague: C.H. Beck.

Kühn, Zdeněk. 2011. *The Judiciary in Central and Eastern Europe: Mechanical Jurisprudence in Transformation?* Leiden: Brill.

Madsen, Mikael Rask. 2015. "The Legitimization Strategies of International Judges: The Case of the European Court of Human Rights". In *Selecting Europe's Judges. A Critical Review of the Appointment Procedures to the European Courts*, edited by Michal Bobek, 259–78. Oxford: Oxford University Press.

Madsen, Mikael Rask, Pola Cebulak, and Micha Wiebusch. 2018. "Backlash against International Courts: Explaining the Forms and Patterns of Resistance to International Courts". *International Journal of Law in Context* 14 (2): 197–220.

Majerčík, Ľubomír. 2016. "Czech Republic: Strasbourg Case Law Undisputed". In *Criticism of the European Court of Human Rights: Shifting the Convention System: Counter-dynamics at the National and EU Level*, edited by Patricia Popelier, Sarah Lambrecht and Koen Lemmens, 131–54. Cambridge: Intersentia.

Matczak, Marcin, Matyas Bencze, and Zdeněk Kühn. 2010. "Constitutions, EU Law and Judicial Strategies in the Czech Republic, Hungary and Poland". *Journal of Public Policy* 30 (1): 81–99.

Molek, Pavel. 2013. "Judikatura ve správním právu". In *Judikatura a právní argumentace*, 2nd edition, edited by Michal Bobek and Zdeněk Kühn, 377–416. Prague: Auditorium.

Office of the Public Defender of Rights. 2018. "Doporučení veřejné ochránkyně práv ke společnému vzdělávání romských a neromských dětí". Accessed 21 January 2019. www.ochrance.cz/fileadmin/user_upload/DISKRIMINACE/Doporuceni/Doporuceni-desegregace_86-17-DIS.pdf.

Papoušková, Tereza. 2018. "Nastolování agendy u Ústavního soudu: Kdo a na základě čeho vybírá, které případy projednat a které odmítnout? [Agenda Setting at the Constitutional Court of the Czech Republic: Who Decides and How Which Cases are Decided on merits?]" *Jurisprudence* 27 (6): 3–21.

Papoušková, Tereza. 2019. "Nastolování soudní agendy: případová studie Ústavního soudu České republiky [Setting up Judicial Agenda: A Case Study on the Constitutional Court of the Czech Republic]." Ph.D. thesis, Brno: Masaryk University.

Peppers, Todd C., and Christopher Zorn. 2008. "Law Clerk Influence on Supreme Court Decision Making: An Empirical Assessment". *DePaul Law Review* 58 (1): 51–78.

Petrov, Jan, and Katarína Šipulová. 2016. "Mezinárodní lidskoprávní smlouvy v judikatuře obecných soudů: Nejvyšší soud a Nejvyšší správní soud [International Human Rights Treaties in case Law of the General Courts: The Supreme Court and Supreme Administrative Court]". In *Mezinárodní lidskoprávní závazky postkomunistických zemí: případy České republiky a Slovenska [International Human Rights Obligations of Post-communist Countries: Cases of the Czech Republic and Slovakia]*, edited by Ivo Pospíšil and Vladimír Týč, 141–65. Prague: Leges.

Pin, Andrea. 2019. "The Transnational Drivers of Populist Backlash in Europe: The Role of Courts". *German Law Journal* 20 (2): 225–44.

Procházka, Antonín. 2008. *V boji za ústavnost: Ze vzpomínek bývalého ústavního soudce [In Fight for Consitutionality: From the Memories of Former Justice]*. Brno: Centrum pro studium demokracie a kultury (CDK).

Rutledge, Peter B. 2007. "Clerks". *The University of Chicago Law Review* 74 (1): 369–406.

Schorm, Vít Alexander. 2018. "Několik poznámek na okraj tématu a samotného projektu „beyond compliance" [Several Remarks on Topic and on Project 'Beyond Compliance']". In *Beyond Compliance: Implementace rozhodnutí mezinárodních lidskoprávních těles na národní úrovni [Beyond Compliance: Domestic Judicial Implementation of the International Human Rights Case Law]*, edited by Hubert Smekal and Ladislav Vyhnánek, 191–202. Prague: Wolters Kluwer.

Smekal, Hubert, and Katarína Šipulová. 2014. "*DH v Czech Republic* Six Years Later: On the Power of an International Human Rights Court to Push through Systemic Change". *Netherlands Quarterly of Human Rights* 32 (3): 288–321.

Sumption, Jonathan. 2011. "Judicial and Political Decision-making: The Uncertain Boundary". *Judicial Review* 16 (4): 301–15.

Swanson, Rick A., and Stephen L. Wasby. 2008. "Good Stewards: Law Clerk Influence in State High Courts". *Justice System Journal* 29 (1): 24–46.

Tate, Chester Neal, and Torbjörn Vallinder, eds. 1995. *The Global Expansion of Judicial Power*. New York: New York University Press.

von Staden, Andreas. 2018. *Strategies of Compliance with the European Court of Human Rights*. Philadelphia, PA: University of Pennsylvania Press.

Vyhnánek, Ladislav. 2017. "A Holistic View of the Czech Constitutional Court Approach to the ECtHR's Case Law". *Heidelberg Journal of International Law* 77 (3): 715–43.

Vyhnánek, Ladislav, and Robert Jakubíček. 2016. "Roles and Responsibilities of Assistants and Advisors at the Czech Constitutional Court". In *The Role of Assistant-Magistrates in the Jurisdiction of Constitutional Courts*, edited by Augustin Zegrean and M. A. Costinescu, 67–70. Bucharest: Universul Juridic.

Wind, Marlene. 2016. "Do Scandinavians Care about International Law? A Study of Scandinavian Judges' Citation Practice to International Law and Courts". *Nordic Journal of International Law* 85 (4): 281–302.

Part III

Broader repercussions

9 Beyond judicial compliance

Domestic courts in the ECHR regime

Many proposed solutions to the European Court of Human Rights' (ECtHR or Strasbourg Court) caseload, legitimacy, and implementation crises are related to the operation of domestic courts. More specifically, domestic courts are trusted to diffuse the ECtHR's conclusions within their jurisdiction, filter eventual European Convention on Human Rights (ECHR or Convention) violations and remedy them at the national level, and thereby decrease the number of applications incoming to the Strasbourg Court, strengthen the implementation of the Convention, and positively affect the ECtHR's legitimacy.[1]

In order to assess the feasibility of these expectations, this book has probed deeply into the practice of the apex courts in Czechia, analyzed various levels of domestic judicial engagement with the Strasbourg jurisprudence, and detected ways in which domestic judges actually treat the ECtHR's case law in their day-to-day practice. The previous chapters have uncovered the frequency of citing the Strasbourg rulings, prevalent modes of arguing with the ECtHR's case law, and the broader effects it has had on selected areas of domestic law.

This final chapter builds on these findings but takes a step further. It aims to reflect what these insights imply more generally for the Strasbourg human rights regime and how they relate to recent legal-political trends taking place in the Council of Europe (CoE), specifically in the (post-)transitional countries in Central and Eastern Europe (CEE). In particular, this chapter revisits the above-mentioned hope placed in domestic courts and assesses domestic courts' actual capacity to contribute to a brighter future of the ECHR system. Although the empirical part of this book dealt mostly with the Czech apex courts, we put the Czech experience in the broader context of developments in the group of (post-) transitional countries of CEE, which entered the CoE only in the 1990s. Nevertheless, any generalizations must be made carefully and take account of local legal, political, and social specificities.

As we argued in Chapter 1, socio-political state-level factors such as regime type, legal infrastructure, and countries' reputational concerns all affect implementation of international human rights law. The CEE region has recently undergone significant changes on this level. Many CEE countries have shown significant leaning towards the rule-of-law backsliding, and nationalist, populist, and even authoritarian tendencies. Although the Czech case provides only limited evidence regarding these developments, this chapter takes these socio-political trends into account since they are of critical relevance for the discussion about the role of domestic (apex) courts in the ECHR regime. Domestic courts can use the ECtHR doctrines to counter the populist/authoritarian/nationalist tendencies. Yet, domestic courts are regularly targeted and captured by the populist governments. Consequently, there is a danger that captured courts will resent or even abuse the ECtHR jurisprudence.

In brief, we argue that domestic judiciaries represent important actors in the Strasbourg regime. However, they can use the ECtHR's case law for both good and bad. We show that, on the one hand, domestic judges can in good faith adopt the ECtHR's doctrines and diffuse its conclusions among other stakeholders, filter ECHR violations and thereby reduce the docket of the ECtHR, translate the ECtHR's principles and conclusions into a domestic context so that they reflect and fit into the domestic legal culture, use the ECtHR's case law as a shield against domestic actors who encroach upon human rights, and ultimately rely on the Strasbourg jurisprudence in their fight against abusive constitutionalism. We call these strategies the bright side of the domestic judicial treatment of the Strasbourg case law. On the other hand, there is also a dark side, as domestic judges can fight against the proliferation of Convention rights, as interpreted by the ECtHR; challenge the ECtHR as such; or even abuse the Strasbourg case law domestically to arrive at conclusions that would not have been accepted by the ECtHR itself. We briefly visualize the bright and dark sides in Table 9.1.

Table 9.1 The bright side v. the dark side of the use of ECtHR case law

Bright side	*Dark side*		
Adoption of ECtHR doctrines	Refusal of ECtHR doctrines		
Diffusion of ECtHR conclusions	Pushback	Backlash	Withdrawal
Filtering ECHR violations	Legitimacy challenges		
Mediation/translation of ECtHR conclusions into domestic context	Widening gaps between domestic and international human rights protection		
Shield against opposing actors	Capturing domestic courts		
Extra layer of protection against abusive constitutionalism	Decreased partnership capacity	Rising judicial resistance against the ECtHR	Abuse of Strasbourg case law

Source: authors.

In the following sections of this chapter, we expand on individual strategies on both sides of the continuum. Section 9.1 focuses on the bright side. First, we argue that domestic judicial implementation of the ECtHR's standards in transitioning countries can make a particularly significant difference on the ground and genuinely increase the protection of human rights. Acceptance of the Strasbourg jurisprudence by domestic judges in such a context is not automatic though,[2] and hence we identify factors that may help to overcome their indifference and resistance. Second, we show that if the Strasbourg case law is deeply embedded in the reasoning of domestic courts, it may operate as a shield against politicians who pursue nationalist or authoritarian policies, and it may even serve as bulwark against abusive constitutionalism. Section 9.2 then turns to the dark side. Drawing on the pushback–backlash–withdrawal trichotomy, it shows that domestic judges may disagree with the development of the ECtHR's case law. Depending on the level of disagreement, they can resort to pushback or even backlash against the Strasbourg Court. In the long term, this may legitimize the state to withdraw from the Convention entirely. Furthermore, domestic judges may also rig the ECtHR's case law in order to justify the illegitimate decisions that serve ruling domestic politicians. Finally, Section 9.3 discusses the future challenges in domestic judicial implementation of the ECtHR's case law in the (post-) transitional context.

9.1 The bright side

In this section, we analyze the positive effects of domestic judicial engagement with the Strasbourg case law. First, we show that the Strasbourg Court makes a difference on the ground and that domestic judicial use of the ECtHR's case law has greatly improved human rights standards in transitioning countries. At the same time, we show that it is not always easy to persuade domestic judges – in the CEE context especially, judges embedded in the mindset of the communist-era judicial methodology – to actively engage with the ECtHR's case law. We thus identify several contingent circumstances that may help to overcome the initial resistance or indifference of such judges, such as improving the language skills of domestic judges as well as those of their law clerks, providing judicial training on the ECHR in the local language, publishing textbooks and in-depth commentaries on the ECHR that are tailored to a given jurisdiction and its particular problems, creating analytical departments at domestic apex courts that continuously monitor the Strasbourg Court's case law and inform domestic judges about new relevant ECtHR rulings, and selecting an active Government Agent who sensitively communicates the repercussions of the ECtHR's jurisprudence to domestic judges. Second, we show that if the Strasbourg case law is deeply embedded in the reasoning of domestic courts, it may operate as a shield against politicians who pursue nationalist or authoritarian policies and it may even serve as bulwark, albeit arguably only for some time, against abusive constitutionalism.

9.1.1 The Strasbourg Court makes a difference

The ECtHR and domestic judicial implementation of its rulings have hugely contributed to the advancements in human rights protection and the rule-of-law observance in the CEE (post-)transitional countries. Scholars have labelled the Strasbourg Court's case law as a human rights handbook providing transformative guidance to the CEE courts (Çali, Koch, and Bruch 2013, 981; Ziemele 2016, 498). Sometimes, CEE lawyers even looked up to the ECHR jurisprudence as to a "lantern of the law" (see Bobek et al. 2013, V). The areas most affected by the ECtHR are those heavily influenced by the previous non-democratic context. This context had led to the emergence of a specific mindset regarding these issues. Those areas include the non-existence of domestic human rights remedies, lack of practice in balancing human rights and the public interests, insufficient protection of political rights, and detention (Ziemele 2016, 496–7).

Our research supports these claims and shows that the apex courts adopted many human rights doctrines originating in the ECtHR's case law. Acceptance and application of these doctrines by apex courts subsequently led to their (more or less) successful diffusion and domestication in national legal orders and to filtering out numerous ECHR violations by remedying them at the national level. Finally, apex courts have also been instrumental in translating the often abstract ECtHR doctrines into the national constitutional context, thereby mediating between the international and the national in the ECHR system (see Paulus 2014; Ulfstein 2016, 57; Petrov 2018a, 531).

Mostly lacking domestic inspiration, the transitional countries' apex courts adopted numerous ECtHR-inspired legal doctrines by direct application of the Convention, ECHR-conforming interpretation of domestic laws, and filling the gaps existing in domestic legislation. To name a few examples, the Constitutional Court (CC) introduced ECtHR-influenced methodology for balancing privacy rights and free speech in the context of defamation (see Chapter 7). The Supreme Administrative Court (SAC) transplanted the Strasbourg Court's approach to judging lawfulness of political parties' dissolution (see Chapter 6). The Supreme Court (SC) largely embraced the ECtHR's case law on assessing judicial delays and lengthy proceedings (see Chapter 5). Other (post-)transitional countries in the CoE have reported similar trends, especially with respect to their constitutional courts. The Croatian Constitutional Court, for instance, changed its strengthened procedural rights in eviction proceedings in response to the Strasbourg Court's case law, which led to improvements in the application of the proportionality analysis, even by ordinary courts (Turković and Omejec 2016, 119–20; Petrov 2018a, 511).

Our micro-level analysis showed that often the adoption of the Strasbourg-inspired doctrines by apex courts led to their gradual diffusion and acceptance by lower courts too. The SC, for example, issued an important interpretative guideline unifying the ordinary courts' approach to the removal of children from parental care, implementing the ECtHR's judgments in *Wallovi* and in

Havelkovi.[3] Czech legislation later embraced these standards as well (Petrov 2018b, 153–54). The SAC used Article 6 ECHR jurisprudence to "patch" the imperfect legislation, and it elevated the protection of procedural rights before administrative bodies and administrative courts to a higher level (see Chapter 6). The CC's approach to defamation gradually penetrated the case law of ordinary courts too (see Chapters 5 and 7; and Kosař 2011). Beyond these examples, there has been a more general effect of Czech apex courts' increasing citation of the Strasbourg Court's case law. The frequent supporting use of ECtHR references in apex courts' argumentation has diffused the awareness about the ECtHR's rulings and contributed to the ongoing gradual standardization of ECHR-argumentation in domestic jurisprudence (see Chapter 8).

Additionally, apex courts have to some extent substituted the Strasbourg Court and filtered out eventual ECHR violations. In the past decade, for instance, the CC followed the *res interpretata* effect of the Strasbourg jurisprudence and accepted the existence of the positive right to effective investigation (see Chapter 7), thereby providing opportunities to resolve these cases at the domestic level. The SC has corrected the compensation awarded by lower courts for lengthy proceedings in order to comply with the ECtHR's standards (Chapter 5; and Kosař and Petrov 2018, 416). The SAC assesses the privacy and family-related claims of asylum seekers on a daily basis, using ECtHR-inspired doctrines (see Chapter 6).

Nevertheless, apex courts have not always merely passively accepted the ECtHR's conclusions. They have also made efforts to "translate" vague ECtHR doctrines and concepts to the detailed context of Czech law, thereby helping to mediate the national and the international dimensions of the ECHR regime. Recently, the SC dealt with a controversial issue of *non bis in idem* regarding the concurrence of criminal and administrative sanctions. It took account of the ECtHR's new case law and "translated" the Strasbourg Court's judgment in *A and B v. Norway*[4] into the context of tax frauds in the Czech law.[5] The SAC, especially during the first years of its functioning, adjusted the abstract procedural principles stemming from Article 6 ECHR to the particularities of Czech administrative procedure (see Chapter 6). Finally, the CC's most recent approach to balancing privacy rights and freedom of expression combines both ECtHR and domestic elements (see Chapter 7).

On the other hand, the Strasbourg Court's positive influence facilitated by the apex courts was neither immediate nor automatic. The macro-analysis shows that it took a while for Czech courts to get accustomed to using the ECtHR's case law. Similarly, as in other CEE jurisdictions (e.g., Horwitz 2009, 535; Garlicki and Kondak 2016, 325–7), the very foundations of the Czech constitutional jurisprudence were more inspired by foreign, especially German, constitutional law. Accordingly, the CC has built heavily on the German constitutional jurisprudence ever since the early 1990s and only started citing the Strasbourg rulings more frequently in the 2000s due to the rising volume of the Strasbourg case law and numerous structural and contingent circumstances (see below). The situation was different with the two Czech supreme courts. As a younger court established only in 2003, the SAC was quicker in becoming accustomed to engaging with the Strasbourg case law in its argumentation. The SC's position, on the contrary, illustrates the post-communist judiciaries' initial hesitation to engage with international human rights law. This setting was not exclusive to the Czech Republic – the differing approach to the ECHR and human rights law in general between old post-communist courts and new post-transitional courts was typical for the CEE region (Župančič 1998). Most commonly, it manifested in the "judicial wars" between the old supreme courts and newly established constitutional courts (Sadurski 2014, 35–43). The difference in engagement with human rights law between the old and the new courts also manifested in countries that established new administrative jurisdictions only after democratic transition – such as the Czech Republic (Chapter 6) or Latvia (Mits 2016, 218).

The case of the Czech Supreme Court best demonstrates the legacy of the communist approach to judicial methodology, in particular the hesitance towards the judicial application of human rights norms and international law. In relation to the Strasbourg case law, some SC judges even questioned the normative force of the ECtHR's rulings (Chapter 5; and Kühn 2005). This judicial methodology, labelled by Kühn (2011) as "mechanical jurisprudence", was strong at the SC, but definitely not exclusive to it. In fact, it has been a common issue in a number of CEE countries where judges of ordinary courts resisted new constitutional and human rights doctrines and interpretative canons (Krzyżanowska-Mierzewska 2008; Uzelac 2010; Kühn 2011; Bobek 2015; Kosař and Petrov 2017, 606–7; Černič 2018).

Thus, becoming accustomed to engaging with the ECtHR's jurisprudence has been facilitated by numerous contingent circumstances. Insights from the study of Czech apex courts are useful in deciphering the scope and effects of such circumstances. We have identified some of these factors in Chapter 2, but the Czech case study revealed their nuances and context-dependence.

First of all, the language skills of individual judges and their law clerks matter (see Chapters 5–7; and Kosař and Petrov 2017). Even though the ECtHR has recently significantly improved access to its case law in more than the two original languages and has started publishing translations of its judgments and decisions into various languages on its website, the majority of the Strasbourg case law is available only in English or French (see Chapter 2). Furthermore, no matter how many of the ECtHR's rulings are translated into local languages, judges are more willing engage with the Strasbourg case law when they are comfortable with either English or French and can reread and reflect on the key passages of the ECtHR's rulings by themselves. Alternatively, if judges themselves are not fluent in English or in French, they should have an incentive to hire law clerks who can remedy this weakness[6] (Kosař and Petrov 2017). This is particularly important in CEE, where many top jurists in their fifties and sixties, including constitutional court justices, do not speak foreign languages fluently (Malenovský 2011, 187; Kosař 2015, 143–44). Special courses on legal English with the focus on ECHR may also help sitting judges. However, in the long run, a nuanced engagement with the Strasbourg case law by domestic judges can be achieved only if language skills are taken into account in the selection of new domestic judges.

Second, a well-staffed secretariat or a specialized analytical department at the apex court can significantly improve the use of the Strasbourg case law and be of help in overcoming eventual non-compliance with the ECtHR case law caused by a lack of awareness. Such a secretariat can provide research support for the justices regarding Strasbourg case law and partly remedy the limited language skills of judges and their teams. In the Czech Republic, all three apex courts went further and established specialized analytical departments that focus primarily on the analysis of international law, European Union law, and foreign law (see Chapters 5–7). Their role in "translating" the Strasbourg case law into the Czech context cannot be overestimated. More specifically, the analytical departments alert the judges when a new Strasbourg judgment against the Czech Republic is issued. They provide the justices with monthly summaries of the new Strasbourg rulings against other countries. Moreover, at the request of an individual justice, they conduct individualized research on the Strasbourg jurisprudence tailored to a particular case (Kosař and Petrov 2017).

Third, the Czech case study confirms that judicial training, textbooks on the Strasbourg system of human rights, and the ECHR commentaries in the local language are crucial for spreading the knowledge of the ECtHR's case law among judges. However, in order to be really effective and capable of overcoming domestic judges' resistance, they must be tailored to the needs of judges and fine-tuned to the local context. Let us start with the textbooks and commentaries. In the 1990s, only the translation of Vincent Berger's collection of ECtHR's case law (Berger 2003) and a few law review articles engaging with individual ECtHR rulings were available. This was enough for Czech judges to roughly familiarize themselves with the Strasbourg jurisprudence, but these sources were insufficient for direct use by judges who needed a condensed distillation of key principles and how they apply to various circumstances. For instance, in the defamation context, domestic judges needed to know which particular sentences (with complete quotes) were considered by the Strasbourg Court as statements of fact and which as value judgments. Berger's collection included too few examples of this distinction and did not contextualize them. Moreover (due to its obvious focus on the ECtHR's rulings relevant for France) it did not include many cases[7] deemed crucial for the Czech context. In the early 2000s, a monograph on the ECtHR's case law by a Czech author working at the ECtHR's Registry (Hubálková 2003) made significant progress, as it included ECtHR transitional justice cases and was tailored to the Czech audience. But it still missed the direct quotations from the ECtHR's rulings and was more of a textbook-style publication. It was only the 2012 commentary on ECHR by leading Czech human rights scholars[8] (Kmec et al. 2012) that provided what Czech judges need: the German-style commentary with a succinct summary of key principles governing each Convention article, the myriad references to the ECtHR's case law, direct quotations from key ECtHR judgments that can be easily transplanted to the Czech court's ruling "as is", identification of general trends as well as internal inconsistencies in the Strasbourg case law, and a thorough discussion of the peculiar cases against the Czech Republic, such as the *D.H.* judgment[9] or judgments concerning lustration and restitution of property. This story shows that translation of foreign books and commentaries on the Convention is a good first step, but domestic scholars are necessary to produce a tailored ECHR commentary that reflects the needs of domestic judges. As regards up-to-date information about recent case law of the ECtHR, the dissemination activities of the Government Agent's Office are highly relevant (see Petrov 2018b, 159).

Similarly, judicial training must be tailored to the local context and reflect the urgent needs of domestic judges. This does not mean that foreign scholars and ECtHR judges should not provide such training, but our lesson from the Czech case study is that we also need domestic interlocutors (domestic judges or scholars who know domestic substantive law as well as procedure) to effectively transmit the principles stemming from the Strasbourg case law and translate them to the Czech context. In Czechia, such tailored judicial training has often been prepared in cooperation with the Government Agent's Office before the ECtHR.

This brings us to another factor that may affect domestic judicial implementation of the Strasbourg case law, namely the Government Agent. The Czech case study shows that if the Government Agent is proactive and widely respected by judges, they will outsource judicial training on the ECHR to him/her, involve him/her in searching for solutions to the interpretative problems, and listen to his/her solutions (see Chapter 5; and Kosař and Petrov 2017). This is not to say that judges will always follow the Government Agent's proposals, nor that they should, but rather that the Government Agent's unique insider knowledge of the functioning of the ECtHR and its judges may help domestic judges to find robust and long-lasting solutions that fully address the ECHR problems.

9.1.2 Strasbourg case law as a bulwark against abusive constitutionalism

Since the end of the Cold War, some of the new (post-)transitional CoE countries have been threatened by backsliding towards authoritarianism (Levitsky and Way 2010). More recently, the CEE region has experienced a steep rise of populist political actors with anti-pluralist and even authoritarian tendencies (Müller 2016; Bugarič 2019; Halmai 2019). In the past decade, the CEE populist governments used the instruments of constitutionalism actively in order to get rid of limitations to their power. This phenomenon, labelled by different authors as abusive constitutionalism (Landau 2013), populist constitutionalism (Landau 2018; Blokker 2019), autocratic legalism (Scheppele 2018), or constitutional retrogression (Ginsburg and Huq 2018), has been highly relevant for the effectiveness of the ECHR system. On one hand, populist rule is at odds with many of the values on which the CoE is built

(Jagland 2017). Populist constitutionalism then endangers many of the principles underlying the ECHR, such as pluralism and minority rights protection (Petrov 2020), in particular in cases of the authoritarian type of populism that flourishes in CEE (Bugarič 2019). On the other hand, the Convention and the ECtHR's case law can provide an important resource for countering abusive constitutionalism and populist reforms that endanger fundamental rights and the rule of law. Domestic courts can make use of the ECtHR's jurisprudence as a shield against populist actors with authoritarian tendencies. Moreover, if the ECtHR doctrines are well embedded in the domestic public law, they can serve as an extra layer of protection against abusive constitutionalism and can promote pluralist values that are suppressed by populist constitutionalism.

One of the first CEE regimes on the backsliding route was Vladimír Mečiar's government in mid-1990s Slovakia, which pursued numerous illiberal policies and was distinctive for its nationalist, populist, and authoritative style that shifted the country towards competitive authoritarianism (Levitsky and Way 2010, 91). The Slovak Constitutional Court became one of the major actors opposing Mečiar's reforms (Procházka 2002a, 168). However, the Slovak Constitutional Court was not yet a well-established actor, was heavily criticized by the governmental representatives, and thus had to strategically navigate between deference and occasional activism. In this setting, the constitutional judges made use of the ECtHR's jurisprudence as a shield against the opposing actors (Procházka 2002b, 218; Bobek and Kosař 2010, 138). Referring to the ECHR dimension of the case allowed the Slovak Constitutional Court to bolster its argumentation and partially shift the government's criticism to the ECtHR – an international court that was out of the government's reach.

The logic of the ECtHR's case law as a shield was also used by the Polish Constitutional Tribunal in the 2005–2007 period when the populist Law and Justice Party led by Jarosław Kaczyński governed. The Polish Constitutional Tribunal was one of the major opponents of Kaczyński's reforms and annulled, for example, a statute altering media oversight and the government's efforts to toughen lustration mechanisms (Sadurski 2014, 360). In the latter case, the Tribunal used the ECtHR's rulings as extra support for its conclusions. As Garlicki and Kondak (2016, 326) explained, the Tribunal referred to the ECtHR's case law and decided separately on the conformity of the new lustration legislation to the Convention. As a result, the Tribunal partially shifted the responsibility on the supranational level.

The rule-of-law backsliding, however, went much further in the 2010s, especially in Hungary (von Bogdandy and Sonnevend 2015) and Poland (Sadurski 2019a), but also in Romania (Perju 2015), Bulgaria (Vassileva 2019), Slovakia (Kosař, Baroš, and Dufek 2019), and other countries. Even Czechia, widely considered the most resistant of the Central European countries to attacks on the separation of powers, is far from immune. The winner of the 2017 parliamentary elections, and current Prime Minister, Andrej Babiš (Haughton, Havlík, and Deegan-Krause 2017), prefers not only to "run the state like a firm" (Jandourek 2013; Kopeček 2016; Hloušek and Kopeček 2017), but also to weaken the checks on his powers and policies (Hanley and Vachudová 2018; Kosař, Baroš, and Dufek 2019). It is thus very likely that the recent case law of the ECtHR concerning structural issues as judicial independence will stand in his way.

These countries' backsliding stories are quite well known, especially Viktor Orbán's "constitutional Blitzkrieg" against the judiciary and other independent agencies in Hungary (Kovács and Tóth 2011; Halmai 2012; Landau 2013; Tushnet 2015; Uitz 2015; Kosař and Šipulová 2018) and Jarosław Kaczyński's packing of the Polish Constitutional Tribunal and purging of the Supreme Court (Garlicki 2016; Koncewicz 2016; Sadurski 2019a). We look more closely at the role of the use of the ECtHR's case law by domestic apex courts in the backsliding context. The rise of populist constitutionalism and the rule-of-law backsliding has been caused by an extremely complicated mix of social, political, and legal reasons. Responding to these trends is accordingly difficult and challenging. Still, the Strasbourg Court has already addressed some of the issues closely related to the typical populist policies, including migration policies (especially in the context of Articles 5 and 8 ECHR), protection of non-governmental organizations under Article 11 ECHR, protection of journalistic freedom and media pluralism under Article 10 ECHR, and, increasingly, even questions regarding domestic judicial design.[10]

Countering those populist policies, which are highly problematic from the point of view of the fundamental rights and the rule of law, is particularly challenging though. First of all, the ECtHR's interventions regularly come rather late. In *Baka*,[11] for instance, the Strasbourg Court's Grand Chamber ruled on the termination of the applicant's mandate as President of the Supreme Court more than four years after the termination had taken place. In such circumstances, when the measure criticized by the ECtHR is a fait accompli, it is extremely hard for the ECtHR's ruling to reverse the measure. Moreover, the populist ideology and communication strategy are well placed to portray the Strasbourg Court as a foreign elitist institution intervening in domestic matters and deforming the will of the people (see Petrov 2020). As a result, the reputational concerns change and the populist leaders might even use the international judicial interventions in their favour and present themselves as the true defenders of national sovereignty and democracy (Kosař and Šipulová 2018, 107; Candia 2019). In addition, although gradually strengthening, the system of supervising compliance with the Strasbourg Court's judgments and decisions does not seem to be strong enough to prevent minimalist compliance on the part of the populist governments.

Nevertheless, the ECtHR's rulings addressing the rule-of-law backsliding can represent a useful resource for domestic courts if they seek to counter the abusive populist reforms. As this book has shown, domestic courts have developed numerous human rights and rule-of-law safeguards based not only on national constitutional law, but also on adopting the ECtHR's doctrines. Accordingly, many of the domestic constitutional safeguards are intertwined with the Strasbourg jurisprudence and, therefore, embedded in international law. As such, well-established ECtHR case law can represent an additional layer of protection against abusive constitutionalism as well as a "counter-populism measure" (Hostovsky Brandes 2019). Moreover, references to the ECtHR's case law can contribute to maintaining pluralism – often suppressed by populist constitutionalism – in the public debate (Hostovsky Brandes 2019). Although the populist governments can amend constitutions, adopt completely new constitutional documents, and even void all the constitutional case law pre-dating the new constitution,[12] they cannot easily denounce international human rights jurisprudence advanced by the Strasbourg Court. In this vein, the Hungarian Constitutional Court increasingly turned to the ECtHR's case law and other international human rights law sources shortly after Viktor Orbán electoral victory in 2010, seeking standards outside of the government's reach (Polgári 2016). Such a trend, however, faded somewhat once the Hungarian Constitutional Court was staffed with judges nominated exclusively by the government's nominees. This brings us to another dimension of domestic courts' position in the ECHR system. National apex courts' high capacity to contribute to the Strasbourg system's effectiveness and legitimacy also has a dark side – this capacity can be turned against the Strasbourg Court and initiate resistance against the ECtHR and widen gaps between the domestic and the Strasbourg level of human rights protection.

9.2 The dark side

The ECtHR and implementation of its case law by domestic apex courts have definitely improved the human rights situation on the ground in the (post-) transitional countries. However, as the previous section suggested, there have always been limits and obstacles to the full effectiveness of the ECtHR's case law. Recently, major challenges related to the rise of abusive and populist constitutionalism added to the mixture of obstacles threatening the effectiveness of the ECHR regime. This section analyzes what we call the dark side of domestic judicial engagement with the ECtHR's jurisprudence and maps how national judges can add to the resistance against the Strasbourg Court.

9.2.1 Backlash, pushback, and withdrawal

Domestic courts do not always qualify as the greatest compliance partners of the ECtHR. Sometimes, this might come as a natural consequence of their judicial nature and limited capacity to address systemic problems, especially if they are related to broader social and political trends. Implementation of the *D.H.* case[13] is a good example. *D.H.* concerned the segregation of Roma children in elementary education. The issue has been related to legal rules regulating the placement of pupils to mainstream and special education. More generally, however, it has been largely affected by social and cultural factors and prejudices. Although courts have intervened and focused on the conditions of compensation for past discrimination (see Chapter 8), they hardly contributed to tackling the overall problem and its roots.

Besides the limited capacity to remedy systemic social issues, domestic courts also possess powers to resist the ECtHR's case law. As discussed above, (post-) transitional countries experienced initial resistance against international human rights law related to the legacy of "mechanical jurisprudence" inherited from the previous regimes (Kühn 2011), which originated mainly in the "old" post-communist courts (see Chapter 5). Although this legacy still affects the judicial mindset in the (post-)transitional countries of CoE (see Emmert 2012; more generally Bobek 2008), the Czech experience shows that a number of structural and contingent features (see Section 9.1) can contribute to standardizing the judicial engagement with the Strasbourg case law.

More recently, however, the resistance against the ECtHR has changed. Rather than the historical legacy, recent instances of judicial resistance can be explained by quite natural "interlayer irritation" in the multi-level human rights regime (O'Cinneide 2010, 25; Benvenisti and Harel 2017), by differing legal opinions on particular human rights issues, and also, more critically, by differing overall views of relations between constitutionalism, democracy, human rights, and national sovereignty (Petrov 2018a, 528). In order to shed more light on different types of resistance against international courts, Madsen, Cebulak, and Wiebusch (2018) distinguish between *pushback* and *backlash*. By *pushback*, they understand instances of ordinary resistance or situations

> in which some audiences are unsatisfied with the (new) contents of the law as developed by an [international court], and they seek to push back against it with the goal of reverting to an earlier or different legal situation. Yet, crucially, they do not seek to challenge the [international court]'s authority as such .
>
> (Madsen, Cebulak, and Wiebusch 2018, 202)

Backlash, on the other hand, is conceived as extraordinary resistance

> not only targeting the contents of the law itself, but also targets the institutions as such and their authority. [...] It can be described as a more revolutionary resistance, as it seeks an institutional transformation or even a suspension or closing of an institution.
>
> (Madsen, Cebulak, and Wiebusch 2018, 202–203)

The Czech case shows that there was, especially in the first decade of the Czech democracy, initial resistance of judges against international human rights law as a novel instrument piercing the veil of domestic law. This initial resistance amounted to something more than an isolated pushback. On the other hand, it is difficult to label it as a backlash. We rather see it as a (post-)transitional phenomenon linked to a more general legacy of the persisting (post-)communist mindset of some judges (see Bobek 2015).

Yet, our research (Chapters 5–8) shows that when Czech judges refer to the Strasbourg case law, they follow it in the vast majority of cases. In the 2010s, however, several instances of pushing back against the ECtHR's conclusions occurred. Two cases of court-led pushback on the part of the SAC demonstrate that, depending on further factors, pushback originating in domestic courts can be both profitable and highly challenging for the Strasbourg Court. In 2012, the SAC refused to follow the ECtHR's take on *non bis in idem* adopted in *Zolotukhin* (see Chapter 6). In this dialogue, the SAC proceeded according to the values enshrined in the Strasbourg jurisprudence, but contested the ECtHR's interpretation and warned the Strasbourg Court of possible consequences of its conclusions for the legal orders where several concurrent administrative proceedings might occur as well as for legal orders with dual sanctioning systems (administrative and criminal). From the short-term perspective, the SAC did not comply with the ECtHR's judgment in *Zolotukhin*. From the long-term perspective, however, the Strasbourg Court might have even profited from these insights and used them to further develop its jurisprudence. In fact, the ECtHR took some of this criticism into account when deciding *A and B v. Norway*.[14]

Another pushback from the SAC came in 2019 in a judgment concerning transgender persons' rights.[15] As explained in Chapter 6, the SAC refused to follow the ECtHR's ruling in *A.P., Garçon and Nicot*,[16] which had stated that refusing a change in civil status on the grounds of failing to undergo a surgical treatment leading to sterilization amounts to violation of Article 8 ECHR. The SAC referred to the concept of judicial dialogue and refused to challenge the Czech legislative status quo based on the requirement of surgical treatment and sterilization. Although still falling within the category of pushback, as defined by Madsen, Cebulak, and Wiebusch (2018), this instance of the SAC's resistance was much more problematic. Even though the SAC shielded itself with the idea of judicial dialogue, in fact it did not engage extensively with the Strasbourg Court's reasoning; rather, it refused the ECtHR's conclusion because the majority of the Czech society allegedly preferred the strictly binary account of sex. Such an approach provides a greater challenge for the Strasbourg Court's authority since it was based on voicing the (alleged) local resentment against broadening the LGBTI rights protection and loosening the concept of sex, rather than on mere concerns about the functioning of public administration as in the previous case. Also, regarding the way the judicial dialogue was approached, the judgment presents a problematic precedent for Czech courts' future engagement with the Strasbourg case law. It is a reminder that even Czech judges, usually ECtHR-friendly, can resort to court-led pushback against the ECtHR in future. Yet, the effects of the SAC's transgender ruling should not be exaggerated, as it is subject to the CC's review and, since it provides rather few arguments (besides the prevailing social view) and lacks a thorough engagement with the ECtHR's legal reasoning, it might also eventually be overturned by the SAC's Grand Chamber.

Looking beyond the Czech cases, the above-mentioned practices of abusive and populist constitutionalism are highly relevant for the debates about the effectiveness of and resistance against the ECtHR as well. On the most general level, the populist court-curbing decreases domestic courts' partnership capacity in implementing the Strasbourg case law (Petrov 2018a, 525–6). Within the Hungarian constitutional reform, for instance, access to the Constitutional Court was limited, as were the court's competences (Scheppele 2015). Resulting from a number of procedural and organizational measures adopted by the populist government in Poland, the Constitutional Tribunal was held in paralysis and, for some time, was barred from effectively reviewing new legislation (Sadurski 2019b, 65). Soon after, the government targeted the Polish Supreme Court's autonomy, too (Kovács and Scheppele 2018). Decreasing the apex courts' authority and autonomy is highly problematic both generally and in the context of the domestic judicial implementation of the Strasbourg case law since the courts' capacity to decide cases (including those with ECHR dimensions) effectively and autonomously is decreased.

Second, the changing political context may encourage greater resistance against the ECtHR on the part of domestic courts. In 2015, the Russian Constitutional Court reviewed the Law on Ratification of the ECHR. The Russian Constitutional Court did not abolish the law. However, it declared that neither the Convention nor its interpretation by the Strasbourg Court took precedence over the Russian Constitution.[17] Subsequently, the Russian Parliament followed the Constitutional Court's suggestion and gave the Constitutional Court a new competence to declare the execution of an international obligation impossible if it contradicted the Constitution. In a way, this mechanism made the implementation of the ECtHR's judgments and decisions in Russia subject to the Constitutional Court's consent. So far, the Russian Constitutional Court has used the competence twice, declaring the Strasbourg rulings in *Anchugov and Gladkov* (concerning prisoners' voting rights) and in *Yukos* (concerning the ECtHR's remedial order addressed to the Russian government to compensate the victims) non-executable (see Aksenova and Marchuk 2018; Petrov 2018a, 517–8). As Madsen (2019) put it, "[d]epending in practice on how systematic and frequent this doctrine will be used by Russian courts, principled resistance has potentially been turned into backlash and a severe challenge of the authority of the ECtHR in Russia". What is particularly interesting in this series of Russian cases is that it is a court-inspired backlash rather than backlash driven directly by the executive.

In Europe, we have not seen withdrawal from the Convention recently, despite the occasional threats of leading politicians from the United Kingdom, Russia, and other CoE member states. As a result, there has not been a domestic court-inspired or court-led withdrawal either. Many would perhaps consider such action as fantasy in Europe. However, the Latin American experience shows us that this is not as unlikely as it seems at the first sight (Soley and Steininger 2018; Contesse 2019). For instance, the Venezuelan Supreme Court's judgment urged the Chávez Administration to denounce the

American Convention on Human Rights on constitutional grounds, which Hugo Chávez then did in 2012. This is a prime example of a court-inspired treaty exit (Huneeus and Urueña 2017). A few years later, the Dominican Republic Constitutional Tribunal's 2014 judgment held that the Dominican Republic's acceptance of the jurisdiction of the Inter-American Court of Human Rights had been unconstitutional, which resulted in a court-led treaty exit (Huneeus and Urueña 2017). These two examples clearly show that domestic courts, and constitutional courts in particular, can be employed, once captured, as legitimizing tools that justify withdrawal from the regional human rights treaty. Of course, only the future will tell us whether European populist or authoritarian leaders will resort to this strategy. Yet, it cannot be discarded.

In sum, most manifestations of the "dark side" view of domestic courts in the ECHR system are highly problematic for the proposed solutions to the ECtHR's caseload, implementation, and legitimacy crises based on the idea of subsidiarity and shared responsibility. On the most general level, the populist court-curbing decreases domestic courts' partnership capacity in implementing the Strasbourg case law. Additionally, it might encourage domestic judicial resistance against the ECtHR's jurisprudence and add to broader legitimacy challenges against the Strasbourg Court. Finally, experiences from other regional human rights regimes indicate there is even a possibility of captured courts abusing international human rights jurisprudence. The following section focuses on this scenario in the European context.

9.2.2 The judicial abuse of the Strasbourg case law

Apart from the well-established backlash–pushback–withdrawal triad, judges can also abuse the very Convention articles. Once the judiciary is captured the way it is in Hungary and Poland, one can easily imagine that judges can abuse the criminal procedural aspects of the right to fair trial to thwart criminal prosecution of pro-government politicians. Similarly, the right to free elections can be used to annul the term limits. This might sound like a stretch, but the Latin American experience tells us that this is a real possibility. For instance, in 2017 the Bolivian Constitutional Court, the Plurinational Constitutional Tribunal, used the American Convention on Human Rights to strike down constitutionally mandated presidential term limits (Huneeus 2019).

The trick here is that such abusive use of the Convention rights benefits the given individual and hence it is difficult to bring such a dispute to the ECtHR,[18] which does not have the power of abstract review, nor that to decide on competence disputes or hear the complaints brought by the government. That is also the reason why authoritarian government in CEE might be tempted to resort to such judicial abuse of the Convention rights.

One may object that human rights are inherently good and cannot be misused in this way. Unfortunately, they can, like almost any other concept of modern constitutionalism, and CEE provides several examples of such misuse recently. For instance, Viktor Orbán skilfully abused the concept of constitutional identity[19] in order to defy the European Union's policy towards migrants.[20] More recently, the Slovak Constitutional Court rigged the doctrine of unconstitutional constitutional amendment[21] to block any possibility of introducing security clearance for judges, one of the few available meaningful accountability checks for the Slovak judiciary,[22] which suffers from numerous issues (Kosař 2016). The Polish Constitutional Tribunal, once captured by Kaczyński's protégés, also started to bend various constitutional concepts (Castillo Ortiz 2019; Sadurski 2019a).

The Slovak and Polish examples show that while in Europe domestic courts are generally conceptualized as the last line of defense for the liberal democratic constitutional order, it is not that uncommon for judges to issue rulings that instead intentionally attack the core of liberal constitutionalism. David Landau and Rosalind Dixon (2020) call this practice *abusive judicial review*. They show that would-be authoritarians at times seek to capture courts and deploy them in abusive ways as part of a broader project of democratic erosion, because courts often enjoy legitimacy advantages that make their anti-democratic moves harder to detect and respond to both domestically and internationally.

So far, the most obvious judicial abuses of human rights have been reported from Latin America (Dixon and Landau 2020). Only the future will tell us whether this phenomenon finds traction in Europe as well. However, we deemed it important to raise this issue in this book pre-emptively. Post-communist countries have a long history of instrumental use of law and courts, and the instrumental use of the Polish Constitutional Tribunal to legitimize controversial governmental policies (Sadurski 2019a) suggests that current CEE leaders will not shy away from using courts as positive aids in their endeavor (Castillo Ortiz 2019, 69).

This finding also has important repercussions for the recent suggestion that the ECtHR should adopt a (more) procedural review of domestic courts' rulings, if they engage with the ECtHR's case law. According to its proponents, this procedural turn is supposed to address subsidiarity concerns raised by several CoE member states (especially, but not exclusively, established democracies), which believe the ECtHR's review is too intrusive, and to reduce the ECtHR's docket (Çali 2016; Gerards and Brems 2017; Spano 2018). However, the procedural review of domestic rulings by the ECtHR might work only if domestic courts engage with the ECtHR's jurisprudence in good faith. In contrast, if a domestic court acts in bad faith and abuses the Strasbourg Court's jurisprudence, the ECtHR might need to switch back to the fully-fledged substantive review, even if the domestic court extensively cites the ECtHR's rulings. It is not our intention to explain here how to determine that a domestic court acted in bad faith, which is one the most difficult tasks in constitutional law and theory (Pozen 2016). Typically, procedural irregularities such as blocking competing evidence, or entirely novel or bizarre approaches to domestic law, are important indicators of bad faith (Pozen 2016; Dixon and Landau 2020). Future research should build on these insights from constitutional theory and adjust them to the Strasbourg system of human rights.

9.3 Conclusion: The future is in the eye of the beholder

Our case study showed that the Strasbourg jurisprudence is deeply embedded in the decision-making practice of all three Czech apex courts. It is a good example how domestic courts can diffuse the ECtHR's standards and operate as filters, which narrow down the number of ECHR violations and reduce the ECtHR's docket. Despite the initial indifference of the communist-era judges and occasional pushback, the Czech apex courts have done a good job in translating the ECtHR's standards into Czech law. This has in turn significantly improved Czech human rights standards. In this sense, there is hope that the Convention-conforming interpretation of Czech law became an integral part of judges' mindset and that the ECtHR's case law cannot be uprooted easily.

On the other hand, the recent developments in Hungary and Poland revealed that the judicial branch has been unable to tame anti-constitutional forces and protect the Central European *Rechtsstaats*. The judiciary turned out to be surprisingly weak once the struggle became real (Kovács and Scheppele 2018; Kosař, Baroš, and Dufek 2019). What is more, populist leaders managed to capture the courts quite quickly as they dismissed their opponents on the bench and packed the apex courts with their protégés. The packed apex courts may no longer be the natural domestic allies of the ECtHR. On the contrary, they might become the main obstacles to implementation of the Strasbourg standards and the centers of anti-ECtHR resistance, like in Latin America. To our knowledge, there is no comprehensive study of the changes in judicial treatments of the ECtHR case law before Hungarian and Polish courts after the rise of Viktor Orbán and Jarosław Kaczyński to power to prove or disprove this scenario. Our book provides a framework on how to address this development conceptually, as well as the method for analyzing it empirically.

Notes

1 See the Introduction and Chapters 1 and 2.
2 Such judicial resistance might also take place in established democracies, but for different reasons.
3 SC, no. Cpjn 202/2010, opinion of 8 December 2010, reacting to ECtHR, *Walla and Wallová v. the Czech Republic*, no. 23848/04, judgment of 26 October 2006; *Havelka and Others v. the Czech Republic*, no. 23499/06, judgment of 21 June 2007.
4 ECtHR [GC], *A and B v. Norway*, nos. 24130/11 and 29758/11, judgment of 15 November 2016.
5 SC [GC], no. 15 Tdo 832/2016, decision of 4 January 2017.
6 Some justices of the Czech Constitutional Court go even further and intentionally hire former members of the ECtHR's Registry, which gives them a clear competitive edge regarding the knowledge of the Strasbourg case law (Vyhnánek 2017).
7 For examples, the ECtHR's judgments concerning transitional justice measures such as restitution of property.
8 Two out of four co-authors of this commentary clerked at Czech courts for many years and thus they know how judges work and what they need.

9 ECtHR [GC], *D.H. and Others v. the Czech Republic*, no. 57325/00, judgment of 13 November 2007.
10 See Kosař and Lixinski (2015). In the context of abusive constitutionalism see ECtHR, *Ерményi v. Hungary*, no. 22254/14, judgment of 22 November 2016; *Baka v. Hungary* [GC], no. 20261/12, judgment of 23 June 2016; and Kosař and Šipulová (2018). Recently, the Strasbourg Court also gave notice to Poland of several applications related to recent changes to the Polish judiciary. See the proceedings in *Xero Flor w Polsce sp. z o.o. v. Poland*, no. 4907/18 (concerning appointments to the Polish Constitutional Tribunal); *Broda v. Poland*, no. 26691/18, and *Bojara v. Poland*, no. 27367/18 (both concerning premature discontinuance of the term of vice-presidents of a regional court).
11 ECtHR [GC], *Baka v. Hungary*, no. 20261/12, judgment of 23 June 2016.
12 This was the case in Hungary. The Fourth Amendment to the Constitution determined that the case law made before the force of the new constitution ceased to be in force. That erased the mandatory force of the judge-made constitutional law of Hungary (Sólyom 2015, 29).
13 ECtHR [GC], *D.H. and Others v. the Czech Republic*, no. 57325/00, judgment of 13 November 2007.
14 ECtHR [GC], *A and B v. Norway*, nos. 24130/11 and 29758/11, judgment of 15 November 2016 (some of the SAC's reservations were communicated by the Czech government as a third-party intervener; see § 95).
15 SAC, no. 2 As 199/2018–37, judgment of 30 May 2019.
16 ECtHR, *A.P., Garçon a Nicot v. France*, nos. 79885/12; 52471/13 and 52596/13, judgment of 6 April 2017.
17 Russian Constitutional Court, no. 21-П/2015, judgment of 14 July 2015.
18 There is simply no directly injured party.
19 On the concept of constitutional identity, see Rosenfeld (2010), Jacobsohn (2010), and Orgad (2015).
20 See Halmai (2017) and Uitz (2016).
21 On the doctrine of "unconstitutional constitutional amendment" see Roznai (2017) and Albert (2019).
22 Slovak Constitutional Court, no. PL. ÚS 21/2014, judgment of 30 January 2019. See also Domin (2019) and Drugda (2019).

References

Aksenova, Marina, and Iryna Marchuk. 2018. "Reinventing or Rediscovering International Law? The Russian Constitutional Court's Uneasy Dialogue with the European Court of Human Rights". *International Journal of Constitutional Law* 16 (4): 1322–46.

Albert, Richard. 2019. *Constitutional Amendments: Making, Breaking, and Changing Constitutions.* New York: Oxford University Press.

Benvenisti, Eyal, and Aron Harel. 2017. "Embracing the Tension between National and International Human Rights Law: The Case for Discordant Parity". *International Journal of Constitutional Law* 15 (1): 36–59.

Berger, Vincent. 2003. *Judikatura Evropského soudu pro lidská práva [Case Law of the European Court of Human Rights].* Prague: IFEC.

Blokker, Paul. 2019. "Populism as a Constitutional Project". *International Journal of Constitutional Law* 17 (2): 536–53.

Bobek, Michal. 2008. "The Fortress of Judicial Independence and the Mental Transitions of the Central European Judiciaries". *European Public Law* 14 (1): 99–123.

Bobek, Michal, ed. 2015. *Central European Judges under the European Influence: The Transformative Power of the EU Revisited*. Oxford and Portland, OR: Hart Publishing.

Bobek, Michal, and David Kosař. 2010. "The Application of European Union Law and the Law of the European Convention of Human Rights in the Czech Republic and Slovakia: An Overview". In *The National Judicial Treatment of the ECHR and EU Laws. A Comparative Constitutional Perspective*, edited by Giuseppe Martinico and Oreste Pollicino, 117–50. Groningen: Europa Law Publishing.

Bobek, Michal, Jiří Kmec, David Kosař, Jan Kratochvíl et al. 2013. *Dvacet let Evropské úmluvy v České republice a na Slovensku [Twenty Years of the European Convention on Human Rights in the Czech Republic and Slovakia]*. Prague: C.H. Beck.

Bugarič, Bojan. 2019. "Central Europe's Descent into Autocracy: A Constitutional Analysis of Authoritarian Populism". *International Journal of Constitutional Law* 17 (2): 597–616.

Çali, Başak. 2016. "From Flexible to Variable Standards of Judicial Review: The Responsible Courts Doctrine at the European Court of Human Rights". In *Shifting Centres of Gravity in Human Rights Protection*, edited by Oddný Mjöll Arnardóttir and Antoine Buyse, 144–60. Abingdon: Routledge.

Çali, Başak, Anne Koch, and Nicola Bruch. 2013. "The Legitimacy of Human Rights Courts: A Grounded Interpretivist Analysis of the European Court of Human Rights". *Human Rights Quarterly* 35 (4): 955–84.

Candia, Gonzalo. 2019. "Regional Human Rights Institutions Struggling against Populism: The Case of Venezuela". *German Law Journal* 20 (2): 141–60.

Castillo Ortiz, Pablo J. 2019. "The Illiberal Abuse of Constitutional Courts in Europe". *European Constitutional Law Review* 15 (1): 48–72.

Černič, Jernej Letnar. 2018. "Impact of the European Court of Human Rights on the Rule of Law in Central and Eastern Europe". *Hague Journal on the Rule of Law* 10 (1): 111–37.

Contesse, Jorge. 2019. "Resisting the Inter-American Human Rights System". *Yale Journal of International Law* 44: 179.

Dixon, Rosalind, and David Landau. 2020. "Abusive Judicial Review: Courts Against Democracy". *UC Davis Law Review* (forthcoming).

Domin, Marek. 2019. "A Part of the Constitution Is Unconstitutional, The Slovak Constitutional Court Has Ruled". *Verfassungsblog*, 8 February 2019. Accessed 15 June 2019. https://verfassungsblog.de/a-part-of-the-constitution-is-unconstitutional-the-slovak-constitutional-court-has-ruled/.

Drugda, Simon. 2019. "Slovak Constitutional Court Strikes down a Constitutional Amendment – But the Amendment Remains Valid". *I-CONnectblog*, 25 April 2019. Accessed 15 June 2019. www.iconnectblog.com/2019/04/slovak-constitutional-court-strikes-down-a-constitutional-amendment-but-the-amendment-remains-valid/.

Emmert, Frank. 2012. "The Implementation of the European Convention on Human Rights and Fundamental Freedoms in New Member States of the Council of Europe – Conclusions Drawn and Lessons Learned". In *The European Convention on Human Rights and Fundamental Freedoms in Central and Eastern Europe*, edited by Leonard M. Hammer and Frank Emmert, 597–645. Hague and Portland, OR: Eleven International Publishing.

Garlicki, Lech. 2016. "Disabling the Constitutional Court in Poland". In *Transformation of Law Systems in Central, Eastern and Southeastern Europe in 1989-2015*, edited by Andrzej Szmyt and Bogusław Banaszak, 63–78. Gdansk: Gdansk University Press.

Garlicki, Lech, and Ireneusz Kondak. 2016. "Poland". In *The Impact of the ECHR on Democratic Change in Central and Eastern Europe: Judicial Perspectives*, edited by Iulia Motoc and Ineta Ziemele, 305–29. Cambridge: Cambridge University Press.

Gerards, Janneke, and Eva Brems, eds. 2017. *Procedural Review in European Fundamental Rights Cases.* Cambridge: Cambridge University Press.

Ginsburg, Tom, and Aziz Z. Huq. 2018. *How to Save a Constitutional Democracy.* Chicago, IL: University of Chicago Press.

Halmai, Gábor. 2012. "From the "Rule of Law revolution" to the Constitutional Counter-Revolution in Hungary". In *European Yearbook of Human Rights*, edited by Wolfgang Bedenek, Florence Benoît-Rohmer, Wolfram Karl et al., 365–82. Vienna: Intersentia and NWV - Neuer Wissenschaftlicher Verlag.

Halmai, Gábor. 2017. "The Hungarian Constitutional Court and Constitutional Identity". *Verfassungsblog*, 10 January 2017. Accessed 15 June 2019. https://verfassungsblog.de/the-hungarian-constitutional-court-and-constitutional-identity/.

Halmai, Gábor. 2019. "Populism, Authoritarianism and Constitutionalism". *German Law Journal* 20 (3): 296–313.

Hanley, Seán, and Milada Vachudová. 2018. "Understanding the Illiberal Turn: Democratic Backsliding in the Czech Republic". *East European Politics* 34 (3): 276–96.

Hloušek, Vít, and Lubomír Kopeček. 2017. "Entrepreneurial Parties: A Basic Conceptual Framework". *Czech Journal of Political Science* 24 (2): 83–91.

Hostovsky Brandes, Tamar. 2019. "International Law in Domestic Courts in an Era of Populism". *International Journal of Constitutional Law* 17 (2): 576–96.

Horwitz, Morton J. 2009. "Constitutional Transplants". *Theoretical Inquiries in Law* 10 (2): 535–60.

Hubálková, Eva. 2003. *Evropská úmluva o lidských právech a Česká republika [European Convention on Human Rights and the Czech Republic].* Prague: Linde.

Huneeus, Alexandra. 2019. "Human Rights Law and Non-Liberal Politics". *AJIL Unbound* 113: 380–84.

Huneeus, Alexandra, and René Urueña.2017. "Treaty Exit and Latin America's Constitutional Courts". *AJIL Unbound* 111: 456–60.

Jacobsohn, Gary J. 2010. *Constitutional Identity.* Cambridge, MA: Harvard University Press.

Jagland, Thorbjørn. 2017. "Understanding Populism and Defending Europe's Democracies: The Council of Europe in 2017". *Council of Europe: Speeches 2017*, 24 January 2017. Accessed 18 June 2019. www.coe.int/en/web/secretary-general/-/understanding-populism-and-defending-europe-s-democracies-the-council-of-europe-in-2017.

Jandourek, Jan. 2013. "Babiš chce řídit stat jako firmu. To asi nepůjde, stát není firma [Babiš Aims to Manage the State like a Firm. That Won't Work, the State Is Not a Firm]." *Reflex on-line*, 6 September 2013. Accessed 15 July 2019. www.reflex.cz/clanek/info-x/51716/babis-chce-ridit-stat-jako-firmu-to-asi-nepujde-stat-neni-firma.html.

Kmec, Jiří, David Kosař, Jan Kratochvíl, and Michal Bobek, eds. 2012. *Evropská úmluva o lidských právech: komentář [European Convention on Human Rights: A Commentary].* Prague: C.H. Beck.

Koncewicz, Tomasz Tadeusz. 2016. "Of Institutions, Democracy, Constitutional Self-defence and the Rule of Law: The Judgments of the Polish Constitutional Tribunal in Cases K 34/15, K 35/15 and Beyond". *Common Market Law Review* 53 (6): 1753–92.

Kopeček, Lubomír. 2016. "I'm Paying, so I Decide – Czech ANO as an Extreme Form of a Business-Firm Party". *East European Politics and Societies* 30 (4): 725–49.

Kosař, David. 2011. "Justiční Mafie II" ["Judicial Mafia II"]. *Soudní Rozhledy* 17 (8): 311–14.

Kosař, David. 2015. "Selecting Strasbourg Judges: A Critique". In *Selecting Europe's Judges: A Critical Review of the Appointment Procedures to the European Courts*, edited by Michal Bobek, 120–61. Oxford: Oxford University Press.

Kosař, David. 2016. *Perils of Judicial Self-Government in Transitional Societies.* Cambridge: Cambridge University Press.

Kosař, David, Jiří Baroš, and Pavel Dufek. 2019. "The Twin Challenges to Separation of Powers in Central Europe: Technocratic Governance and Populism". *European Consitutional Law Review* 15 (3): 427–61.

Kosař, David, and Katarína Šipulová. 2018. "The Strasbourg Court Meets Abusive Constitutionalism: Baka V. Hungary and the Rule of Law". *Hague Journal on the Rule of Law* 10 (1): 83–110.

Kosař, David, and Lucas Lixinski. 2015. "Domestic Judicial Design by International Human Rights Courts". *The American Journal of International Law* 109 (4): 713–60.

Kosař, David, and Jan Petrov. 2017. "The Architecture of the Strasbourg System of Human Rights: The Crucial Role of the Domestic Level and the Constitutional Courts in Particular". *Heidelberg Journal of International Law* 77: 585–621.

Kosař, David, and Jan Petrov. 2018. "Determinants of Compliance Difficulties among 'Good Compliers': Implementation of International Human Rights Rulings in the Czech Republic". *The European Journal of International Law* 29 (2): 397–425.

Kovács, Kriszta, and Kim Lane Scheppele. 2018. "The Fragility of an Independent Judiciary: Lessons from Hungary and Poland – And the European Union". *Communist and Post-Communist Studies* 51 (3): 189–200.

Kovács, Kriszta, and Gábor Attila Tóth. 2011. "Hungary's Constitutional Transformation". *European Constitutional Law Review* 7 (2): 183–203.

Krzyżanowska-Mierzewska, Magda. 2008. "The Reception Process in Poland and Slovakia". In *A Europe of Rights: The Impact of the ECHR on National Legal Systems*, edited by Alec Stone Sweet and Helen Keller, 531–602. Oxford: Oxford University Press.

Kühn, Zdeněk. 2005. "K otázce závaznosti rozhodnutí Evropského soudu pro lidská práva pro domácí soudnictví [On the Binding Effect of ECtHR Case Law on Domestic Judiciary]." *Právní rozhledy* 13 (1): 1–7.

Kühn, Zdeněk. 2011. *The Judiciary in Central and Eastern Europe: Mechanical Jurisprudence in Transformation?* Leiden: Martinus Nijhoff Publishers.

Landau, David. 2013. "Abusive Constitutionalism". *University of California Davis Law Review* 47 (1): 183–260.

Landau, David. 2018. "Populist Constitutions". *University of Chicago Law Review* 85 (2): 521–43.

Levitsky, Steven, and Lucan A. Way. 2010. *Competitive Authoritarianism: Hybrid Regimes after the Cold War.* New York, NY: Cambridge University Press.

Madsen, Mikael Rask. 2019. "Resistance to the European Court of Human Rights: The Institutional and Sociological Consequences of Principled Resistance". In *Principled Resistance to ECtHR Judgments – A New Paradigm?* edited by Marten Breuer, 35–52. Heidelberg: Sringer.

Madsen, Mikael Rask, Pola Cebulak, and Micha Wiebusch. 2018. "Backlash against International Courts: Explaining the Forms and Patterns of Resistance to International Courts". *International Journal of Law in Context* 14 (2): 197–220.

Malenovský, Jiří. 2011. "L'indépendance des juges internationaux". In *Recueil des cours de l'Académie de droit international de la Haye*, Vol. 349, 9–276. Leiden: Martinus Nijhoff.

Mits, Mārtiņš. 2016. "Latvia" In *The Impact of the ECHR on Democratic Change in Central and Eastern Europe: Judicial Perspectives*, edited by Iulia Motoc and Ineta Ziemele, 201–33. Cambridge: Cambridge University Press.

Müller, Jan-Werner. 2016. *What Is Populism?* Philadelphia, PA: University of Pennsylvania Press.

O'Cinneide, Colm. 2010. "Human Rights within Multi-Layered Systems of Constitutional Governance: Rights Cosmopolitanism and Domestic Particularism in Tension". *Irish Yearbook of International Law* 3: 19–44.

Orgad, Liav. 2015. *The Cultural Defense of Nations: A Liberal Theory of Majority Rights.* New York: Oxford University Press.

Paulus, Andreas L. 2014. "From Implementation to Translation: Applying the ECtHR Judgments in the Domestic Legal Orders". In *Judgments of the European Court of Human Rights – Effects and Implementation*, edited by Anja Seibert-Fohr and Mark E. Villiger, 267–84. Baden-Baden: Nomos.

Perju, Vlad. 2015. "The Romanian Double Executive and the 2012 Constitutional Crisis". *International Journal of Constitutional Law* 13 (1): 246–78.

Petrov, Jan. 2018a. "Unpacking the Partnership: Typology of Constitutional Courts' Roles in Implementation of the European Court of Human Rights' Case Law". *European Constitutional Law Review* 14 (3): 499–531.

Petrov, Jan. 2018b. "Legislativní reakce ČR na judikaturu ESLP [Legislative Responses of the Czech Republic to the ECtHR's Case law]". In *Beyond Compliance: Implementace rozhodnutí mezinárodních lidskoprávních těles na národní úrovni [Beyond Compliance: Domestic Judicial Implementation of the International Human Rights Case Law]*, edited by Hubert Smekal and Ladislav Vyhnánek, 137–59. Prague: Wolters Kluwer.

Petrov, Jan. 2020. "The Populist Challenge to the European Court of Human Rights". *International Journal of Constitutional Law* 18 (forthcoming).

Polgári, Eszter. 2016. "The Hungarian Constitutional Court's Case with the ECHR: An Ambivalent Relationship". *Verfassungsblog*, 22 June 2016. Accessed 15 June 2019. https://verfassungsblog.de/the-hungarian-constitutional-courts-case-with-the-echr-an-ambivalent-relationship/.

Pozen, David E. 2016. "Constitutional Bad Faith". *Harvard Law Review* 129 (4): 885–955.

Procházka, Radoslav. 2002a. *Mission Accomplished: On Founding Constitutional Adjudication in Central Europe.* Budapest: Central European University Press.

Procházka, Radoslav. 2002b. "Európsky dohovor o ľudských právach v slovenskom ústavnom poriadku [The ECHR in the Slovak Constitutional order]." *Časopis pro právní vědu a praxi* 10 (3): 215–19.

Rosenfeld, Michel. 2010. *The Identity of the Constitutional Subject: Selfhood, Citizenship, Culture, and Community.* London: Routledge.

Roznai, Yaniv. 2017. *Unconstitutional Constitutional Amendments: The Limits of Amendment Powers.* New York: Oxford University Press.

Sadurski, Wojciech. 2014. *Rights before Courts: A Study of Constitutional Courts in Postcommunist States of Central and Eastern Europe.* 2nd edition. Heidelberg: Springer.

Sadurski, Wojciech. 2019a. *Poland's Constitutional Breakdown.* Oxford: Oxford University Press.

Sadurski, Wojciech. 2019b. "Polish Constitutional Tribunal under PiS: From an Activist Court, to a Paralysed Tribunal, to a Governmental Enabler". *Hague Journal on the Rule of Law* 11 (1): 63–84.

Scheppele, Kim Lane. 2015. "Understanding Hungary's Constitutional Revolution". In *Constitutional Crisis in the European Constitutional Area: Theory, Law and Politics in Hungary and Romania*, edited by Armin von Bogdandy and Pál Sonnevend, 124–37. Oxford: Hart Publishing Ltd.

Scheppele, Kim Lane. 2018. "Autocratic Legalism". *The University of Chicago Law Review* 85 (2): 545–83.

Soley, Ximena, and Silvia Steininger. 2018. "Parting Ways or Lashing Back? Withdrawals, Backlash and the Inter-American Court of Human Rights". *International Journal of Law in Context* 14 (2): 237–57.

Sólyom, László. 2015. "The Rise and Decline of Constitutional Culture in Hungary". In *Constitutional Crisis in the European Constitutional Area: Theory, Law and Politics in Hungary and Romania*, edited by Armin von Bogdandy and Pál Sonnevend, 14–45. Oxford: Hart Publishing Ltd.

Spano, Robert. 2018. "The Future of the European Court of Human Rights – Subsidiarity, Process-Based Review and the Rule of Law". *Human Rights Law Review* 18 (3): 473–94.

Tim, Haughton, Vlastimil Havlík, and Kevin Deegan-Krause. 2017. "Czech Elections Have Become Really Volatile. This Year Was No Exception". *The Washington Post*, 24 October 2017. Accessed 15 July 2019. www.washingtonpost.com/news/monkey-cage/wp/2017/10/24/czech-elections-have-become-really-volatile-this-year-was-no-exception.

Turković, Ksenija, and Jasna Omejec. 2016. "Croatia". In *The Impact of the ECHR on Democratic Change in Central and Eastern Europe: Judicial Perspectives*, edited by Iulia Motoc and Ineta Ziemele, 110–35. Cambridge: Cambridge University Press.

Tushnet, Mark. 2015. "Authoritarian Constitutionalism". *Cornell Law Review* 100 (2): 391–461.

Uitz, Renáta. 2015. "Can You Tell When an Illiberal Democracy Is in the Making? an Appeal to Comparative Constitutional Scholarship from Hungary". *International Journal of Constitutional Law* 13 (1): 279–300.

Uitz, Renáta. 2016. "National Constitutional Identity in the European Constitutional Project: A Recipe for Exposing Cover Ups and Masquerades". *Verfassungsblog*, 11 November 2016. Accessed 15 June 2019. https://verfassungsblog.de/national-constitutional-identity-in-the-european-constitutional-project-a-recipe-for-exposing-cover-ups-and-masquerades/.

Ulfstein, Geir. 2016. "The European Court of Human Rights and National Courts: A Constitutional Relationship?" In *Shifting Centres of Gravity in Human Rights Protection*, edited by Oddný Mjöll Arnardóttir and Antoine Buyse, 46–58. Abingdon: Routledge.

Uzelac, Alan. 2010. "Survival of the Third Legal Tradition?" *Supreme Court Law Review* 49 (2): 377–96.

Vassileva, Radosveta. 2019. "Is Bulgaria's Rule of Law about to Die under the European Commission's Nose? The Country's Highest-Ranking Judge Fears So". *Verfassungsblog*, 23 April 2013. Accessed 15 July 2019. https://verfassungsblog.de/is-bulgarias-rule-of-law-about-to-die-under-the-european-commissions-nose-the-countrys-highest-ranking-judge-fears-so/.

Von Bogdandy, Armin, and Pál Sonnevend, eds. 2015. *Constitutional Crisis in the European Constitutional Area: Theory, Law and Politics in Hungary and Romania*. Oxford: Hart Publishing Ltd.

Vyhnánek, Ladislav. 2017. "A Holistic View of the Czech Constitutional Court Approach to the ECtHR's Case Law". *Heidelberg Journal of International Law* 77 (3): 715–43.

Ziemele, Ineta. 2016. "Conclusions". In *The Impact of the ECHR on Democratic Change in Central and Eastern Europe: Judicial Perspectives*, edited by Iulia Motoc and Ineta Ziemele, 491–502. Cambridge: Cambridge University Press.

Župančič, Boštjan. 1998. "Od souboje ke smlouvě, aneb co vlastně ustavuje ústava?" [From Combat to Contract: What Does the Constitution Constitute?] *Právník* 137 (6): 476–98.

Appendix

Codebook of meso-level analysis of the rulings of international human rights bodies in the case law of the Czech apex courts (Constitutional Court, Supreme Court, and Supreme Administrative Court)

Version 1.0 (2019-09-13)

Introductory remarks

Unit of analysis

The unit of analysis is a section of a national judicial ruling dealing with a human right enshrined in a provision of an international human rights treaty, if the section contains a reference to at least one decision (or judgment) of an international human rights body. If the given section of the national judicial ruling includes a reference to decisions of several international human rights bodies then the section represents parallel units of analysis whose number corresponds to the number of mentioned international human rights bodies (hence to the number of international human rights treaties whose human rights were concerned).

For example:

> *Czech restitution laws favouring access of Czech citizens to restitution was also recognised by the European Court of Human Rights in the decision of the spouses P. and G. in the case of G. and Gá v. the Czech Republic, application no. 39,794/98, 10 July 2002 and in the decision of P. and Pá v. the Czech Republic, application no. 38,645/97, 10 July 2002 both published in the Case-law Journal of the European Court of Human Rights, 4/2002. The Supreme Administrative Court is aware of the Human Rights Committee's different opinion, but it is bound by Czech laws and case-law of the Constitutional Court of the Czech Republic and the European Court of Human Rights enabling different approaches to restitution and reparation of grievances committed by the Communist Regime relating to citizenship.*[1]

This passage contains a reference to two international human rights bodies (the European Court of Human Rights ["ECtHR" or "Strasbourg Court"] and the Human Rights Committee). It should therefore be coded as two units of analysis.

Assessment of values and categories

While assessing particular values and categories, it is necessary to follow what a domestic court says it is doing. Even if, based on his own expertise, a coder knows that a quoted decision or judgment of an international human rights body is interpreted by the scholarly community differently than a domestic court concludes, only the domestic court's interpretation is determining. However, if a coder encounters such cases, he records them in a "comments" column.

I. Identification of national rulings

A. Court

Code

1 – The Constitutional Court of the Czech Republic

2 – The Supreme Court of the Czech Republic

3 – The Supreme Administrative Court of the Czech Republic

B. ID

Fill in the field with a respective case file number.

C. Date

Fill in the field with the date of the ruling (not the date of publication: or the date of entry into force, nor the date of availability) – it is located at the end of a national judicial ruling after the final instructions. Fill in the date in the dd. mm.yyyy format, with no spaces and with added zeros, i.e. 04.05.2016.

II. References to an international human rights treaty and body

A. Treaty ID

Fill in the field with the code of the international human rights treaty and its international human rights body that a domestic court refers to. E.g., fill in the field with the code for the International Covenant on Civil and Political Rights if a domestic court refers to the Human Rights Committee. Fill in the field with the code for the European Convention on Human Rights ("ECHR" or "Convention") if an ECtHR ruling is referred to, etc.

Code

1 – European Convention on Human Rights (European Convention)

Note: At this moment, only the ECHR and ECtHR are coded at the meso-level.

B. ID Provision

Fill in the field with the code of a particular provision of an international human rights treaty that an international human rights body ruling refers to. In the case of the European Convention on Human Rights, see the ECHR coding sheet (Excel table). In all other cases, fill in the field only with the article number of the relevant provision. Moreover, a provision of a relevant convention must be also filled in if a court refers only to a judgement and a relevant treaty provision is not mentioned.

Exception: There is a residual category in the case of the European Convention on Human Rights (ECHR coding list: 0) covering situations when a domestic court refers to a ruling of an international human rights body and a reference is not directly linked to the specific right guaranteed by the European Convention – i.e. reference to the test of legality and legitimacy without a link to a specific right.

C. ID International human rights body

Fill in the field with the code for the international human rights body that a domestic court refers to.

Code

1 – European Court of Human Rights

Note: At this moment, only the ECtHR is coded at the meso-level.

D. ID international ruling

Fill in the field by identifying the ruling (one or several) of the international human rights body that a domestic court refers to. The field is filled in verbatim from how the ruling of an international human rights body is quoted by a domestic court in its ruling. A coder copies this identification from a national ruling; no other information (date, complaint number, etc.) is considered – this is the "copy and paste" method. Where a domestic court does not refer to a specific ruling of an international human rights body, i.e. it refers generally to its decision-making activity, fill in NA.

> The value of *a generic quotation* (see Category F. Carefulness of reference to ruling of international human rights body) always corresponds to the *NA* coding in the ID category of an international ruling.

III. Use of reference to a ruling of an international human rights body

A. Part of a national judicial ruling

Fill in the field with the code of a part of a national judicial ruling when a reference is made to a decision or a judgment of an international human rights body.

A narrative part of a domestic court's ruling contains a recapitulation of the facts of a case, its procedural aspects and the content of the submission of the litigants. If a reference to a ruling of an international human rights body appears only in a *narrative part* of a ruling and a domestic court does not make a reference in its reasoning *sensu stricto* (i.e. in the part which contains a legal assessment of a case by the domestic court itself, see below), then it is only a reference in the narrative part. We abide by the formal criterion of the part of a ruling in which a reference to an international human rights body appears.

Note: Narration in reasoning – occasionally, a domestic court may refer to an international human rights body in the part of its ruling that is formally described as a reasoning (legal assessment by a court), but a reference is made only in a sentence recapitulating objections of litigants or procedural aspects or facts. If a coder encounters such a situation, he mentions it in a "comments" column. Example:

> *The appellant further argued that the lower courts had violated his right not to be punished twice for the same act (Art. 40(5) of the Charter of Fundamental Rights and Freedoms, Art. 4 of Protocol 7 to the European Convention), and referred to the judgment of the Grand Chamber of the European Court of Human Rights – Zolotukhin v. Russia […]. The Court has examined this objection and has come to the conclusion that it is unfounded ….*
>
> (hypothetical example)

If a domestic court did not comment on the case *Zolotukhin v. Russia*[2] while assessing objections, it is a reference to the ruling of the international human rights body only in the narrative part.

If a reference to a ruling of an international human rights body appears in an actual legal assessment of a case by a domestic court, not just in a narrative (recapitulative) part, then *it is a reference in a domestic court's (majority) reasoning*. This is the case when a domestic court merely refers to a ruling of an international human rights body, as well as cases when a domestic court focuses on the details of a ruling of an international human rights body. If a reference to rulings of an international human rights body appears both in the narrative part and in the reasoning of a domestic court, it must always be *coded only as a reference in the reasoning of a domestic court* (a reference in the reasoning of a domestic court overrides a reference in the narrative part).

If a reference to the international human rights body appears only in a separate opinion of a dissenting or concurring judge, then *it is a reference only in a separate opinion*. Generally, we do not deal with references in separate opinions in meso-analysis, but if a sample of domestic court rulings contains a reference to an international human rights ruling only in a separate opinion, a coder selects value 3 and the rest of the field is filled in NA.

Code

1 – reference only in a narrative part
2 – reference in a domestic court's reasoning
3 – reference only in a separate opinion

If a coder selects 1 (reference only in narrative part) or 3 (reference only in a separate opinion), all of the following categories are automatically NA.

B. Treaty party (country) against which a referred ruling of an international human rights body was issued

Depending on the addressees of rulings of international human rights bodies that a domestic court refers to, fill in the field with the code.

Code

1 – if a domestic court refers to rulings of an international human rights body when parties are states other than the Czech Republic.

For example: (1) A domestic court in a unit of analysis (see above) refers only to the ECtHR's case *Zolotukhin v. Russia*. (2) A domestic court in a unit of analysis (see above) refers only to decisions and judgments of the ECtHR concerning dissolution of political parties, while in any of the referred rulings of international human rights bodies the Czech Republic was not the party.

2 – if a domestic court refers to rulings of an international human rights body when the only party was the Czech Republic.

For example: In the judgement of the Supreme Administrative Court ("SAC"), no. 5 A 145/2001-58 of 4 March 2004, reference is made only to the case of the European Court of Human Rights, *Bucheň v. the Czech Republic.*[3]

3 – if a domestic court refers to rulings of an international human rights body when the Czech Republic and other States are parties to the proceedings.

For example, the Constitutional Court of the Czech Republic ("CC") in the case no. III. ÚS 1136/13 (*J. S.*, judgment of 12 August 2015) refers to the judgment of the Grand Chamber of the European Court of Human Rights in the case of *D.H. v. the Czech Republic*,[4] as well as the case law of the European Court of Human Rights dealing with other countries (*Larkos v. Cyprus*[5], *Oršuš and Others v. Croatia*[6], ...).

NA – in the case of a generic quotation, i.e. when a domestic court refers to the decision-making activity of an international human rights body without specifying a particular ruling.

C. How the international human rights ruling is followed

Fill in the field with a code depending on the position of a domestic court in relation to a referred ruling of an international human rights body, whether it follows it, distinguishes from it, or refuses its conclusions. While coding, the default position is that a domestic court follows a ruling of an international human rights body. Even if a domestic court only refers to a ruling of an international human rights body in brackets and does not comment on it in more detail, it is assumed that it follows its conclusions. "Following" also includes situations when a domestic court develops the conclusions of an international human rights body in a way that results in greater protection of rights than the international human rights body itself did (while coding, such cases should be mentioned in the "comments" column). **Following simply represents a default value within this category.**

Only if a domestic court explicitly states that it will not follow the conclusions of a referred ruling of an international human rights body, even if it is applicable to the case, it is *a refusal*.

E.g. the SAC in its judgement no. 1 As 125/2011-163 of 11 January 2012 expressed the principle of *non bis in idem* in the context of administrative punishment, namely the concept of offense. The court noted the development of the Strasbourg case law, culminating in the ruling of the Grand Chamber, *Zolotukhin v. Russia*. Despite the fact that the ECtHR in the this judgement rejected the approach which emphasises the legal characterisation of the two offences is too restrictive on the rights of the individual, the SAC, on the contrary, stated that perpetrator's conduct is to be assessed primarily on the basis of the its legal qualification and legal qualification of its significant consequences. The Supreme Administrative Court stated that a strict following of the concept of conduct in accordance with the *Zolotukhin* judgment could lead to

> *situations when certain interests and values could not be protected by administrative authorities, even if those authorities are specifically required to protect them. The unacceptability of such a situation would be particularly evident at the time when an offender would first be sanctioned by an administrative body for a rather insignificant consequence of her behaviour, which would, however, thwart the possibility of her punishment for other, more severe and more serious consequences.*

The concurrence of administrative and criminal proceedings might therefore lead to "*the abandonment of administrative sanctioning in favour of criminal prosecution (in the narrow sense)*", which is a development that "*the ECHR certainly did not intend to bring*". The Supreme Administrative Court thus rejected the conclusions adopted by the Strasbourg Court and did not follow its approach in the *Zolotukhin* case. At the same time, however, it reflected that case law, discussed it and outlined reasons why it considered the conclusions of the ECtHR as inappropriate in relation to administrative prosecutions.

If a domestic court explicitly states that conclusions of a referred international human rights body's ruling are not applicable to a case at hand (whether on the grounds of facts or law), it represents *distinguishing*. Thus, a domestic court does not apply conclusions formulated by an international human rights body because according to a court's reasoning, they are not applicable to the case – for example, because of a different factual basis or because an international human rights body's ruling concerns a different legal element, etc. For instance, the SAC in its judgement no. 5 Afs 50/2012-39 of 13 December 2013 ruled that a minority shareholder is not legally entitled to bring action against the Czech National Bank's decision concerning the request of a main shareholder for a consent with justification of the amount of a consideration from the exercise of the right to buy participatory securities. The applicant quoted the ECtHR's case law concerning the squeeze-out and protection of minority shareholders' rights and the SAC stated that "*none of those procedural situations dealt with by the European Court for Human Rights and quoted by the applicants address the issue that the Supreme Administrative Court deals with in this matter*".

> If a coder chooses 2 or 3 (distinguishing or refusal), he copies the passage (paste into "note" column) that concerns distinguishing or refusal.

Code

1 – Following

2 – Distinguishing

3 – Refusal

D. Influence of the international human rights ruling on domestic ruling

Fill in the field with a code depending on how the application of a ruling of an international human rights body affects the reasoning of a domestic court. Influence can be either supporting or substantive. An outcome of litigation is not relevant to this category. The influence of a ruling of an international human rights body on the argumentation of a domestic court is important.

The category of *a supporting influence* refers to cases when a domestic court makes a reference to a ruling of an international human rights body without such a reference having a substantive influence on the construction of a domestic court's argumentation. **The supporting effect is therefore the default value** to be selected if elements of a substantive influence are not met. Supporting influence is particularly the case when a domestic court refers to a ruling of an international human rights body generally during the interpretation of content or the nature of a given law, without a further linkage directly related to the present case. Typically, this is the case when a domestic court in its reasoning explains the constitutional and international background of the right in question without going into further detail.

For example: the SAC, judgment no. 1 As 53/2011-109, 27 July 2011. First, the SAC defined the \constitutional and international basis of the right to education. For this purpose, it also referred to the ECtHR's judgment in the so-called *Belgian language* case[7] (see Paragraph 23 of the national judgment). Subsequently, however, the SAC did not explicitly work with the ECtHR case law and based its own reasoning and legal conclusions (that the decision of a nursery school to terminate pre-school education is subject to review by administrative judiciary regardless of a founder of a nursery school) from national law.

Cases of supporting influence also occur if a domestic court bases its argument in national law and subsequently justifies it with a reference to a ruling of an international human rights body in order to prove that the reached conclusions are also in accordance with international human rights law ("ornament"). In general, cases of supporting influence are typically, but not necessarily, characterized by a smaller space devoted to argumentation with international human rights rulings. Example of ornament: the CC, judgment no. Pl. ÚS 12/14, 16 June 2015, Paragraph 49:

> *Similarly according to the case-law of the European Court of Human Rights, the protection of legitimate expectations, i.e. the protection of the claim the eligible person has legitimate expectations to, is also an integral part of property law,. The central criterion for the assessment of the existence of such legitimate expectations is the consideration of individual and specific circumstances of the case, which gave rise to to legitimate expectations such as the property interest protected by Article 1 of the Additional Protocol to the Convention (judgment of the Grand Chamber of the European Court of Human Rights in Anheuser-Busch Inc. v. Portugal, application no. 73,049/01, 11 January 2007, par. 63–65, or the judgment of the European Court of Human Rights in Glaser v. the Czech Republic, application no. 55,179/00, 14 February 2008, par. 50–52).*

The category of *substantive influence* includes cases when a reference by a domestic court to a ruling of an international human rights body substantially affected the argumentation of a domestic court. We consider the main indicator of a substantive influence to be whether a domestic court subsumed the present case (or the facts of the case) under conclusions or criteria resulting from a referred ruling of an international human rights body. Typically, a domestic court would refer to conclusions an international human rights body ruling and subsequently, it would use these conclusions to assess the case at hand.

For example: the CC in its judgement no. I. ÚS 860/15 of 27 October 2015 first used the ECtHR's case law to define what constitutes inhuman or degrading treatment within the meaning of Article 3 ECHR (Paragraph 53 et seq.). In the rest of this part of the judgment, the CC considered whether the facts of the present case fulfilled the prohibition of inhuman or degrading treatment as interpreted by the ECtHR. In other words, the CC first interpreted general principles and subsequently subsumed the present case under these principles. Therefore, such a references constitutes an example of a substantive influence of an international human rights ruling.

The rule of subsuming applies also in constitutional review of the legislation before the CC. Even though generally, in constitutional review cases the CC does not subsume the facts of the case under the ECtHR case law principles (especially if it is an abstract review), it can still review the national legal norm according to conclusions derived from the case law of international human rights bodies.

For example: the CC in its judgment no. Pl. ÚS 45/04 of 22 March 2005 annulled Section 242(2) of the Code of Criminal Procedure for its breach of Article 5(4)

ECHR. First, the CC, with numerous references to ECtHR rulings, explained what Article 5(4) ECHR requires in relation to the right to be heard. Subsequently, the CC concluded that the then-legislation in the Code of Criminal Procedure did not comply with such standards and annulled the provision of the Code. The Constitutional Court thus subsumed the characteristics of the Czech legislation under the conclusions resulting from the ECtHR's case law and concluded that the Czech Code of Criminal Procedure did not meet these requirements.

The value of a substantive influence also has a negative definition. Supporting references (ornaments) cannot be identified as of substantive influence even if there is a hint of subsumption. Typically, this will be the case of a brief argument (one or two sentences long) that an international human rights ruling referred to by a party to a dispute cannot be applied to the present case. Although a domestic court in such a case decides whether to subsume the case under standards established by an international human rights body, a coder will not categorise it under a substantive influence if the reference to an international human rights body is brief and of little relevance to the rest of the case. However, the coder will highlight such cases by a brief description in the "comment" column. For instance, the Supreme Court ("SC") judgment no. 30 Cdo 3534/2014 of 26 November 2014:

> *The judgment (cited above) of the European Court of Human Rights (ECtHR), in the case of Bořánková v. the Czech Republic, application no. 41,486/98, 7 January 2003, is not applicable to the case, because in the present case the injured party is, in contrast to the injured party in the ECtHR judgment, the owner of the property in question. The Supreme Court concludes that regarding the claim to compensation of alleged material damage ad 1) and 2), the contested decision of the Court of Appeal is in accordance with the established case-law of the Supreme Court and finds the extraordinary appeal in this part inadmissible.*

If both supporting or substantive influence of rulings of an international human rights body is found within a unit of analysis, it is necessary to choose the substantive influence that prevails in such cases.

Code

0 – Supporting influence

1 – Substantive influence

If a coder inserts 1 – a substantive impact – in the next step she selects Technique E (application of a ruling of an international human rights body by a domestic court). If a coder selects 0 – a supporting impact – she skips step E (fills in NA) and proceeds to categories F J.

E. Legal technique of applying the international human rights case on domestic ruling (only in cases of substantive influence)

Invalidation of a domestic legal norm – This is a situation in which a domestic court (only the CC has such a competence in the Czech constitutional system) concludes that a provision of domestic law violates a provision of an international human rights treaty – as interpreted by the referred ruling of an international human rights body – and therefore invalidates the domestic legal norm. E.g. the abovementioned CC judgment no. Pl. ÚS 45/04 of 22 March 2005.

Primacy (in case of conflict) and application of international human rights norm – This is a situation in which a domestic court concludes that national provision is in conflict with a provision of a treaty – as interpreted by the referred international human rights body – and this conflict cannot be ameliorated by interpretation. Accordingly, a domestic court, pursuant to Article 10 ECHR, directly applies provisions of an international human rights treaty instead of a contradicting statute. E.g. the SAC in its judgement no. 6 As 55/2006-96 of 11 July 2007, concluded that the exclusion of the service allowance under the Act on Security Information Service from judicial review is not in contradiction with the Czech Charter, however, it violates Article 6(1) ECHR within the scope of the ECtHR's judgment in the case of *Pellegrin v. France.*[8] The Supreme Administrative Court therefore concluded that the decision of the Security Information Service is subject to judicial review based on the primacy and direct application of Article 6 ECHR.

Conform interpretation of national law with international human rights norm – This is a situation in which a domestic court concludes that there are several lines of interpretation in relation to a specific national provision and an international human rights treaty – as interpreted by an international human rights body – will fundamentally affect which line of interpretation will be applied. In such cases, a domestic court reinterprets national legal provisions so as to bring it into line with a provision of an international human rights treaty as interpreted by an international human rights body. This is a narrow category. It does not cover all cases in which a ruling of an international human rights body affects national legal practice. It covers only cases when a domestic court states how the specific provision of national law must be interpreted in future, as a result of a ruling of an international human rights body. E.g. the SC in its opinion no. Cpjn 202/2010 of 8 December 2010 stated that the provision on the regulation of institutional care of the child (§ 42 of Act no. 359/1999 Coll., on social and legal protection of children) must be interpreted in such way that "*the reason for an order for the institutional care of a child cannot be only material shortage of a family, and especially its poor housing conditions*".

Application of a ruling of an international human rights body in order to fill in a gap or complement the national legal norm. This is the situation when the application of an international human rights ruling has a substantive influence on a domestic court's reasoning and influences certain changes in national law, but not through one of the previous techniques (invalidation, non-application or reinterpretation of a national legal norm). In such cases, a domestic court applies substantive conclusions of an international human rights body's ruling on domestic law and domestic legal practice without having an immediate impact on a specific legal norm of the national law. The specific national legal norm often remains in the background, and a domestic court instead applies principles established by an international human rights body to assess the case. Thus, the application of an international human rights ruling has a substantive impact on a domestic court's argumentation and on a national legal practice, since it introduces principles of an international human rights body, but does not directly affect a specific national legal norm. E.g. the CC in its judgment no. I. ÚS 860/15 of 27 October 2015 extensively cited the ECtHR's case law in order to infer criteria and subsequently assess the compliance of an intervention of the Police of the Czech Republic with the prohibition of torture. The Constitutional Court thus complemented the national law by means of the standards introduced by the ECtHR, as it specified a set of standards concerning the limits of the use of coercive means by the police. However, at the same time, this was not an example of a conform interpretation as defined above.

Blessing (validation) of domestic law via a ruling of an international human rights body. This category covers cases when a domestic court bases its argumentation primarily on a ruling of an international human rights body and explains why the related right guaranteed by an international treaty **has not been violated** and why national law/practice is in accordance with international law. E.g. the SAC in its judgment no. 6 Ads 41/2008-67 of 7 October 2009 summed up the criteria stemming from the ECtHR's case law which sets the limits of acceptable criticism of judges. Subsequently, it subsumed the facts of the case at hand under those criteria and concluded that the applicant's right to freedom of expression had not been violated. Typically, the CC's judgment dismissing the petitions will also fall under this category.

The *remaining category* includes those cases of substantive influence of rulings of an international human rights body that do not fall under any of the 1–5 categories. This category also includes **refusal** (see Category C above) and **distinguishing** (see Category C above) from the international human rights body's ruling, if it has a substantive impact on a domestic court's argumentation (we assume this will be the case in an overwhelming majority of cases). Furthermore, it includes **transformation** of international human rights body's case law – i.e. cases when domestic courts use ECtHR's rulings "more creatively", and tailors the findings of an international court (which is remote from a domestic law) to the national law's needs (they can of course do so for different reasons and the effect of the ECtHR's case law in a national milieue might be strengthened by appropriate setting into the national legal context or, on the contrary, the effect of the ECtHR's case law might be reduced through its narrow interpretation and minimalist projection into the national law – an example of transformation is the German Constitutional Court's ruling on preventive detention. A coder highlights such cases by inserting word "transformation" in the comments and notes column.

Code

1 – invalidation of domestic legal norm

2 – primacy (in case of a conflict) and application of an international legal norm

3 – conform interpretation of a national provision with international human rights norm as interpreted in a ruling of an international human rights body

4 – international human rights ruling filling a gap in domestic legislation (specification/complementation of national law)

5 – blessing (validation) of national law

6 – remaining category

NA – no substantive impact (supporting impact)

F. Level of the detail of the reference to a ruling of an international human rights body

Fill in the field with a code depending on the form that a domestic court uses to refer to a ruling of an international human rights body.

A generic reference is a reference to an international human rights body as such without quoting a particular ruling of the body. For example:

> *the Constitutional Court in the present case considered whether the decision of the District Court complies with the requirements of Art. 5(4) of the Convention, as understood by the European Court of Human Rights providing a binding interpretation of the Convention, which according to Article 10 of a Constitution enjoys primacy and direct applicability over provisions of ordinary laws.*[9]

In the case of *a reference to a particular ruling of an international human rights body*, it is essential that a domestic court does not refer only to an international human rights body as such or to its case law in general, but to a particular ruling of this body. At the same time, however, the domestic court does not go into details – i.e. it does not quote directly or refer to a specific part of the ruling. E.g.

> *such a conclusion follows from the ECtHR's case-law, which found in judgement Haas v. the Netherlands (application no. 36,983/97, 13 January 2004), that the right to inherit does not on its own follow from Art. 8 of the Convention. Similarly, in the case Bourimi v. the Netherlands (application no. 28,369/95, 3 October 2000), the ECtHR stated that the right to family and private life does not on its won include the right to inherit unless there are other significant circumstances.*[10]

Reference to a specific part of a particular ruling of an international human rights body. A domestic court refers to a specific part of a particular ruling of an international human rights body – to a particular point, paragraph, or section of a ruling. A domestic court thus seeks to specify the source of the conclusions of a ruling of an international human rights body to which it refers. For example,

> *according to the European Court of Human Rights, the notion of necessity requires that a restrictive measure corresponds to a pressing social need and that the measure is proportionate to the legitimate aim pursued (judgment of the European Court of Human Rights, Wingrove v. the United Kingdom, application no. 17,419/90, par. 53, 25 November 1996.*[11]

If a reference to the international human rights body rulings with different levels of detail is found within a unit of analysis, it is necessary to code the highest level of detail occurring in the unit of analysis ("the winner takes all" rule).

Code

1 – a generic reference to an international human rights body and its case law

2 – a reference to a particular ruling of an international human rights body

3 – a reference to a specific part of a particular ruling of an international human rights body

G. Direct quotation from a ruling of an international human rights body

Within this category, a coder assesses whether or not a domestic court has made a reference to an international human rights body's ruling directly. A direct quotation means that domestic court directly uses (copies) a part of a text (it is usually visually separated by quotation marks, italics or a separate paragraph) from an international human rights body ruling. It also includes a direct quotation of an international human rights ruling through literature (for example, if a domestic court copies a direct quotation from a commentary on the ECHR and explicitly states the commentary cites the ECtHR's case law). For example, as noted by the ECtHR,

> *in certain circumstances the two rights may come into conflict and it may be considered necessary, in the period preceding or during an election, to place certain restrictions, of a type which would not usually be acceptable, on freedom of expression, in order to secure the "free expression of the opinion of the people in the choice of the legislature.*[12]

Code

0 – absence of a direct quotation from a ruling of an international human rights body

1 – direct quotation from a ruling of an international human rights body

H. Space devoted to a reference to a ruling of an international human rights body

Fill in the field according to the scope of a quoted ruling of an international human rights body in a reasoning of a ruling of a domestic court. Note: It is necessary to focus on a passage devoted to a reasoning which use the international human rights ruling; this does not include arguments referring *only* to a relevant international treaty or its individual provisions.

Code

1 – small (up to 100 words)
2 – significant (more than 100 words)

I. Existence of cross reference

Fill in the field with the value depending on whether a domestic court refers to a ruling of an international human rights body directly or via a recapitulation and summary of domestic courts' case law. It does not necessarily need to be a quotation of its own previous case law referring to international human rights bodies – this category also covers a situation when domestic court refer to a ruling of another domestic court, which contains a reference to an international human rights body's ruling, e.g. when the SC or the SAC "takes over" the reference to ECtHR's by quoting rulings of the Czech Constitutional Court. **The default value is that a domestic court itself directly refers to an international human rights body.**

I. 1 presence of a direct link

Code

0 – absence of a direct reference to an international human rights body

1 – a direct reference to an international human rights body (default)

I. 2 presence of an indirect link

Code

0 – absence of an indirect reference to an international human rights body (default)

1 – an indirect reference (a reference to an international human rights body through quoting a domestic court's rulings)

J. Reference to literature

This category analysis whether a domestic court, *in direct connection* with a ruling of an international human rights body, also refers to expert literature, i.e., if it draws information concerning an international ruling from literature, comments or discusses this literature, etc. If a domestic court uses such a reference refers in this sense to literature, we distinguish whether it is national or foreign literature and whether it is a commentary form of literature or another source (an article, a monograph).

Code

J.1 Application of national commentary literature

0 – no reference to national commentary literature

1 – a reference to national commentary literature

J.2 Application of other national literature

0 – absence of reference to other national literature

1 – reference to other national literature

J.3 Application of foreign commentary literature

0 – no reference to foreign commentary literature

1 – reference to foreign commentary literature

J.4 Application of other foreign literature

0 – absence of reference to other foreign literature

1 – reference to other foreign literature

Notes

1 SAC, no. 6 Ads 155/2009-42, judgment of 16 June 2010.
2 ECtHR [GC], *Zolotukhin v. Russia*, no. 14939/03, judgment of 10 February 2009.
3 ECtHR, *Bucheň v. the Czech Republic*, no. 36541/97, judgment of 26 November 2002.
4 ECtHR [GC], *D.H. and Others v. the Czech Republic*, no. 57325/00, judgment of 13 November 2007.
5 ECtHR, *Larkos v. Cyprus*, no. 29515/95, judgment of 18 February 1999.
6 OCtHR, *Oršuš and Others v. Croatia*, no. 15766/03, judgment of 16 March 2010.
7 ECtHR [Plenary], *Case "relating to certain aspects of the laws on the use of languages in education in Belgium"*, nos. 1474/62; 1677/62; 1691/62; 1769/63; 1994/63 and 2126/64, judgment of 9 February 1967.
8 ECtHR, *Pellegrin v. France*, no. 28541/95, judgment of 8 December 1999.
9 CC, no. I. ÚS 589/05, judgment of 2 November 2006.
10 SC, no. 30 Cdo 1982/2012, judgment of 24 September 2014.
11 SAC, no. 6 As 167/2015-37, judgment of 2 December 2015, § 24.
12 See ECtHR [GC], *Bowman v. the United Kingdom*, no. 24839/94, judgment of 19 February 1998, § 43; and SAC, no. 6 As 167/2015-37, judgment of 2 December 2015, § 25.

Index

Page numbers in italics refer to figures, those in bold refer to tables

For Product Safety Concerns and Information please contact our EU representative GPSR@taylorandfrancis.com
Taylor & Francis Verlag GmbH, Kaufingerstraße 24, 80331 München, Germany

www.ingramcontent.com/pod-product-compliance
Ingram Content Group UK Ltd.
Pitfield, Milton Keynes, MK11 3LW, UK
UKHW020016200926
475702UK00014B/1917
9781032173207